OCTAVIUS BROOKS FROTHINGHAM, GENTLE RADICAL

OCTAVIUS BROOKS FROTHINGHAM

Octavius Brooks Frothingham, Gentle Radical

J. Wade Caruthers

THE UNIVERSITY OF ALABAMA PRESS
University, Alabama

Library of Congress Cataloging in Publication Data

Caruthers, J   Wade.
    Octavius Brooks Frothingham, gentle radical.

    Bibliography: p.
    Includes index.
    1. Frothingham, Octavius Brooks, 1822–1895.
I. Title.
BX9869.F83C37   288'.092'4 [B]   76-18079
ISBN 0-8173-5166-3

Contents

Illustrations

Preface

Well past the midpoint of the twentieth century, some theologians were still reexamining the traditional Christian myths and symbols, still questioning the relevance of instituted religion; others were advocating a study of man rather than a futile search for a vaporous and mystical God. Unitarians, who had long since pondered these questions, were still asking, "Can Liberals Worship?" and "Are Unitarians Christians?", asserting that what was needed was a theology for the liberal church.[1] The "Post-Christian Era" was a term used increasingly to describe a stage in man's thinking about ultimate and eternal matters.

The time-lag has been long between twentieth century concern over the status of Christianity and the initial impact of nineteenth century religious radicalism. This movement took form and was given expression between 1820 and 1890. By questioning orthodox Christian concepts such as the Trinity, miracles, the nature of an omnipotent deity, sin, atonement, the after life, and interpretations of the Bible, the radicals enlarged upon the Puritan tradition and increasingly addressed themselves to the individual conscience and its relationship to the social questions of the age. The religious radicals were not, by and large, social reformers. Very few were abolitionists, members of the women's rights movement, or active in the labor movement. Yet all yearned for the end of slavery and hoped for equality and social justice. They tended to be molders of thought rather than activists. Their appeal was to the mind and conscience of the individual.

Casual students of the American intellectual tradition are familiar with the names of William Ellery Channing, Ralph Waldo Emerson, and Theodore Parker. Little is known, however, of the generation of radicals that came on the scene during and after the Civil War, complementing the ideas of their famous predecessors, and in some cases going beyond them. Octavius Brooks Frothingham (1820–1895) was the undisputed leader of this group. Steeped in Kant, Hegel, Schelling, and Fichte, he expanded the tradition, already begun in America, of Biblical criticism and the newer concept of a nondenominational, non-Christian humanism. In so doing he helped reinterpret much of the Christian dogma in terms of modern scientific, literary, and historiographical knowledge. The pulpit and the press were his weapons; the Free Religious Association, of which he was an organizer and first president, was his channel to confront the old order and persuade his generation to accept the "Religion of Humanity."

Although Frothingham held pulpits in North Church, Salem, Jersey City, and New York, where he established his fame as a pulpit orator, he was more than a brilliant preacher. He spread the abstract ideas of free religion and wrote biographies of leading figures of his time and a history of New England Transcendentalism, a standard work today. His scholarly writing in theological journals was balanced by a versatility which gave him a reading audience in secular periodicals among intellectuals, literary critics, and connoisseurs of art and the stage.

In spite of Frothingham's prominence in radical theological circles between approximately 1850 and 1880 and his position of leadership among the generation that followed Parker and Emerson, his renown suffered a gradual eclipse shortly after his death in 1895. By the time of World War I it can be said that he was virtually forgotten, save by relatives and surviving colleagues. The only published scholarship about him has been Professor Ahlstrom's able introduction to the Harper's Torchbook reprint of his *Transcendentalism in New England* (1959). Strangely, the works of many of his contemporaries and younger colleagues who had looked to him for inspiration are the ones cited or quoted by modern scholars dealing with religious radicalism in the nineteenth century or examples of spokesmen in the Free Religious Association.

It had been a fifty-one year journey, beginning in 1843 when Nathaniel Langdon Frothingham, the father of Octavius, sat as committee chairman to examine Parker for "heresy" for his shocking sermon, "The Permanent and Transient in Christianity," to 1894 when Minot J. Savage, recruited to free religion by Octavius Frothingham, presented a successful resolution at the annual Unitarian Association meeting to drop from the preamble of the denominational constitution the specific Christian orientation as a basis for a "Unitarian Creed." From the beginning to the end of the epic journey the question had been: How free was liberal religion? As free as all out-of-doors, as broad as humanity itself, was the answer of Frothingham and his fellow radicals. That the Unitarians grew into this universal concept, followed by many other formally orthodox denominations in the twentieth century, establishes Frothingham's place in the history of religious ideas in America. As such, he deserves a prominent place in the American intellectual tradition.

It cannot be claimed that this work is a definitive biography of Octavius Frothingham. No personal papers exist, destroyed perhaps at his own request. No family records were found, no diary, mementos, nor family pictures, little of his personal life, nothing of his wife Caroline. Personal letters used were available in collections of his many friends and colleagues, fortunately preserved in numerous manuscript rooms in New York, Massachusetts, Connecticut, and Maine. About one-half of his three hundred sermons survive in print and, of course, all his magazine articles and published books are readily available. This work, then, is an intellectual biography rather than a study of a man's personal life. Yet all significant personal material has been included in order to bring his obscure lineaments into a sharper focus.

It is hoped that this biography will restore him to the place in history that he merits—that of the major figure in the development of radical religious ideas in the post-Parker era of nineteenth century America.

My sincere thanks are extended to the many librarians and archivists for their patience and help during my researches in the Essex Institute, Salem, Massachusetts; Longfellow Manuscript Room, Bowdoin College; Archive Room, University of Rochester; Massachusetts Historical Society; Houghton Library and Archive Room, Harvard Library; Harvard Divinity School Library; Concord Free Library, Concord, Massachusetts; Rare Book Room, Boston Public Library; Manuscript Room, Columbia University; New York Historical Society; New York Public Library; Beineke Library, Yale University; Vital Statistics of Massachusetts, State House, Boston; and Boston Atheneum. My special appreciation is extended to the staff of the UUA, 25 Beacon Street, Boston, for their permission to use the Unitarian-Universalists historical collection. To the library staff of my own Southern Connecticut State College I give credit for help in arranging interlibrary loans of essential material. My colleagues in the History Department helped me by their conversation, patience in listening, and critical comments at various stages in the research and writing. The Department Secretary, Miss Emma Armonath, was a great help in some of the typing, proofreading, and correspondence connected with the writing. My thanks also are due to The Reverend Wayne Shuttee, Unitarian Minister, Hamden, Connecticut, who gave me a few early guidelines for my research. The Reverend Ronald Mazour, former minister, North Church, Salem, Massachusetts, was of great help in guiding me to the primary documents of that church. My wife, Gwynette Caruthers, endured the rough draft, listened, and advised well during the whole process.

Cheshire, Connecticut   J. WADE CARUTHERS

HERMAN MELVILLE'S ELEMENT WAS THE SEA WHERE
TO SAIL WAS TO THINK AND TO SAIL FAR
WAS TO THINK DEEPLY.
EMERSON'S GLORY WAS IN THE WOODS,
IN THE CATHEDRAL OF THE FOREST, WHERE
THE KNAPSACK OF CARE FELL FROM ONE'S BACK.
FROTHINGHAM'S METIER WAS INTELLECTUAL COMBAT
IN THE CITY—IN THE ARENA OF MEN.

I

Enlightened Puritanism: His Heritage

H E WAS BORN FREE AND LIVED IN the "nick of time," as the transcendentalists were wont to say, yet like his cousin, Henry Adams, the cultural milieu was as overpowering as though he were born to strict orthodoxy.[1] The Brahmin boy and youth grew and developed in the environment of the Boston literati and among men who wielded political and economic power. For a youth of his class and time, his career was inevitably to lead him in one of three directions: to State Street and a life of business, to Beacon Street for a career in politics, or into the ministry. Regardless of the career chosen, the path was foreordained by tradition and class affiliation. It would be Boston Latin School, Harvard College and, for those choosing the ministry, Harvard Divinity School.

Octavius Brooks Frothingham, second of five children, was born in Boston November 28, 1822, to Nathaniel Langdon and Ann Gorham Brooks Frothingham. His brothers were Thomas Brooks, the eldest, and two younger brothers, Edward and Ward. Ellen, the only girl, was born in 1835, thirteen years after Octavius. His mother was the daughter of Peter Chardon Brooks who died in 1849, distributing his considerable fortune among his seven children.[2] Nathaniel Langdon Frothingham, Minister of Boston's First Church from 1820 to 1850, was descended from a long line of farmers and entrepreneurs, his own grandfather being a coachmaker in Boston until 1791.[3]

The Frothingham name was established in America in virtually the first year of the Massachusetts Bay Colony. A William Frothingham migrated with Winthrop's group in 1630 and became one of the original settlers in Charlestown. The family branched out to Jamaica, Massachusetts, upstate New York, and New York City. The name appears on the muster rolls of the Continental Army though none seems to have achieved any fame or notoriety in the eighteenth century. The English connection was lost, for no Frothingham name is recorded there after 1750.[4]

The name itself goes back to mythical times in England. According to family records, Frothe, a Danish legendary name, came into England during one of the many Norse incursions and later appears in the "Doomsday Book of 1086." It literally means "the home of Froth's people" (Frothingham). There was recorded a North Fordingham (sic) in the area, later known as Yorkshire and South Frodingham in what is now Hull. The Frothinghams became feudal landholders, some acquiring titles and the status of knighthood. Apparently, the William Frothingham who sailed with Winthrop's fleet was of lesser position though he paid his passage and became a freeholder in Charlestown. While the Frothingham name disappeared from English records, it took root in America.[5]

ONE

When Octavius was born, his father was well established as the minister of Boston's First Unitarian Church, then located in Summer Street. The family resided in the comfortable manse a short walk away. Reverend Nathaniel Langdon Frothingham moved in the highest social and intellectual circles where the Frothingham name commanded respect. Himself a product of Harvard College and Divinity School, he was a contemporary of such Unitarian Divines as George Ripley, William E. Channing, Andrews Norton, and Convers Frances. Waldo Emerson was an intimate friend and frequent dinner guest. In later life Octavius Frothingham recalled the impression of "Ralph Waldo Emerson who often sat at my father's table diffusing the radiance of serene ideas, the heralding of the divine age that was to come." [6]

As a child, young Frothingham occasionally caught a glimpse of Daniel Webster "who," he recalled, "used to stalk past our house, the embodiment of the Constitution, the incarnation of law, the black locomotive of the train of civilization." [7] Charles Sumner, uncle by marriage, destined to be the great abolitionist senator from Massachusetts, was in law school during Octavius' boyhood. Edward Everett, another uncle, had a career in public life and was to be president of Harvard College for a time. Young Octavius grew up in an atmosphere of aristocracy and conservative Unitarianism. In later life Frothingham observed that the high social position of his father's generation tended to make the merchants, politicians, and judges consider social reform a delicate subject. The ministers in the group, with the exception of Theodore Parker, showed deference to powerful figures in their congregation. They admired Daniel Webster, who personified the "high minded" Federalist tradition—those that loved union more than they hated the divisive subject of slavery. To young Frothingham, his father's generation represented the old Massachusetts tradition that opposed democratic institutions and subscribed to John Winthrop's dictum that "the best part of the community is always the least and of the least part, the wiser are still less." [8]

Yet there was something in the young boy's environment that encouraged him to break out of the shell of a complacent Boston Unitarianism. Ironically, as we shall see, it was the milieu of Boston Unitarianism itself, enriched by Boston Latin School, Harvard College, and Divinity Hall. This part of his life spanned the years 1834 to 1847. During these thirteen years Boston became a center of abolitionism, the Transcendental group organized and dispersed, and Brook Farm was established and abandoned. The clipper trade with China boomed. Henry Thoreau took to the woods, though few noticed at the time. Waldo Emerson delivered his Divinity School address and many heard. Theodore Parker was virtually "excommunicated" by the Boston Unitarian Ministerial Association. As Boston lost its commercial supremacy, it remained for a time America's intellectual capital. As New York City rose to challenge Boston's pretentions, Octavius Brooks Frothingham would pursue his intellectual development, as a sort of pilgrim's progress, in that city.

TWO

Little can be recaptured of Frothingham's childhood. There is no reason to believe it was far different from that of any other upper-class boy born in nineteenth century Boston. His own *Recollections and Impressions,*[9] unlike his cousin Henry's memoirs,[10] are modestly brief on details of his personal life.

One gets the feel of his early home life, spent in the atmosphere of enlightened puritanism. Wine was consumed at the table where his mother would mildly chide his father for using the last bottle of his favorite red Italian wine, warning that he would miss it when it was gone. Poems were read aloud, the best literature was available and frequently discussed. Prayers and Bible reading were held at low key in the manner of the upper-class Unitarian families of that age. Though Octavius' father was pastor of First Church, he seemed not to impose religious doctrine. We can imagine the Frothingham children attending church and church school regularly, yet more in a spirit of social expectations rather than fear of falling from grace of failing to achieve salvation. The home offered love and intellectual stimulation controlled by a mild orthodoxy.

At age twelve (1834) Octavius entered Boston Latin School, beginning the path trod by many American greats. Waldo Emerson and Octavius' uncle, Edward Everett, had been graduated in 1811. Two others, later to be Frothingham's older colleagues in Unitarian controversies, preceded him by a few years: John T. Sargent in 1823 and James Freeman Clark in 1825. A year later Charles Sumner graduated, followed by Wendell Phillips in 1827. Edward Everett Hale was graduated in 1835, the year that Octavius finished his first year.

Boston Latin School, a two-story building with a peaked roof and a church-like steeple, stood on the south side of School Street. When Octavius enrolled, the building was twenty-two years old and was to house

the school until 1844. It seemed appropriate enough that young Frothingham attended in the same building, no doubt occupying the same desks
as had Waldo Emerson less than a quarter of a century earlier.[11] Octavius
enrolled in October of 1834. Thomas Brooks, his older brother, had
withdrawn the previous spring after a mediocre record in "recitation" and
a good record in "conduct." Though few details are available concerning
Octavius' life in the school, *Rank Books* for each year indicate a brilliant
record of even achievement between 1834 and the year of his graduation
in 1839.[12] The tutors ranked students each month for achievement in
conduct and recitation, supplemented by a curious system of points
accumulated at the end of the student's career. One assumes the latter
category, "recitation," refers to academic achievement, to use modern
parlance. In the first year (1834–35), twelve-year-old Octavius received
for recitation seven firsts, two seconds, one third, and one fifth. In
conduct he was first each month. His second year, in a class of twelve, he
was ranked first in both recitation and conduct. So it went through the rest
of his stay at Boston Latin School, with his receiving more firsts in
recitation than lesser ratings and rather consistent firsts in conduct. One
dramatic exception was noted in May, 1837 when he was ranked seventh
out of eleven classmates in conduct.[13] Unfortunately, the reasons for his
fall from grace was not recorded. Had they been, an interesting facet of
young Frothingham's personality would emerge. We can be content with
the fact that his superiority and perfection revealed a human flaw at age
fifteen. At the end of his six years at the Latin School Frothingham was
graduated second in a class of probably nine boys. He had accumulated
1,879 "points" to 1,889 points recorded for a certain C. W. Eustis. Later
records show that Eustis died in 1842, probably during his junior year at
Harvard College. How brilliant a career was cut off when Frothingham's
classmate died will never be known.

The curriculum of Boston Latin School was classical, basically secular
with the theological overtones of earlier days dropped away. Certainly the
record of declamation contests, on annual "Visitation Day," show a political and literary orientation in sharp contrast to Calvinistic emphasis in the
years that Cotton Mather attended.[14] On July 22, 1837, Octavius delivered his declamation on extracts from Edmund Burke's speech on conciliation. On the same program he was part of a "trialogue" taking the part
of Walch, Salidin and attendant being portrayed by two other classmates.
At the August Visitation Day in the same year Frothingham recited
"Emmett's Defense." One month before his graduation in 1839, at the
annual Declamation Day contest, Octavius took the part of Louis in
Bulwer's "Dialogue from Richelieu." Who won the contest was not recorded.[15]

The young man, soon to be seventeen, was solidly grounded in classical
languages, mathematics, literature, poetry, history, and forensics. He was
ready for Harvard College.

THREE

The presidency of Josiah Quincy was well underway. A landscaped campus had begun to emerge. The student's pigpens, and privies had given way to more civilized and academic facilities. Halworthy Hall, where Frothingham roomed for three of his four years, stood prominently on the campus with its dignified Georgian architecture.[16] Students who were influenced by Swedenborg, the theological mystic, and German Idealism began to attack "Lockean sensationalism" and cold reason based on empirical evidence. Emerson had delivered his *American Scholar* address two years before Frothingham began his freshman year. The *Divinity School* address given the year before was still reverberating on the campus. Transcendentalism was in the air as undergraduates and Divinity School students began questioning the "orthodox Unitarianism" represented by William Ellery Channing.

When Octavius Frothingham appeared on the Harvard campus in the fall of 1839, the college was no longer a narrow higher school devoted exclusively to training proper Bostonians and future members of the clergy. It was in its late "Augustan age" as Samuel E. Morison has called it.[17] Twenty years before George Tichnor, Edward Everett, and George Bancroft, the first generation of American scholars to be trained in Europe, had finished their grand tour, studied in German and Italian universities, and returned to Harvard in 1819 to reform the system. Although Bancroft and Everett soon resigned their teaching posts, Tichnor stayed on, attempting to persuade President Kirkland and the Harvard Corporation to create an academic atmosphere at Harvard College which would make it second to none in America by adopting certain European practices. Incomplete as many of Tichnor's reforms were, ending in the resignation of President Kirkland, and despite a battle among the fellows of the corporation and Tichnor's own resignation in 1835, changes did occur. The stilted recitation gave way to lectures, broad reading replaced textbook memorization, and a few elective courses were introduced. Some departments were established in the disciplines, most notably in Tichnor's field of literature, poetry, and belles-lettres.[18] W. H. Prescott, the elder Dana, Edward Everett, and Andrews Norton, the "Unitarian Pope," moved Harvard into the nineteenth century. In the fall of 1839 young Frothingham and his seventy-five classmates began exposure to this intellectual atmosphere and, in the words of Emerson, the mild Unitarianism of pale negations.

The faculty, ten in number, was not an undistinguished lot—the product of the conflict among the trustees and the thrust of Tichnor's reforms at the end of the "Kirkland era." President Josiah Quincy, whose tenure spanned Frothingham's undergraduate years, did the college a "sort of violent service," as Emerson recalled and "was a lubber and Grenadier among our clerks." [19] The Honorable Joseph Story headed the

fellows of the corporation. His colleagues were Lemuel Shaw, Charles
Loring, John N. Lowell, and Reverend James Walker of the Divinity
School. Professor of Rhetoric was Edward T. Channing. Reverend Henry
Ware, D.D., served both the college and the Divinity School. The Latin
tutor was Charles Beck; Greek tutors were Cornelius Felton and Charles
Wheeler. Benjamin Pierce was tutor in mathematics and natural
philosophy and Joseph Lovering taught mathematics. Most notable was
Henry Wadsworth Longfellow, Professor of Poetry and Letters, the suc-
cessor to Tichnor himself, who had resigned four years prior to
Frothingham's enrollment.[20]

The intellectual fare was a combination of the old and new. Still based
on the medieval trivium and quadrivium, the curriculum of Harvard
during Frothingham's years there also reflected the Tichnor-Bancroft
innovations. The Greek and Latin classics were heavily stressed in the first
three years. Mathematics began with algebra and geometry, based on
tutor Benjamin Pierce's own famous text, and branched out into practical
mathematics, analytic geometry, and theory of numbers. Modern language electives appeared in the sophomore year, natural philosophy in
the last two. In the junior and senior years, Cousin's *Psychology* and Locke's
On Understanding were read. No American or European history appeared
in the curriculum. Apparently the college authorities felt the young men
had sufficient acquaintanceship with this discipline after studying Knight-
ly's *History of Greece and Rome*. Chemistry and astronomy comprised the
sciences in the junior and senior years, with a smattering of the physical
principles of sound. Grammar, rhetoric, exercise in forensics, and theme
writing ran through the entire four years. The men were exposed to a
study of the U.S. Constitution and the best classical economic thinking
from Say's *Political Economy* in the senior year. How much outside reading
was done in the best current books of the early nineteenth century was no
doubt a personal matter between tutor and students or perhaps influenced by the student's family background. The senior year was enriched
by required lectures in various disciplines. The Harvard Catalog for
Frothingham's senior year records lectures on law, probably by Joseph
Story, in natural philosophy and mathematics by Benjamin Pierce, and
literature and poetry by Henry Wadsworth Longfellow.[21]

In the charging lists of Harvard College Library are many indications
that Frothingham did not read widely as an undergraduate. During his
freshman and sophomore years, 1839–40 and 1840–41, the records show
no book withdrawals. In the following year his classmates, Samuel
Longfellow and Thomas Wentworth Higginson, withdrew six to eight
works on history, physics, and religion. In the spring of the year 1841
sophomore Frothingham withdrew three volumes on the writings of
Pascal and Southly. The records for his junior year (1841–42) show no
library withdrawals but numerous ones by T. W. Higginson and Samuel
Longfellow. Frothingham charged out nine books between December

and May of his senior year, 1842–43, including Schiller's *Wallenstein* and works of Homer, Scott, and Byron. Library use is not the only indication of intellectual activity to be sure. Frothingham's home, which he no doubt visited on weekends, was well furnished with books useful to a Harvard student. This was not the case with Thomas Wentworth Higginson, who borrowed more frequently. It is significant to note that the intellectual fare offered undergraduates by the college library did not include the "radical" German books.[22] Rather it was characterized by the time-honored "great books" in the traditional liberal arts fields. The intellectual climate at Divinity School would be somewhat different.

Apparently the college grew but little during Frothingham's stay. President Quincy changed but few things from the "Kirkland era." There were ten faculty members listed in his senior year as there had been four years earlier. Only two new names appeared in the faculty roster replacing two who resigned. Frothingham entered in a class of seventy-six freshmen and graduated in a class of thirty-three seniors. The "attrition," as we would say today, was high; the faculty turnover was low. Harvard was stable. Was it static?

It was lively at times. President Quincy's annual reports to the corporation gave an official view of the academic tone and style of undergraduate behavior during Frothingham's undergraduate years. During his freshman year, 1839–40, the President's report reflected satisfaction with the "quiet," "faithful" pursuit of studies which he called "exemplary." The next year all was quiet until June when the college fence and a worker's shed for the building of Gore Library were set on fire, burning the "latter to the ground." Quincy, baffled by such "wanton" acts, assured the corporation that the offenders were punished appropriately, but did not elaborate. Another highlight of the year was a group of students who "threatened nonattendance at recitation"—in short, a student strike—unless "a college official" was fired. Frothingham's junior year was an orderly one until July when a "bomb shell" was set off "about midnight" in University Hall "doing great damage to adjoining rooms." Poor Quincy was again at a loss as to the reason for such "untoward" acts but assured the corporation the situation was well in hand. Except for the usual pranks of setting bonfires on the steps of college buildings, emitting catcalls after hours, and drinking too much at club meetings, the rest of Frothingham's undergraduate days were in the official reports relatively quiet. The usual undergraduate resistance to things spiritual was shown in the increased attrition rate at required prayers and Sabbath observances. In Frothingham's freshman year 10 out of 76 skipped prayers. By his senior year the figure had increased to 33 out of 68 students. These cold statistics appeared without presidential comment. No doubt the pattern was the rule rather than the exception.[23]

Frothingham, unlike Henry Thoreau and Thomas Wentworth Higginson, left few impressions recorded of college life. Higginson, who was later to become a Divinity School classmate of Frothingham and to be his close friend and colleague over the next half century, recorded impressions of certain tutors and aspects of college life.[24] Perhaps Frothingham's impressions were similar, though he was two years behind his friend at Harvard. Higginson described President Josiah Quincy as aloof and "stand offish." Longfellow was genial and informal, having a close relationship with his students. Higginson considered Jared Sparks an "unimaginative teacher." He describes parties, dancing, backgammon, and singing with certain Cambridge and Boston young ladies, during which he often "had a miserable time." [25]

On Exhibition Days there were programs and athletic feats with prizes, where wine was drunk and cigars smoked. Phi Beta Kappa Day was also celebrated with orations and prizes. Elizabeth Peabody's bookstore on West Street in Boston was the place to get the latest "German books" which were apparently unavailable in Harvard Library. Occasionally Margaret Fuller held her famous conversations here. One can safely assume that Octavius Frothingham participated in at least some of the activities described by his friend, Higginson. Of the numerous undergraduate clubs one wonders which attracted Octavius. It is doubtful if the Hermetic Society or Natural History Club devoted to science appealed to him. The Hasty Pudding Club, which Emerson had considered too snobbish, probably did not include Frothingham in its membership, although his friend, Samuel Longfellow, was the secretary for one year.[26] Then there was the Porcellian for gay blades who enjoyed convivial evenings and various spoof societies such as Knights of the Square Table, Navy Club, and Med. Fac., a satirical group who had mock ceremonies, awarded spurious degrees and citations. This type of humor probably would have appealed to Frothingham but no record exists of his membership.[27] It is more likely that Octavius was lone performer in those activities in which he excelled—declamation and forensics. At the end of his junior year in 1842 he, along with John Kingman, was awarded the Boylston Prize for declamation, with the Honorable Senator Samuel Hoar as one of the judges.[28] Music was another great interest and strength of Frothingham along with public speaking. He was a member of the University Choir and its president during his sophomore year.[29] This was a convivial activity that he and his classmates recalled as being among their warmest memories of college years.

Henry Thoreau, who was graduated two years before Frothingham entered, took a more jaundiced view of his college days at Harvard. In response to the suggestion that Harvard taught all the branches of learning, he quipped, "Yes . . . all the branches and none of the roots." [30] At another time he scored the Harvard grounding in natural philosophy and mathematics which he said, in spite of it not one of his classmates could navigate a rowboat down the Charles River. Perhaps this ex post facto comment can be discounted without a discredit to either Henry Thoreau or the college, one official of which considered him as a student to be a "solitary idler." [31]

Frothingham was not an idler nor was he inclined to look back bitterly on his Harvard days. Neither was he the warm social man of Higginson's type. His relations with his tutors and most classmates must be described as being a bit "offish." Yet more than a half century later Josiah P. Quincy, historian and lawyer, recalled an unidentified classmate as saying,

> He was a close and conscientious student and one of the first eight in the class. But he was far from being a dig and gave and took his full share of social enjoyment. He sang favorite songs with capital effect, and there were very few general occasions of the Phi Beta Kappa or other undergraduate festivities that he did not set the table in a roar by a ballad called "Hamlet" or delighted the more sober by Dicken's song of the "Ivy Green." He was bright and cordial in his manners, always greeting you with a smile.[32]

In spite of Higginson's account of Henry Wadsworth Longfellow's warm and informal relations with his students, young Frothingham did not share in this apparently. During the early years of his Salem ministry, Frothingham had the occasion to write to Longfellow offering a letter of introduction for a friend which began stiffly, "My Dear Sir, I hope I am not taking too great a liberty in introducing to your notice Adolph Casatanant from Martinique. . . ." [33] A few years later Frothingham was asking for an answer to his note about a certain Mr. Scherb which he had not received.[34] Later he did take the liberty of asking Longfellow to recommend a mutual friend for a position at Bowdoin as Professor of Belles Lettres.[35] What his opinion of Longfellow as a Harvard professor was is unknown.

His formality toward Professor Longfellow is curious. The professor's younger brother, Samuel, was a classmate and close personal friend of Frothingham. During college years Sam lived at famed Craige House with his older brother's family. There is no doubt that Frothingham visited the home socially as something more than merely another of Longfellow's literature students. Later in life, it is true, he was to denigrate the poet's work. Yet he must have enjoyed the small, intimate, seminar-style class Longfellow conducted in a carpeted room around a table in University Hall.[36]

The only surviving opinion of Frothingham's Harvard mentors is that of Reverend James Walker who joined the Harvard and Divinity School staff in 1839, the same year that Frothingham enrolled as a freshman. Walker was popular with the young men, solicitous of their welfare, kind and patient in answering their questions. Frothingham, influenced by him, considered him "reasonable," "non-dogmatic," "moderate" in tone, yet preaching, at times, in the radical tradition of Jonathan Mayhew.[37]

Unlike his friend Higginson and other young men of his century, Octavius Frothingham left behind no diary or journal. One can piece together bits of evidence and only speculate about his years at Harvard. His name appears from time to time in the college records, but it was mostly a routine type of entry. His mathematics course was waived in his sophomore year. As a freshman, he and fifteen others were allowed to cut chapel and "worship with his family." In his junior year things livened up a bit when he and his roommate, White, were "privately admonished" by President Quincy for "noise in their room." He was fortunate for at the same time another was "publicly admonished" for "turbulence in class and shooting a pistol in his room." On Exhibition Day his name, like those of his classmates, appeared as giving a Latin oration or a rendition in English of "Vaublanc at the Erection of a statue in honor of Napoleon." His essays and orations were meticulously copied in beautiful handwriting he never again tried to match. Finally, in August, 1843, when he was ready to be graduated, he was rated along with others as a "highly distinguished" student. He passed the "highest course in Latin and Greek" in September. As a matter of course, he and twenty-eight others were accredited for the M.A. degree three years later, in August, 1846.[38]

There is no doubt that his record was a distinguished one. Majoring in "Greek, Latin, Rhetoric, Political Economy and History" he was graduated in the top few of a class of thirty-three young men. The college events of the summer of 1843 were the usual ones for observing the end of the four year career of a graduating class. Class Day on July 13 was marked by the prayers of Reverend James Walker, music by the band, a recitation by Eben Carlton Sprague, a poem by Henry Dwight Sedgwick, and a sentimental rendition by the class of "Old Bonnie Doon" followed by "Auld Lang Syne." [39] This was routine enough. One wonders with what spirit Octavius entered into these sentimental expressions of regard for Alma Mater. The Harvard Class Book, partly written by classmates at graduation time, filled in through subsequent years, shows a strong ambivalence in Frothingham's attitudes. Two pages appear in his handwriting which suddenly breaks off with a notation by William A. Richardson, class secretary, "removed at his [Frothingham's] request." Page five begins again in his handwriting in the midst of an intense passage about college fellowship, etc. Suddenly it breaks off and resumes as a terse entry, "My biography is now finished. I was born, went to school . . . claim only a corner of memory and affection of classmates. . . . ." In another hand, the rest is a sketchy catalog of dates and events in his early years after graduation.[40] If this indicates hostility toward his college experience it did not seem to keep him away from his 20th and 50th reunions which he attended in 1863 and 1893.[41]

The traditional graduation ceremony, routine in form, was memorable in some respects. After the graduation dinner, the thirty-three graduates,

speakers, and guests filed to the First Unitarian Church on the corner of
Church Street directly across from Massachusetts Hall.[42] A newspaper
reporter from a Boston paper observed the event. The audience and
graduating class listened to disquisitions from each graduate accompanied by the usual prayers and invocations. The salutatory oration was
delivered in Latin by Octavius Brooks Frothingham. The young man rose
and faced the distinguished audience which included the "venerable"
John Quincy Adams, a member of Harvard Corporation. "The young
gentleman who gave the salutatory oration saluted him as one entitled to
the homage of the University." [43] One can assume that young Frothingham was well aware of Adams' presence and had prepared his remarks
well in advance. Adding additional lustre to the occasion were honorary
Doctor of Laws degrees conferred on William H. Prescott, George Bancroft, and Jared Sparks. Ezra Stiles Gannett received a Doctor of Divinity
degree. A few days later the annual Phi Beta Kappa anniversary was held.
Frothingham, as a new member, was undoubtedly there.[44]

So far in Octavius' life it is difficult to see how the seeds of radical
dissent, to be so characteristic of his career, were implanted. Certainly
Boston Latin School, followed by four years at Harvard College, were
regular enough. Unfortunately, we can never know what the personal
and unique experiences of his early years contributed. As he sat and
watched George Bancroft, lately part of the "radical" Jacksonian movement, and Jared Sparks, whose ministerial career had been launched by
William Ellery Channing, honored by Harvard College, he must have
pondered his own future. No doubt the example was not lost on him. The
next phase was to be three years in Harvard Divinity School where liberal
influences can be more clearly seen.

FOUR

On September 25, 1842, one year before Octavius Frothingham entered Harvard Divinity School, Theodore Parker wrote to Convers Francis relating a conversation he had held with a Mr. Withington concerning
the state of teaching at Divinity Hall. The "school bears a new aspect . . .
it has a new soul." He congratulated Francis who had been appointed
Professor of Pulpit Eloquence and Pastoral Care a few months earlier for
his part in creating the new atmosphere. Parker felt that the Unitarian
denomination had "first-rate scholars" like Frothingham (Nathaniel
Langdon) and Upham "but among the young men there was a "want of
sound study." He advised Francis to broaden theological study, to institute a broad library, reminding him that the purpose of the ministry was
to promote "truth and goodness." "Is not theology about where natural
science was before Bacon," he asked? "Shall we leave the reformation of
theology to the orthodox or do our part?" He asked Francis to "pardon a

boy's advice" and ended by decrying ministers who spend their time visiting "old women in the parish" rather than seeking truth by preaching, precept, and study.[45]

Parker's radicalism is well known but behind the import of this letter was long and complex debate within the Unitarian denomination itself, which caused new winds to eventually stir Divinity Hall. The controversy itself was a logical extension of the Arminian conflict within Calvinism itself. This had come to the surface in William E. Channing's famous 1819 sermon at the ordination of Jared Sparks in Baltimore. Radical in his day, Channing had stressed the Arminian impulse of free will and inquiry as a modification of predestination and revelation without really challenging all the tenets of Calvinism or the viability of miracles. The controversy broke open anew and in a larger context as Octavius Frothingham was preparing to step onto the stage. It overlapped his late Boston Latin School and early Harvard years. Andrews Norton, "Unitarian Pope," former Divinity School professor, and George Riply, his former student and minister of Purchase Street Church, Boston, were the chief antagonists.[46]

The battle of sermons and pamphlets between Norton and Riply was waged from 1836 to 1840. Essentially the issue was between Transcendentalism and Rationalism. The nature of miracles was involved as it always had been, but the debate involved far more than pure theology. Norton represented the rational, empirical approach supported by the psychology and philosophy of John Locke. George Riply as a transcendentalist stressed intuition based on German and French Romanticism. Although Riply had plenty of vocal support among such transcendentalists as Emerson, Parker, Orestes Brownson, and James Freeman Clark, Andrews Norton and the orthodox majority of Unitarians carried the controversy dubbing the transcendental views "heresy" and a threat to Christianity. A year after Emerson's famous Divinity School address, Andrews Norton was asked to speak to the graduation class. His sermon was a "declaration of war against radicals and a move to consolidate Unitarian forces. . . ."[47] Clearly it was a rebuttal to Emerson's address of the previous year in which he accused both Emerson and Riply of infidelity.

George Riply resigned from the ministry in 1841, leaving Norton as spokesman for the Unitarian majority which included Nathaniel Langdon Frothingham. A few years later this made it possible for the denomination to present a solid front against Theodore Parker at his "heresy trial." Yet, there were two notable exceptions—Convers Francis and James Walker. These men were sympathetic to the transcendentalists and the German school of philosophy and theology. These men were the Divinity School professors of Octavius Frothingham and his generation. Although the controversy between the "Lockean sensationalists" and "intuitive transcendentalists" consolidated conservative Unitarians by driving key men from the association, it helped produce a generation of radical young men who entered the Unitarian ministry with attitudes of scepticism and revolt. As we shall see, the conflict lay the groundwork for the eventual founding of the Free Religious Association by Octavius Frothingham and his contemporaries.

By the time Frothingham had finished Harvard College in 1843 and was entering Divinity School, the abolition movement had become an abrasive issue within Unitarianism. Although most of the abolitionists were transcendentalists or Calvinists, very few Unitarians joined the movement. Wendell Phillips thought that the ministers avoided the issue to please wealthy parishioners and to placate southern slave-holding brethren. Regardless of the reason, abolitionists of Wendell Phillip's frame of mind regarded them as part of the "black hearted ministry." During Frothingham's first year in Divinity School the Unitarian Association voted down a resolution proposed by Samuel May for declaring slavery unchristian on the grounds that no support should be given the "diabolical spirit" of William Lloyd Garrison.[48] Such a stand must have presented a sorry spectacle to the impatient young men in Divinity Hall. But Samuel May, one of the few Unitarian abolitionists, was soon to encourage the young Reverend Frothingham in his radicalism and William Lloyd Garrison, Jr. was to be a colleague of Frothingham in the Free Religious Association.

Moribund though the denomination might seem, Divinity School itself was described as being vaguely liberal, steering a middle course "between the orthodoxy of Andover and the rationalism of Germany." [49] Founded in 1819, the year of Channing's sermon at Jared Sparks' ordination in Baltimore, the school was the continual concern of Harvard authorities. Dean John G. Palfrey was writing all though the 1820s and 1830s about the need for a well-financed, autonomous school with an adequate staff and library.[50] Divinity Hall was built in 1824 on a faraway section of the campus "embedded in a rustic woodland" where students both lived and studied. Harvard was never intended to be a Unitarian seminary, but due to the efforts to avoid sectarianism, it tended to be Unitarian in spirit from the beginning and was so quite noticeably after 1819.[51]

Frothingham himself, in later years, acknowledged the liberal influence of Reverend Convers Francis and Professor Noyes. Yet he considered Divinity Hall to be a "half monastic" atmosphere. Frothingham entered Divinity Hall when the school was in a difficult period, being starved financially and "overburdened" intellectually with only a three-man faculty—Henry Ware, J. Convers Francis, and Reverend Noyes.[52] Oblivious to Emerson and Brook Farm, the school taught a conservative Unitarian doctrine and thought Theodore Parker "a bugbear." [53] Nevertheless, Parker's theology must have been part of the unofficial curriculum. Thomas Wentworth Higginson related an encounter with his classmate Frothingham after the students had been debating the question "Is Theodore Parker a Christian?" As Higginson and Frothingham met later at the woodpile behind their dormitory, both agreed that Parker needed no denominational label and could stand on his own views. Frothingham's rejoinder was ". . . that is the way I view it. I am perfectly willing to be called a Frothinghamian." [54] Later Parker and Frothingham were to become close friends though Frothingham eventually felt that he had "gone a great deal beyond . . . Parker." [55]

The same could be claimed for many in Frothingham's generation at Divinity School. It was a lively group, beginning their theological training in times of change. "The leading men of the Harvard class naturally gravitated to the Divinity School," recalled T. W. Higginson with perhaps some lack of modesty. "There I met such men as Thomas Hill, later president of Harvard, William Alger, Samuel Longfellow, Samuel Johnson and Octavius B. Frothingham." [56] There were others, such as James Richardson, Secretary of the class of '43, whom Frothingham described as "a brilliant wreath of fire . . . which seemed every moment to be on the point of becoming a star, but never did." [57] Frothingham's special friends in Divinity School were T. H. Higginson, Samuel Longfellow, and Samuel Johnson, who gave the class oration on Graduation Day July   , 1846.[58] These friendships were to last throughout their stormy lifetimes of religious controversy.

It was a good time to be entering Divinity School. The bicentennial of Harvard College was celebrated that September of 1843. A large tent was spread out in front of Halworthy Hall, where Octavius had spent the last four years. The campus swarmed with mayors of Massachusetts towns and governors of neighboring states. There were toasts and cigars. Speeches were made. Senator Webster was there. Dr. Oliver Wendell Holmes gave an amusing spoof on the Alma Mater. Edward Everett, Frothingham's uncle and governor of the state, gave an address.[59]

It was also a good time to be entering the Unitarian ministry. "The Transcendental movement was then at full tide," recalled Samuel Longfellow later. The germ of it had been already in Channing's sermons; Emerson had printed *Nature* and the early addresses at Cambridge, Dartmouth, and Waterville—this last his complete expression of spiritual pantheism, and had collected and edited the chapters of *Sartor Resartus;* Dr. Walker had given his Lowell Lectures on Natural Religion; Boston Unitarian circles were still riled over Theodore Parker's "heresy trial" of the previous January which had resulted in his "virtual excommunication" from the association.[60]

It was in this atmosphere that Frothingham and his Harvard classmates presented themselves to the Divinity School on the first Friday after their commencement exercises in August, 1843. They had to prove their soundness of "morals and seriousness of character" and be examined in Latin, Greek, the first four books of Xenophon's *Anabasis,* Locke's essays, and other works of "intellectual philosophy." As if four years at Harvard College were not enough, a mastery of Paley's *Moral Philosophy* and mastery of works in logic, rhetoric, geography, and mathematics had to be demonstrated. With these hurdles passed, the would-be ministers must possess copies of the Old and New Testaments "in the original language" of the approved Greisback edition.[61] It is significant that the Griesback version of the Bible was required at the Divinity School. Johann Jacob Griesback was a pioneer in German New Testament criticism and an authority used by Joseph Buckminister prior to his appointment as Dexter lecturer in 1811. Although Buckminister died before he could take the Dexter chair, the topic of Biblical criticism was introduced into the curriculum of the Divinity School a generation before Frothingham's time.[62]

Although Frothingham never had anything positive to say about his Divinity School education his classmate, Samuel Johnson, found the students interesting if sometimes boring with an excellent library and a great deal of freedom to select "partly by [one's] own judgement." [63] Actually, it was a prescribed curriculum including Hebrew, Criticism and Interpretation of Scripture, Church History and Polity, composition and delivery of sermons, and duties of the pastoral office. Yet a balance of viewpoints was attempted among the diverse subjects of Natural Religion, Evidence of Revealed Religion, and Systematic Theology. The curriculum was also a balance between theory and practice. There were required exercises for upperclassmen in extemporaneous speaking, and seniors preached weekly during summer terms in the "Village Church" where Octavius had given the valedictory address in 1843. Public lectures by invited speakers were also a part of the experience and attendance was required by all Divinity students.

President Josiah Quincy, who would retire during Frothingham's middle year in Divinity School, reported a faculty of three Divinity professors in 1843. Convers Francis, as Parkman Professor of "Pulpit Eloquence and Pastoral Care," taught Natural Religion, Ecclesiastical History, Church Polity, Delivery of Sermons, and Duties of the Pastoral Office. According to Frothingham's later judgment it was the stimulus and direction of Francis that carried Longfellow, Higginson, and Johnson "into the transcendental ranks." [64] Reverend George Noyes, as Hancock Professor of Hebrew, Oriental Languages, and Dexter Lecturer in Sacred Literature balanced Reverend Francis' point of view with his classes in Critical Interpretation of the Old and New Testaments, Evidence of Christianity (revealed religion presumably), and Dogmatic Theology. No mention was made of Reverend James Walker's teaching responsibilities other than his dual responsibility of teaching in both Harvard College and the Divinity School. Reverend Henry Ware, Jr. was still active, though what he taught was not mentioned in President Quincy's reports.[65] However, Samuel Longfellow recalled "Thursday evenings" with him as a regular part of the Divinity School experience, observing that he was a conservative Unitarian of the James Walker type.[66]

In spite of Frothingham's memory of Divinity School as being "half monastic" and Samuel Johnson's complaint that Dr. Convers Francis was "very uninteresting," the young divinity students were offered balanced viewpoints in theology, philosophy, and ethics. There was no basic change in the curriculum during Frothingham's stay at Divinity Hall but efforts continued to improve the school and expand the library by financial donations.[67]

The "informal curriculum" such as Theodore Parker's speeches and social controversies being debated in society outside of Harvard College had more influence than can be recorded. But it was the freedom to read and study independently that stimulated the young men at Divinity Hall. Surprisingly Frothingham did not read as widely as some of his classmates. During his first year he drew out seven books including Baxter's *On the Soul* and Butler's *Grottus*. His friend, George Bartol, whose older brother Cyrus Bartol would later help in founding the Free Religious Society, read nothing but works of literature. Two other classmates, Johnson and Richardson, withdrew *Augustinian Pelagianism,* Whately's *St. Paul,* Luther's *Table Talk,* and Goethe's works by Coleridge. As during his undergraduate days, Frothingham's reading increased in his second year. Nineteen books are recorded as withdrawn by him. This was his most impressive list including Dr. Potter's *History of Christianity,* Jones' *St. Mark, Augustinian Pelagianism,* Gilpin's *Wycliff,* and a work by H.E.G. Paulus, a German New Testament critic.

At the same time, Bartol and Longfellow were reading literature, Higginson read *Wealth of Nations,* German literature, and the works of Hegel, while Theodore Parker, enjoying the library privilege of an alumnus, read Fluge's *Theolog Wissenschaft.* Between September and May of Frothingham's senior year (1845–46), he withdrew eight books. Although it was essentially the same theological fare he had consumed previously, there was one notable exception—Frederiech C. Straus' *Leben Jesu* (1838) which topped the list.[68] From the evidence available, this was Frothingham's only venture into German criticism of Christianity while at Divinity School. Library lists show no evidence of Harvard possessing the critical works of J. G. Eichorn, J. G. Von Herder, or J. J. Griesback, authorities at this time in the new field of New Testament criticism. However, Professor Francis and Professor Noyes were familiar with these German scholars and probably used their ideas in lectures to their classes. It can be assumed that Professor Convers Francis brought up the subject in his course, Natural Religion, but apparently Frothingham did not follow through with much reading on the subject. Higginson, on the other hand, was reading works of Schelling and those of the religious mystic Swedenborg which would later influence Frothingham by way of Theodore Parker. In a word, he was not advanced in his theological thinking at this time if his reading can be used as a measure. It is likely that his classmates, Higginson, Johnson, and Longfellow were more widely read than he and edging closer at this time on toward religious radicalism.

This may not be a fair estimate of his views, however, when one considers a series of lectures on the Bible he delivered to a ladies' group in Salem, Massachusetts in the spring of his junior and senior years in Divinity School. Just how he came to do this is not clear. Perhaps he was recommended by some professor at Harvard to fulfill the request of the Salem women or perhaps it was his famous "Unitarian name" and his Harvard reputation for brilliant scholarship. It is clear that he spent a great deal of time preparing his "lessons," drawing from some reading of German scholarship as well as, no doubt, his class notes from Divinity School lectures. One of the group, a Miss Eliza Davis Bradlee, recorded his remarks in meticulous detail, filling four volumes of composition books.[69]

The Bible is not an inspired book, he told them at the first meeting. The Gospels were a product of the times, written by ignorant men who fully believed in Jesus and had everything to lose by propagating their faith. He then contrasted the four men, Matthew, Mark, Luke, and John as to style and context for writing what they supposedly wrote:

> . . . the Bible is not necessarily an inspired volume—but it is highly valuable—and I should reverence it as containing sublime principles—although I might not subscribe to all its sentiments . . . it was written by Jews and often subject to their prejudices—therefore would I read and study it as I would any other book—with mind alone—ready to investigate—making constant use of common sense and reason.[70]

As for Jesus, he disposed of his supernatural beginning but elaborated on the man's work as a spiritual leader. From that point, the young Divinity student cast doubt on certain miracles, yet defended the value of them in a certain context of an historical time. Apparently this was a bit too much for his listener, who wrote in response to his views of Jesus and miracles, "Mr. F. does not believe in Jesus nor the resurrection—how then can we constantly listen to him." She had no objection, however, when he continued with the suggestion that devils should be cast out as being entirely too crude and unnecessary for modern religion. Devils, suggested Frothingham, are symbolic ways of referring to the present-day prevalence of "slavery and drunkenness."

The lectures must have been exciting for both teacher and pupils. Frothingham, if Eliza Bradlee's notes are to be trusted, gave them the best Transcendental-Unitarian interpretation of the Deity and religious creeds. "The Transcendentalists believe there is no God—that the soul is everything—it possesses an all-creative power in itself. They are governed by a sense of right—verities as they term them—to which all are bound to submit." As for the Christ idea, Frothingham gently pointed out to the ladies that Paul had raised the idea of "Christ as high as possible" and that "pagans" combined the idea with their own myths, broadening the concept for a wider appeal among the people of the Greek and Roman world. He hastily added that the present age is not "ripe" for a fair and true evaluation of this development. Characteristic of his later style of skepticism, he admitted that Unitarianism has no creed, only opinions which may be no more true than Calvinistic views. There is some value and truth in all creeds:

> I would not receive an opinion merely from its being Unitarian—or reject it for its Calvinism or because it favors any particular doctrine—I conceive good in every form of religion . . . Unitarianism does not by any means contain all of Good. The only Unitarian opinion I advocate is the liberality which it grants in interpreting the scriptures—but this is the rock over which it may be destined to stumble—many have gone so far as to give up everything which is religious—have become mono-maniacs almost.[71]

As the lecture continued through the spring of 1845, the young Divinity student seemed to draw back from his role as radical innovator in the minds of his female pupils. One is tempted to speculate that he discussed the content of his lectures with Divinity School professors or, perhaps more significantly, with his own father. Two years later, in Salem, Reverend N. L. Frothingham would warn his son against saying too much.

In his last lecture of the year he justified belief in the Trinity in classic Unitarian style, "without mysticism, without confounding the three-in-one or one-in-three." The authority of Christ is essential and cannot be dispensed with he finally told the ladies. One cannot be a Christian, no matter how good, without acknowledging the mission of Christ. Yet as Parker and others have said, all will get salvation without such a belief. However, in complete contradiction to this earlier disposal of the idea of the divinity of Jesus he told the group, "The whole account of the resurrection is so impregnable that we cannot but believe it." [72]

Was his last lecture of the series a "recantation" or simply a reflection of a young man's mind in process of growth with ideas yet unformed? At any rate, the ladies invited him back the following year for a series of lectures on the Apocalypse.[73] He subjected the book of Revelations to "internal and external" criticism. "Let us set aside," he told his class, "the thousand and one prophecies of the coming of Martin Luther, Napoleon Bonaparte or Ghengis Khan which ingenious critics have found in the book of Revelations." He rejected the authenticity of the Apocalypse as did German criticism and set aside the notion that John wrote it. The Apocalypse

was an inspired book of poetic art and not written for evangelical purposes. It was written, he thought, in a time of trouble, which threatened
the Jewish nation with extinction. The symbols of the Temple's destruc-
tion, the seven-headed beast on the "head of the beast," had particular
reference to the impending doom of Jerusalem, the seven hills of the seat
of Roman power, and Nero himself as its beastial head. The Apocalypse
then is not valuable for religious truth or as a "minute prediction" of the
future victory of Christianity. Lacking both religious truth and historical
validity, the Apocalypse is a tract for the times, written under the press of
urgency of Roman persecution and falling away of Christian adherents all
over the Empire. The book, therefore, is no longer usable because its
work is done, "as Christianity itself might yet be when *its* work is done." As
dogmatic as this may have sounded to the ladies, Frothingham ended his
remarks modestly as befitting a young Divinity School student then without official office.

> As yet the whole subject [of these books] is much in the dark—and at some
> future time I may be better able to explain them than I am now—at present I
> am mainly indebted for my information to Mr. Stuart who is indebted to the
> Germans—the German books upon the subject not being within my
> reach—and it is therefore not unreasonable to hope that we also may in
> some distant manner come to understand them.[74]

The lectures over and his goodbyes said to his ladies of the class, he
received a letter of thanks and a four-volume work of unknown title. His
group appreciated his "full and impartial" examination of the Bible in his
first labors in the ministry. It was signed by nine women as his "grateful
and affectionate pupils." [75] In a long, sentimental reply four days later,
Frothingham thanked them for the volumes and apologized for "an
occasional severity" for which he promised he had already repented.[76]

FIVE

This experience must have been the highlight of his Divinity School
experience. The trial preaching in Salem made him well known in that
city and led him to his call, the following year, to North Church. Otherwise his three years at Divinity School were uneventful. Even President
Quincy's annual reports were routine summaries and statistics concerning college affairs and bland comments about the "peaceful, successful"
years. Waldo Emerson made an occasional appearance to borrow books
and hold informal talks with students but gave no more Divinity School
addresses. Frothingham's father, Rev. N. L. Frothingham, came out from
Boston periodically to examine undergraduates in foreign languages,
invariably giving a "good report" to the President. Suddenly in the spring
of Frothingham's middle year at Divinity Hall, President Quincy an-

nounced in a blunt note to the corporation that he would retire.[77] By the fall of 1846 his successor was named. He was Frothingham's uncle, the Honorable Edward Everett, twice governor of the state, U.S. Envoy to England, European educated, and world traveler. He had accepted the appointment with reluctance [78] and some feeling of distaste as a position he considered a comedown in his career in public life. Everett also considered himself unqualified and unfit for such a position. Yet Emerson described his role as like "Pericles in Athens . . . a man of 'perfect utterance and radiance of thought who could lift the rudest undergraduates to new learning.' " [79] Actually Everett was right. His term as president was brief and unpleasant. Unpopular with students and contentious with the corporation members, he resigned within two years. The *Boston Post,* as quoted in the *Salem Gazette,* regretted his resignation as being due to the "intractability of the students," adding that apparently the "B-boys are too strong for the government." [80] Octavius Frothingham had nothing but respect for his Uncle Edward. It was he who listened to his pregraduation sermon in the "Village Church" in the summer of 1846 and taught him to speak without notes in the extemporaneous manner—a skill that helped Frothingham become one of the greatest preachers of the age.

His trial sermon was approved by the Divinity School professors and President Everett. His graduation essay was prepared. On Visitation Day the thirteen Divinity School graduates, along with the graduating seniors and graduates of other schools, participated in the traditional ceremony in the Unitarian Church across the street from the Harvard campus. The graduation essays of Frothingham's class of 1846 are missing from Harvard College records. Had they been saved, it would be possible to get a glimpse of the thinking of these young men as they began their careers in the ministry.[81] Ten of the thirteen graduated and spent the rest of their lives in quiet ministerial posts and were never heard of again. Not so for Octavius Frothingham and his friends, the "Sams"—Longfellow and Johnson. Higginson would follow a year later.

II

The Clam Bed and Beyond:
Salem and
Jersey City Years

THE YOUNG MINISTER HAD BEEN in Salem five years when he wrote to George E. Ellis, editor of the Unitarian *Christian Examiner,* thanking him for the opportunity to write articles and reviews for publication. "I made [the offer to write] in a state of intellectual despond, feeling that in this clam bed of Salem, I may be relapsing into a condition of perilous inertness [and] mental rust." [1] Why he harbored such fears is not clear. He had been active enough with his writing for the *Examiner,* as a member of the School Committee, and Chairman of the Salem Lyceum. Even more exciting years were to come with the "Anthony Burns Affair" which contributed to the break with his congregation.

It is true that Salem by 1847 had long since passed the peak of her commercial glory. Although the first industry had been established more than twenty years earlier, Salem was far from being the bustling industrial city that many New England towns were by the 1840s.[2] Yet Salem, a town of 20,000 at this time, was far from being isolated from New England thought or national events. The Mexican War was on as Frothingham took over his office in North Church. A scanning of Salem papers in these months reveals a tone of hostility to the war and a feeling of humiliation for the nation in being involved in the invasion of Mexico. The town reacted sensitively. Less than a month after Frothingham's ordination, Samuel Johnson, then living in Salem, spoke against the war in Boston Square Church in Salem.[3] Similarly, the slave question touched the town on a sensitive nerve and was not ignored. A few months after the Mexican War speech by Johnson, the Female Anti-slavery Society sponsored an appearance of William Wells Brown, a fugitive slave who spoke, along with Samuel Johnson and William Lloyd Garrison, at the Lyceum Building.[4]

The young minister faced a congregation made up of the middle class and elements of the intelligentsia of Salem. Some lived on inherited wealth from the sea trade; most were entrepreneurs, shopkeepers, and professional people. Typical of the group were two men who were leaders in the affairs of the church during Frothingham's tenure: John H. Nichols, surveyor and auctioneer, and George Wheatland, Justice of the Peace. It was a group conservative in its politics and complacent in religious beliefs. It was a "good parish" and an "ideal environment for study," recalled Frothingham in later years. "But the life was almost too quiet for me as circumstances presently proved." [5]

Even North Church, standing on a stately Essex Street two doors from the famous "Witches House," seemed a monument to the past. Erected in 1836, the building was constructed of Quincy granite in the early English Gothic style.[6] In Frothingham's time, before the Tiffany windows were added, the building no doubt had a modest and slightly puritanical appearance. The congregation, "gathered" in 1629, was an offshoot of the First Congregational Society, and for a short time had been the church of Roger Williams.[7] In 1772, a year before the Boston Tea Party, part of the congregation split off, established North Church, and became Unitarian.

It was in this building at 11 A.M., on March 10, 1847, that the young Divinity School graduate was ordained after a few months of trial sermons in various places. He came to the church under the best possible auspices. The former pastor, Reverend John Brazer, had died the year before in February, 1846. The congregation had turned down a Reverend D. Ingersoll and, in September, 1846, decided to invite candidates to preach not more than four Sundays for each individual. By December 19 the Proprietors Committee recommended inviting Octavius Frothingham to be the pastor. Nine days later the society voted 63 to 1 in favor of calling him to their church. By January, 1847, Frothingham's acceptance was confirmed, his salary set at $1,500 per year.[8]

ONE

An ordination was always a solemn occasion when the elders impressed the rising young minister with the awesome responsibility of his new office. Octavius' father, Nathaniel Langdon Frothingham, up from Boston for the occasion, assisted Dr. Parkman of Boston, Rev. T. T. Stone of Salem, and Rev. George Putnam D.D. of Roxbury.[9] He preached the ordination sermon: "Rightly Dividing the Word of Truth." Sermons must be in keeping with the impulse of the age, considering the impact of science and truth as a progressive thing. Yet truth "must be sifted," admonished his father, "interpreted" in levels for different people. Little of substance can be added to religious truth. "Your duty," he warned, "is to interpret it and divide it 'rightly.' " Rev. Frothingham warned the young man that innovation is not the role of the minister; special causes or tastes should not affect the interpretation of existing truth. He ended with this:

May God give you grace to divide the word rightly, my son, in the place where you are honored to stand, and wherever that task, difficult as it is, will be only a part, not even the most important part . . . of your sacred obligation. . . . The Virtue is in the seed and not in the sower's hand.[10]

"Do not say sharp or frivolous thing," said Putnam, "but try to avoid alienating your congregation; yet be a scholar and cultivate your intellect." Subsequent events proved these to be two contradictory pieces of advice. However, young Frothingham seems to have followed more closely the advice of Dr. Putnam than that of his father.

Nathaniel Langdon Frothingham, Minister of First Church, Boston, since 1820, had come to personify conservative Unitarianism. Moving only slightly beyond William Ellery Channing, who disclaimed original sin, the Trinity, and allowed some play of Free Will, N. L. Frothingham took his theological ground against Theodore Parker's "Natural Religion" and his political activism. He also opposed both Parker, who established his own Free Church, and John Freeman Clark, who advocated such establishment outside of the Unitarian Association. His approach to social activism went no further than serving as the Vice-President of the Massachusetts Bible Society for several years.[11] Essentially N. L. Frothingham was a literary man, hymn writer, and poet. The book withdrawals from Harvard College Library are indicative of his intellectual tastes. Eight to twelve volumes a year were borrowed, ranging from Mandeville's *Free Thought* to a Greek and Latin lexicon. Save for the work of Goethe, no German authors in philosophy or Biblical criticism were borrowed. Novels, plays, or works of poetry made up the bulk of his reading during his son's formative years.[12] In contrast, it is interesting to note that George Ripley was borrowing and reading works of Kant and Fichte. Likewise, Emerson was borrowing works in German philosophy and theology, while Parker was reading everything from Marco Polo to Adam Smith and Schelling.

As his son recalled years later, he was "offish" to Waldo Emerson's invitation to the organization meeting of the Transcendental Club.[13] He declined with a polite note expressing his regrets that he could not join "you Olympians" saying "I would rather have you by yourself or with two or three elect spirits." [14] A low key but steady correspondence passed between him and Emerson during the years 1827 to 1867, three years before Nathaniel L. Frothingham died. The theme was usually literary, thanking Emerson for a volume of essays, commenting on a poem or literary piece in a current journal, chiding him for not appearing as guest speaker at First Church, and once actually accepting a dinner invitation to the Saturday Club.[15] He was typically provincial in the manner of Boston-born of that era. In spite of wide familiarity with the wonders of Florence, Venice, Geneva, Rome, and Paris, he could still say, ". . . give me my little Boston before them all." [16] His poem eulogizing Webster and his fondness for Longfellow's "Building of the Ship" displayed a conservative brand of Whig nationalism. Often it was his wont to quote Milton's famous lines on liberty:

> That bawl for freedom in their senseless
>   mood
> And still revolt when truth would set
>   them free
> License they mean when they cry liberty
> For who loves that, must first be wise
>   and good.

Octavius Frothingham recalled his youthful reaction in later years. "How often have I heard those lines cited, as if the truism they contained settled the whole matter of freedom!" [17] Yet freedom was the legacy of the father to his son. "The true liberal Christian," wrote N. L. Frothingham, "is he who can, in the first place, believe he may be wrong while firmly believing he is right." [18]

The ordination, attended by two hundred persons according to a local account, was a service "of a high order and gave satisfaction to a large audience." It was followed in the afternoon by a "collation" in Hamilton Hall for guests and out-of-town strangers.[19] No one can know what the young man thought as he sat and listened to his father deliver the ordination sermon on that March day in 1847. Was this the source of his undogmatic yet confident encounter with Free Religion in later years? Surely he recognized "the lyrical view of religion," which was a result of his father's literary dimensions, "as the beginning of the new era whose end is not yet, the initiation of a freer movement of mind which detaches intellect from all dogmatism and insures a perfect freedom." [20]

The ordination was over. The father, knowing his son, feared the results of his restlessness of mind, his potential for radicalism fresh from Harvard Divinity School. The Rev. N. L. Frothingham felt it quite appropriate to hand his son at once a legacy of religious freedom and a warning to "rightly divide the 'word of truth.' " The meaning was clear: do not rock the theological boat.[21]

TWO

Thirteen days later, March 23, 1847, Octavius married Caroline Elizabeth Curtis of Boston. Little is known of the occasion of their acquaintance and courtship. Caroline was the daughter of Caleb and Caroline Curtis, originally of Maine but by then a substantial Boston merchant family. Doubtless he had met her at some Boston social occasion as an undergraduate or Divinity School student. It seemed an impeccable match in the Boston Brahmin tradition. The couple moved into the modest but comfortable brick manse for the North Church minister on

Carpenter Street, a short street opening from Federal Street and in Frothingham's time ending in the open country along the shore of North River. No more that six family homes lined the street, with a seaman's bethel on one side of the manse and an orphans' home on the other.

The neighborhood, scarcely changed today, was in the "best part" of Salem, between Chestnut Street, famed for elegance and architecture, and North River, where the village met the open countryside. The houses were of a Federalist or early national period style and less elegant than those on Chestnut Street. Located in close proximity to the street and to one another, they gave the impression of a solid upper-class neighborhood. The young minister could walk in ten minutes to North Church along the tree-lined streets. Depending upon the route chosen, he could pass the houses of some of the wealthy and famous Salem residents of his day. If he chose to walk the length of Federal Street in which Carpenter Street opened, the Pierce-Nichols house was passed. After a right turn on North Street, the former house of Nathaniel Bowdich, the famed Salem supercargo navigator and later Harvard College trustee, was passed. Turning the corner of Essex and North Streets, the house of Judge Corwin of witch-trial fame stood (Witches House). Another famous old house built by Dr. Ebenezer Putnam in the 18th century stood between "Witches House" and the church. A prominent landmark on the other side of the church was a mansion built by George Ropes, a wealthy merchant and shipbuilder.[22] The area bounded by Federal, Essex, and North Streets was a neighborhood of houses forty to sixty-years-old. It was a mellow, well-established neighborhood in its prime from the standpoint of family use and architectural elegance. In the 1840s, as now, it would seem to be an ideal location for a life of speculation and preaching and for raising a family.

Frothingham left few comments and no records of his family life. The vital statistics of Massachusetts record the birth in Salem of a daughter, Elizabeth Bowdich Frothingham, on January 27, 1850.[23] There is every indication that the young minister and his family lived a model life as example and symbol of what might be expected by the congregation in a small, conservative community. As might be expected, the manse on Carpenter Street was open to friends, parishioners, and strangers alike. The young minister with his wife were expected to guide and support the life of the church as well as act as an informal social agency in the community. In spite of Frothingham's growing feeling of isolation and boredom, he plunged into the intellectual and cultural affairs of Salem. As a young daughter, "Bessie" grew and endeared herself to the friends and neighbors, and the young minister established himself as the beloved pastor of North Church. His radicalism and restlessness grew apace, yet he parted company with his congregation with regret and moved on reluctantly, as we shall see, to larger opportunities. Meanwhile, much work was at hand in Salem to challenge him.

Frothingham had succeeded Rev. John Brazer whose twenty-six-year tenure extended from 1820 to 1846. His ministry had seen the building and dedication of the new North Church building in 1836. The church building, at Frothingham's arrival, had stood only eleven years but was apparently in need of repair and renovation. By September, 1847, after a brief spring in the pulpit, he wrote to Rev. George Bartol, a classmate and then minister in Lancaster, Massachusetts, that he had completed a sea-side fishing vacation which was "pleasanter than fishing for men," especially now in "strange water" now that the church was shut down for repairs. He complained that the large temporary hall swallowed up his audience.[24] This happened because shortly after his ordination ceremony the Proprietors decided to install a new organ and a balcony in the rear of the church. This involved extensive renovation and a vast amount of woodwork and skilled finishing.[25]

As if mechanical problems were not enough for the new minister, he was also partly responsible for the forthcoming meeting in Salem of the Unitarian Association. In October, he invited Bartol and his wife to make their headquarters with him and Mrs. Frothingham on Carpenter Street. He confided that the meeting might be good for the cause (but) "we both might have inclinations in the other direction ... anyway we can talk." [26] A local account of the "Autumn Conference" mentioned the names of the men who dominated the deliberations: Rev. Henry W. Bellows, Rev. John Freeman Clark, Rev. Dr. George Putnam, Rev. Ezra Styles Gannett, and Rev. Briggs. This was the conservative leadership against which Frothingham and his young colleagues revolted in 1867. The meeting dealt with procedural matters and expressed opinions in favor of "peace," "freedom," and temperance.[27] Yet, a later account, in editorial form, spoke of "Unitarians and the War." The "Autumn Conference" passed a memorial against the Mexican War, later printed in Boston and circulated publicly.[28] Although it seemed to Frothingham that the old leadership was firmly in control, perhaps the Unitarian Association was less moribund than he and the younger men thought. Looking back through the spectrum of Frothingham's later activities in Free Religion and resignation from the Unitarian Association, however, one is tempted to read harbingers of his early thoughts in this direction. I believe it is safe to assume this. If true, the letter to Bartol is probably the earliest recorded sentiment for a Free Religious Association. But this was twenty years in the future.

THREE

A more immediate task during his first year in Salem was to prepare and deliver one of the sixteen lectures in the Lyceum Series during the 1847–1848 season. The topic was "Bishop Berkley," a lecture performed in good company. Nathaniel Hawthorne was corresponding secretary that year and Mark Hopkins had spoken on "Language." Frothingham was followed by Louis Agassiz, who spoke on "Animal Creation and Glaciers."

The Salem Lyceum, established in 1830 and the building on 35 Church Street built the next year, was a platform for some of the most brilliant people of the age. Carl Bode has said that the Lyceum at Concord, where Thoreau was the corresponding secretary, was the "most intellectual" in the country but that Salem was "almost equally noted." [29] In the ten years prior to Frothingham's arrival in Salem, a sampling of speakers shows such figures and topics as Jared Sparks on "The American Revolution," Convers Francis' "Practical Man," and Horace Mann on the "Education of Children." A broader view of the entire history of the Salem Lyceum shows some 853 lectures given between 1820 and 1879. To list the names of the speakers is to call the roll of figures in the intellectual and political history of the period. Included were Daniel Webster, Rufus Choate, Edward Everett, Theodore Parker, Henry Bellows, Ralph Waldo Emerson (who spoke 28 times), Oliver Wendell Holmes, Sr., Charles F. Adams, John Quincy Adams, James Walker, Caleb Cushing, Wendell Phillips (16 times), Charles Sumner, James Freeman Clark (8 times), Edward Everett Hale, George W. Curtis, Fanny Kimble, George Bancroft, and several "local people," including O. B. Frothingham.[30]

A sampling of the years during which Frothingham participated shows the intellectual company in which he traveled. By 1853 he was President of the Lyceum. That year Starr King spoke on "Property," George Curtis on "Young America," Rev. Henry Ward Beecher gave "Manifestations of the Beautiful," and Rev. Henry Bellows' "New England Festival" added an inspirational and religious touch to the annual offerings. Frothingham, having been abroad the previous summer, spoke on the subject "Europe." Wendell Phillips, the great reformer, and David Wasson, who later helped found the Free Religious Association, were also in the lecture series. The following year, 1854–1855, Frothingham was again President of the Lyceum but did not present a lecture. This was also his last year in Salem. He was invited back three times, however, after he had parted company with his North Church congregation. During his first year in Jersey City (1855–1856) he returned to lecture on "Carlo Barrow," following Samuel May's presentation of "Magna Carta of New York" and preceding Theodore Parker's "Social Progress."

The following year, 1856–1857, Frothingham discussed "Epicurus, The Philosophy of the World." Samuel May, the Unitarian abolitionist, spoke on "Social Progress." Moncure D. Conway, Frothingham's future Free Religious Association colleague, presented a lecture; Theodore Parker spoke on "Benjamin Franklin"; James Russell Lowell gave "Dante"; and Emerson presented "Work and Days." The following year,

Frothingham's next to last year in Jersey City, was also his last appearance in the Salem Lyceum. Beecher was there again, speaking on "The Laws of Sympathy." Frothingham gave "The Conservative." The previous lecture was delivered by Waldo Emerson which was his famed "Conduct of Life." [31]

His Lyceum appearances were over but he had made an impact beyond the confines of Salem and stimulated his own intellectual progress. One can imagine the young minister in the Lyceum Hall, a "boxy" building of "Greek" adaptation,[32] unusually impressive with its seven hundred seats surrounding the platform in semicircular tiers. Directly overhead in the center of the ceiling was a ventilator hidden by a romanticized version of Apollo in his chariot pulling the sun across the heavens in bas relief. It was here that he introduced Emerson, and saw and heard him in action. Here he and Parker, already acquainted, met as equals. He listened to Webster, Sumner, and Edward Everett Hale as political voices of the age.[33]

It was probably at the Lyceum that Frothingham met David Wasson. There is no reason to doubt that the two of them, in numerous conversations with Samuel Johnson, Samuel Longfellow, perhaps with Theodore Parker, their mentor, dreamed and planned a Free Religious Association outside of the Unitarian Association.

One wonders what he thought of Henry Thoreau, who in Frothingham's later *History of Transcendentalism,* received a mere parenthetical reference. In this Lyceum young Frothingham got his first experience in the arena of great minds. It was to stand him in good stead for a broader stage and wider field of action during his New York years. But before that, there was still much to do in Salem.

FOUR

On April 8, 1848, he was elected to the Salem School Committee. His selection for this important town function, along with Rev. T. T. Stone and William F. Nichols, is some indication of the favorable impact he had made in the community during his first year. His activities during the first two years on the committee are not too clear, but by 1850 he was Chairman of the Visiting Committee, responsible for the actual supervision of the several schools in the town. Frothingham's personal responsibility was the supervision of the "Evening Free School," established for children of the poor who for various reasons did not attend the regular public schools. In his first annual report he felt that the girls' section was going well but the boys' division was of "doubtful success" due to the unruly "boys of the streets" over which the teachers had no power but "patience and kindness." Yet the school must go on, he felt, as he asked for continued support.[34]

Two years later, with the Evening Free School in the fifth year of existence, Frothingham felt that it was no longer an experiment but "successful beyond expectations." He pointed out other New England towns such as Portsmouth, New Hampshire, Boston, Roxbury, and Newburyport (Massachusetts) where, according to his friend Thomas Wentworth Higginson, the Free School had taken root. In spite of the tentative success, he was apparently apprehensive about the future of the school. Much of his 1852 report was a plea for more tax support to educate those who had "the misfortune to be poor [so that they] should not also be ignorant." To bolster his argument to the town authorities he attacked the "myth" that the United States was ahead of parts of Europe in universal education. He compared Salem with European cities where "mobs of unruly youths [are seen] running the streets." Although he was not clear as to what European cities he was referring or whether he had been a first-hand observer, Horace Mann could have done no better in stating the case for free compulsory public education.[35]

The following year (1853) the Evening Free School fell on hard times. The director seemed to have mismanaged the money, the boys were unruly, and the school closed down for a while. Frothingham's report was short and blunt, warning the town to support free education to "avoid neglect of the poor in a town singularly free of pauperism." [36] Things were no better the next year. Frothingham's report, his last on the Free School, was an even more desperate plea for public support of education of the "lower orders." They must be saved from "priest and partisan" and taught to vote wisely. Actually he was stating the case for civic education and equal educational opportunity. He warned of the dangers of neglecting the poor, pointing out the cost of ignorance and its threat to society. Why discriminate against the poor, he asked, by spending $400 per pupil in the public day schools and $100 per pupil in the evening division? [37]

Apparently Frothingham asked to be relieved of his responsibility for the Free School after this last plea to the School Committee. The following year the school report shows a brief comment from him as supervisor of the Classical Department of the high school. He expressed a general approval of the curriculum designed "for those headed for Harvard." [38] He was on familiar ground here. Yet his earlier work for the Free School was not in vain. On December 30, 1854, the *Salem Observer* noted the reopening of the Evening Free School with regular teachers hired under the direct supervision of the School Committee. The following spring the school report recorded a more successful year and increased appropriations.[39]

This was his main contribution to the public school system of Salem, but not quite all. In September of his last year in Salem he spoke at the dedication of the "Normal School." A spokesman for the State of Massachusetts proposed a toast to the Salem School Board: "May they labor in unison with the Board of Education to promote the cause of public instruction in the community." The young minister, speaking for the

School Committee of the town, responded, congratulating Salem for getting a state supported school to train teachers. It would be good, he thought, for the Salem system to be in close proximity to the supply of trained teachers. It would also be good for women to have a chance, as the "fair sex, for a fair education, fair wages, and fair dealings in society free from unjust restraints of the law." There were no mental restraints on women, he was sure, only social barriers. Gracefully returning the toast to the Salem Normal School, he ended his remarks with these words: "Though [women] cannot command a flagship, it is more intellectual work to command the man that does." [40] The women's rights movement, though in the air, was not central to Frothingham's thoughts at the time; thus he saw public school teaching as the main opportunity for women.

FIVE

The young minister selected his activities carefully. The Lyceum and School Committee must have occupied a great deal of his time in addition to his parish duties and, as we shall note, his scholarly writing. Frequent notices of meetings and published membership lists of the Bible Society failed to record his name, which must have pained his father down in Boston.[41] During the Mexican War years, a group calling themselves "Friends of Peace" ran notices in the local papers offering themselves as free speakers on the war question. In the list of more than twenty names, including those of William Henry Channing, Rev. Briggs, Samuel May, and his schoolmate T. W. Higginson, Frothingham's name never appeared.[42] Nor did he seem to ever have participated in local ordination ceremonies.[43] He did manage to keep up his Harvard contacts as one of the Boylston prize judges for declamation.[44] The Salem Choral Society, founded in February, 1855, also claimed him as a member of the "Council of Advisors." Dedicated to promoting sacred music, it gave concerts and had a corporate existence into which ladies could be invited as "complimentary members." [45]

The choral society and Lyceum were probably the only stimulating activities in the intellectual life of Salem. However, Frothingham had his Boston connections which were distinguished. On March 20, 1849, a printed invitation went out from Bronson Alcott to certain "esteemed Gentlemen" to form a club or college for the "study of ideas and tendencies proper to the Nineteenth Century" and to further the "ends of good fellowship." [46] A week later an organization meeting, attended by sixteen of the sixty people originally invited, was held to form the "Town and Country Club." There is no record that Frothingham was one of the group, which included Theodore Parker, Ralph Waldo Emerson, Thomas Wentworth Higginson, and William Henry Channing. Yet, a few weeks later, the first substantive meeting was held, attended by Frothingham, Theodore Parker, William Henry Channing, John Freeman Clark,

Cyrus Bartol, and John Weiss. The latter two were instrumental in forming the Free Religious Association in 1867. The topic of discussion for the
first meeting was the "women question which after much discussion was
left in an 'unsettled way.' " [47] Nineteen of the sixty people originally
invited to form the "Town and Country Club" are virtually a roll call of
intellectual leaders in the Transcendental, Abolition, and Free Religious
Association movements. Included in Bronson Alcott's invitation list of
March 20, 1849, were Ralph Waldo Emerson, William Lloyd Garrison,
Theodore Parker, William Henry Channing, Henry Hedge, John
Freeman Clark, Starr King, John Weiss, T. W. Higginson, Henry
Thoreau, Stephen Foster, Oliver Johnson, Samuel Johnson, A. D. Mayo,
C. K. Whipple, and Samuel May.[48] Unfortunately, no consistent record of
the meetings of this group exists. It soon fell apart, according to Henry
Commager, because of bankruptcy.[49]

The nucleus then formed the elite "Saturday Club," excluding Theodore Parker and, by his own choice, Octavius Frothingham.[50] Many of the
younger ones lived to form the "Radical Club" after the Civil War, sometimes referred to as the "second transcendental movement," of which
Frothingham was a member for a brief time (see Chapter VIII).

Much more amusing and of greater future significance was the "Hook
and Ladder Club," an informal group of young ministers recently out of
Divinity School. Frothingham recalled later that it met irregularly but
hilariously in the manner of the "Spoof Club" of Harvard College. The
irrepressible John Weiss unwittingly gave the group its name one day
when he seized the garden hose on the lawn of one of the members and
thoroughly soaked Johnson, Higginson, and Frothingham.[51] This re-
leased a chain of banter referring to themselves as holy firefighters
putting out devilish fires and ascending to heaven by divine ladders. But
not all of their time was spent in comic relief from their solemn profession.

Premonitions of many things were in the air. Among his Lyceum and
"Hook and Ladder" colleagues, as well as to George Bartol earlier, it is
certain that Frothingham had talked of a free religious movement of
some type. Higginson, in the year that the "Town and Country Club" was
founded, stated reasons why a "Free Association" should not be formed:
lack of sympathy, premature times, technical difficulties, etc. Yet two
years later he was expressing favorable reaction to his own Free Church in
Worcester, Massachusetts.[52]

By 1854 others of Frothingham's generation of young ministers were
corresponding about the possibilities of a free movement outside of the
Unitarian Association. Apparently Theodore Parker had asked David
Wasson, whom Higginson considered the most radical of all, a man who
issued "wild sounds," to give him a list of names of those who might favor a
"Free Association." He declined, due to his limited acquaintances, asking

Johnson to do so.[53] A month later, Wasson again wrote to Johnson, recalling a conversation he had had with Parker about getting together to test sentiments concerning an association. He had also been in contact with Frothingham who, for reasons we shall see, seemed reluctant to start a free church movement. In some disappointment, Wasson confided to Johnson that Frothingham had been meditating on the subject but had not answered his last letter agreeing upon a day of meeting. "I have not heard from him since. I do not expect to hear from him. . . ." [54]

A lively correspondence took place between Frothingham and Samuel Johnson. Of the few letters that exist written to friends, the "Dear Sam" letters usually dealt with pulpit exchanges, requests for a speech, or an invitation to visit. During Frothingham's early years in Salem, he depended a great deal upon the friendship and intellectual support of Johnson. In 1849, while Johnson was still living in Lynn, Massachusetts, preaching at his "Free Church," Frothingham invited him to come and preach "for a poor pittance" and to stay with them at the Carpenter Street manse, adding persuasively that it would be "high treason to visit anybody but a pantheist." [55] The following summer, with plans in the making for a lecture series at North Church, Frothingham appealed to Johnson for help:

> Come to strengthen my own position and attract people to my church. . . .
> Since I am on the Board of Management . . . I am anxious to have matters
> arranged early in order to forestall the thinkers.[56]

No record of the lecture series survives. It can only be assumed that Frothingham was attempting, outside of his pulpit and Lyceum platform, to introduce radical ideas of religion and philosophy to the people of Salem. He invited the help of Samuel Johnson, who later was active in the Free Religious Association and became the American authority on Oriental religious philosophy through his three-volume work.

The Female Anti-Slavery Association of Salem was continually after Frothingham as a speaker. Just how active he was with the group is difficult to say. From 1852 through his Jersey City years to 1859 there was correspondence between him and Miss Adeline Roberts, treasurer and corresponding secretary of the society.[57] This usually took the form of brief, formal notes accepting a speaking engagement, arranging a convenient date, or polite refusals to speak. It would seem that Frothingham was much sought after by the abolition ladies, but was usually reluctant to commit himself.[58] This may have been due to his natural aversion to organized "causes." Certainly he was not lukewarm on the issue of slavery. Through his Salem years many of his colleagues of his age were active on abolitionism. He developed a strong personal, but not uncritical, friendship with Theodore Parker through the Lyceum work and by personal contact with him in Boston, one would assume.[59] Yet until his famed

"Anthony Burns" sermon in 1854, his antislavery work appears to have been in a low key. He was busy enough, as we have seen, and his parish duties came first.

SIX

Much of the business of the church was routine but time consuming for a young minister who preferred to spend most of his time in reading and contemplation. Yet he faced up to the problems of the small church for which the Proprietors Record shows less than one hundred stockholding members or pew holders. The church itself seated scarcely two hundred people. Raising money through pew rentals with the related problem of collecting rents, selling those at public auction which were in arrears, electing church officers, and maintaining the church building were perennial questions of discussion and decision. Allocating money for church music, selecting a new hymnal, and changing the order and hours of the Sunday services also occupied the time of the minister and church officials. In addition to the new balcony and organ installed in the fall of 1848, a Sunday School building and vestry were planned and built during the spring and summer of 1853.[60]

Frothingham evidently had the support of the governing body of the thriving church. During the same period of church expansion, money was provided to have a substitute minister in the absence of the regular pastor. At the same time, Frothingham's request for more light in the church was complied with. One June 12, 1853, the Proprietors Committee report recorded the ominous statement that "the society have observed with deep regret the failing health of their pastor." It was voted to grant him a six-month leave with full salary and to raise money for a substitute minister. Frothingham makes no mention in his own memoir of his troubles during this spring. Apparently it was a difficult time with overwork and commitments in many directions aggravating the dread tuberculosis, called a "bronchial infection." He did go abroad in the New England manner to regain his health. Alone in the summer of 1853, he toured England, Scotland, Holland, the Rhineland, Switzerland, and Italy.[61] It will be recalled that seven years later Theodore Parker went to Europe for the same reason but never returned. Frothingham's ailment was apparently cured or arrested upon his return in the fall of 1853. From then on events seem to have accelerated. Two years later he would be in Jersey City, but meanwhile the parish work went on.

Frothingham had the facility for working simultaneously in several directions. He could work in community affairs, plunge into the midst of theological or social controversy, and at the same time be the humane pastor and teacher of his parishioners. His very great concern for children is evident from the interest he showed in the North Church Sunday School. Unlike most ministers, he acted for a time as his own Sunday

School Superintendent.[62] He addressed the children personally each Sunday and supervised the reading material to assure a broad coverage of religious and literary topics of interest to children. Scanning the book topics in the Sunday School library one is impressed by the variety and relevance of the books. Audubon, *The Naturalists,* a book on dogs, *Swiss Family Robinson,* and other adventure stories were available. Bible stories and, of course, the favorite book of the nineteenth century for humorous, mild didacticism, *Tales of Peter Parle,* were prominent. History, Christmas stories, a child's version of Shakesperean heroes, and a book entitled *How to be a Lady* characterize the list.[63]

Children were drawn to Frothingham, who made vivid and lasting impressions upon them. Martha Nichols, probably the daughter of John H. Nichols of Frothingham's church committee, recalled years later the feeling that she and the other children had toward the young minister. In the autumn of 1853 when Frothingham had returned from Europe the children had composed and prepared a special hymn for him. When the children rose and sang it as a surprise it "unnerved him, and he sank into his chair, with his head in his hands." [64] Yet children did not run and cling to him. Rather they had a feeling of awe. One child is reported to have asked if he were not the Angel Gabriel.

His gentle, warm relations with the adults of the congregation was also evident. He was in the habit of spending long hours at the church or in the manse on Carpenter Street listening to individual woes, helping people, arranging for meetings, and planning for the various church activities. Typical of his way were gracious letters to various ladies of the church addressed as "My Dear Friend," assuring the group he would meet with them or if he could not, asking to be "absolved" and to notify the people "so as not to inconvenience them." [65] But there were issues to face and a society to confront. In this area personal relations and ministerial warmth were put to the test. Here Frothingham and his congregation began to feel the conflict inherent in the advice of Reverend Putnam at his ordination: "Do not say sharp and frivolous things, avoid alienating your congregation, and cultivate your own intellect." [66]

SEVEN

He never was in the habit of saying frivolous things but as his intellect developed so did his convictions and his willingness to express them. During his first year at North Church he was "directed" to observe communion with these specific words: "All members desiring communion with Christ . . . join in celebrating the Lord's Supper." A year later he was voted down by the Proprietors in his request for "less frequent communion to be held in the afternoons." [67] It is clear that from the beginning of his ministry Frothingham, like Emerson at Third Church in Boston earlier, attempted to abandon what he considered a meaningless ritual and bring his congregation into modern Unitarian thought and practice. The alienation had begun.

Frothingham's own account of the growing situation, written years later, is somewhat indirect but hints at more than one reason. Slavery was an issue "impossible to evade" with Parker, Phillips, and Garrison thundering. The Anthony Burns affair in Boston divided the parish. Speaking in the third person, he recalled: "The situation on both sides became uncomfortable and he accepted an invitation to another city, where he could exercise his independence without check or limit," adding enigmatically that Transcendentalism was in the air and Emerson "led the dance of the hours." [68] There was more to it than slavery.

Martha Nichols, in her memorial paper read in 1896, mentioned Frothingham's visit to Theodore Parker in Salem. It was a ministerial errand to enlist Parker's help in retrieving a runaway husband of one of Frothingham's parishioners. Conversation inevitably followed. Frothingham borrowed some of Parker's books and, informally, one can suppose, some of his ideas and rhetoric. Rev. Edward J. Young, in a memorial paper for Frothingham before the Massachusetts Historical Society, stated bluntly that Frothingham left Salem over the Burns affair in Boston and because he had refused to give communion after the episode. Also, he began to read "certain books until he finally adopted the views of Baur and the Tübingen school." [69] Parker introduced Frothingham to the ideas of this school of radical theology.

The order of events in the Parker-Frothingham relationship is not clear. Did he meet Parker at the Salem Lyceum or in his Boston study? Did he know Parker personally and read his borrowed books before attempting to eliminate communion in his church? Probably not. Did he get his antislavery feeling from Parker? Not primarily, it is safe to say, yet Parker certainly reinforced his views.

Even before Frothingham complained to George Ellis about his boredom in Salem he was confiding in Parker that it was his example that kept him inspired in the "clam bed" and eased the pain of the alienation from his own father.

You know how I am placed; in the midst of Hunkerdom! No word of sympathy or comfort reaches me from a single person. I do not say of station and influence but of solid influence and weighty character. Even the elect women, those true reliances of a young minister, withdrew from me their slim and sentimental support with here and there a solitary exception. At home you know how it is. I do not speak of it. I hate to think of it. I even dislike to go into my father's house. I say this in no complaining spirit but only as explaining the hearty comfort and refreshing joy that your words and example give me. . . . Sometimes I confess my faith does waver, but not for any long time. Let me acknowledge most humbly that much of its steadiness and persistency are due to you. When I come to see you it is to the end that it may be increased and confirmed. . . . You do me good, and that is more than can be said of many a person who certainly never offends me by any moral exaggerations.[70]

Parker, of course, influenced all of the men of Frothingham's generation who were still in Divinity School, where Parker's "natural religion" and abolitionism was often the informal subject of debate. Frothingham's own account of Parker's influence thirty-five years after the episode is inconclusive. In his *Recollections and Impressions* he entitled a chapter "Crises of Belief." It was the Parker contact he acknowledged while in Salem and the reading of Frederick C. Baur that introduced him to the higher New Testament criticism. A new basis for Christian convictions emerged as he discarded the Deity of Christ, Atonement, and Perdition. Theism remained, he said, yet he did not wholly accept Parker's "trinity of God, Immortality, and the Moral Law." Frothingham felt, rather, that man had a spiritual nature which created beliefs. He placed more emphasis on great religions and cultures of the world with their saints and seers. His mind was shaped by the teachings of Schleirmacher, Fichte, Constant, Cousin, Carlyle, Goethe, and Emerson. Parker's learning, he felt, "was copious rather than discerning." [71] After fifty-five years it is impossible to say how much of his thought came from his career in the Free Religious Association and how much had been absorbed from Theodore Parker by the time of his break with North Church. If his memoir is to be taken at face value, it would appear that he had no doubt of Parker's inspiration. He concluded the section in the third person: ". . . the young minister undertook to take his congregation within, but without success; so he went elsewhere. This action proceeded from the faith Parker instilled." [72]

The popular knowledge of Frothingham, gleaned mostly from remarks of contemporaries long after the fact, states that the capture of Anthony Burns caused his break with his church. It was a combination of causes to be sure. Even before the Burns affair the Proprietors Committee met to consider a communication from the pastor stating that he was considering leaving his post. At a general meeting of pew holders, a resolution was drawn up expressing their feelings toward Frothingham:

> We understand he has been invited to a distant place . . . we feel he should know about [our] affection, confidence, respect inspired by his ministrations among us for the past seven years. . . . Therefore resolved: That warm sentiments be conveyed to him [and] that the group would deeply deplore his leaving.[73]

To support the sense of the meeting, the resolution was ended by a list of Frothingham's strengths and virtues. It was enough to embarrass a modest man but he stayed—for a while.

Three weeks later, Sunday, June 4, 1854, he stood up in the North Church pulpit and denounced the rendition in Boston of the runaway slave named Anthony Burns. The city had been seething over the affair, the third such since the passage of the Fugitive Slave Act four years before. Burns had shown up in Boston in May where he was captured and put in jail to await the arrival of his master, a Colonel Suttle of Alexandria, Virginia, and to await the ruling of Judge Edward Loring, Commissioner for the enforcement of the Fugitive Slave Act. It was an angry meeting in packed Faneuil Hall where the crowd heard Theodore Parker and Wendell Phillips. Vague plans were made to storm the jail and release Burns. Parker and others attempted to control the crowd before it became a mob. Police lines were broken and the jail was stormed, but it was no use. Poor organization and confusion resulted only in a battered door. Thomas Wentworth Higginson, down from Worcester, got a bloody chin from a police sabre. A policeman lay dead from a wild shot, its origin unknown. Burns was still a captured slave. Parker and other leaders were threatened with arrest and facing a court trial. The decision on Anthony Burns was foregone. Judge Loring ruled to uphold the federal law and return Burns to Virginia in custody of Colonel Suttle.

It was on the morning of Friday, June 2, that Burns was marched from the courthouse jail under military guard to the harbor. Crowds hissed the detachment of Marines sent from Charleston Navy Yard. Bells tolled and onlookers sang derisively "Carry Me Back to Old Virginny." This ended the Anniversary Week of religious celebrations and meeting of the Anti-Slavery Society. The timing could not have been more dramatic.[74]

Anniversary Week had drawn ministers to Boston from all over New England. Many, of course, were eye witnesses of the Burns affair, if not actual participants. No one now knows if Frothingham was there. There is no evidence that he was at Faneuil Hall or at the courthouse attack. It would be quite unlike him to have been in the midst of such physical action. His field of action lay elsewhere. It is quite likely that he remained in Salem, physically removed, studying the reports of what happened and formulating his Sunday sermon. In the short forty-eight hours that elapsed between the reenslavement of Burns and Sunday morning, he had composed his remarkable discourse—"The New Commandment." This was his Anthony Burns sermon which proved to be the turning point of his career and the climactic event leading to his decision to leave for "a distant city."

June gives a delightful appearance to the New England scene. Federal Street, Salem, lined with trees in full leaf and yards with lilacs barely gone by breathed an atmosphere bucolic, conservative, almost unreal. Who knew that the young minister, as he walked down that street on the June 4th morning was going to confront what Parker had called the "hideous snake" of slavery coiled in "obscene embrace" with the "worm of New

England condonence and indifference." The classic Federalist facades of
the Federal Street houses must have seemed to Frothingham almost to
sneer as he passed on his way to confront his congregation and his own
conscience.

The church must have been packed, possibly with many visitors. He
stood up behind the high, massive pulpit in the dark panelled, almost
Gothic sanctuary. Frothingham's thoughts can be imagined as he looked
out on his congregation, seated in their rented, high-walled pews, enclosed, apart from their neighbors. Did it remind him of slave pens and
the sectarian spirit? These had been on his mind for several years and
were the subject of the discourse he was about to deliver. The sermon was
Biblical enough—at least in the beginning. "A New Commandment I give
unto you; that ye love one another; . . . all men know that ye are my
disciples if ye have love for one another." (John XIII:34–35) "A New
Commandment indeed," easy enough to follow in serene times in
"academic groves" but "when before was it ever spoken to troubled and
persecuted men, by one who was hated and hunted for his life?" "When
before was it ever addressed amid pressing dangers. . . . ?" Certainly not in
Roman times or seriously pursued among the Hebrews or at any time in
history, said Frothingham. By now the congregation must have known
what was coming. He launched a vigorous attack on Christianity itself. It
was Christianity historically and in the present that has subverted the
injunction of Christ to love one another. To be a Christian one must
merely believe. Churches concerned with protecting creed concern themselves with membership lists and distinctions between the "elect" and the
"unregenerate."

> Believe . . . clamour the churches—believe the trinity; believe the atone-
> ment; believe the divinity of Christ; . . . believe in the Bible and the miracles
> . . . believe and pray and you need not trouble yourselves with the casting out
> of the demons that possess you. . . .

The system of Christianity itself was the enemy. Its spread had meant only
the spread of sects.

> Each new branch of the vine has been a new heresy. . . . Each denomination
> represents a quarrel. . . . How many spires are pushed up into the skies
> through spite?

He attacked the sectarian spirit, the blind defense of dogma, and the
insistence on belief rather than the simple expression of love and
brotherhood as a test for Christianity. The hollow forms of church organization and performance of meaningless rituals were condemned.
Reminiscent of Emerson's criticism of church ceremony back in his own
ministry and later in the Divinity School address, Frothingham attacked

the Communion as a symbol of conformity of belief rather than a sign of
brotherhood. Doctrinal controversy, writing of belief and policy against
opposing sects seemed to him to be the reason the "New Commandment"
was often ignored.

> How strange a controversy does Christian history furnish upon the idea of
> Christ. How plainly does it prove that Christians may be guilty of any
> atrocity, if they only hold fast the faith, and that the purest life saves none
> who have incurred the slightest taint of heresy.

The history of the Catholic and Protestant Churches was called into
testimony upon the failure of religion to soften the human heart. These
were episodes of atrocities long past, admitted Frothingham, yet he
warned that "things are not substantially better now." The churches in
America both North and South were blind to "the most hideous institutions now existing under the sun." The Southern churches apologized for
it; the Northern churches were silent upon it; persons who attempted to
abolish it were, "for the most part, unconnected with the church." Then
came the hard-hitting message followed by a Biblical parody:

> But the churches of the country deem themselves no less Christian on this
> account. Nay, they regard themselves all the more, and all the more pecul-
> iarly Christian in their indifference to philanthropic enterprise—
> Christianity, we are told, is a scheme of redemption for the miraculous
> regeneration of human souls; the Christian is one who holds the orthodox
> faith, believes in the supernatural being and power, and in the vicarious
> merits of Christ; and it is the duty of the Church to explain and defend its
> doctrines, to bring people to its sacraments, and make them assent to its
> creeds. The great company of disciples has nothing to do with the abolition
> of those evils which express human rage and hatred, and ordain malice,
> pride and selfishness as permanent institutes of society. But where is the
> New Commandment?

Certainly it was not in Boston during the recent "Holy Week," said
Frothingham. There was Christianity there but not religion. There were
Bible Societies, Sunday Schools, and Missionary Societies; there were
preachers and Christians moving about from meeting to song fest, clutch-
ing hymn books, prayer books, and Bibles; sectarianism was in high voice
defending the trinity, atonement, and sin, original and otherwise. "Duties
to the Hindus and the Cherokees, the best mode of instructing children in
the doctrines of the Gospel, and gathering them into the fold of Christ"
were subjects of main concern when "in the very center of the city, in the
very halls of Christian justice *Christ himself* in the person of one of the least
of his disciples, was arraigned before Pontius Pilate." The illusion was
clear: Anthony Burns faced Judge Loring. The "Procurator" sat surrounded by "mercenary soldiery" and asked the accused if he had in fact

called himself a King who had absolute "dominion over his own person . . . and the natural right to come and go as he would." The accused claimed the sovereignty over his own body and will and was condemned, and guarded "by nearly two thousand armed men is led alone our modern *via dolorosa* toward the place of infamy and pain beyond the city." Even as Frothingham preached, Burns was a prisoner aboard ship in Boston Harbor waiting his return to Virginia and slavery.

Where was the Church? Where was the "New Commandment," he asked. Certainly it was not in Boston; neither was it in Salem. Yet Frothingham's moral indignation did not lead him to the kind of one-dimensional fanaticism that was characteristic of the abolitionist. What could have been done in Boston the previous week? His answer was a rather mild one, typical of the nineteenth century school of "individual uplift" reformers: to "feel like Christians," to express brotherhood, to create an atmosphere into which the slave catcher would not dare enter.

> Here my friends is the simple issue. The cause of humanity—the anti-slavery cause—is the cause of Christ, inasmuch as it involves directly the principles of brotherly love. In every scourged and vilified slave, I see a person crucified. 'Inasmuch as ye did it unto the least of these, ye did it unto me.' " [75]

It was over. One can guess that it was a silent, grim-faced congregation that filed out, attempting to say something pleasant to conceal the mixed emotions. Some were stunned by thoughts never confronted before, others were angry, some had injured feelings, all perhaps felt more than a little guilty. The young minister felt apprehensive as to whether he had gone too far. Looking for moral support and a friendly face, he went to Boston the next morning to talk to Theodore Parker who had his own troubles in the Burns affair. To Frothingham's surprise he found his friend, dressed in a house robe, calmly tending his flower garden.[76] Their conversation, it can be safely assumed, dealt on the Anthony Burns capture, Parker's impending trial, and Frothingham's angry sermon of the day before. It seems unlikely that Parker encouraged him to modify his stand taken in the sermon. Nevertheless he returned to Salem in a calmer frame of mind. He never "recanted" but when the discourse was later printed, he felt it necessary to add a prefatory note moderating somewhat his attack on Christianity by recognizing some of the "benefits and blessings" Christianity had given to the world. Even the churches of America, he thought in retrospect, were not quite as guilty as he had implied in the sermon: "The Christian church of this country tolerates, *if it does not defend and support,* the institution of slavery, and discourages efforts to remove it." [77]

In the heated atmosphere of the spring of 1854, there were angry protests against the sermon. Some were in private conversations, others in the printed word. One anonymous person, presumably not of North Church membership, calling himself a "layman," went to the trouble of publishing a review of the "New Commandment" discourse. Though it was printed in Boston, it was obviously intended for a Salem audience.[78] It was a direct refutation of the New England tradition of "political sermons." Opposing the use of pulpits for political causes, he attacked Frothingham's entire intellectual position that Christianity was an eclectic body of man-made forms and symbols adding up to a dogma extracted from morality and ethics. He wrote, to support his criticism, reiterating the fundamentalist position that Christianity is based on facts of revelation and Christ's sacrifice and is not a human philosophy. The Church then was not a political instrument to abolish slavery or even criticize it. It should encourage and comfort rather than stir up strife. Though slavery is to be lamented, the role of the churches is to serve both master and slave. The Harriet Beecher Stowe image of the religious faith of Uncle Tom was the model of Christian faith. What devout Christian would not, if necessary, be a slave and suffer with Uncle Tom, if he could only enjoy with him the power of faith and consolation in Christ? The anonymous critic thought that this was sufficient and that churches did not need "christianizing at the hands of Mr. Frothingham and Theodore Parker." [79] Oblivious of the obvious contradictions in his argument, he then launched into an open defense of slavery, quoting St. Paul and lifting rhetoric from J. C. Calhoun, George Fitzhugh, and Chancellor Harper. This pamphlet represents the thinking typical of those who would be offended by the Anthony Burns sermon. It is safe to assume that this element of opinion was fairly widespread. How many people in his congregation felt this way is difficult to say.

Frothingham's sermon itself was printed "at the request of the Standing Committee," according to the title page of the printed version. This would imply an official sanction from the church's governing body. The *Salem Gazette,* one of the three biweeklies of the town, ran a full account of the sermon introduced by long excerpts of pertinent parts and expressions of thanks to their "friends of the *Observer's* office for publishing OBF's sermon on Burns." In their opinion "the discourse [was a] frank, bold, able . . . exposition of the author's view of Christian duty . . . showing how little churches have followed their duty in Christian ethics." [80]

This was the end in Salem, though one year remained. Fortunately, North Church closed at the end of June for the summer. Perhaps some of the tension had been eased by the time the society reconvened in September. The summer was probably spent at his father's country home in Burlington, Massachusetts, where other brothers and younger sister Ellen often converged for the summer reunion. Dr. Nathaniel Frothingham, four years retired from Boston's First Unitarian Church, was a man of conservative views yet gentle in his judgements and judicious with advice. He always supported his minister son in his work, though not really agreeing with his advanced views. He was known to have said at one time, "I am perfectly satisfied with my son." [81] Family councils and a New England summer in the country might have been therapeutic after the abrasive weeks in June. Yet young Frothingham was heard to say, following the Burns affair, "That great stone church stands in my way; I cannot stay and keep people out of their pews." [82]

It is safe to assume that when he returned to Salem in the fall of 1854 he found the congregation divided and falling away in church attendance if not in membership. He felt he had failed. His last year at North Church was not a happy one. No longer on the school committee or the Lyceum board of directors, Frothingham was looking for a new arena of action. New Jersey seemed a possibility once more. By early spring he was writing to his old Divinity School friend, Samuel Johnson, asking for advice. "Pray give me your opinion of the people at Jersey City and give them to me at once." [83] Actually he had all but made up his mind at this writing. Johnson's reply could scarcely have returned before he gave his letter of resignation to the Proprietors Committee on March 26. "I have received a second invitation from the Unitarian Society in Jersey City and have accepted after full deliberation." There was an overtone of deep regret at leaving the people but he did not evade the real reasons for leaving. Without mentioning them, he continued, "It has seemed to me for some time past that a new and different sphere would be more congenial to my habit of mind and the views I hold of my profession . . . grant me an honorable discharge from the place that has meant so much. . . ." The rest was a matter of form. The Proprietors accepted his resignation for the end of April with deep regret and best wishes. The acceptance was of a long resolution written in elaborate, moving style which read like a citation for outstanding and valorous service. His friend, John H. Nichols, signed it as the Proprietors Committee secretary.

His resignation was a community event noticed by the newspapers of Salem. The *Observer,* always close to North Church affairs, printed the letter of resignation and the committee's response including a long list of Frothingham's achievements and virtues. The *Gazette* announced the departure with "regret." The *Register* announced his resignation and gave a brief account of his farewell sermon, "The Eternal Life." [84] It was an inspirational, noncorrosive message. In good transcendental style Frothingham assured his flock that human life should be based on eternal values. Jesus, who never died, personified the eternal life which is also inside individuals. Since Heaven was in Him and is also within the human being, the temporal life of Jesus is unknowable and irrelevant.[85] At a Lyceum meeting held a few days after his departure from the city a resolution was passed thanking him for "able, courteous work" in developing the Lyceum programs and expressing regret at his departure.[86]

There is every reason to believe that this was a general feeling among the people in Salem who had known and worked with Reverend Octavius Frothingham. Yet the people of North Church must have breathed easier during the peaceful year following the Anthony Burns sermon. What had he really accomplished? He himself had expressed a sense of failure in not having "brought his congregation along" with his antislavery views and advanced religious philosophy. Probably his greatest impact was on the children and in personal contact with his people. No criticism can be found for his lack of compassion, patience, understanding, and devotion to his flock. His intellectual powers and his sincerity were never doubted. As to his success in moving the minds and hearts of his followers toward antislavery and to a more radical position in religious views there can be no real measure. A speaker at the Three Hundredth Anniversary of First Church, of which North Church was a branch, gave him full credit:

> Frothingham was a brilliant preacher and an intellectual leader in the denomination rather advanced in his views . . . [North] Church took on several new forms of activity. . . . I have always considered that the coming of Mr. Frothingham was the real turning point in the Church . . . from that of an old established New England parish to that of a modern religious society.[87]

EIGHT

Jersey City was still a country town in 1855, yet to Frothingham it appeared to hold promise as a place where his liberal religion could be preached and his intellectual powers could expand. The invitation to come there had been extended the year before, as we have seen, but this time it was more urgent and the need for making a change was obvious. Rev. Henry W. Bellows, of All Souls Church in New York, had been instrumental in recruiting Frothingham for the Jersey City post. Bellows, born the same year as Theodore Parker and twelve years Frothingham's senior, left Framingham, Massachusetts in 1847, the year Frothingham came to Salem.[88] He had followed the career of the young minister and had become acquainted with him through the Salem Lyceum, the annual Unitarian Conferences, and the New England roots they both shared. Except for Frothingham's growing reputation as a brilliant speaker and his outspoken views on slavery, it is difficult to know why Bellows was particularly interested in urging him to come to Jersey City in close proximity to his own area of influence. Bellows was a key figure in the Unitarian Association with which the younger ministers of Frothingham's generation were increasingly becoming disenchanted. Perhaps Bellows did not realize this at the time. In his ideological views Bellows was neither a conservative in the Evangelical sense nor a conservative of the school of Frothingham's father, but a "liberal Christian" with the "Broad Church" views shared by Rev. James Freeman Clark, Frederick Hedge, Ezra Styles Gannett, and others who never sympathized with the Free Religious Association, later led by Octavius Frothingham.[89] This was all in the future when, in Frothingham's own words, he received an invitation from Rev. Bellows to come, "seconded by a cordial representation from Jersey City." [90]

His prospects seemed favorable for an open-minded approach to religion. The Society was already Unitarian when he arrived and a new meeting house was being built. No records of the size of his congregation exist, but he attracted people from New York City who came out to the church which had just dropped the communion service and become dedicated "to a large rational faith." [91] The communion ritual was dropped, he recalled later, not on Emerson's grounds, but because it divided rather than united the people. It implied a "righteousness and grace which did not exist." His own views as he took over the Jersey City Society were, he recalled,

> scarcely Unitarian, not even Christian in a technical sense or in any other, but a broad "signification." It was theism founded on the Transcendental philosophy, a substitution for the authority of Romanism and of Protestantism. . . . It most successfully tided over the gulf between Protestantism and Rationalism. Parker used it with great effect. It was the life of Emerson's teaching. It animated Carlyle. It was the fundamental assumption of the abolitionists and all the social reformers.[92]

By the middle of May the Frothingham family was established in Jersey City, and the minister had preached his inaugural sermon. No record of it survives, but Rev. Bellows was there and heard it. Commenting in the *Christian Inquirer,* which he edited, he congratulated the Jersey City Society for having a minister of such "piety and strength of beliefs" but mildly warned them of his criticism of the "Myths of Christianity" which he implied Frothingham could not accept.[93] Clearly the sermon was not to Bellows' taste.

Frothingham's new church was ready for use in the fall. On a Wednesday night in mid-September he spoke at the dedication ceremony on "The Uses of the Sanctuary." The terminology itself seemed conservative enough as did much of the rhetoric of the sermon. "My Christian friends," he began, the "dear superstition" about the "house of God" being set apart from secular ground had uses in the past but sets up a false destination between "evil and good," and between "secular crimes and iconoclasm." The use of the church is to study religious truth and not dogma. It is indeed a "house of God, a place to study divine wisdom" but "I wish for myself that it were not even called Unitarian. . . . I should be glad if it bore no sectarian name whatever, so we could honestly earn for it the title of being a place where the being of God is worshipped and the truth of God is sought." "Truth is in all creeds," he continued, but paraphrasing for a different meaning his father's ordination advice to him eight years before, it must be "sifted out and rightly divided." The church he thought was a place of peaceful worship but also an arena for challenge and intellectual encounter. This was a sermon that could be taken two ways. It had a traditional base but offered the new challenge of liberal religion.[94] Increasingly, Frothingham would use the term "radical faith" and drop theological vocabulary.

While he was becoming established in his new church and expanding his reputation as a radical preacher, he did not ignore the antislavery cause. Although Boston was a center of abolitionism, in the New York area one could speak out more directly without offending audiences. During his first fall in Jersey City, Frothingham wrote a tract for the Anti-Slavery Society which originally was probably a lecture. Following sound antislavery doctrine he opposed the colonization schemes then being proposed in some quarters. It was a "plot to rid the country of free Negroes" he felt. It would actively entrench slavery and be an advantage to the large slave holders. All of the large plantation owners such as "Judge" Washington, John Randolph, and Henry Clay had advocated African colonization, he pointed out. The late Daniel Webster came under his attack for advocating it. Free Negroes, he thought, would also suffer because they were not equipped nor did they have a desire to emigrate to Liberia.[95]

By the spring he was in New York before the Anti-Slavery Society again. This time he was angry, sarcastic, ironically humorous, and eloquent at times. He was in good company. On the platform with him were "old tired soldiers of a noble cause" who had fought the good fight through so many weary years. Disclaiming any chance of contributing new ideas to the cause or new plans of action, he reiterated the old abolitionists' purpose and praised their work. "No thought is old until its work is done," and "at no time is the work of the abolitionist more urgently needed than now." In literary style, quoting Tennyson's law, "The path to duty is the path of glory," he praised those who had trod that path:

> The Serene Phillip, Accomplished Knight of the Crusade with practiced eye thrusts his keen unerring rapier into . . . every sophistry and without an effort lays in the dust the most majestic lie. The hearty Sumner flinging off his cumbrous garments one by one meets the challenge of the Phillistines with the cheerful alacrity of David. Clear-eyed Gerrit Smith looks right through the tangled web of congressional sophistry. . . . Parker champions the new Church and with an undaunted look confronts all the demons face to face, and never misses his blow.

But not all followed the "path to glory." There were the "Mammon worshippers" or defenders of slavery and, worst of all, the "palterers" or compromisers. Each came under Frothingham's oratorical blows. The

"Mammon worshippers" follow the path of desire. "He is a practical common sense man; he is for things that work well, plans that succeed, enterprises that pay. . . ." "This man soon rids himself of his angels" by convincing himself that "only bold pretenders" would sacrifice self-interest to "empty notions of conscience." The defenders of slavery, another breed of men turned on by the antislavery cause, say "Evil be my good." They patronize the Bible to support slavery as a divine institution:

> You know who they are who rave and bluster about abolitionists and write truculent letters to Northern ministers and lecture committees. Some of these people are genial, dashing, rioting, reckless men, good humored, fiery, with great relish of animal life and no appreciation of the spiritual.

As Frothingham's speech rolled on it became evident why he never joined the abolitionist society although he participated in its work. Saving his heaviest blows, not for the slave owners whom he never considered evil men, but for the compromisers, he launched into a rousing jeremiad. These people were the most harmful to the nation, he felt, these Northern men with Southern principles who exhaust all sophistry to appear to be "serving God but really serving the devil."

> These people wish to be on both sides—to get God's blessing and the Devil's plums, to be nominally on good terms with Conscience, while practically they indulge desire . . . He despises moral cowardice . . . he is brave enough; he only believes *honestly* that discretion in his case is the better part of valour. . . . He loves justice and humanity . . . but he is persuaded that these great ends cannot be permanently advanced inconsistently with a wise, solid, unselfish, conservation of private interest. Of course a man must obey the law of God . . . but he is not so rash as to imagine that he himself is to be a private interpreter of that law. . . . God-fearing men made the laws of the State; and the common sense of the 'vox populi'; is that not too the word of God? This pious talk is only palterer's make believe.

Recalling his own encounters with the "palterers" in his North Church society and elsewhere, Frothingham levelled verbal blows at all classes of palterers. The politicians were guilty of it. No worse result of compromising was the one of "1850, when Commerce gained a victory of conscience and Christ's image, carved in ebony, was sold for Southern votes . . . practical religion commended in the name of cotton." The epithet "doughface" did not appear in his speech, which implied as much. "Is it not possible," he asked, "that the Presidency of Henry N. Wise of Virginia might be a heavier blow to the slave power than the Presidency of Millard Fillmore?" Answering his own question with a Biblical figure of speech, the answer was yes. "Satan loses half his Power when he shows his tail. In the garb of a fine gentleman he finds conquest easy." His point was clear. The real political enemies to the antislavery cause were Northern politicians such as Fillmore and Buchanan and not John C. Calhoun or Henry Wise.

The merchant, said Frothingham, was sure of course that the cause of civilization was the cause of trade. Although slavery was a part of the cotton business, it was "doomed to perish with the advance of civilization." He scornfully added, "He is an abolitionist only if he does not work in the same fashion as those that assume the name, because then action is 'suicidal,' tending to disturb the relations of trade, whose cause is identical with that of liberty." On the other hand, he continued, "the lawyer is sure that the entire safety of society depends upon the maintenance of law." The lawyer is also a sophist. He abhors slavery and the laws are imperfect, but they must be upheld. The Constitution and the federal laws protect slavery and cannot resist its extension, says the lawyer, "so he draws a deep sigh, construes the law as rigidly as possible to make sure it is not evaded, talks of the essential principles of conservation, meaning hunkerism and Southern patronage, and stands ready to pocket the bribe of any kidnapper who needs his services as defender of the Constitution." With gentlemen, on the other hand, Frothingham observed, "taste is a substitute for conscience." To them the antislavery men are vulgar, too noisy, lacking high-toned ideals of "respectable life." The gentlemen go to great pains to prove "themselves immaculate."

To Frothingham the clergy, of course, were the most guilty breed of palterers. His diatribe against them was pieced together from the personal experience of his fellow clergymen, including perhaps his own father and Rev. Henry Bellows. They hide behind pious phrases, claiming their duty to be the saving of souls rather than preaching politics. While abhorring slavery in "whispered private conversations," they slyly slip the word "bondsman" or "chattle" into their abstract prayers, thus "pouring out their conscience in dribbles." Yet, after a sharp attack, Frothingham, in his characteristic way and much unlike Theodore Parker, spoke compassionate words for his fellow clergymen. Be gentle with them, he asked the audience of abolitionists. Have mercy on their natural timidity and encourage them to speak out against slavery. Judge them for their moral stand but judge them gently. "If they are worth judging, they are worth saving."

The speech thus far must have consumed the best part of an hour, yet he was not through. His heaviest volley remained to be fired at the deadly enemy itself—the "slave power, alas, to what a dreadful state has [it] reduced us! It has made slavery a new art and elevated compromising of conscience to a refined science." The "new gospel of compromise" has had its casualties and even its martyrs. In oblique reference to Daniel Webster, he asked, "Did it not bring down the great son of New England in sorrow to his grave?" Slavery was war! declared Frothingham. Its very nature breathes belligerence and aggression. It has already brought armed men to the streets of Boston. It has armed congressmen with bowie knives and pistols. It has ridden in Kansas with rifle and bullet to conquer a territory. It has bred a warrior class whose "maxim is might is right," noted for their

> dashing recklessness, the hot blooded chivalry, the lavish generosity, the fiery sense of honour, the careless gaiety, the frank, easy, good nature, the impetuous passion, whether of love or hate, the swaggering grace, the luxury—all mark the soldier. Such qualities are peculiar to feudal society, which is military. Slavery is ever breathing menaces of war. On the slightest provocation it offers battle.

What was to be done about "this utterly immoral and demoralizing" institution which was the "blackest sin in sight of heaven?" War must be faced with war, warned Frothingham but a war with weapons more deadly than swords and guns. Words should be our weapons, he thought: "Words of truth that will [slay] error, brave words that are battles half won which slay not the body, but wicked spirits that possess the body." [96]

The prolonged applause that undoubtedly came was from an audience that did not need to hear the speech. They were already "true believers." Yet it must have helped rally their spirits and solidify their feelings in the atmosphere of the Kansas—Nebraska Bill. It was an election year offering a choice between the Democrat James Buchanan and John C. Fremont of the newly-formed Republican Party. In retrospect, historians have seen much significance in the election of 1856 when parties began to polarize and the Republicans for the first time took a stand against the extension of slavery. Frothingham was not impressed. To him and his old friend, Samuel Longfellow, it was "six of one and half a dozen of another" and assurance of "Civil War in Kansas before the Spring." [97]

Actually it had already started. The bloody incidents between pro and antislavery factions in the spring of 1856 had provoked Senator Charles Sumner's indictment of the South in his famed "Crime Against Kansas," delivered on May 26, a few weeks after Frothingham's own address before the Anti-Slavery Society. Antislavery people at large and New England intellectuals in particular were outraged when the news came that Senator Sumner had been caned into unconsciousness by the avenging Representative Preston Brooks of South Carolina. Frothingham stood before his congregation on the morning of June 1, 1856 and delivered an angry sermon, "The Last Signs." How much longer must we wait to realize the true nature of slavery, he asked. These are the last signs of slavery:

> The pride, lust and lawlessness of the slave holders using their familiar weapons—bowie knives, bloodhounds, pistols, halters, riots, mob executions, duels, assassination in the streets, auction sales of women and children. For thirty years we have heard tales of bloody horror, of suicides, huntings, scourgings, burnings and orgies of devilish lust. Cannot we all see the signs of the times?

Slavery is a "bloody hand that has first seized Texas, then Kansas, and has now reached into the Senate chamber itself." Do not think, he warned, that this attack is simply an attack on a Senator. "The blow is aimed at all of us. The bleeding Senator is representative of bleeding liberty." The issue was larger than Kansas or the life of an individual man, he thought. "Beating a white Senator is no more than a poor black man—it is humanity that is at stake—race has no part in our indignation." What was to be done? Wage war—not violent war but the war of conscience against the evil of slavery. Where was the church? It was dead, too busy worshipping dead saints to honor living ones, too busy saving souls to save living men. His targets were both the Protestant evangelical sects and the Catholics who in Hoboken had just received a box of bones from Rome, allegedly those of St. Quienten.[98] It was a rare performance. By contrast, the Anthony Burns sermon, two years earlier, seemed mild.

The New Jersey sojourn was a depressing period for Frothingham. Dull parish duties serving dull parishioners palled on him. Except for occasional trips into New York to speak before antislavery meetings and pleasant summers back in New England, his main stimulation seemed to be contacts with New England friends.

A month after his arrival in Jersey City, he wrote to Emerson expressing regrets that he could not contribute money which Emerson had requested to assist Bronson Alcott. He had been in the Alcott home and was indebted to him, he pointed out, but could not afford a contribution due to the expense of moving and an income which was "never large." Sermons did not pay nor had books and articles brought him income. He was grateful, however, for the friendship of Emerson's brother who also resided in Jersey City.[99] He wrote to Emerson from Burlington, Massachusetts, the family summer homestead, that his congregation was an undistinguished group of uncultured people but that he wanted to do "all he could for them." Would Emerson come down and speak before them in the fall for a "modest pecuniary reward?"[100] Characteristically Emerson was reluctant to commit himself or for long periods to even answer Frothingham's letters. Finally, through the fall and winter of 1856 a date was arranged on which Emerson was to appear as a part of a lecture series for Frothingham's congregation. It was impressive, a list including national Unitarian figures, old Lyceum acquaintances from Salem days, and Divinity School classmates. Frothingham gladly confirmed the date for February, 1857, and hoped that "the skies be merciful and steam effective."[101]

His correspondence with Samuel Longfellow contained friendly words of sympathy for one another and arrangements for pulpit exchanges, promising to "come East" if Longfellow would "come middle."[102]

Letters were written to Wentworth Higginson about books and mutual friends such as David Wasson whose health was precarious—"an excellent man" thought Frothingham in September, 1857.[103]

Two months later he complained to Higginson that he was "a lone man almost cut off from his kind, except the very ordinary kind that compose a parish. I have scarcely had a communication . . . with a sympathetic [ear]. New York is altogether too distant for society . . . and Jersey is utterly faithless." Hours were spent in "getting up" the weekly sermon, difficult work, Frothingham admitted, because "my ideas are so far off . . . and speech is slow—study is pretty much suspended for lack of sympathy." Yet he was engaged in wirting an article on F. C. Baur for the *Christian Examiner* which would be published, he thought, if it was "not too alarming." Although it was probably true that Jersey City was not the most stimulating place, part of Frothingham's malaise was due to "a most extraordinary and fearful exodus" of people threatening his "congregation with depletion." These were hard times. The depression of 1857, as it was later called, was on. Frothingham had lost twenty-five people since the onset of the panic and feared that many more would move away in the "spring to Milwaukee or elsewhere west, leaving me sole occupant and flat incumbent of the church." New Jersey, he predicted, "would be a living no more." He was in the depths of despair, certain that he would soon be like the man when ready to sit down who had the chair pulled away, forcing him to "sit with something more than unceremoniousness." His great disappointment was that his people were not ready for "liberal views of radical ideas." New York City was no better, being a conservative market and warehouse town. The attempt to form a "Free Society" the previous spring failed for him due to the financial "throws" but would not succeed anyway, he thought, "with a preacher very much better qualified than I am or should be." There were also other reasons—a disagreement among the "materialist, spiritualist, positivist," and "wide awakers with flowing beards." Since the diverse groups could not agree on a "no creed-no pope . . . type of debating society," the result was nothing. In despair he confided to Higginson that he might as well return to New England, to an orthodox parish "where a safe man is wanted—a man who has never been to Tübingen nor present at a district convention nor committee himself on the war and rights question." Perhaps he could supply vacant pulpits, as an itinerant preacher concerned only with litany and "philosophic preaching," he thought. This dark mood lasted only a moment as he added hastily, "The worst feature of it . . . is the look of vacuity that comes with it—as if one could not command a permanent stand. I am not like that and I shan't try it." Yet he continued with wry comments on the unreliable press reports on the economy and the futility of the ministers' "crusade against the Gin shops" in Jersey City. The real issue, he told Higginson, who doubtless agreed, was the propaganda for slavery and the great need for political leadership in the abolitionists' cause. "The abolitionists need a talisman—they have prophets enough and of the best." One bright spot in the "panic," thought Frothingham, was the hope that if cotton fell low enough to ruin the slave system perhaps free labor could take its place. On literary subjects he was on sure ground, thanking Higginson for a letter by David Wasson, about a book by James (the Elder) and various books of poetry and magazine commentary. He considered Wasson brilliantly "witty" and considered James' style arid as if exposed too long in the atmosphere of "the lecture hall." Yet his personal situation preyed on his mind. "I have men to comfort" and an example to set "for my people as well as I know how." Did he think he could persuade them to "behave like men and to be better another time?" He doubted it when there was more than could be done for the poor and Boston ladies were playing the "Puritan matron" and ladies in New York were "spending their husbands' money on piles of cheap things which they could never wear in their lives." Frothingham ended his lament to Higginson with a second plaintive plea to supply him with facts and information concerning their mutual concerns and to find him a position in New England.[104]

It was not to be. New England had to wait for retirement years. By February of his last year in Jersey City he wrote to Higginson again that he did not like New Jersey or the people, and he also doubted his own capabilities. Forming a "Free Society" seemed a good way out but he doubted that he could do it.[105] Unknown to him, his place of ultimate fame lay close at hand.

His last year in Jersey City was increasingly unhappy. Even as he was confiding his feeling to Wentworth Higginson, the Frothinghams were expecting their second child, which contributed to his feelings of anguish. A son was born July 3, 1858, and lived but eighteen days.[106] This event added a dimension of tragedy, not uncommon in those times, to the Frothingham family. To further add to his gloom was his last sad meeting with Theodore Parker who was on his way abroad. How gaunt he looked as they sat at dinner at Astor House in February, 1859; how depressing to stand at the end of the pier as he sailed away.[107]

Frothingham was determined to get out of Jersey City where his ministry had always been "uphill work." [108] Concrete efforts were made during the fall and winter of 1858 to establish a society in New York for him. By spring it was all but settled. Rev. Henry Bellows, who had been instrumental in getting the New Jersey post for Frothingham, was the key figure again. The main problem seemed to be the delay in coming to a final decision on the formal announcements of the founding of the society and its meeting place. A committee, apparently coordinated by Bellows, was looking for a suitable hall and was preparing for a meeting in Bellows' own church to make the final decisions. Meanwhile, Frothingham, caught between two congregations, was impatient. "My Dear Friend," he wrote Bellows, "allow me to put in a personal consideration and do not quarrel with me if I suggest that my position is getting more awkward every day," being caught between two parishes and obliged to answer within a few days. Pressing the issue, he inquired if a meeting could be held "this Saturday" to decide (1) whether the new society would be fairly permanent and with "every sensible" guarantee of sympathy and material aid, and (2) whether it "shall be under my direction and with my aid." These points could be decided, he urged, "early as well as late" with the details later. "Let me know something . . . right away." [109] Frothingham feared control by the older man who was a prominent figure in the administrative affairs of the Unitarian Association. He was also becoming increasingly impatient with Rev. Bellows' deliberate, conservative way of doing things.

Yet the project was successfully completed. By May, Frothingham was established in New York City, writing to Bellows about a wayward parishioner, John Collins. "The New Bedford scheme for him fell through" but perhaps Frothingham's father in Boston could do something for him. He and Bellows were perplexed as to what to do with Collins—put him in the Army? Send him to Blackwells Island? Make him a cook? What should we do about "our brother," he asked! [110] His parish duties had begun routinely enough. His activities in and out of New York for the next twenty years would be far from routine.

NORTH CHURCH, SALEM

III

Arena of Ideas:

Theological Journalism

THE *Christian Examiner,* FOUNDED IN 1824 by William Ellery Channing, was virtually the official organ of the Unitarian Association. Not that there was one line of dogma to propound, but the editors and contributors were usually New England Unitarians representing various shades of accepted theological belief. Rev. George Ellis, Divinity School classmate of Theodore Parker was prominent in the Unitarian Association and editor of the *Examiner* from 1847 to 1855. Even Henry Bellows considered him a conservative Unitarian arrayed against the "heretical wing," [1] which Frothingham would come to lead although these lines would not be drawn until after the Civil War. In the decade and a half previous to the split among Unitarians, the *Examiner* afforded a broad ground upon which divergent views could be expressed. Frothingham's first ventures into scholarly journalism were two contributions to the *Examiner* written in his last few months in Divinity School. His writing for this journal would total twenty-eight articles spanning the nineteen years from 1846 to 1865.

In a remarkably erudite article which appeared in July before his graduation from Divinity School, Frothingham reviewed Rev. J. R. Beard's *Historical and Artistic Illustrations of the Trinity.* [2] He followed Rev. Beard's classical and early Christian origins of the Trinity, and concluded wryly that since the Council of Nicene said little about the Holy Ghost, it must have come "from some dark corner—fitting its nature." A month after his graduation the *Examiner* carried a short article by Frothingham, "Justification by Faith." [3] Written while still a student, in it he expressed the "anti-sensationalist" school of thinking, pointing out that the doctrine was one of "spiritual and religious progress." "To believe is enough" he thought, expressing himself in such theological terms as "Christ, the Redeemer." It was a Biblical interpretation, without references, showing the stage of his thinking as he began his ministerial career. Two years later, in a review of the book, *The Incarnation,* he seemed to agree with the

Unitarian, Samuel Taylor Coleridge, that Christ, the Redeemer, was "the mediator for sinful man." [4]

ONE

In the spring of his fourth year in Salem, his review of Robert Wallace's *Unitarianism in the Sixteenth and Seventeeth Century,* reflected little change in his theological thinking. After a severe attack on Wallace for being a dull author and for presenting an "episodic" and fragmented view of Unitarian history, he wrote an erudite essay, doing what he accused the author of failing to do. He demonstrated a thorough knowledge of Socinius and the extinction of Unitarianism in Poland during the Reformation. Frothingham stated that he did not sympathize with the socinian system because he felt it was inconsistent with the belief in Christ the Redeemer, which he apparently still clung to at this time. With an ambiguity which would become typical of his thinking, Frothingham modified his criticism of socinianism by writing that he did sympathize with the movement that would encourage a scientific look at religion and a more philosophic view of theology.

He had expressed his misgivings to Editor George E. Ellis two months before the article was published. Was he too "severe" on Wallace, he asked. Hoping that the article would be satisfactory, he offered to "add, subtract or amend" as Ellis might request.[5] Apparently Ellis, conservative though he was, gave the young minister free expression. Frothingham closed his review with a bold plea for a modern religion. "Sooner or later we must have a rational religion and a scientific theology; a religion grounded upon the moral and spiritual constitution of man, and a theology conformed to the principles and facts of human reasons." [6]

As the March, 1851 issue of the *Examiner* came out, Frothingham was corresponding with Ellis about his next scholarly effort in theological journalism. He promised to write the two articles on "Christology" Ellis had requested, preferring this topic to one on Thomas Paine, who, he thought at this time, "should be left alone." [7] A lively correspondence ensued between the two concerning the content and interpretation which they both considered a bit controversial for the *Examiner.* By May, Frothingham had completed one article to be entitled "Christ of the Jews" according to their "compact," warning Ellis that he had expressed his own views for which the magazine need not be responsible. His second article was to be "Christ of the Gentiles" which he hoped would be published together with the first article in the November, 1851 issue. He hoped that the editor would not be "alarmed at the radicalism" of the article, adding that "the *Examiner* [might] safely contain certain heresies if they mingle not with its life blood. . . . [I] hope to hear from you soon and favorably." [8]

He did hear soon but apparently not too favorably. A week later he was writing Ellis that he had revised the article and elaborated his views of

German Biblical criticism but rejected Ellis' suggestion that the article end
with a "religious tone." His next thought to Ellis was to apologize for the
small inaccuracies, expressing the hope that he would learn how to write
"for the press." [9] The debate between Ellis and Frothingham continued
through the summer as the manuscripts were passed back and forth. The
fastidious Ellis was still not satisfied with the article as the publication
month for the first article arrived. Frothingham had accepted Ellis'
"suggestions and help for improvement" but insisted the opinions expressed must stand, quickly adding that they were not really his but "foreign
opinions" which did not commit the *Examiner.* Although Ellis was to publish
the articles which might "ruffle quiet waters," Frothingham assailed the
smugness and conservatism of Christians. He ended his letter with the
backtracking apology, "Excuse this little burst of indignation." [10]

But this did not end the matter. Two days later Frothingham was still
defending the opinions expressed, reiterating that they were a synthesis
of foreign opinions and that a Mr. Peabody of the editorial board had
made "a most unwarrantable surmise" in assuming that Frothingham
really agreed with the opinions of foreign writers. Yet he was willing to
"let it stand and take criticism." [11] Toward the end of September with the
fate of the article still undecided, he wrote to Ellis: "I hope I have
succeeded at last in making my meaning clear. If I have not, it must be that
I have no meaning to express." Enclosed in this exasperated letter was a
revised beginning for the article and a closing thought thanking Ellis for
the trouble in "amending and correcting [the] poor manuscript." [12]

TWO

Few critics would ever accuse Frothingham of not making his meaning
clear. Indeed, clarity was one of the most notable characteristics of his
writing. Was Ellis overcautious and hypercritical or was Frothingham at
this stage, in fact, a "muddy" writer? The editor of the *Christian Examiner,*
of course, knew that the views of the young Salem minister were a bit too
radical for the magazine, yet to his credit he published Frothingham's
articles. Since this was Frothingham's first venture in scholarly writing,
Ellis, the cautious editor and taskmaster, probably deserves much credit
for helping Frothingham clarify his thinking and develop a lucid writing
style.

His two articles on "Christology" were literary gems. The first, published in September, 1851, was entitled "Christ of the Jews." "Biblical
criticism," he stated, "is an experimental science. You can only say what
general positions in it are about settled, not what special truths are
demonstrated." After thus disarming his reader, he acknowledged the
influence of such German writers as Schwegler, Baur, Zeller, Planck and
Schwitzer, all of whom had "greatly furthered the cause of Critical Science." The Christ idea had progressed through four stages, he thought.

The Messiah idea of the Jews, being too primitive and narrow to appeal to a broader world less influenced "by graceful speculations from the East," thus evolved into the exalted Christ of Peter's first epistle. "Why the change?" he asked.

> While Christianity was mere Judaism, the Messiah would do, but it expanded to include all mankind. Jesus had to expand from a local Messiah to a symbol of wider appeal. . . . Christ could not be stationary in men's thoughts. That the field of his operation was gradually enlarged from the narrow borders of Judaism to the wide boundaries of the world, from the political affairs of an insignificant state to the spiritual interests of all human souls, is an established historical fact. . . . We should expect his own nature to expand in like degree.[13]

There is no doubt that Frothingham agreed with the German school of criticism and added his own insights from history, science, anthropology, and his philosophical skepticism in spite of his disclaimers at the beginning of the article. As he had instructed his ladies' class in Salem during his last year in Divinity School, the idea of Christ came from legend, controversy, cultural reflections, opinion and apocrapha. "Ideas of it [changed] with modern thought."

Enlarging on this theme in the second article, "Christ of the Gentiles, he stated his radicalism boldly:

> The Hebrew Messiah . . . could no more satisfy the intellectual Greeks and the Cosmopolitan Romans that the theocratic hope cherished by the devout in Jerusalem would content the speculative philosopher at the school, or the worshipper at the shrine of Apollo.[14]

He sketched for his readers the views of the Tübingen school of New Testament criticism. Christ was invented by Paul to die for man's sins and had little in common with his mythic origins as a Jewish Messiah.

> The heathen nations would have nothing to do with this Hebrew Messiah. . . . If they accepted Christ it must be on grounds wholly independent from his national character. There were two ways of bringing the two parties together: one, the extension of the redeemer office; the other the elevation of his person. Paul adopted the first of these methods; John adopted the second.

Frothingham concluded that Christ had evolved in men's minds as an intellectual idea from the carpenter's son to the "Divine Logos." It was an historical development of about two centuries of New Testament writing. In one last paragraph Frothingham summarized his thoughts on the Christ of the Gentiles":

. . . the missing Christ has preceded his person. His nature has preceded his function . . . (sinners, reformers, all individuals of various moral and mental states have used him). . . . He is the actual of our ideal. More than this, he cannot be . . . less than this he cannot be until our ideal is enlarged beyond today's imagination.[15]

Frothingham had wanted the two articles to be published in the same issue of the *Examiner*. Ellis and his editorial board members decided otherwise. Frothingham, already sensitive over criticism of style and interpretation, wrote sarcastically that he thought his writing was seriously impaired by separating the two articles. "The old *Examiner* is putting me off," he told Ellis, "to save its reputation." The "old *Examiner* is hard put for articles" to put in a "left over" from the last volume. The journalistic trick of the continued story" had been resorted to, he thought. His anger spent, Frothingham characteristically cooled and added conciliatory words for having questioned the judgment of Dr. Ellis and Dr. Putnam of the editorial board.

In looking over what is written I am afraid I have said too much about an unimportant matter—but it must go as it is and find its excuse in your candor and kindness.[16]

By the time the second article, "Christ of the Gentiles," appeared, the controversy was set aside and Frothingham was speculating to Ellis about his next writings. He had read Straus' *Leben Jesu* and works by Sweglein and Freurbach but felt his "unmetaphysical brain" was not up to such broad subjects. He would prefer rather suggestions for a lighter theme.[17] It was to be a book review of Hofman's *The Christ of the Apocryphal Gospels*. "It is finished, such as it is," he informed Ellis. He was flattered that the editor thought it good but felt it necessary to repair his contacts with the *Examiner* for the future. "If you think my pen does you no discredit, I beg you will remember that it is at your service." [18]

He was critical of Hofman's book which had "slight blemishes" due to the "credulous" author who seemed to search for evidence of Christ's divinity. His review became an essay, apparently reflecting Frothingham's own view of the apocryphal Gospels. They were not inspired, not enlightened, and not works of art but simply evidence of the stage of religious thought of the time. No new ground was covered in his appraisal.

They disclose the working of Christian thought . . . and furnish pregnant suggestions respecting the composition of the greater books which tell all we know of Christ, and relate the earlier movements of that faith which, in Aftertime, assimilated to itself the thought and reference of the civilized world.[19]

Six months later the restless Frothingham was asking Ellis for another writing assignment. Perhaps, he wrote to Ellis, he could do an article on Schwegler or Freurbach or any subject which he might suggest.[20] Ellis replied that he might do another article on New Testament criticism.[21] It turned out to be a review of C. T. Bunsen's *Hippolytus and His Age* (4 volumes)—"a most vexatious small job" thought Frothingham.[22] Nevertheless it was agreed upon, along with a pulpit exchange, for March or April. It was a confused essay, where Frothingham seemed to be critical of Bunsen's use of sources in placing the date of the Gospel of John but at the same time hoping that Bunsen had "demolished" Baur and Schwegler—the Tübingen school of theology—a body of thought for which he had previously shown affinity.[23] Perhaps he was intimidated by the presence of an article in the same issue by the editor, G. E. Ellis, Henry Bellows, Orvill Dewey, and his own father, N. L. Frothingham.[24]

The next article caused Ellis his usual editorial pains. A lively exchange took place during the last days of March about "Man and Nature in Their Religious Relations," to come out in the *Examiner* of May, 1853. It was too long, Ellis thought, but Frothingham was reluctant to cut, offering to pay for the extra space. Several members of his clergy association had read it, he reminded Ellis, and had "commended it very highly." He insisted that it go into the May issue "without strangulation" but on second thought suggested ways it could be cut, provided his own expressions, which had caused him "no little trouble," could be kept.[25] He hoped the editor would like it. Apparently he did. The result was a remarkably bold examination of the Proposition of Original Sin in the theory of man's fall and redemption. There was no Biblical or theological justification to support such a theory, he stated. Quoting St. Augustine, Jacob Bohme, and Milton's *Paradise Lost,* he concluded that the "vulgar theory of man's fall and redemption" was of "recent origin" with no sound basis. "It takes man out of history," he claimed, and makes him a creature of theologians' brains, "a metaphysical" and "theological deduction."[26] In the nineteenth century it was a common belief that the "pre-Adamite" condition of the world was a sign of original sin and the fall of man. Frothingham took issue with this myth.

> . . . The most fatal objection to the common theory respecting causal connection between nature and man is found in the very obvious fact, that all signs of corruption in the natural world . . . existed ages before man appeared upon the globe. The pre-Adamite earth was grim, gloomy and deadly to the last degree. The sulphurous sparks, the eras of earthquakes, flood submersion, volcanos, hurricanes, subterranean fire, atmospheric convulsions, were drawing to a close before the human race was formed. . . . The surface of the globe was a rocky waste. Tempests vexed the air. . . . The most hideous monsters abounded. . . . What shall we say of the iguanodon, that enormous lizard? . . . He ought to have been one of the earliest products of original sin. And the pterodactyl! His appearance

would indicate that he was the first to bear the brunt and wrench of man's transgressions. . . . The bird gave him his head and neck, the bat his wings, the crocodile . . . his snout. . . . This horrible creature would sit upon trees during the lonely night, with his wings folded, or would hop dismally about, like a huge bird.

No, said Frothingham,

such monstrosities did not long co-exist with man; kindly nature for the most part had finished her rough experiments in Creation, had dispatched the more coarse and clumsy work before the time of his appearing and when his nobler form came well-moulded, from her hand, she was already clearing away the old rubbish and burying it under the mountains.

Frothingham claimed facts have refuted the theories of geologists behind which "lurk theological theories" of the fall of man. There was no fall, he wrote.

Progress is the law of life; progress not even, uniform and rectilinear, but steady and constant; progress from feeble and rude beginnings onward. Upward and not downward, has been the tendency of nature from its commencement.[27]

Man himself has compiled with this process, thought Frothingham. Though in doubt about the theory that he was "the next step above the orangutan," he was sure that his nature appeared in imperfect form and that the "law of development is the law of man."

As Frothingham approached his last year in Salem, he and Ellis planned an article on "Scientific Criticism of the New Testament." The usual debate took place between the two. The first draft was not to Ellis' liking and Frothingham suggested that someone else might do better. Yet he revised it with the suggestion that if it were not satisfactory he had been satisfied with the writing of it whether it was published or not. On second thought he offered to "remove objections" as far as he could without recasting the whole paper and modify the content if Ellis' "fears continued unabated." [28] The cautious editor was appeased, yet his fears were understandable. The article was not so much a discussion of scientific criticism of the New Testament as a slashing attack on the moribund and confused state of Unitarian thought, as Frothingham saw it. "How can so much confusion of doctrine come out of the same Bible?" he asked.

Andover and Cambridge annually send forth their classes of young men with two distinct gospels, both claiming to be the gospel of Christ as revealed in scripture. These young men preach essentially opposite and contradictory views of the divine being and providence—of human nature and its origin; . . . of the character and office of Christ—of man's mortal and immortal existence in all its relations—and each party maintains that his doctrine is taught to the letter of the word. There must be some mistake here.[29]

Frothingham leveled his attack against Unitarian equivocation on New Testament criticism. They made "feeble protests" against the orthodox Protestant view of the Bible as an inspired book, yet claimed inspiration of thought stemming from it; rejected the evangelical creeds, yet clung to a creed themselves; failed to study the New Testament like any other book and approach it with an unbiased mind. Science must be applied, wrote Frothingham, lest a "battle of tongues" enuse. Like Francis Bacon, who applied science to natural law, science must be applied to "mental and moral philosophy." "Observation must precede theory" so that the Bible may be studied not as Christian apologetics but as a product of the evolution of ideas through an historical period. His attack on Unitarians' "pale negations" must have grieved his father and pleased his contemporaries who would later engage in the futile battle over the Unitarian Creed, leading to the establishment of the Free Religious Association thirteen years later.

While vacationing in the summer of 1854 at his father's summer home in Burlington, Massachusetts, he wrote to Ellis offering to review a book if one could be sent up from Boston.[30] The result was an innocuous review of a volume of sermons by Rev. T. T. Stone, a contemporary of Frothingham who had just left his Salem pulpit over a "crisis of conscience." Frothingham wrote in the *Examiner* that he liked the purely religious tone of Stone's sermons, ending his review with the words "Christian and Divine Life." [31] It was almost like a bland epilogue to his controversial article on Biblical criticism of the previous year.

THREE

Frothingham published nothing in the *Examiner* for more than three years. He broke his silence in the January, 1858 issue with what Samuel Johnson called "an admirable statement on the Tübingen school" of theology and its chief spokesman, Dr. Ferdinand Christian Baur[32]—the man and philosophy which had influenced Theodore Parker. Baur's New Testament criticism was admired by Frothingham for its detachment from "superficial questions of Virgin Birth and Resurrection" and because he analyzed the Bible as a literary critic from the standpoint of an evolving literature during the formative years of Christianity.[33] Frothingham's extended discussion of Baur's thought and quotations from his writings was similar to the articles on "Christ of the Jews" and "Christ of the Gentiles" in previous issues of the *Examiner*.

His next article was a composite review of three books: D. Van Ott Fock of the University of Kiel, *Socinianism* (2 volumes), 1847; George E. Ellis, *A Half Century of the Unitarian Controversy*, Boston, 1857; and James Martineau, the English religious radical, *Studies in Christianity*, Boston, 1858.[34] Whether Frothingham or editor Ellis selected the volumes is not clear. Together, thought Frothingham, they represented a spectrum of

Unitarianism—what it was, what it is, and what it is to become. After a brief notice of each book, he launched into the question of Unitarian development and scripture. It had gone through a developmental stage, he pointed out, but at present was ambiguous and equivocal as to the nature of Jesus and not outspoken at all on modern historical and literary methods of Biblical criticism—his old quarrel of previous articles. Still, he thought, the Unitarian ideas had progressed to the point of "morbid self-criticism" and had "opened the book for examination." Yet it had far to go, he continued, in spite of the influence of Locke, Milton, Clarke, Priestly, Buckminster, and the Wares. Curiously, he omitted Theodore Parker from his list of minds influential in the development of Unitarianism. At present, he thought the Unitarians had at last overthrown the Oriental despot of primitive Christianity and enthroned the ideal of divinity within humanity. His essay, a mixture of flights of literary imagery and hard factual blows, was a challenge to the Unitarians of his times.

As the last article came out, Frothingham was already preparing another essay review of three theological works. It was published in January, 1859, during his last busy year in Jersey City as he was negotiating his move from there to New York City. "Imagination in Theology" analyzed the works of Von Ludwig Feuerbach, Rev. J. R. Beard, and Von Dr. K. R. Hagenbach. He used Feuerbach's intuitively transcendental point of view to criticize the logical outcome of too much imagination. There were too many "fantastic tales and meaningless symbols," he wrote, woven around the man Jesus, and about concepts of the atonement, incarnation, and immortality. All of these were products of "oriental paganism," he thought, passed on to a "late barbaric culture" in Europe.[35] Here he spoke less like a Transcendentalist and more like a Rationalist, a progression of thought of which he was to be accused later.

FOUR

His move to New York City shortly after the publication of this article did not seem to interrupt the flow from his pen. In spite of the press of duties attending the establishment of the new church and the outbreak of the Civil War, he produced a long, erudite article entitled "Epicurus and Epicurians," published in July, 1861. It was a rather amusing article tracing the Epicurian school of philosophy, its aims of pleasure, its attempt to exorcise superstition and unnecessary pain, its almost stoic simplicity. Frothingham followed the logic of Epicurianism down through history, developing a tongue-in-cheek moral blast at New York society in 1861:

> The modern Epicurus, in his ordinary estate, is a well-bred man of the world, with some amiable common-sense, and an unsounded capacity for enjoyment. . . . If an American, he is probably a New Yorker, and by

profession almost anything you will, provided it be merely profession. You may meet Epicurus, out of business hours, on Broadway, in a print-shop or a bookstore; in the evening, in his opera box or at the club. About the details of his life there is a little mystery, which scandal has long been trying to dissipate, which charity is willing to leave undisturbed. To all appearance, his style of living is moderate and elegant; evidently arranged with a view to securing all the luxury that is consistent with agreeable physical sensations. Having no fondness for domestic cares or family responsibilities, he is by choice a bachelor, like his ancient master, though if Cupid smites him with a golden arrow, diamond-pointed, he gracefully submits to the holy bond which unites to him a woman's beauty and fortune, and consents to charge himself with the duty of preserving the one and spending the other. The social tastes of Epicurus are rather exclusive, though not perhaps strictly select. The great unwashed are his aversion; but one would judge, from two or three of his intimates, that he had no deadly antipathy to impurity so long as it did not appear on the skin. Our friend, who has travelled, observed, and meditated much, is a great philosopher. He can talk finely about the equality of human conditions, the nice distribution of happiness in every human lot, and the compensations to be found in all human estates. It is really beautiful to hear him enlarge on the simple pleasures of the poor, the immunities of the disfranchised, the privileges of the lowly, and the innocent joys of the enslaved. So profound is his faith in Providence, that he will not see that anything in the universe needs correcting. We have heard him maintain, over his sherbet and Madeira, that the world would be well enough if men would only let it alone. He has no patience with philanthropists and reformers; he has no faith in saints and heroes—not he: they are knaves and pretenders, all of them—do more harm than good. As for chivalry, disinterestedness, and all that, every man of common sense knows it is nothing but self-love in showy disguise. Everybody has his price; we all get what pleasure we can; and we avoid pain if we can. A great philosopher. It is astonishing what a reputation for wisdom he has acquired by simply assuming that all men are knaves, and that frailty's name is woman.

In politics, as in morals, our philosopher is conservative. In fact, he hates politics and politicians, and annually threatens to leave the country for England or France, where the government is strong enough to protect property and the rights of gentlemen from socialists and radicals. The people, he thinks, ought to be governed. Laws which the well-to-do of all time have found perfectly satisfactory, ought to be satisfactory still, and ought to be preserved by force, if need be. Once, the privileges of the finer clay were respected; but now the earth is plagued by enthusiasts, who talk about their consciences, and are forever reminding people of certain eternal principles of equity, humanity, and the like. Nonsense. Life is a compromise—a perpetual compromise between pains and pleasures, goods and ills. And your grand patriots and benefactors are simply men whose great luxury is the indulgence of their own self-esteem, and who "value money and social rank less than the pleasure of venting their spleen and making a sensation."

Epicurus is seen occasionally at the church where the best soprano in town is to be heard, and the pink of the fashion is to be seen, and he is quite sure that the preacher will say nothing to create an unpleasant sensation. No one, indeed, ever suspected him of excessive piety. Some of his friends have frankly confessed that his attachment to the forms of worship perhaps exceeded his love of religion. But it is shameful for those horribly earnest people out of doors to say that he has no more faith in Christianity than the Grand Turk. For has he not a great dread of heresy and innovation? Does he not abhor the New Lights? Is he not a staunch friend of religious institutions, and has he not often been heard to say that the Church was quite invaluable as an instrument of conservatism, as a means for keeping the ignorant and passionate under some salutary restraint? When he speaks of the impossibility of knowing anything about the secrets of the universe, and the uselessness of speculating upon the causes and essences of things, his conversation is really edifying to all comfort-loving souls. And so large is his charity that, in his tolerance, all religions are alike to him: one is no more true or venerable than another; he has a theory that they are all, at last, the same thing. And to show that this is not mere theory, he actually changed his religion two or three times in Europe, in order to gain admission to certain holy cities and shrines belonging to the Turks. He is beneficent too. He contributed last year to the ragged schools, saying wisely that it was better to pay a dollar for prevention than ten dollars for cure; that poor schools were cheaper than jails, and teachers less expensive than officers. It is so painful for him to contemplate suffering, that he often flings an alms to a street beggar with an air which seems to say that it costs him less to give than to refuse. He disapproves, in the abstract, of grave social wrongs, even when they do not affect himself. And such is his love of peace and quietness, that he would be glad to hang and shoot everybody who disturbs the settled tranquillity of the public mind. He is a kind, pleasant, patronizing, gracious gentleman, with the softest voice and blandest manner and handsomest words you ever knew, and it is a shame to call him a materialist and an atheist, a man of such affability and delicacy.[36]

It was a jeremiad. Yet not content to end on such a note, Frothingham typically gave the Epicurians their due. Thanks be to them, he wrote, for their attempts to relieve the world of anxiety and to make the world an easier, softer place for man. But also thanks to them "for their sad confessions that the pursuit of happiness is fruitless" and that men cannot be transformed into butterflies.

By September, 1861, he had reviewed Robert Alfred Vaughan's *Hours With the Mystics* (London, 1860).[37] Mysticism he equated with transcendentalism. It was the philosophy of Parker and Emerson, he thought, which emphasized the indwelling God, the spirit of Christ and not the man, and the Pantheistic view that God was in nature. He praised mysticism because it "lifts us above words rather than makes us faithful to [a creed]." Here he is clearly a transcendentalist accepting the *a priori*, intuitive point of view as an essential part of religion and philosophy.

His next venture in Biblical criticism was a review of a book by a layman
and retired soldier, General Hitchcock's *Christ the Spirit: Being an Attempt to
State the Primitive View of Christianity* (New York, 1861). Frothingham was
pleased that the author had quietly asserted the mythic nature of Jesus
without the torturous labors of Frederick David Straus. He agreed that
the author was correct in portraying Jesus as a figment of Essene mythol-
ogy which literalists then later seized upon to turn into a literal symbol.
Christ is pure spirit, agreed Frothingham, and appears everywhere. He
dwells in the Duomo of Milan, and in the Quaker meeting house in Salem.
The Catholic priest presents him in the sacrament of Transubstantiation;
the Unitarian "communes" with him in his simple memorial rite; the
Silent Friends have him nearest of all. Frothingham admitted Christ must
have a form for the use of man. Yet the form, he objected, often hides the
substance as a type of idolatry. Frothingham hoped the spirit of Christ
would not be lost in smashing the idols.

> We have no intention and no desire to act the part of destructives. We would
> never shatter an idol that revealed a God. But knowing as we do know how
> many see no God behind the idol—knowing as we do know how many,
> believing the historical Christ to be shattered, fear that the real Christ is
> gone—we would passing by the others as not needing what we have to say,
> speak our word of encouragement to these. We have wished to detach the
> immortal person from his temporal environment; we have wished to show
> how little he has been injured by the falling of his house made with hands;
> we have wished to make him appear walking triumphantly over its ruins.[38]

The following year of 1863, the turning point in the Civil War and the
year Frothingham dedicated his first church building in New York, three
of his articles appeared in the *Christian Examiner:* one a light review, "The
Pulpit in the Past," of an inconsequential book; another a review of Henry
Ward Beecher's sermons, "Altar, Pulpit and Platform"; the third a review
of Ernest Renan's *Life of Jesus.*[39]

Frothingham wrote a long discourse on the power of the pulpit as
opposed to the popular platform without actually mentioning Beecher in
the content of his sermons. Preaching was gaining in power he pointed
out, although the clergy had lost many functions. The role of the pulpit,
he thought, was to express moral laws and hold up values to the world.
"Establishments dread the pulpit," he felt, for the "voice is mightier than
the pen."

Frothingham's review of Renan's *Life of Jesus,* which caused a "flurry of
excitement for the extreme audacity of its thought," was probably the
most thoroughgoing and devastating treatment of this famous work. As
late as 1928, John Haynes Holmes of All Souls Unitarian Church in New
York gave it a glowing account, considering it the last, definite work on
the life of Jesus. Frothingham also established this by stating that it was the

"last word of naturalism in its attempt to describe Jesus." But he said more. The book made no attempt to analyze, he wrote, but merely to maintain the theological myth of Jesus. Renan had avoided the rigors of historical and literary criticism, thought Frothingham, a literal approach which had been "destroyed earlier by the German school of Straus and Baur." The book was a work of art, admitted Frothingham, but was a "romance" of no more historical value than the Gospels themselves upon which the life of Jesus was based. Renan's treatment, to Frothingham, was "external," too shallow, too rational—a "charming" tale but missing the point of the "spiritual dimension of Jesus." This critique shows the inherent conflict between Renan, the French Rationalist, and Frothingham, the American Transcendentalist in the Darwinian Age. Said Frothingham,

> Perception is an interior thing. It is the mind that sees. The best eyes will be of little use where there is no speculation in them. . . . A great person manifests himself in and through his external history, but [it] is not by mastering the facts of his external history that you will apprehend him. In that way you will be pretty sure to misapprehend him. We must interpret the history of the man rather than the man by the history. . . .[40]

Here the transcendentalist speaks a word of doubt about the scientific rationalism of his age. He also seems to doubt his own beliefs in the validity of the "law of development" expressed by him elsewhere in terms of evolutionary theory. In attacking Renan's *Life of Jesus* he rejected the linear concept of evolutionary theory. Man had a soul, he thought, before he began evolving.

> The spirit explains the body, the soul answers questions about the senses . . . you cannot leap from nerve to thought, from organ of knowledge to the faculty of knowledge, nor can you come by surprise on the soul, by feeling your winding way along the convolutions of the brain.[41]

Biblical criticism was the theme of "The Evangelist Debt to the Critic," a review of W. H. Furness' *The Veil Partly Lifted and Jesus Becoming Visible,* published in the May, 1864 issue of the *Christian Examiner.*[42] In his usual style, Frothingham felt that Furness had written a charming book defending the Jesus of the four Gospels of Matthew, Mark, Luke, and John, but lacked the perception of analysis of Renan, Baur, and Straus. Going beyond the author of the book under review, he reexamined all levels of New Testament criticism. On the literary and historical level, Straus was advanced but missed the allegorical dimension; theologically, Baur's treatment was pernicious; Furness and Renan both lacked intuition. Reiterating his point of previous articles, he felt that the "real Jesus" was impossible to recapture and it was needless to do so. Those who searched for Jesus the man missed the poetry and symbolism of the four Gospels. The Evangelists, wrote Frothingham, were in fact poets and theologians and not chroniclers.

The orthodox scholars accepting the ancient interpretation of the church, assumed two positions: first that the Gospels were history, second, that the history was supernatural. Rationalism, rejecting the second of these assumptions, still insisted on the first and received the Gospels . . . on the plane of natural events.

Although this missed the point of allegory and myth, Frothingham saw value in this level of criticism from the standpoint of the development of ideas. "Let Furness bring the hammer, Renan his drill, Baur his acid; who decomposes most shall find most." [43]

Moving from theology to philosophy, the November issue carried his review of Ephriam Frothingham's *Philosophy As Absolute Science*. [44] The reviewer, no relation to the author, recommended the book to all thinkers as a useful "master key" to the dualisms in philosophic thought. Emerson's comment about marriage as the bond of two opposing forces, and Henry James, the elder's *Substance and Shadow* which attempted to present the dichotomy in human dilemmas, were referred to in justification of the validity of Ephriam Frothingham's approach to philosophy.

Rev. I. I. Hecker, a Catholic priest, came under heavy attack from Frothingham in his January, 1865 *Examiner* review of *The Order of Saint Paul the Apostle and the New Catholic Church*. Hecker, who at the age of twenty-four had visited Brookfarm for a summer, had criticized the establishment and such transcendentalists as Waldo Emerson and Margaret Fuller for their emphasis on individualism and belief in intellectual progress as being anathema to the Paulist Fathers' attempt to "capture" America and make it more democratic. Frothingham reacted strongly against Hecker's allegation that Protestantism means authority and elitism, while Catholicism means democracy. The "neo-Catholic church" in New York, Frothingham wrote, was a facade for the same old medieval institutions, ostensibly modernized to capture nineteenth century America. He did not entertain Hecker's thought that Catholicism was better suited to American democracy than Protestantism. "Protestantism means individualism which means liberty; Romanism means centralization which means authority. This is the whole story. . . ." In elaborating his argument against Hecker's claim that Catholicism embraced democracy, Frothingham reviewed the recent do-nothing movement.

There was a time when, in a momentary crossing and mingling of the religious and political streams, the Catholics appeared as the champions of individual liberty and personal rights, and the Protestants seemed to be on the side of the narrow, exclusive, oppressive "Native American" policy. But this was an accident as was evident from its unproductiveness. The immense influx of the Irish population, their speedy appropriation and illegal naturalization by the Aristocratic party which bore the democratic name, because they were not democrats and used it as a lure to these poor fugitives from an oppressive and monarchical government, excited the reasonable

apprehensions of sincere republicans, who foresaw danger to republican
institutions in the wholesale admission of ignorant foreigners to the rights
of citizenship, in the bribery that was connected with it, and the consequent
monopoly of power over the masses by a few unprincipled demagogues. It
happened that immigrants were nearly all Catholics.[45]

In the climate of the Civil War, Frothingham equated the Democrats
with the Southern aristocracy and the Republicans with the party of
freemen and free soil. He felt Catholicism would retire from its old haunts
with the fall of the Southern slave system and the victory of the North.
Although certain areas, such as the Southwest and some cities, would
continue to be attractive to Catholics, he was sure that it would not spread
because it was "not a portable but stationery religion . . . too cumbersome
to go into a saddlebag." On the other hand, Protestantism was a "Northern spirit" of freedom, a natural religion whose "missionaries . . . travel
faster than the brothers of the Order of St. Paul. They are industry,
enterprise, intelligence, knowledge, the awakened capacities of man." [46]
The anti-Catholic blast was rather typical of the radical Unitarian of
Frothingham's time. It also had another basis. After more than five years
in New York City, Frothingham, the transplanted New England intellectual, was doubtless suffering "culture shock" from the Irish and other
recently arrived ethnic groups. Although it would be unhistoric to label
Frothingham a "know-nothing," he was anti-Catholic from an intellectual
and theological point of reference. This theme recurs in later sermons
and social commentary during Frothingham's New York "ministry."

FIVE

His last appearance in the pages of the *Examiner* was in the July, 1865
issue. Two essay reviews of books were of major significance for revealing
the stage of his thinking as he was making his reputation as an intellectual
leader and just prior to his involvement in the founding of the Free
Religious Association. One essay, a review of J. S. Mills' *Examination of Sir
William Hamilton's Philosophy,* reflected his gradual change from transcendentalism to an affinity for a more scientific view of philosophy; the other,
"The Drift Period in Theology," was a composite review of three current
books on theological thinking which also indicated his cautious but growing affinity for a scientific theism.[47]
Frothingham carried on a disputation between the two exponents of
conflicting philosophies in dealing with J. S. Mills and William Hamilton.
Hamilton, the intuitive transcendentalist was arrayed against Mills, the
psychological, scientific philosopher. Frothingham, age forty-two, ten
years after his Salem experience and the Theodore Parker influence,
admitted that the intuitive, transcendental philosophy had been swept
aside by naturalism and rationalism. J. S. Mills had abolished Sir William

Hamilton. Regretfully, but with his characteristic flexibility of mind, Frothingham recognized John Stuart Mills as

> a thinker of what is called in modern speech the psychological school, to which belonged also Professor Baur of Aberdeen and Herbert Spencer. Under the old classification he would be called a sensationalist as distinguished from a Transcendentalist. . . . but . . . the nomenclature [may] fail to do anything but misrepresent.

As much as he admired Mills' psychological, sensational view as a fruitful approach to a rational, scientific religious philosophy, he still felt that transcendentalists such as William Hamilton or Theodore Parker came out with answers similar to the sensationalists. Views of good and evil, immortality and divinity, could be both proven by the senses and known intuitively. Frothingham would never completely clarify his views of this difference in philosophic approach, much to the confusion of his colleagues and delight of his critics who later would accuse him of "recanting" his radical views of religion.

The lead article of the issue "Drift Period in Theology," however, followed consistently the idiom of naturalism. Alluding to drift periods in geology when seas move and the earth is in upheaval prior to a new formative change in the earth's crust, Frothingham, in the language of evolutionary theory, wrote that man's mind changes in philosophic and theological points of view. Theology he felt was in a "drift period" as yet unsettled but clearly tending toward a pantheism based on science. It would not be an austere scientific theism which would be too intellectual for most people who feel more than they think. But he was sure that a rationalism based on science would prevail.

> The tendency is already, and will be more and more, to abandon theological methods in the treatment of moral and spiritual, even of the theological and Christological subjects; to dispense with theological phrases, and approach all topics from the scientific point. From the known, inferences will be drawn from the unknown. Literature will apply its laws to the Bible. Human nature will give the key to the character of Jesus. Creation will explain the Creator. The order, harmony, and beneficence of the physical and social world will be demonstrated in a way that none can dispute; and all controversy about the divine attributes will become obsolete.[48]

Frothingham thought the drift period in theology, though characteristic of the western world, was particularly noticeable in nineteenth century America. In thoughts reminiscent of De Tocqueville, he described the unsettled quality of American religious thought:

> In America, the unrestrained liberty of the people in all the departments of life, their complete emancipation from establishments and traditions, their

entire absorption in practical pursuits, their general and eager intelligence, their fertility, their self-reliance, have wrought an insensible change in all habits of mind, usage, and feeling. Nothing can stand still in the powerful current of their common energy. Disintegration goes forward everywhere. The people are not unreligious; on the contrary, they are "very religious"; but they are always desiring "some new thing." The word "progress" is continually on their lips. They move all over. While the feet run, the soul runs also. They carry their houses with them. The Americans are driven by the Spirit, and go whither they know not. They are, under Providence, men of destiny, hardly knowing what they mean, what they wish, what they believe, or what they worship. They drift in masses, the sport, apparently, of the winds which blow where they list. They are irresponsible for their creed. They "believe as they go along"; and they go along so fast that it is not easy at any moment to say, "Lo here!" or "Lo there!" The masses distance the leaders. The teachers toil on after pupils. The guides follow, and bring up in the rear. Nobody can talk fast enough to say what is in the people's minds. They feel further than he sees. The great elements of influence travel and impel more rapidly than individual thinkers can march. Trained, cultivated, and careful thought must act the part of conservative. The minds that go in advance of the great public, and seem to guide it, are minds that are more sensitive than the rest of the finer currents of thought that permeate and control the century; minds more readily detached from their old connections, more responsive to breaths of air, and more nimble in following out the direction that is appointed.[49]

Clearly, one of the sensitive minds in tune with the "finer currents of thought" controlling the century was that of O. B. Frothingham himself. Already established, at this writing, for five years in New York, he was to go on to his reputation as one of the leading intellectual preachers of the age. He had been eager enough to leave Jersey City for a larger audience and a greater challenge. He found it in New York City.

IV

The Pulpit Voice:
New York Ministry

RECALLING HIS CONGREGATIONS DURING the twenty years in New York, Frothingham described them as "composed of all sorts of people. There were Unitarians, Universalists, 'Come Outers,' spiritualists, unbelievers, all kinds, anti-slavery people, reformers generally. But this, as being incidental to the formation of every liberal society, was not objected to." [1] Although founded in the spring of 1859 at the invitation of Dr. Bellows, Dr. Osgood, and others of the New York Unitarian Association as the Third Congregation—Unitarian Society, the group gradually moved away from any denominational affiliation and became finally in 1870 the Independent Liberal Church (ILC) of New York. During the first four years (1859–1863) the society rented Ebbit Hall. In 1863 a church building was constructed and occupied until the spring of 1869. The new church building, with acoustical problems, never suited Frothingham who also objected to the ecclesiastical surroundings of the structure which really did not suit the "genius of the new society." The church was sold and the group moved to Lyric Hall between Forty and Forty-First Streets on Sixth Avenue across from Reservoir Park, now Bryant Park. "During the week it was a dance hall," he recalled, "but on Sundays it was arranged for religious purposes." Movable seats, a small organ, and a desk on a small platform were added "to a large room fifty by one hundred feet." [2]

It was during the Lyric Hall years (1869–1875) that Frothingham himself, as we shall see, moved out of Unitarianism and into the Free Religious Movement. The group also had long ceased to be a Unitarian congregation. There were people of Catholic training, many of Protestant training, some with no religious training whatsoever, atheist, secularist, positivists—always thinking people with their minds uppermost. It was a "church for the unchurched." [3]

Masonic Temple on the corner of Twenty-Third Street and Sixth Avenue was the scene of the last years of Frothingham's Independent Liberal Church (1875–1879). "Clavering," a pen name for a *Boston Journal* writer, described the building and its atmosphere on a Sunday morning:

> The Sunday services conducted by the Rev. Octavius B. Frothingham at the new Masonic Temple attract large congregations of the most intelligent men and women in our community.
>
> The hall that has been leased by the Independent Society, whereof Mr. Frothingham is pastor, is situated on the corner of Sixth Avenue and Twenty-third Street, and reached from the latter thoroughfare by a broad, massive stairway of polished marble, adorned with classic emblems in bronze of the fraternity by whom it was lately reared.
>
> It is a simple hall, and the bare, white walls are yet innocent of any touch of color, and while waiting for the beginning of the service the eye rests neither on them nor on the two rows of heavy columns that blossom into the foliated terminal capitals of Corinth, but seek repose and find it on the organ front, which faces the congregation, and is exquisitely decorated in every brilliant and beautiful color that an autumn sunset could lend.
>
> I speak of this organ particularly because it has so long been the custom to cover organ fronts with inappropriate and gaudy gilding, and it is a genuine source of delight to observe a perfect harmony of color before the harmony of sound begins.
>
> There are about a thousand opera chairs in the hall, and opposite there is a dais, on which are placed a reading-desk supported by a single column, together with a small walnut stand and several armed chairs, the blue covers of the latter affording another grateful gleam of color. At the foot of the desk mosses and the large leaves of some familiar garden plants are usually placed, above which a few clusters of brilliant flowers mingle with the smilax and ivy that creep toward the top. A nosegay, arranged with artful careless-ness, is generally to be seen upon the stand, close to which is the pastor's chair.[4]

Frothingham referred to the size of his congregation as "never large" yet there were probably eight hundred to one thousand people in attend-ance each Sunday. Many were intellectual leaders in New York City during the decade of 1860 to 1870. On his Board of Trustees through the years were: James H. Morse, minor poet headmaster of a boys' Latin school, a close friend of the Frothinghams; Oliver Johnson, editor of *Independent Weekly Tribune,* editor of *Christian Union,* and biographer of William Lloyd Garrison; George Haven Putnam of the G. P. Putnam's Sons publishing house; and Calvert Vaux, architect and designer of Central Park. George Ripley, former head of Brook Farm and retired Unitarian radical preacher from Boston, attended often after joining the staff of the *New York Herald Tribune.* Edmund C. Stedman, author, jour-nalist, and man of letters; Henry Peter Gray, an artist; C. P. Cranch, a poet; and Dr. F.A.P. Barnard, president of Columbia College, were all part of Frothingham's "church for the unchurched." Horace Greeley, down from Chappaqua, was sometimes seen in the congregation "with eyes half-closed but not missing anything," and occasionally annoyed when the children stuffed his greatcoat pocket with a copy of a sermon Frothingham had preached on "Immortality" with which the *Tribune* editor disagreed.[5]

ONE

How did Frothingham hold such an intellectual but diverse group together? During his Salem and Jersey City years, he had complained that his congregations had fallen away. This was not the case in New York. What were the sources of his ability to draw his people in and stimulate their minds week after week for twenty years? E. C. Stedman, his personal friend and a trustee of the society, contrasted him with Emerson, who had settled in the provincial town of Concord as Frothingham had made his New York establishment "a modern oracle and shrine." He had also taken on the mantle of Theodore Parker by seeking a wider audience in New York as Parker had done in pre-Civil War Boston. To Stedman, Frothingham was the "purest New England type . . . a clear link with the strong intellectual, theological impulse (though not doctrine of Colonial times) . . . a latter day Calvinist type that would have died for his faith but advanced modern ideas." [6] His pulpit style was based not on oratorical tricks but on appeals to the mind. His prayers, making no pleas for self-centered desires for salvation and personal immortality, challenged the individual mind and conscience directly. His sermons were as "compact as Emerson's, though better structured." In contrast to the florid pulpit manner of the "established preachers" Frothingham adopted the low key, conversational way of the puritan plain style, though Stedman did not use the term.

Another contemporary, James Morse, explaining Frothingham's pulpit style to Felix Adler, thought part of his success was due to his ability to speak extemporaneously from brief notes "rarely consulted." He could sense his audience and depend upon the inspiration of the moment for proper phrasing, "arranging his address in an order perfectly logical, illustrating richly, putting in half-memorized dates, quotations abundantly, yet finding opportunity to watch his audience whose inattention or puzzlement he must meet on the spot with some satisfactory anecdotes. . . ." [7]

Stedman, more interested in content than delivery, felt that the secret of Frothingham's appeal to the intellectual audience was his broad pluralistic approach to theology, philosophy, and social ethics. The intellectual atmosphere created in Masonic Hall, said Stedman in 1876,

> was drawn from the anthology of sacred theology: Christian, Jewish, Hindu, Persian and Oriental. Each idea was valued and used appropriately and relevantly. Historical analysis, comparative religion, literary criticism and linguistics were used to make his discourses triumphs of pure reason.[8]

Judge George Barrett, another parishioner, had an affinity for Frothingham as a preacher because of his controversial fairness. He invariably understood the facts upon which his own position rested while he gave full and adequate expression to his adversary's argument. Those with whom he disagreed continually complained that Frothingham seemed to understand their philosophical positions better than they did, "something," said Josiah Quincy, "that can scarcely be said of Wendell Phillips, William Lloyd Garrison or Theodore Parker." [9]

From the days of the rented Ebbit Hall in 1859 to the final spring of 1879 in Masonic Hall, Octavius Frothingham held the pulpit that appealed to the intellectual community of New York City and established his reputation as one of the memorable preachers of the age. The same Boston journalist who had described Masonic Hall caught the intellectual atmosphere at the height of Frothingham's fame.

On a recent Sunday, when I was one of an expectant throng, these observations were made, and I know from inquiry that they may be applied generally. The hall was nearly full, and the organist (a lady) was already seated when Mr. Frothingham walked quickly up the aisle, through a side door and out upon the dais at the moment when the opening voluntary upon the organ was commenced. At its close, after a slight pause, an appropriate selection—from the "Creation," I think—was sung by the quartet choir, and then, when the last note had ceased to reverberate, the pastor stepped to the desk, raised a small volume in front of his breast, and turning over the leaves said in a low, distinct voice, "Will you listen to the reading from the Indian Scriptures?"

After reading with exquisite expression and distinct emphasis numerous proverbs, many of them singularly terse and beautiful in their composition, he paused for a moment, and then, "this from the Arabic," continued the reading of truths which the translator has made universal knowledge. This custom is varied I believe only in the selection of the matter; sometimes our Bible is used, and sometimes "the Bible of others."

Then another hymn, and Mr. Frothingham arose and stood at the desk to pronounce the opening prayer. His always earnest face bore an expression of intense feeling, and for more than a minute he remained motionless, with clasped hands, slightly upturned face, and closed eyes. Presently his lips began to move, though for an instant no audible sound escaped them, and he may have been but searching and concentrating his own mind. When the first word reached my ear the stillness in the hall was perfect save the sound of the speaker's voice, and throughout the delivery of the prayer it remained unbroken.

The earnest expression of Mr. Frothingham's face when he rose seemed to command everyone's attention; his silently moving lips caused them to strain the ear to catch the first faint sound, and when the full, serious voice bore forth the appeal for goodness, and truth, and virtue, and brotherly love, and strong humanity, not a word was lost. It was no supplication for the alteration of eternal laws, nor any unmeant confession of abject worthlessness and misery, but a noble, manly aspiration to men and women to act worthily and well on earth.

When ended, Mr. Frothingham resumed his seat, seemingly somewhat exhausted, his left elbow upon the table, and his head resting upon the open hand that partly shaded his face, while the faint tones of the organ that had taken up the end of his prayer were lost in silence.

Then began the discourse. Probably most readers of the Boston *Journal* know something of Mr. Frothingham's glittering oratory, which at first attracts hearers who are afterward charmed by the pure gold of candor, integrity, and truth, which is its foundation. His logic is always inductive if not always consecutive; and though he may not hold his hearers from point to point of his argument, still if they question for a moment it is only while waiting for the answer which surely comes. He uses no sophistical syllogisms to really mystify while seeming to convince, and he throws on his own opinions the white light of investigation whereby to discern the truth. He does not rend asunder the prejudices of others with the blow of a trip-hammer, but rather penetrates them with the keenly-cutting anger, letting light through. The wounds he inflicts are always kindly meant, as the surgeon's who cuts out the cancer to save the life.

Once he said of one of his own arguments, "Call it iconoclasm, image-breaking if you will; but every idol is a mask, and to shatter the idol is to reveal the God."

Some of Mr. Frothingham's finest efforts have been made in discussing topics connected with the conduct of life and the various social relations; and into these subjects he enters with an integrity of purpose that alone could inspire such enthusiasm as he invariably displays. In the discussion of matters of faith or theology he is inclined to mordacity, and denounces with biting satire what he regards as baleful superstitions; and as he stands alone among our pulpit orators in avowed belief, the temptation to level his bitter shafts must be often resisted, for he speeds them but seldom.

His discourse is always characterized by intensity; and by reason of his marvellous powers of imagery is rarely without the adornment of some vivid word-picture that lives in the hearer's mind in brightness and beauty.

People who oppose Mr. Frothingham on other than theological grounds declare that among a community as pure and unselfish as he would have them it might be possible to live up to all his precepts; but that to the work-a-day world they are far-offish and transcendental, while his friends claim that however he may be removed from the sphere of common human-ity he never fails to render the world he lives in attractive and fascinating, nor to lift his hearers, for a time at least, from their pains and cares, and lead them to higher aspirations and nobler resolves.[10]

TWO

In spite of the brilliance with which he preached and the apparent success of his New York establishment, Frothingham's attitude was ambiv-alent. He continually had gloomy second thoughts about his role as a radical preacher and the permanent impact of his ministry in the Independent Liberal Church. He often confided to friends that he was an optimist on Saturday night and a pessimist on Monday morning.[11] Although this attitude probably came from his self-critical nature he had reason to be pessimistic about his role in New York. His small group was surrounded by what he called the popular religions. Henry Ward Beecher in Brooklyn probably held the largest audience. There was John Hall of the Fifth Avenue Presbyterian Church to which many of the social elite belonged. Thomas DeWitt Talmadge of the Dutch Reformed Church in Brooklyn preached to throngs of people. His own Unitarian colleague, Dr. Henry Bellows of All Souls Church, held center stage for the conservative Unitarians of the Boston stamp, characteristic of his father's day. In the nation were commanding figures such as Cardinal Gibbons of Baltimore, Maryland, shepherding large numbers of Catholics, and Washington Gladden of Columbus, Ohio, liberal in the "social gospel" but orthodox in theology and denominational matters. Then there was Dwight Moody preaching in the Hippodrome to large audiences who would gather periodically in an enthusiastic atmosphere of religious fundamentalism.[12] As we shall see, Frothingham felt surrounded and virtually alone in his struggle against the appeal of the "popular" religions.

Yet he struggled better than he knew in propagating liberalized views of religion and its role in human affairs. George Haven Putnam, publisher, considered him more influential "than any other American as being representative of the liberal faith." [13] Peter Dean, the English biographer of Theodore Parker, considered Frothingham, at the height of his fame in 1877, the most intellectual preacher which America possessed.[14] There was no doubt that Frothingham's attempt to bring Christianity to terms with evolutionary theory and modern Biblical criticism put him a generation ahead of the mainstream, as were his coreligionists Frances E. Abbot, William J. Potter, William White Chadwick, Samuel Johnson, Samuel Longfellow, and Thomas Wentworth Higginson.[15]

As we have seen, he had been moving in the direction of a free nondenominational religious society in his thinking at least since his Salem days. Although his New York church was chartered in 1860 as the Third Congregational Unitarian Church, the bylaws implied a less sectarian free religious society on the order of Parker's in Boston, Higginson's in Worcester, and Johnson's in Lynn—all organized prior to Frothingham's:

> . . . established for the support of public worship, the maintenance of religious faith, liberal, intelligent and progressive, the cultivation of religious life, individual and social, insisting always upon the freedom of individual opinion in all matters of religious faith, . . . it is expressly understood that no . . . assent to any covenant be required. . . .[16]

This, indeed, was a covenant in itself but a free and open one sufficient for

the pursuit of the "new faith." Since Frothingham was more interested in
the process of inquiry in the search for truth, we must now ask: What was
meant by the "new faith" and its interchangeable term, "new theology"?
How did the radical preacher deal with the theological categories as the
intellectual leader of his free society? How did Frothingham's theological
and philosophic position fit into the religious thought of the American
intellectual tradition?

THREE

During his twenty-year ministry in New York, Frothingham elaborated
his meaning of the "new theology" in innumerable sermons. His major
argument against Christianity was that it was not a developing idea but an
idea already developed, organized, instituted. "A complete investigation
of the subject," he wrote two years before his retirement, "will probably
reveal the fact that Christianity owes its entire wardrobe, ecclesiastical,
symbolical, dogmatical, to the religions that preceded it. The point of
difficulty to decide is in what respects Christianity differs from the elder
faiths." [17]

To him it meant an attempt to modernize traditional Christian unity.
He searched for new interpretations and truths linking literal views of
Christian symbols and myths. He attempted to bring religion to terms
with the scientific views of the nineteenth century. To him the doctrine of
evolution held one key to understanding the process of the intellectual
and ethical progress of man. He also tried to balance the scientific theory
of development with the older transcendental view of the intuitive, *a priori*
mode of thought. By never rejecting theism he never fully accepted the
view that science was the only key to reason and no truth lay outside of
science. The supreme wisdom, he thought, lay within the human mind
rather than coming from some transcendent God. As a transcendentalist
he believed God was within man and nature; as an evolutionist he was sure
all the forces of nature and society were working toward a progressive,
humanistic end. Yet the key to progress was human effort, for ethics and
truths grew out of human experience. He could be called an exponent of
theistic humanism. His "new theology," then, was a synthesis of elements
of Deism, transcendentalism, and Darwinism, with a strong overlay of the
puritan spirit.

But it was more than this. As we shall observe more fully later, he was
also influenced by the Swedenborgian mode of theological thinking. He
admitted his debt to Theodore Parker for introducing him to the thought
of Emanuel Swedenborg who led Parker himself and many of his followers in Frothingham's generation to be inclined toward the intuitional,
inner light approach to spiritual knowledge. Established in England in
1783 as the "new church," it became one source of inspiration for American transcendentalists. As Frothingham developed his ideas in New York,

his early dissatisfaction with the barrenness of Christianity grew. Increasingly he viewed it as a form of sectarianism in itself. Accordingly, he showed a growing affinity for the ethical and spiritual literature of other world cultures. He attempted to synthesize common ideas, symbols, and myths from all the world religions. He began to view religion as an universal truth transcending all times and places. The "religion of humanity" became the label for the "new theology" and was the central focus of the Free Religious Association which he was soon to lead.[18]

Frothingham's theological position, radical though it seemed to most of his contemporaries, fits squarely into the Free Thought movement in the American tradition. The same philosophies that turned Frothingham to theistic humanism turned others to atheism or agnosticism. Sidney Warren has used the device of the political spectrum to classify positions of Free Thought: atheism as "left wing," agnosticism as "center," and Free Religion as "right wing." As "right wing" free thinkers, Frothingham and his coreligionists rejected atheism, respected the writings and utterances of such English agnostics as Matthew Arnold, George Elliot, Samuel Butler, and the American Robert Ingersol, but retained their affinity for religious forms and symbols. "They combined radicalism in their fundamental outlook on life with a basic spiritual consciousness which at once rendered them free thinking and religious." [19] As a freethinking spokesman at Lyric Hall and the Masonic Temple, Frothingham became the leading pulpit voice for the "religion of humanity." Regardless of modern views of his place in "right wing" Free Thought, he was referred to by contemporaries as the "radical preacher," as he indeed considered himself.

He had been established in New York but a few months when the *New York Evening Post* quoted a part of his sermon on the "broad church" movement. It was a disclaimer to the rumor that the Unitarians were going back to orthodox symbols. Although he admitted that a few would like to, he would be extremely reluctant to do so. Liberal religion, he felt, was not ready for symbols. If ever it is to be done it should not borrow from tradition but develop its own. "Our motto must be spirituality, freedom, simplicity . . . until the spirit vouchsafes to us new revelations." [20] Yet his vocabulary of disclaimer was orthodox, a style of his which caused much confusion and misunderstanding in press reports of his public addresses. Two years before his retirement the *New York Evening Telegram,* commenting on "Radicalism in New York," raised the cry of atheism. Mr. Frothingham drew "some of the most intellectual men and women in New York," they observed, "and to some extent is the favorite of actors and actresses who feel him more sympathetic to their profession than orthodox preachers." They doubted, however, if he and Felix Adler were actually atheistic and admitted that "Mr. Frothingham's sermons are always good." [21] He was not an atheist, but a radical he was.

It is possible to catch the flavor of his thought as he led his congregation in weekly discourses on (1) the status of Christianity and the churches, (2) special events, (3) social issues, (4) evolution and human nature, (5) Jesus and Christ, (6) concepts of God, (7) death and immortality, (8) faith and revelation, (9) prayer, (10) atonement, (11) sin and social ethics, and (12) children and religion.

FOUR

1 The Status of Christianity and the Churches   As a radical whose thought had long been tending in the direction of a free church, he naturally had most to say about the status of the church and the plight of Christianity in his day. During his travels abroad in the summers of 1873 and 1877, Frothingham visited the old churches and cathedrals of Europe and England. It seemed to nourish his radical views. They were masses of stone, relics, and symbols whose original meaning had been lost. "There is a danger," he told his congregation, "incident to all institutions that are maintained . . . the danger of substituting observance for thought . . . the present task is to transfer sentiments that have been instituted to the mind itself, to rescue and revive ideas that have been buried under masses of stone." [22] The goal of a "free faith" is to free the mind from the bondage of fear and superstition. As each "layer of sectarianism has rooted out the superstition of the previous one," now comes the rational religion with Theodore Parker its greatest prophet and Emerson the freest mind of all. Rational religion puts fear in its proper perspective in relation to the natural world and frees the mind of fear. "For what is there to be afraid of except fear itself?" [23] Radicalism is the root of a free faith. The radical, said Frothingham, does not destroy; he goes to the roots; he questions but does not confuse. "He stands four square to all the winds that blow."[24] The free faith is the safest creed. It is safer than the written Bible. It is safe because it is "changeable, fearless, and closer to humanity." Resorting to nautical language, Frothingham likened the rationalist to the navigator in the open sea—a safer place to be than hugging a dangerous coast.[25] In the "Gospel for Today" [26] Frothingham compared the old and the new faith. The old Gospel was for salvation of men from sin while Jesus represented submission and other-worldness. The new faith accepts no redeemer save man's own intelligence. The new faith came about from education, liberty of conscience, and intellectual progress. The new faith evolves, gradually casting aside miracles, priests, and saints. It needs no unique events or special books.

> It seeks a supreme will in the ordinary texture of the world, rises above clarity, toleration, embraces radicals of all religions and cultures: Mohamet, Zoroaster, Confucius, Pythagoras, "infidels of the Enlightenment," challenges skeptics to create, atheists to live divinely. . . .[27]

Christianity came under his attack for stressing an artificial dualism in all things and presenting life as a thorny path to the grave. There was good in evil, fetters could become sails, and Calvinism itself had some redeeming aspects, properly interpreted. The human body was not a "prison house for the soul" and the expulsion from paradise was really an opportunity to seek truths and become human.[28] What is the role of the church and minister in pursuing radical religion? Churchgoing has the same function as attending art galleries or concert halls. It is part of the poetry of religion. Prayers are to people rather than to God. The sermon is

> . . . directly intellectual . . . addressed not to the emotions but to the intellect. The preacher is not priest but prophet. He takes religion out of the temple and performs a teaching function. He addresses himself to subjects men should not forget—the nature of man, the purpose of life, death and immortality, and the search for perfection. He attempts to apply ideas to the needs of the hour.[29]

One of the most distressing things to Frothingham was the prevalence of revivalism and popular religion. "Why does it prevail?" he asked in a sermon. Partly because of the natural tendency to believe what is taught from the past—a natural reverence for antiquity, but mainly, he thought, because "the corner stone of popular religion is the poor." Implying that pie-in-the-sky religion promised a reward in heaven while the burdens of the world are to be endured, Frothingham came close to saying that popular, evangelical religion was an opiate of the people. "The strikers last summer (1877)—unbelievers many of them in all religions, still unconsciously accepted this tradition—the kingdom of heaven is for us; for the toilers, for the poor, for the unpaid—for those who have no opportunity." This is pernicious, thought Frothingham, to hold out religion as an escape. Popular evangelical religion deadens the sense of self-help and self-improvement. But times have changed. "The new faith, founded on man's consciousness of his power . . . will emerge . . . and prevail," [30] he hoped.

In spite of his periodic moods of pessimism, he felt that orthodoxy was doomed and that "reasonable religion" would win the allegiance of men. "The Rising and Setting Faith" he entitled one sermon in which he lashed out at Henry Ward Beecher, who spoke on "practical subjects" and Dwight Moody, who appealed to the heart rather than to the head.[31] He attacked the "revival factory in Brooklyn," calling it "sentimental religion," though it was not clear whether it was Beecher or Moody he was referring to. "It is not a revival of old religion we need but a new creation, new faith and new hope. . . ." [32]

Frothingham was convinced that sectarianism was a major obstacle to the realization of the new faith. There were times when he felt that sectarianism was dying. At other times he was not so sure. At the height of his activities in the Free Religious Association, he preached optimistically that

> the wars between the churches will cease, sectarian hatred must be at an end, religionists will no longer clutch religioinsts by the throat and drag them down. All truth seekers, believers, doers, aspirers, workers will be confessedly one body, one fellowship, one family contending zealously to bring in a new order of things. This is the spirit of the new faith. . . . The new faith will accept nothing less than cordial and full appreciation of every earnest endeavor that is made by any honest thinker or worker for humanity.[33]

He did not say if he thought Moody and other evangelists were also honestly working for humanity.

In a more pessimistic frame of mind later, he declared that Christianity itself was the most serious form of sectarianism standing in the way of free religion. The sectarian spirit would never die, he declared, as long as Christianity exists, which like "every system . . . claims for itself the sole possession of divine revelation." Yet he felt that evolutionary theory, properly used, and science, properly applied, would eventually bring all people to leave Christianity for a "religion of humanity." [34]

Frothingham's radical departure from the interpretation of Christian forms naturally put him in opposition to organized religious institutions and their organizers. He called them Pharisees who are of no special class but of every class. There are Pharisees in law, the theater, education, business and, of course, among the clerical profession. These are arrogant people who denounce those who disagree with them. Some of his choicest opponents with whom he did theological battle were, in his opinion, in this category.[35]

He was severely critical of the efforts of the world meeting of Protestant clergy and the Evangelical Alliance in the fall of 1873. In his opinion these groups were attempting to preserve outmoded creeds which were based on unfounded myths and appeals to unthinking people. Such efforts should be opposed by "Free Religion . . . [which would] make men indifferent to the still, sad music of humanity." [36] Occasionally he attacked Catholicism in a sense of bewilderment at its holding power over the hearts of men. The beauty of the cathedral and mass, he thought, was illusory; the appeal to the heart and emotion was deadening; the central place of authority in Catholicism was outdated. "Why should religious truths," he asked, "be thought of as absolute comforters and mysterious; it is incompatible with our own secular view: The only final authority is reason . . . the human mind in the nineteenth century has outgrown Catholicism," he asserted.[37] He feared the loss of secular society with the growth of Catholic power. The struggle in England in the 1870s was of great interest to him. Although he acknowledged Cardinal Newman's quip that he would "first drink to conscience, then to the Pope," another Catholic authority, unidentified, was quoted by Frothingham as saying, "Freedom of conscience is freedom to accept religious truths." "Who can claim supremacy on conscience?" asked Frothingham. He denied that any living institution had the right to define divine law. He saw the coming battle between instituted authority versus rational authority; historical versus human authority; priest versus principles." "Let the two camps be massed," he said militantly, "formal authority versus rational authority; send the weak to the rear and victory will perch on the banners of the enemies of instituted authority." [38]

His optimism was usually of short duration. Basically he was pessimistic about the possibility of religious domination ever reaching an age of reason or a common ground of rational religion as he would define it. Even the efforts in 1874 of the Unitarians and Protestants to agree upon a faith were doomed to failure, he believed. All of their various faiths were mutually exclusive. He declined to participate in any ecumenical movement and to "embarrass those who disagreed" with him.[39]

2 Special Events   Special events, about which all preachers were expected to make appropriate remarks, gave Frothingham the opportunity to air his views in dramatic fashion. The grief and trauma of the Civil War required frequent funeral sermons. Here his views of death and immortality came forth. The dead, he felt, being martyrs in a sacred cause, achieved immortality and did not violate the principle of nonviolence as in the case of the Quakers. The ideal of peace was served by killing the monster of war and its twin, slavery. As a comfort to the bereaved mothers, he assured them it was better to have had sons who died in a good cause rather than to have "wastrel youth" to grieve over.[40]

One of the most traumatic events of Frothingham's New York career was the draft riot in July of 1863. He had heard the gunfire, had seen the burning buildings, and was shocked when his own parishioner, Horace Greeley, barely escaped a lynch mob. In spite of his own brush with street hoodlums, who roughed him up and stole his watch, he took the long view of the event in a sermon a few days later in "The Morality of the Riots." "No terms can be kept with rioters," he said sternly.

> They must be put down by the swiftest and most crushing force. The swifter and more crushing the more merciful. This is the only way to deal with them. That is understood: the law of self-preservation declares it. . . . Yet force must be held in balance. There is no necessity here for glorifying soldiers or magnifying the office of the howitzer. Let not the short reign of terror from below tempt us to pray for a reign of terror from above. Carbines and sabers are necessary tools; but they are very ugly tools in modern cities. I do not rejoice at the picket-guard that clatters in front of my door. This is the place for calm words and thoughts of charity.[41]

Refusing to invoke the old doctrine of human depravity, he attempted to explain the causes of the riot. It was partially the issue of conscription aggravated by the practice of buying exemptions which many of the poorer class justifiably resented. The deeper cause, continued Frothingham, was the lack of understanding among the masses of the real meaning of the war. Because of their ignorance, especially among the "foreigners," they did not see that the cause of the slave was also their cause. It had been ever thus throughout history. The people often oppose their best interests, seek to kill their own benefactors. They must be treated with forebearance, he said, educated and forgiven, "for they know not what they do."

When Senator Charles Sumner died in March, 1874, Frothingham used the opportunity to compare his life's work with other "saints" of the past. Rejecting the Catholic and Protestant concept of sainthood, he eulogized Sumner as a living saint in his day who renounced the worldly reward of popularity by advocating human equality. He was, thought Frothingham, a "saint of humanity." [42] Horace Greeley, editor of the *New York Tribune* and Frothingham's parishioner, was also eulogized in a sermon as a "worshipper of humanity." [43]

News of Theodore Parker's death reached America in May, 1860. Frothingham had been in his new post less than a year when he had to rise to the occasion and deliver a sermon on the work and ideas of his mentor of Salem days. His passing was a blow to the slaves and friendless, said Frothingham. "Why are the lips of the public organ silent?" Because "critics fear to offend those who loved him; those who loved him are too stunned." Frothingham was one of the first to speak out. It was far from being a eulogy. Parker was no great theologian, far from original, and his "absolute religion" would not bear close analysis. Although a shallow thinker, we should "bless Theodore Parker," thought Frothingham, "for smashing idols and liberating the God within," for emancipating our minds from fetters of the past, for distinguishing between theology and religion, between faith and belief. What was Parker's weakness? Frothingham's answer was a harsh appraisal that shocked and offended many who loved Theodore Parker. He was brash, reckless, and narrow, thought Frothingham. His compulsion for knowledge, to probe, to oppose, made him often miss the point; he could not see other points of view.

> In construing the letter of the beliefs he sometimes missed the spirit. . . .
> There seemed to be no twilight region in his mind in whose cool and starlit recess he could escape from the glare of his unsleeping intelligence which forced him into seeing every object in sharp outline and with every object its long and heavy shadow.[44]

Those who felt that Frothingham had recanted by repudiating his teacher might have been reassured by subsequent sermons, especially his

Divinity School address in the summer of 1868. Delivered exactly thirty years after Emerson's famed address, it was solidly in the Emerson-Parker tradition of radical Christianity. Frothingham attempted to point out to the Divinity School graduates the challenge facing the ministry and also to inspire them as to its urgency and dignity as a profession. There is no chasm, he assured them, between the traditional and false division Christianity has insisted upon between God and man, man and reason, infinite and finite, life and death, the natural and the supernatural. The only real gulf is between the human and animal elements in man himself. The role of the minister is to reconcile this chasm and "abolish the separatism between things human and things divine." He warned them that they were to be prophets and not priests and that theirs was an "austere calling."

It means work, study, thought, care. It is pretty sure to mean things worse than these. You must not complain because others fare more sumptuously, and wear costlier garments than you. You must not whine because you cannot live as well as your parishioners. Be satisfied to live in simple nobleness with your humanity. You do not enter the ministry to be rich or famous or luxurious. The less of all that you may be the more you are faithful. Estimate your loyalty by the earnestness of your battle. The prophets have often been called to make bread out of stones. The ministry is not a *paying* profession: they who wish it might be, do not understand it; they who hope to make it so, had better leave it. We can well spare those young men who avoid it for more lucrative pursuits. Prize the human absolutely, supremely, solely; but never confound the human with the secular. Do not imagine, that, by imitating the secular dress and manners, you are broadening your humanity: you are not. You are merely incurring the danger of confounding the lower humanity with the higher. Humanity is not a slouched hat or a gray coat, a swagger or a cigar. Respect your order, regard its decencies, observe its proprieties, be jealous of its honor. *Culture* and *character,*—be these your mottoes. Do not be ashamed of being ministers. Let men see that you are ministers because you are men, and they will respect your ministry. Do not fret against the limitations which shut you in with all things noble, and only shut you out from some things pleasant. Be tranquil in the atmosphere of serene truths; be happy in the spiritual companionship of the good among the living, of the sainted among the dead; hold fast the unseen hands of the men who have lived and died for their fellows; and listen for every note of that still, sad music which has breathed, and is ever breathing, from those who have borne the cross, and have found in sacrifice an all-sufficing joy.[45]

When the Ethical Culture Society was formed by Felix Adler in New York in 1876 Frothingham took this opportunity to welcome the group and applaud its efforts to study practical problems rather than theological ones. "But isn't there more to Sunday than this?" he asked his congregation. His answer was self-evident.

We came together here mainly not to discuss social questions; not to study the practical problems of existence; not to deal with matters of scholastic or secular learning; we came here, let me say in all sincerity and simplicity, to see if we cannot get a closer sight of the secret of existence."

In a transcendental theme he added that more than "the five senses" are needed to probe life's secrets. We must dream as well as think with evidence. Following up our dreams with duties "will dignify and glorify all our life." [46]

He seldom let a special event go by without using the occasion to strike a blow for some point of ethics or view of radical religion. On Memorial Day, 1873, he delivered an unusual jeremiad against the country where "fraud, plotting, venality, abuse of trusts and the cruel use of power . . . [has] attracted the attention of foreign people and has made us a by-word of reproach." While the nation decorated the graves of Civil War dead, Frothingham inveighed against the "covering up of the sins of the nation with flowers." [47] He began a sermon from Ecclesiastes in response to the Chicago fire of 1871. "Gold is tried in the fire and acceptable men in the furnace of adversity." It was the familiar theme of adversity leading to renewal while the old rubbish is burned away for a fresh start. His discourse was at once a criticism of urban life in America and an expression of hope for better conditions.[48]

In a similar view, but with less optimism, he preached about the Centennial Year celebration in July, 1876. In Philadelphia, he said, paeans of praise have been poured out glorifying inventions, continental expansion, and growth of the nation. He was not impressed. "These things are no evidence of the potency of our republican principle . . . this would come with any institutions." The real question he thought was: Has the nation made progress in achieving its unique creative idea—that of human equality? He thought not. The blacks were far from this status and "hordes of immigration has made a failure of democratic institutions by diluting the ideal of equality and weakening our political blood." Dangerously close to sounding a nativistic note, he modified the thought by blaming venal political parties, both Democrat and Repulican, for failing to adopt a gradual plan of "receiving" foreigners "becomingly." He took a dark view of the nation in the fall of 1876. The technology had thrived yet the political institutions had failed to live up to the promise of 1776.

3 Social Issues Frothingham spoke out but rarely on social questions after the abolition of slavery. Occasionally he observed the plight of the poor, advocating amelioration for "rescuing labor from its sting." [49] Burial reform was of interest to him and he advocated cremation from the standpoint of scientific and historical evidence.[50] When it came to punishing criminals he favored the death penalty, if executions were humane. He hedged on prisons and their effectiveness and seemed to want to isolate the whole problem of crime from social causes.[51]

He was one of the most outspoken critics of religious support of secular activities. There was a movement in the 1870s to insert a religious clause into the preamble of the Constitution to institute prayers in Congress, to establish an official Senate chaplain, along with growing pressure in New York State to use tax money for parochial schools. "Formal Religion and Life" should be kept separate he urged in a forceful sermon of that title. ". . . Here as elsewhere it will be found that human strength is better than superhuman sentiment, that our values are our best gods. . . ."[52]

The condition of the poor during the depression of 1873 aroused his attention. He did not relish this subject but felt it was forced on him by circumstances. Alms giving should be abandoned, he felt. Poverty had always been a part of industrial society, and industrial society must be changed to eliminate the cause of poverty. He was confused as to what the solution should be. On the one hand, he was sure that evolutionary progress would eventually eliminate poverty, yet he knew this would be slow. The answer, he vaguely suggested, lay in the new "social science" methods properly understood and used.[53]

Frothingham lived through one of the most corrupt and crime ridden decades in the history of New York City and the nation. He was aware of the Tweed ring, crime in the streets, and the decline of public leadership characteristic of the post-Civil War era. His reaction was painfully inconsistent. Clearly he was not on sure ground in the "practical question" which he accused Henry Ward Beecher of dealing with so exclusively. The monumental corruption of New York City baffled and angered him by turns. In a quaint, Biblical sermon about Job and piety, he assured his listeners that one "reaps what they sow," that virtue is its own reward, the wages of sin is punishment, and that good will win out at last.[54] Another time he told his audience that he was sure virtue of some individuals could overcome vice of others. Since society is simply one grand individual, society is improved by improving individuals. After this rather vaporous approach to crime and political corruption he turned his displeasure on "lower instincts" of the "depraved class." They must be kept down because they are appealed to by the scoundrels "who come from the refuse of society" to become political leaders. Women can help by direct influence on men, a method more influential than the ballot box, he thought.[55]

The application of Christian ethics he was sure would eventually lead to reform of labor and education, and achieve political rights, social equality, and commercial integrity.[56] Typical of nineteenth century humanitarianism, Frothingham was concerned over "vice." It could not be suppressed, he knew, nor could it be answered that it was an inherited and permanent blight on society. He suggested alternatives to improve the individuals: "coffee instead of gin, tobacco instead of opium" and a religious faith of a new sort. In a word, the "religion of humanity" would be the key to a virtuous society:

> The efforts of teachers, preachers, lecturers, must be directed to the educa-
> tion more than to the entertainment of men and women. And above all, for
> spectral faith in Christ must be substituted a faith in man, hearty, hopeful,
> glowing, winning, which takes people at their best, . . . and a faith like this
> will be possible only when the new religion shall have acquired strength to
> make its ideas prevail.[57]

Vague as his religious answer to reform was, he knew that more was
needed to improve nineteenth century society. In the early months of the
Civil War he criticized the ethic of laissez faire. It had been valid, he
thought, in the days when tyrannical governments laid a heavy hand on
human activities, but in a modern industrial democracy, the laissez faire
approach could not apply. The country could not ignore poverty, crime,
disease, and injustice. Was it not, he asked, the laissez faire ethic that
ignored for so long the monstrous evil of slavery, bringing on the war?[58]

What was the alternative to the laissez faire philosophy? Frothingham
had no answer. Reform parties he was sure would not work. Reformers
themselves were too narrow and fanatical to be effective. The younger
generation of new leaders, he felt, were influenced by the survival of the
fittest philosophy of Darwin. He had reached an unsolvable impasse in his
views of social issues of his day. He viewed "pauperism" as a sort of social
disease of certain groups—a malady to be isolated like any contagion.
Crime was a product, he thought, of certain types of people affected
somewhat by the environment, he admitted.[59] In his mental confusion
about policy and lack of clear-cut knowledge of the courses of social evils,
he always resorted to exhorting his generation to maintain the atmosphere for social reform but to avoid fanatical extremes. Social reform, he
felt, had passed out of the hands of priests and prophets and was now in
the hands of "physiologists, economists, and students of social development." Even these people, as reformers, should avoid dogmatism and the
futile pursuit of "prophetic visions for society." Reform, he thought,
should be based on "rational knowledge rather than an apocalyptic vision." [60]

4 Evolution and Human Nature   He was sure that the new theory of
evolution held the key to both social reform and the "new faith" of which
he was a spokesman. Frothingham felt that he was working in the midst of
an intellectual revolution. The old creeds were giving way to the new one.
Even Unitarianism was being challenged by the "new creed." Theodore
Parker had carried Christianity as far as it would go and now it would
"bear no more attenuation." The new creed, to Frothingham, would be no
mere Christian modification but would go in a new direction with "new
readings of nature and man. The doctrine of evolution, which furnishes

the starting point for the whole theory that offers itself as a succession to Christianity, contains implications of belief that are not friendly to any interpretation of the Christian scheme." But it would not cause a sudden break with the past. "The work of evolution will be effected quietly—and when it is effected the most timid will wonder at their alarm." The "new creed" would differ very little in appearance from the old, but it would liberate people from dogma and encourage men to work for perfection in their lives rather than to wait for immortality. He was sure that many old terms for theological categories would break down and take on new meaning.[61]

It was here that Frothingham made his greatest impact as a radical preacher. In attempting to reconcile the theological and religious concepts with new theories and the "needs of the hour," he did enliven old dogmas with new meaning. On the "nature of man" he had much to say. Man evolved from a low state and was influenced by his experiences and environment. He rejected the concept of the noble savage. Man evolved with society and was an integral part of it. No perfect man had ever evolved nor would he until his social environment approached perfectability. Although he recognized man as a part of nature, Frothingham rejected the naturalist view that he was a mere part of a chemical equation—a part of brute force. Psychology, he recognized, was a new and valid field for understanding human nature, yet his Darwinism, naturalism, and psychological insights were modified by his transcendental predilections—man, though part of nature and a product of society, still had within him a spark of the Divine and a responsibility for his own actions.[62]

5 *Jesus and Christ* "I have a criticism of our radical faith," confided Frothingham to his congregation in the last year of his ministry,

> that it tends to be prosaic . . . in its effort to put away superstition . . . and convert the priesthood of falsity. [We must] take the mask off religion . . . to show how behind all those symbols and forms are lovely visions of beauty, sublimity and truth . . . that much boasted symbol of Christ, purely imaginary . . . wipe away the dust, clear it of the heavy earth that clings to it . . . exhibit it as a symbol which humanity in its best moments had looked to and hoped to realize.[63]

This is what Frothingham attempted to do with the idea of Christ and Jesus in numerous Christmas and Easter sermons. His earlier writings in the *Christian Examiner* had attempted the same scholarly style; in his sermons he did it in eloquent poetic language. Jesus was a natural man, with a Divine spirit, but a man not to be worshipped. Nor was he a savior. but rather a symbol of humanity toward which all men could turn. Jesus was never a Christ, asserted Frothingham, but simply a man around which an oriental myth was built. The story of his miraculous birth, never to be taken literally, is really a poetic symbol of all preexisting morality and what was Divine in man. The "Bible Christian" took it literally and put him in a book; the "altar Christian" enshrined him; and "creed Christians" perform a burlesque on the symbol through their religious ceremonies. Meanwhile, the real spirit of Jesus is hidden away and lost. Yet the celebration of his birth is a useful myth, symbolic though it is, elected from the ages of man, full of human meaning.

Likewise, the story of his death and his mythic resurrection can be used for its poetic and symbolic meaning. His martyrdom, thought Frothing-ham, was symbolic of the agony of men at the hands of other men. History is full of examples of men, ahead of their times and more fully developed than their peers. He saw as examples: Vico in the science of history; Comte in the science of human progress; Channing "offending the Pharisees of his day"; and Parker who "got vilification instead of fellow-ship." The symbol of Jesus' resurrection also had poetic meaning to Frothingham. Certain that the story is not to be taken literally, he was also certain that the concept of resurrection was as old as human life and could mean spiritual resurrection and part of the slow process of becoming human. Despite all the useful symbolism, Frothingham would not base his "new faith" entirely on the concept of Jesus as the symbol of humanity. There were other prophets of humanity in other times and places who spoke more relevantly and effectively to human concerns. The weakness in the Jesus ideology, suggested Frothingham, was that it encouraged "meekness, supineness, and a providential attitude toward life's prob-lems." Jesus suffered, died, and let his enemies do him in. There are times and situations, he thought, which call not for the turned cheek but for militancy.[64]

6 *Concepts of God*   The God of the "new faith" was partly a Deist God, aloof and impersonal, showing itself only in the inscrutable system of evolutionary change, and partly a transcendental God, indwelling, the divine spark of humanity within each individual. In sermon after sermon Frothingham instructed his audience as to the fallacies of seeing God as a superhuman image—a childish and primitive stage, he thought in the developing concept of diety. The ideas of religion evolved along with intellectual progress and the God concept can be understood only in terms of evolutionary theory. Frothingham attempted to break down the barrier between God and man, between things spiritual and things mate-rial. In a sermon Frothingham quoted Emerson's injunction to "Hitch your wagon to a star." "He could have added," he said with some injustice to Emerson, "hitch your star to a wagon and make material things spiritual by pursuing humanity in this life rather than hope for spiritual life later. God is a living force, not in a distant heaven but within the human mind and heart. God is not a man but the human in all men." [65]

The Supreme Being becomes simply man's supreme effort to overcome obstacles and progress socially and intellectually up the evolutionary ladder. Since obstacles to human progress are man-made, God and his Holy Ghost are symbols of natural law and human effort, both necessary for achieving human existence. Fear of God is simply fear of one's own ignorance—the most demonic fear of all, thought Frothingham. Piety, no longer appropriate for thoughtful people, he felt, must take the form of commitment to society and individuals. "Who are the pious of today?" he asked. They are the philanthropists, the Civil War soldiers, the social reformers, the Florence Nightingales, living for some good and worthy end—"this is the piety of this generation," and science is to be the guiding force in the new creed. Frothingham found strong religious sentiments in all the great thinkers as well as in the thought of secular philosophers.

> . . . Bacon and Newton . . . burst into the infinite only to kneel . . . they do not pray . . . but they revere. They do not write confessionals but they avow principles; they call God the unknown and the unknowable. . . . They bring no gifts to his altar but they devote themselves to unfolding his laws.[66]

7 *Death and Immortality*   Frothingham's views on death, immortality, and heaven were in keeping with the "new faith." He took a consistently rational, antisupernatural point of view of this more interesting and persistent problem of human existence—that of dying. Heaven is within man when he acts divinely. John Brown was Frothingham's example, "who had fought his fight and was ready to be offered. The old man [was] not more truly in heaven than he was in that moment." [67] Of the Civil War dead he said that those that died in so holy a cause had reached an immortal existence in heaven, "not on the other side of the grave but on this side of it." [68]

The ideal of immortality was a useful one. Nearly all peoples had believed in some form of it. Likewise, concepts of heaven would help "glorify man" and give him hope. However, the rationalist's "heaven" was an earthly one and his immortality was in terms of human achievement on earth.

> None look forward to heavenly homes who do not make their earthly homes as lovely as they can. . . . Heaven must be a state of mind before it will be a state of existence. Immortality is held to be a gift to all men by virtue of the humanity which they share.

As for death, "it is part of the pulse of human existence," necessary to clear the stage for new generations with new ideas as the old pass on to "sweet and fruitful sleep." [69]

8 Faith and Revelation   Of all the theological categories with which he
dealt Frothingham had the most to say about revelation and faith. His
sermons on these points also reiterated, with different examples and new
contexts, points he made in sermons on other subjects. As one might
expect, the titles, usually couched in orthodox language, were used as a
play on the words of the "popular religion" he so relentlessly attacked.
Revelation came not from a supernatural source or as a religious experience, but from the open mind and spirit of inquiry of the individual
seeking truth. Faith was not necessary for the new creed for it was
replaced by a positive goal: to "bring men to themselves to teach men the
laws of rational development." This he arrayed against the Catholic
purpose of faith to "bring men to submission" and the Protestant faith
that brought men to "believe and be converted." [70]

Disbelief of unbelievers could be applauded because it might lead to
"rational truths." Irreverence was a healthy frame of mind because it
would root out superstition and myths and lead men to study history,
science, biography, and literature—the material for a true religion of
humanity. Scepticism of course was the most favorable mental attitude in
the new faith for then it would matter little whether one believed in the
"Trinity or the Unity" or whatever. "The true attitude of the new Faith,"
said Frothingham, "is that of honorable resistance to what is honestly
believed to be an error . . . [and] warfare against credulity and determination to secure the victory without impairing the nobleness or the beauty
of the truth." [71] To Frothingham, faith was too comforting, revelation an
insult to the intelligence. "The radical faith is an inspirer not a comforter.
Its comfort is in the spirit of truth. It would stir the idle from their
slumber. It would open windows to the fresh wind. . . . Radicalism is
hearty, bluff, and intellectual." [72]

In spite of Frothingham's vigorous proclamation of radicalism, which a
few critics took to be a form of the dogmatism he professed to oppose, he
concluded that the new faith led simply to a "Reasonable Religion." It is
"to be distinguished from religion founded on authority . . . reasonable
religion is distinguished also from religion founded on faith." Warning
that the bald intellectualism of science might be as dogmatic as orthodox
theories, he continued:

> Reasonable religion merely asks that science be liberal, comprehensive,
> generous. . . . Let us have no scientific Popes . . . no scientific priesthood
> at whose confessional piety must penitentially confess its sins against a
> gaseous and unholy ghost. . . . Reaasonable religion is religion in fullest
> sympathy with the whole human mind and with whatever helps to animate
> it, enlarge and enrich it. . . . [It] welcomes aid from literature, the arts of
> painting, sculpture, architecture, music, the drama; seeks an ally in social
> reforms . . . in a word the strengthening of the spirit of humanity which
> alone can be relied on as a permanent remedy for human woes.[73]

9 Prayer   Many of Frothingham's fellow clerics in other denominations thought it strange that part of his Sunday service included a prayer.
What could a rationalist do with such a traditional form of worship? What
kind of a prayer would a radical religionist, a purveyor of the "new faith"
compose and offer to his congregation? None of his prayers have survived
in written form, presumably because they were never written but delivered extemporaneously. However, Frothingham had a great deal to say in
his sermons about prayer as a form of religious expression. As a part of his
assault on "popular religion" he constantly attacked the evangelical
churches' annual "week of prayer." To him this seemed an impertinent
appeal to a supernatural God whose office is to sit on high and listen to
man's complaints and requests. It was also a crude and primitive assump-
tion that a distant God could and would intervene directly and by request
in the affairs of men. These people believed in the "rope and pulley" type
of prayer which brings the right divine response provided the right lever
or rope is pulled. They burn holes in the sky appealing to a nonexistent
deity.

Even the "rationalizing evangelist, Horace Bushnell, devoted a chapter
of his work 'Nature and the Supernatural' to a discussion of this question
and adduces several instances of answers to prayers in the shape of
recovered life and vigor." A Professor Tyndol "proposed an experiment
last summer," recalled Frothingham to his audience, "to test the effectiveness of prayer." Two hospital wards were to be selected and studied
for five years. In one ward, prayer for the patients' health would be
regularly offered; in the other, no prayers were given at all. At the end of
the five years, death and recovery rates would be compared. "The reception to this was not cordial" . . . believers resenting the suggestion but
nonbelievers favoring it. Of course, it would be impossible to test the
efficiency of prayer scientifically, he added tongue-in-cheek, because
"God may not cooperate and medical knowledge may vary." [74]

Yet he was no cynic or shallow nonbeliever in the value of prayer
properly approached. "We must pray rationally," he thought, "for the
humanly attainable. Prayer lifts men out of themselves; puts them in
communion with another; makes them conscious of their common . . .
brotherhood." Prayer urges men toward self-development, to point out
their weaknesses, their dilemmas and possible strengths. Prayer is a
dialogue with one's self; "the prayer and the answer are one." Not
everyone can measure up to the rationalist's standard of the use of prayer.
"Only . . . the devoted man can venture to ask anything of the Supreme
Power; only the man that lays his private passions by, forgets his heat,
dismisses his anger, forsakes his greed, asks nothing for himself, but asks
the things everybody needs, can dare pray." [75] In brief, it would seem that
Frothingham would have only the rationally saved and the elect of the
"new faith" benefit from rational prayer.

10 Atonement   The problem of sin and atonement were other traditional theological problems upon which Frothingham focused the hard
light of rationalism, though modified by his transcendental view of man.
There was no clear-cut distinction between sin and virtue, fidelity and
infidelity, good and evil. Both dimensions resided within the same vehicle
and, "Who is to say?" "Not man," he thought. "We must let virtue and vice
grow together till the end of the world. . . . The human race is one; a line
of beings living and growing through the ages; all its experience belongs
to it; and none can be spared." [76] As for the concept of eternal punishment, he never attempted to give this a rational or humane interpretation.
He disposed of the "barbarous belief" in an angry sermon denouncing the
myth and the religion of Christianity to which the concept of punishment
for sin was so central.[77] Atonement and not punishment was the emphasis
of the religion of humanity. Yet it was not atonement in the traditional
sense. He rejected the idea of a religious martyr dying to atone for a sinful
humanity. This must come from within the efforts of man himself. "The
problem," he thought, "was not forgiveness but repentance. . . . Humanity forgives if the sinner repents by reconstructing his damge." [78]

Similarly, he suggested that judgment is an everyday fact, palpable, and
stern. No gaudy fireworks or calcium lights are required to set off its
features; their naked reality is sufficient. The judgment is not to come; it
is always coming. "It is not a judgment that is to be, but a judgment that
is." [79] Humanity judges itself, defines sin, and offers atonement in
human terms.

11 Sin and Social Ethics   Once in discussing Henry Ward Beecher, "the
great Brooklyn preacher," Frothingham asked the pianist, Rubenstein,
why Beecher had disappointed him. "Because," said Rubenstein, "he
brings religion down to the people instead of bringing the people up to
religion." [80] This uplifting is precisely what Frothingham attempted to do
in his weekly discourses at Lyric Hall and Masonic Temple in New York.
He not only broke down and reinterpreted old theological categories, but
he preached sermon after sermon, appealing directly to the needs and
conscience of his people in his attempt to bring them "up to religion." His
sermons of this type were enlightened, literary jeremiads, calling for
human ethics of a high order.

Unlike his sermons on theological topics, the titles are usually self-
interpreting. "The Gospel of Character," 187__ , attacked the preoccupa-
tion with soul saving and churchgoing of the orthodox whose Sunday
occupation was churchgoing and "selling arms to the French on Monday."
"Modern Irreligion," 187__ , hit at the commercial spirit which had all
men in its grip. Even the clergyman feels that "telegraph poles are tied to
his heart strings. The post office has a hole in his door. The railway train
commands his prompt attendance. Politics levy on his intelligence and
conscience. . . . He must be a man of business." "The Worship of Tools,"

1868, reiterated Emerson's theme that "things are in the saddle and ride mankind." In "Modern Idology," 1873, Frothingham began, "Thou shall offer no false incense. I take these words from one of the oldest of the Hebrew scriptures and make application of them to the last generation of men." The message was clear: Men in nineteenth century New York worshipped power, money, and pleasure.

On the subject of marriage and divorce, he spoke of "The Sacraments of the Home" (1873) and "The Infernal and Celestial Love" (187_). These were jeremiads against greed and lust but also a plea for a free, democratic type of home and family life. Divorce he would accept if "moral affiliations no longer exist." "Paying Debts," 187_, and "Rights and Duties," 1874, were calls for social responsibility. "The Unseen Sources of Character," 1876; "Character: Its Friends and Foes," 1874; and "The Power of the Word Made Flesh," 1873, were all appeals for "goodness" using natural and secular examples from history, literature, and philosophy. Two unusual sermons, "The American Lady" and "The American Gentleman," 1878, employed no theological references, no myths or symbols were unmasked. They were plain-style sermons sketching the lineaments of the ideal American type. The American lady, he thought, should be relieved of drudgery, liberated, but spared sordid activities such as politics. The woman was to be idealized, put on a pedestal, and be "as Beatrice [who] drew with her loving eyes the bewildered Dante toward paradise . . . [Thus] the eternal woman will lure us on." The ideal American man was the upper middle-class citizen who took a measured view of the struggle between capital and labor but whose civic pride led him to support social reform. His ideal American gentleman was Mr. Theodore Roosevelt of New York, the recently deceased father of nineteen-year-old Teddy.

12 Children and Religion   Frothingham was pessimistic about the effectiveness of teaching the "new faith" to children. Yet the Sunday School, as we have seen during his Salem years, was a major concern. In a sermon to the adults, "Religion and Childhood," 1876, he stated his philosophy of religious education and offered advice to parents. Do not indoctrinate but do not ignore religion. Both are equally bad. The first approach would close the mind to rational thought, the second would create a vacuum and a feeling of indifference to things spiritual. The only parts of the Bible suitable for children, he advised, were the parts dealing with personalities and natural things that children could understand. Even some of the myths would be usable provided they were the myths that did not close the mind to further development.

Nowhere did Frothingham strive harder in stripping away dogma and interpreting myths than in his work with the children of his congregation. Each week he prepared a talk to the children with as much care as he used for discourses to the adults. At times his Sunday School talk was a parable dealing with a moral precept or a problem facing children. At other times he attempted to interpret a Biblical story in children's terms and relate it to their lives. Soon after his arrival in New York he published a book of parables of Jesus in language children could understand.[81] Next came a small volume of tales from the Old Testament, paraphrased at a child's level with an overtone of mild didacticism.[82] Encouraged by the reception of this he compiled the *Child's Book of Religion*,[83] containing poems, hymns, and catechism organized around ethical themes relevant to children. Frothingham called this an "experiment" to be used by parents and Sunday School teachers. How successful it was, he never said.

The most appealing writing for children, it would seem, was his *Story of the Patriarchs* (1864) written as Sunday School lessons about Old Testament stories intended, as Frothingham stated, to "give . . . [children] a glimpse of the noble thoughts hid behind their veils." [84] One of the twelve stories in the little volume, which Frothingham thought would do no one any harm, but "may teach a few," he entitled "The Garden." Without mentioning the name of "Adam" and "Eve" or even identifying "Eden" he described a man and woman living in a beautiful spot where everything was done for them and they had nothing to do or to worry about. They, of course, became bored and restless and outgrew their garden paradise and wandered off. Then came the noble thought veiled in the Biblical story, dealt with by Frothingham in sermons to adults at other times: The "fall was not a fall at all nor was it punishment for lost innocence, but the beginning of the human search for truth. The journey from the garden was the process of human evolution.

> They went. The gateway was narrow and long; but at the end of the passage shone the undiscovered mountains. Soon they approached the opening: they eagerly ran forward; they passed it; they issued forth, and found themselves in a new world indeed. A vast plain stretched before them, edged with wild hills and overhung by a gray sky. Dense, gloomy forests skirted the horizon; but no date-trees, no olive-trees, no almond or fig trees were to be seen; no sunny fountains were playing, no graceful animals were sporting; a bleak wind blew across the plain, and, as it touched them, gave them a sensation they had never known before,—the sensation of cold. They shivered and shrank into themselves, and instinctively turned to go back into their garden. It was gone. It had vanished: no trace of it could be found; no wall, no gateway, only a huge blank was behind them. They were alone in their new world.
>
> "What a sad story!" you will say. Yes, my dear children, that is what all people say when they hear it told. . . .

But it was not really sad at all he reminded his young listeners and suggested that it might have been a very good thing that the man and woman did. And why?

. . . I mean this, my children: that all men and women were children once, and children live, or should live, in the world just as those early people lived in the garden. Every man's and every woman's life begins in Eden; every child lives a little while, some a very little while, in Paradise. It does not know it at the time, but afterwards, on looking back, it knows, and sighs.

I could tell you of a time, long ago now for me, when the world was no bigger than my nursery; then it grew as big as the whole house, nursery, parlor, and kitchen; then it took in the yard, the garden, the street; by and by it was as large as the village: but the roads that went away from the village seemed to go out of the world. The heavens seemed just above the house-top, and I could think of no better Father there than my own father and mother. The wind was a whispering of spirits in my ear. The brook which ran through the village sung a sweet song all day. I had no work to do, but was taken care of, just as the lilies are. Where the food came from, the meat and vegetables and fruits, I did not know, and I never thought to ask: they always came; every day, fresh water, pure milk, sweet bread, were set before me: angels—who else could have done it?—brought oranges, apples, figs, dates, raisins; at night a bed was made for me to sleep in, and the kindest of hands smoothed my pillow under my head; in the morning I was met with smiles, and all day long I had nothing to do but enjoy the sunshine, the air, the grass, the toys that were thrown into my lap, the picture-books, rocking-horses, dolls, and games which I neither made nor bought. All things loved me: the dog, which was a parlor wolf, and the cat, which was a nursery tiger, came and played about me without doing the smallest harm: the canary-birds sung to me; the doves cooed; the hens and chickens ate their food from my hand. Summer and winter were equally pleasant to me. When it was cold out of doors, the summer came into the house; a great bright sun rose in the fireplace and shone there all day long; the flowers bloomed in the parlor; soft furs like the fox's skin kept out the frost. Sometimes it happened that I was fretful, discontented, disobedient; then my beautiful world became dark; I did not enjoy the sunshine, or the flowers, or the pleasant walk; my food was bitter; there was no smile on the face of my mother, and no music in the tones of her voice; the kitten ran away from me frightened; the canary moped on his perch; I flung my pets away from me; I broke my toys; O, how miserable the world seemed! I felt as if everybody in it hated me. But the fretfulness passed off, and all was bright again. I was in that garden a long time, and how I got out of it I do not exactly know. I think I must have been carried out of it; for suddenly, before I knew anything about the matter, I found myself outside in the great world, and, strange to say, a little child was sitting on the floor, playing with her kitten, seeming to feel just as I used to feel in my garden. For my own part, I could never find the way back into the garden; and if I could, I suppose it would not be a garden any more, but only a nursery or a kitchen, which I should want to get out of as soon as I could, and go to my study or my workshop down in the dusty street, to find the beautiful things which my little girl thinks are dropped down from the skies. She, dear little heart! is in the garden, and long may she be there, with that in her pure little bosom which shall keep it in bloom the whole year round. Lovely be the flowers!

soft the kittens! delicious the plums and peaches! sweet the song of the
canary! gentle her night's sleep! joyous her day's sport! kind her teachers,
playmates, and friends! and when the gate opens for her to pass out into the
wide, wide world, may she have something in her heart which will make that
a garden too! [85]

Whether the children of his Sunday School received his full message
could be conjectured; however, it seems certain that his personal impact
left permanent memories. Josiah Quincy, a Boston colleague, recalled
that he had the same personal magnetism with children that Theodore
Parker possessed.[86] A lady, recalling Reverend Frothingham for a newspaper article after his death, described the feeling she and other children
had of the "slight figure standing a little above us . . . awesome . . . with
a face we all loved," and the questions he posed for the children to
ponder: What does youth the most harm? What should you be most
willing to lose? What is your favorite story on Jesus? The answers always
came in "matchless eloquence and were never forgotten." [87] "The only
school I can remember vividly," recalled Harriet Stanton Blatch, daughter of the famed women's rights advocate Elizabeth Cady Stanton, "was
attached to the church of O. B. Frothingham in West 40th Street facing
Bryant Park, where the old reservoir stood on the Fifth Avenue side of the
block. The school I thoroughly enjoyed. We were introduced to the Bible
as partly the literature and partly the history of primitive people and Dr.
[sic] Frothingham's weekly address, usually a fable, held his young listeners enthralled." [88]

Another person, probably Martha Nichols who knew Frothingham
during her childhood in Salem and later in New York, recalled his impact
on children outside of the Sunday School.

> The children learned to love and reverence him at Sunday-school, but not
> only there. To one young life at least, and one in such relations is but a sign
> of more, he was the inspiration of every day. The walk to Sunday-school
> with him crowned the week; the delight of taking a note to his house or of
> going there without a pretext stands out like gleams of light against the
> background of dim years gone by. It was the usual thing to ask no question
> of the maid who opened his door; and this privilege must have originated in
> his gracious understanding of childhood, to run breathless up the one flight
> that led to his study door, always open, and then, with almost reverent care,
> to steal in and see whether he were standing and writing at his high desk,
> and if he were, to wait until he was ready with the welcome that always came.
> There to wander among the books that lined the wall to the ceiling, and to
> borrow, with his wise permission, and take home to read, books that seemed
> doubly worth the reading because they were his. When he was away, a note
> scribbled and left on his table must often have made him smile. His smile
> never hurt, even when the maiden of fourteen asked for Mill's "Subjection
> of Women." "Why do you want that, child?" The child confessed that she
> had a benighted friend of her own age who was unable to understand Mill,

and she wished to read her this particular essay, and "explain it" to her.
"You must tell me about it afterwards," he said, with perfect sympathy—
though the smile that twinkled through the sympathy is more apparent now
than it was then.[90]

In his New York ministry the pulpit and Sunday School room were not
the only ways in which he attempted to extend his ideas. There was the
Sunday evening lecture. Here he dealt with current topics of concern to
the general public. "The Education of Women" was the topic of one in a
series on women in society, followed by "Social Conditions of Women and
Should They Vote?" These were informal lectures never published but
occasionally reported in the religious press. Henry Bellows in the *Liberal
Christian* considered them "interesting and powerful discourses." [91]

The pulpit and platform spokesman of the religion of humanity he was.
But this was not all. For eleven of his twenty years in the New York
ministry he was an organizer and leader of the Free Religious Association.
He organized in spite of his aversion to organization; he led, not from a
love of power, but through the force of his commitment to the "new faith"
and his overpowering intellect.

V

New Wine in New Bottles: The Free Religious Association, 1866–1878

"**I**T IS NEW WINE AND IS FAST BURSTING the old bottles . . . it is time to make new and better ones." [1] In these words Francis Abbot, one of the prime movers in the Free Religious Association, greeted its birth in Boston, on Memorial Day, May 30, 1867. The immediate events leading to the meeting in Horticultural Hall began with the growing dissatisfaction of the "radical Unitarians" with the efforts of Henry Bellows, John Freeman Clark, and others to organize a national convention of Unitarian churches. Fearing theological dogmatism as well as exclusion by Bellows from organizational affairs, the dissident clergymen took steps in the fall of 1866 to form a free church movement outside of the Unitarian denomination.

ONE

The scheme of organization was planned at the Beacon Hill home of Reverend Cyrus Bartol of West Church, the older brother of George Bartol of Lancaster, Massachusetts, Frothingham's friend of Salem days. Though older than the young dissidents, Bartol never sympathized with what he feared would be Bellows' attempts at denominational conformity. Also, Bartol, though a personal friend of Bellows, was a radical in the transcendental sense, allowing him a broad sympathy with the young men of the denomination. William J. Potter of New Bedford, Massachusetts, Secretary of the Free Religious Association, recalled at its twenty-fifth anniversary the preliminary meetings leading to its founding.

> It was on almost the last of the October days in 1866 when nine persons gathered in Dr. Bartol's hospitable parlor. . . . We sat in a semi-circle around a blazing wood fire—our host at one end of the circle, near its mantle where . . . he could poke and replenish the fire . . . while he stirred the live coals in our hearts.[2]

Each of the nine around the semicircle spoke in turn. Samuel Johnson of the Lynn Free Church and John Weiss of Watertown both felt that the denomination could not be fought by more organization, that the Unitarian Association could be opposed best by the free work of free and unaffiliated individuals. Sidney Morse, editor of *The Radical* magazine agreed, as did the host of the meeting, Cyrus Bartol. Potter himself, along with Francis E. Abbot, Henry W. Brown, Edward Towne, and George Thayer, a Divinity School student, favored an organization of some sort. "We were five to four for organization," recalled Potter, "yet the company separated with mutual good will and with the purpose to meet again for a further comparison of views." [3] The views had not changed a few weeks later when virtually the same group met and decided to feel out a larger group of "Unitarians and others" as to their sentiments toward a free association. Those that opposed organization agreed not to "put any obstacles in the way."

The duty of preliminary organization fell to Potter, Abbot, and Towne. As they left the Bartol house and "separated on Boston Common, [they] took each others' hands in a mutual pledge to stand true to the purpose which they had at heart until they should see it accomplished." During the meeting just left, they must have discussed the possibility of a leader. This was where Octavius Frothingham entered the picture, a man whose name, said Potter, "would be worth a thousand men." [4] Potter may have written to him and later visited him in New York. It is certain that Cyrus Bartol talked to him late in November and Frothingham considered him "cordial, sympathetic," and indispensable to the free church movement.[5] The feeling must have been mutual for he consented to serve as chairman of a committee and to write an invitation to a larger group for an organizational meeting. This occurred February 7, 1867, again in Bartol's home attended, according to Potter's recollection, by twenty-five or thirty people. Frothingham recalled fifty to sixty Unitarian ministers, laymen, "a few women," Universalists, Quakers, and a "large number of the members of the Twenty-Eighth Congregational Society of Boston, faithful friends of the memory of Theodore Parker." [6] Frothingham chaired the meeting and the committee, Abbot, Towne, and Potter, presented a plan of organization and a draft of a constitution. Thus the Free Religious Association was conceived.

TWO

Scanty evidence exists to explain just why Octavius Frothingham was selected as chairman of the organization committee and later president of the Free Religious Association. Presumably he had made an impact on his contemporaries, young and old, by his preaching in New York, his scholarship in the *Christian Examiner,* his reputation as a radical, and his earlier connection with Theodore Parker. Potter, a quarter of a century later, recalling Frothingham's selection, said,

To have enlisted the aid of one already so distinguished for ability, scholarship, and culture, who was known also as an ecclesiastical and humanitarian reformer, and who had a rare gift for terse and eloquent speech whether in the pulpit or on the platform, was rightly felt to have advanced the cause far toward victory. Mr. Frothingham's invaluable service to the Association afterwards as its first President, and during his eleven years' holding of that office, proved the correctness of this view.[7]

There is no doubt that he had been feeling his way toward a free association outside of Unitarianism since his early Salem days. It is also reasonably clear that Theodore Parker, had he lived, would have led a free church movement of some sort. A year before Frothingham was graduated from Harvard College, Parker wrote to Convers Francis, newly appointed "liberal Unitarian" in the Divinity School, that he anticipated a split in the denomination.[8] It has already been noted that Octavius Frothingham, David Wasson, Samuel Johnson, Samuel Longfellow, and others had been talking and writing about a movement outside of Unitarianism since their Divinity School days. The general feeling among the young group, all followers of Parker, was that the Unitarian conventions were hollow, meaningless affairs; that the denomination was orthodox, that "something must be done" about it. The perennial question was who was to lead such a group of individualists.[9]

The organization of the Unitarian churches envisoned by Henry Bellows was clearly not what Frothingham and other radicals had in mind, though they attempted to go along with Bellows' program as long as they could. During the spring of 1865 when Bellows was laying plans for the New York Organizational Conference of Unitarian churches, Frothingham viewed the proceedings with misgivings. As we have noted and will see further, he and Bellows irritated one another for more than one reason. There was mutual respect, yet Bellows seemed to have respected Frothingham more than was the case of Frothingham's attitude toward Bellows. According to Conrad Wright, he was the major obstacle to Bellows' organizational plan. As the April conference in New York approached.

Bellows got the impression that Frothingham did not mean to come . . . and at that juncture he rather hoped he would not. . . . "Frothingham professes great friendliness," he wrote to Everett Hale, "and tells me he intends no trouble or division—after the convention he will withdraw if he don't [sic] like results—as everybody will! Still I don't think he knows his own mind eno' to be depended [on]. I think he meant well, just now, toward the convention, but is capable [of] bolting or quarreling or contradicting [his] purpose at fifteen minutes notice." [10]

Frothingham understood his own mind well enough. The difficulty was

that Bellows never understood Frothingham's objection to his organizational attempts and his aversion to a constitution that included the words
'"Christian" and "Lord Jesus Christ." It is true that Frothingham had been
conciliatory to Bellows' plan of organization in an address before the
Ministerial Association in Boston a month before the April meeting in
New York. Still, the men who planned the New York meeting—Bellows,
Hale, Mayo, and others—considered Frothingham's cooperation "half-
hearted" and his attendance at the April 5th meeting in New York
"reluctant." [11] Actually his attendance in New York was not at all half-
hearted, though it may have been reluctant. But Bellows was correct in
fearing that Frothingham might try to wreck the organizational plans for
a National Unitarian Association. Frothingham and his fellow radicals
were also probably justified in fearing the dominance of the energetic
Bellows who pushed his plans with the efficiency "of a chief of staff in the
army." [12]

As might be expected, Bellows presented the organizational plan complete with constitution, containing a preamble setting up a permanent
organization to be called The National Conference of Unitarian
Churches. Although no creed was intended in the constitution, the
preamble included such trinitarian terms as "Holy Ghost," "resurrection," and "Jesus Christ our Lord." Bellows, to placate the radicals, proposed a resolution stating that the preamble was not binding on any
member.[13] Nevertheless, Frothingham, at the end of his speech given
previously in Boston to the Ministerial Association, countered the proposal by suggesting a statement that should include "liberal" or "free
church" in the Unitarian Association. His proposal was not adopted and
the preamble and constitution were overwhelmingly adopted.[14]

The constitution was innocuous enough, but the lines were drawn
between organized Unitarianism and the radicals. Frothingham realized
the battle had just begun but Bellows felt the war had been won. Conrad
Wright's admirable study of Bellows' organizational contribution to Unitarianism quoted Bellows exulting to his son after the conference that it
"was an absolute and entire success." Not only was Bellows pleased that
the constitution was adopted, he was triumphant over the "weakness of
the radicals" and that the denomination had "finished naturalism, and
transcendentalism and Parkerism." [15] This revealing statement from Bellows suggests that the radicals were right in suspecting that organizational
efforts would precede attempts to establish creedal conformity along the
lines of a conservative, Channing-type Unitarianism.[16]

Both Frothingham and Francis E. Abbot were disgusted. Stow Persons,
writing symbolically if not factually, described "Frothingham sadly [walk-
ing] uptown [to] persuade his Third Unitarian Society to change its name
to the Independent Liberal Church. . . ." Abbot went back to Dover,
New Hampshire, and tore up a sermon about Christ as the core of

religion.[17] Actually it was some years before Frothingham's church formally disaffiliated from the Unitarian denomination. On a visit in 1870 Higginson was "astounded" when, upon leaving Lyric Hall, he saw a placard reading "Third Unitarian Society" at the entrance.[18]

Frothingham attended the Boston Unitarian Conference in 1874, at which time both he and Potter stated their position as to membership in the Unitarian Association. Potter argued that he could remain in the denomination and still be a free religionist, while Frothingham spoke militantly about the incompatibility of being a member of both. The *Boston Transcript* applauded Frothingham's "straightforward" stand and decried Potter's "equivocation on the issue." Their colleagues were divided. Young W. C. Gannett defended Potter's stand, but no one else of the FRA group followed Frothingham's example of withdrawing from the Unitarian Association.[19]

According to Frothingham's own account, in April, 1875, the congregation voted to drop the Unitarian designation and to become the "Independent Liberal Church." The Unitarian Year Book carried the Third Unitarian Society on its rolls until 1875 when it was dropped, but this was a mere formality. Frothingham had long since disaffiliated intellectually from Unitarianism.

His immediate response to the New York conference engineered by Bellows was his first overt step toward abandoning Unitarianism. The occasion was an angry Palm Sunday sermon in April, 1865, less than a week before Lincoln's assassination.[20] The Civil War was coming to a victorious close and the North was hopeful that a new era of peace and justice would be ushered in. Frothingham used the occasion to contrast hope with reality, to caution his people that great events often lead to disappointing results. He drew a parallel between Jesus' triumphal journey into Jerusalem, followed by his betrayal and death, and the great hopes for nonsectarian religion, followed by its defeat at the recent Unitarian conference in New York.

> All great excitements are disappointing. All mighty movements and convulsions and revolutions are disappointing. We expect much and get little. . . .
> We have just had, in our own circle, an illustration of this truth. It was a significant thing . . . when day by day was bringing news of victory . . . when the armies of the Slave Power were making a hasty retreat. . . . Of this week of all weeks in the year, the Liberal Church in America should hold their first grand national convention. . . . They came, they deliberated . . . they shouted hosannahs. . . . What remains? A piece of ground covered with dry leaves and over them the spirit of truth walking on alone toward a Via Dolorosa. . . . The Liberal Body shrunk from its own principle . . . it held to its old sectarian name with a tenacity never before exhibited. . . .

After a long somber introduction full of Biblical allusions, Frothingham then hit at the Unitarian conference with the much quoted passage, addressing directly the conservative Unitarian leaders:

> There has never been a convention so narrow, so blind, and stubborn as it
> was, so instead of the Liberal Church in America, which we thought we were
> to have, we have the old Unitarian Association, made more Unitarian than
> ever. Instead of a pure fraternity of noble minds, we have a close corpora-
> tion of sectarians.[21]

Although his sermon was perhaps too somber for the occasion, he did not
end on a note of defeat. The conference to be sure was a disappointment
but "perhaps," he suggested, "the uprising of a new spirit of progress will
come all the sooner." [22]

It was true. After the spring meeting in New York, the radicals became
more alienated than ever as the events moved to their final rejection of the
1866 Syracuse Conference. Shortly after Frothingham's Palm Sunday
sermon he wrote to Samuel Johnson asking him to come to see him (if in
the city) "and talk about some things." [23] There were plenty of things to
talk about in the spring of 1865 as Bellows and his group moved toward
organization and even more a year and a half later following the October
10–11 meeting of the newly formed association of Unitarian Churches at
Syracuse. "Something is in the air," he wrote to Johnson two months after
the first meeting at Cyrus Bartol's home in Boston. "Although we must
not move too rapidly a movement for associated religious action must
include all of the finest elements. . . . How far are you willing to go?" he
asked Johnson. "An association without you and Weiss and Wasson and
Bartol" would be a mistake and a failure. "We are both independent," he
reassured Johnson, "and I like it . . . but it seems to me that our separate
candles [could] with advantage be set a little nearer together." Materialists
and intellectualists should associate and make a "wide impression on the
public." To the cautious Johnson, Frothingham posed questions implying
a loose association of independent thinkers: "Could we meet at stated
times? Could we be affiliated in some general way? Could we meet in
formicum under a jealous committee? I would suggest nothing more for I
wish to have the movement entirely free in spirit and in operation." [24]

Frothingham's attempts to move Johnson toward an association reflected the dilemma the radicals faced after Syracuse—how to secede
from the Unitarian organization to form one of their own and at the same
time be unorganized. Indeed, this was one of the weaknesses of the "Free
Churches" such as had been established under Parker in Boston, Higginson in Worcester, and Johnson in Lynn, Massachusetts. Henry Bellows,
who saw this more clearly than most, could never fully appreciate
Frothingham's aversion to the Unitarian Association. This issue, aggravated by earlier events, was a bone of contention between the two men
during the early stages in the founding of the National Association of
Unitarian Churches and as the Free Religious Association was taking
form.

In the fall of 1866, after the Syracuse conference of Unitarian churches, and before the organizational meeting of the FRA had taken place, Frothingham wrote to Bellows in an injured tone complaining that he and a fellow radical, William W. Chadwick of Brooklyn, had been excluded from an organizational meeting of Unitarian ministers called together by Bellows. It is the best statement of Frothingham's own reasons for not joining the Unitarian Association, as well as a warning to Bellows of what was "in the air."

> I saw with some surprise in last week's "Inquirer" the announcement that a local conference of Unitarian churches had been organized in New York under the auspices of the National Conference and in compliance with the general plan of operation.
>
> The meeting of the "Pastoral Association" at which the action was decided on and adopted is said to have been held on the 19th of this month. Our regular monthly meeting was, I remember, adjourned to that date in order that we might hear from you a statement of the affairs of the Inquirer and an account of your success in forming a stock company to take charge of its business. I did not attend that meeting for I was very busy that morning writing the review of [the] History of the Sanitary Commission. But had I received the smallest intimation that any special business was to be brought before the Association, and had the faintest hint been thrown out that a matter so important as the establishment of a local conference was to be considered, nothing would have kept me away. I met [W. W.] Chadwick going to Boston on Monday and his surprise was equal to mine. We both felt that we should have been notified and consulted in a case of the very gravest moment and that the action of the Pastoral Association had placed us personally and officially in a very embarrassing situation. I feel this peculiarly, not that I am hurt or offended or piqued, but I am perplexed at finding myself placed before the public and my own parish in a false position.
>
> Had I been present at the meeting of the 19th as I deeply regret I was not, I should have taken occasion to make a full and frank statement of the reasons why my society was not represented at Syracuse—why I am unable to affiliate with the National Conference in its plans—and why I cannot conscientiously pledge my sympathy or my support to its operation. It is unnecessary that I should write this to you for you know it already; you knew that I am one of the recreants, that I could not accept the Preamble to the Constitution of the Conference; that I have earnestly protested against the attempt at organizing on sectarian principles however attenuated, for sectarian ends however plausible; that the *animus* of the movement was unpleasant to me; that its indications were alarming to the free and undogmatical spirit which I have jealously cherished and which I have assumed to be with the birthright of our faith.
>
> It is impossible for me to take an interest in the kind of propagandism that is contemplated. . . . Not my own sensitiveness merely, but my own judgment tells me that such an endeavor is out of line of our tradition and will not find favor with the masses of the people who cannot make distinction

and who if they take Liberal Christianity at all, will prefer to take it pure and simple with all its radicalism. . . .

My people so far as I know share my persuasions in this regard. They have no desire to enter into the bonds of any "denominational" organization and no disposition to contribute funds for "denominationalism" and its enterprises. I think therefore that I speak for them as well as for myself when I declare to take part in the local conference and announce that we *shall not probably be represented* in the Convention to be held in *your church* next week.

If necessary we must be independent and doubtless and do our own work as we may. We shall not long I think, do it alone: for I already foresee not dimly *either the formation* of some new *association* which will aim at carrying out [some process] which the "Radicals" have at heart.

I do not wish to make a notice in Public about this thing—and I prefer writing this private note in explanation of my conduct. It is not pleasant to be driven to such conduct or such an explanation: but it is a satisfaction to feel that the unpleasantness will be all mine. Mine is also the embarrassment and also the [trouble]. The necessity of defending positions is mine alone. You will be as strong without me as with me—and I must be under the imputation of being incompatible, crotchety—and implacable—but all that must be if it must. I cannot help it—I must be true to myself and to my principles and I should be untrue to both if I allowed myself to be drawn into an organization with the new motives and plans of which I have no sympathy and with whose work I have no healthy concern.

Nothing would give me greater pleasure than to form with our churches in some good social work that might justify our own faith here in New York: and I shall be always glad to feel that in many respects we are if we cannot be one in this particular enterprise.

Cordially yours,
O. B. Frothingham [25]

The patient Bellows apparently answered with a kind note hoping that Frothingham had no suspicion or lack of cordiality toward him and his efforts at Unitarian organization. Frothingham wrote back immediately assuring Bellows of his complete respect for the efforts of the men attempting to organize the association. Yet he did not yield in his opposition to the Syracuse conference that spring or Bellows' recent plan to form a local association of Unitarian churches. He would not join but would put no obstacle in the way of those who would organize, he assured Bellows. Although he ended on a friendly note, he warned Bellows again that

if the left wing can be spread for flight an effort will be made to spread it. Steps will no doubt be taken to ascertain how far an independent organization may be possible. Two conferences have been held at a private home in Boston neither of which I attended, and they elicited nothing definite. Of the "radical" organizers, they will simply organize to do the work which you leave undone—while you do the work they leave undone. Let us shake hands in good faith and feeling.[26]

Both men continued to work in good faith in accordance with their principles but Bellows, it appears, worked with better feeling. Through the pages of his *Liberal Christian* he commented on the events of 1866–1867 leading to the founding of the Free Religious Association, of which he was familiar in spite of Frothingham's indirection. While chiding his friend Cyrus Bartol for creating "ecclesiastical confusion" by opposing the efforts at Unitarian organization, he also understood completely the position of Frothingham whom he thought was "constitutionally disinclined to organization." [27] Later he apologized to Bartol for his "imprudent" comment in the magazine, recognizing his mental constitution as being necessary "in the place [he had] to fill" [28] (West Church, Boston). Here he showed no animus toward this old friend for having allowed the Free Religious Association to be planned in his own parlor. At the same time Bellows feared that a divisive movement, sponsored by the Boston men, would create an undesirable sectionalism in the Unitarian organization,[29] a condition later criticized by Felix Adler within the Free Religious Association itself. Bartol had written to Bellows a few months earlier that there were many liberals in Boston and that Frothingham, knowing a lot about it, could help set up a Unitarian-Universalist congregation there.[30]

In spite of his misgivings, Bellows was forthright in his response to the third meeting in Bartol's house in February, 1867, which was chaired by Frothingham. He was glad no new sect was being formed which would split many good men who are radicals from the conservatives. Both were needed as "meal and leaven in bread." If this statement was wishful thinking, designed as a caution against the very thing Bellows feared, his congratulations to the Free Religious Association must be considered sincere.

> Men so able, accomplished, and thoroughly equipped for the work as Messrs. Frothingham, Johnson, Weiss, and Abbott are, can hardly venture forth into this vast field without making important discoveries and bringing back important and even brilliant contributions to our common faith. We bid them a hearty and earnest Godspeed in their work.[31]

THREE

By February, 1867, the Free Religious Association was virtually in being. In spite of his aversion to organizations, Frothingham took the reins of the presidency energetically enough, though no doubt missing Theodore Parker, whom he and most of his colleagues felt would have led the movement had he lived.[32] It became Frothingham's duty to organize the founding meeting in Boston in May and to arrange for speakers. His immediate task was to enlist the aid of prominent people, laymen as well as clergy, and to persuade his fellow radicals to appear on the platform.

Less than a week after the February meeting at Bartol's house,

Frothingham wrote to Charles Elliot Norton, nephew of George Ticknor and Dante Scholar at Harvard. Because of his prominence in Boston intellectual circles, the committee had asked Norton and Frothingham to draw up plans for an association. The mandate was a broad one and Frothingham was vague in his own mind as to what he and Norton were to do. They had been appointed, he wrote, "to do something or other" but doubted that calling just another meeting to debate would lead to anything but "confusion and disaster." Rather, he thought a precise plan of organization should be drawn up by a few men. It should be exclusive, limited to men

> conditioned on election . . . invited to join whose character and tendencies were well understood as fitting them to be co-workers and not merely hangers on. This much of exclusiveness would be necessary in my judgment to make the movement strong. . . . The nucleus having been formed and the plan of association agreed upon I would call a meeting . . . in next anniversary week in Boston not for consultation but demonstration—to show the number and weight of our hands.[33]

Exclusiveness he did not mind, it would seem, as long as there was uniformity of commitment to free religion. Henry Bellows could hardly have stated the case better for an organized religious body.

Norton's response to Frothingham's letter, though not recorded, was not favorable. A week later Francis Abbot, writing to Norton on another matter, expressed his keen disappointment that Norton had decided not to join the nonsectarian movement which he hoped would be "wide as all outdoors." Abbot, pleading that Norton reconsider, assured him that the movement needed influential laymen "like yourself." [34]

Perhaps he did reconsider. Less than a month before the Boston meeting Frothingham was writing to him to be a platform speaker on the theme of liberty as applied to religion. Although Norton at last turned down the invitation and never joined the Free Religious Association, the letter from Frothingham is significant in showing the stage of the planning of the founding meeting and Frothingham's part in it.

> One meeting will be held in Boston on Thursday of anniversary week—May 30th. The plan is to have a double session, one in the morning for statement and discussion and one in the afternoon for "organization." At the second meeting the interchange of opinion will be perfectly free. At the first meeting it is desirable to have carefully matured thoughts—and therefore it is decided to invite a few gentlemen to speak on the conditions, needs and prospects of Liberal Religion in America under its several aspects—as for instance Unitarianism, Universalism, Spiritualism . . . the new Judaism— the speeches will be compact and pointed and given by men who represent the tendency under review. On the platform we hope to have Robert Collyar, Robert Dale Owen, Dr. Lilienthal, Mr. Wasson, Mr. Abbot and

others. I shall impatiently await an early reply that my mind may be at rest in the affair.[35]

Norton's refusal to participate in the founding of the Free Religious Association is perhaps explained in part by his comment in a letter two months after the Boston meeting. He wrote to a Miss Gaskell that there must be a free, non-sectarian church and that Unitarianism with a future was a step toward this. He also referred to E. L. Godkin, editor of *Nation* as "my near and dear friend," [36] a man who feared that Frothingham was as dogmatic as the dogmatists he denounced.

It was easier to recruit supporters and speakers among the radicals. Both Frothingham and William J. Potter of New Bedford were busy through the winter and spring with correspondence. Potter, enlisting the aid of Mrs. Caroline Dall, wife of a Unitarian minister and activist in many causes, assured her of the advantage of meeting during anniversary week "when many people would be in the city" and that it would not conflict with the American Unitarian Association meeting.[37] Frothingham contacted Francis Abbot about his topic of discussion at the Boston meeting, warning him to avoid speaking for any "ism or point of view"; yet he admitted to Abbot that it is you "or no one for the positivist." Also, could Abbot suggest a woman speaker since they needed one, "if you can name a good specimen." [38]

Earlier in the planning stage Abbot had written his fears to William J. Potter that Frothingham "seemed to be wavering" and thought another call for the meeting should be sent out.[39] He was continually worried about Frothingham's lack of loyalty to the organizational approach, though at this juncture his fears were unfounded. Frothingham had followed through faithfully after the February meeting at Bartol's. The call for the meeting in May had been sent out to religious journals in the nation and newspapers in Boston and New York:

> A Public Meeting, to consider the conditions, wants and prospects of Free Religion in America, will be held on Thursday, May 30, at 10 A.M., at Horticultural Hall, Boston.
>
> The following persons have been asked to address the meeting, and addresses may be expected from most of them: R. W. Emerson, John Weiss, Robert Dale Owen, Wm. H. Furness, Lucretia Mott, Henry Blanchard, T. W. Higginson, D. A. Wasson, Isaac M. Wise, Oliver Johnson, F. E. Abbot, and Max Lilienthal.
>
> (Signed), O. B. Frothingham, ⎫
>   Wm. J. Potter,   ⎬ Committee.[40]
>   Rowland Connor, ⎭

The planning had been well done. The response was good. Shortly after 10 A.M. on the norning of May 30, 1867, in the auditorium of

Horticultural Hall, Frothingham stood and faced a "very large audience" to open the meeting. After explaining briefly the preliminary meetings at the "house of a gentleman in Boston," he rationalized the planning work as an attempt to "save time, endless talk" and "to give point and purpose and balance" to what might be done today. His opening address was really a sermon and a plea for a nonsectarian departure from the "old parties within Christianity." It was a thinly veiled criticism of the work of Bellows in New York and Syracuse. Christiandom, he was sure, had drawn its lines, closing doors through which people could get out. The time for a new departure was at hand and had already begun, he proclaimed.

> Egypt has by multitudes been left. A great exodus has long been going on. The vast armies are on the march. Some are just lighting their first camp fires; some are packing up their luggage for the move; some have just stepped into the Red Sea; others are on the other side. Some are just tasting the waters of bitterness, and some have just plucked the herb which sweetens the waters. Some are out among the sands, wandering about, tired scattered, groping; some are at the foot of the mountain, waiting to hear the trumpet; some have heard the trumpet, and passed on; some have gone beyond the wilderness and touched its utmost verge, and, ascending to the high land, are looking down upon the field before them; others again have gone into the field, have found the promised land, have brought back a report of the fruits and flowers and the people there, have found it a familiar land, the great promised land of the Lord, which the Lord originally gave to all his faithful children; they are at home there.[41]

His Biblical oratory may have sounded strange to the radicals in the audience—theists and nontheists alike; however, it was Frothingham's style to couch his radical views in the language of orthodoxy. Back to more mundane language, he then proceeded to stress the theme of the meeting as being non-sectarian. None of the speakers were asked to represent a particular sect or church. They came as individuals, free to speak from a certain philosophic position. Extreme "left-wing" Unitarians were invited, "progressive" Unitarians, Quakers, Spiritualists, a "modern" Jew, and a scientific theist made up the spectrum of platform speakers. Frothingham mentioned no names of the platform guests until he got to the last category of thought to be represented:

> . . . There are worthy men who are strictly universal, comprehensive, absolute, taking in everything by pure thought, the men of pure intuition, and we have said, "give us one of your men to speak for you." [42]

Everyone knew that he referred to Waldo Emerson, who had come expecting a small committee meeting. With the morning off to a high-toned start, Frothingham then turned to the real business of the day, that of organization. Henry Bellows could not have engineered it any better than Frothingham and the planning group. At a prearranged time he called for a motion to appoint a committee on permanent organization and to bring in any plan "which they decided to recommend." Rev. Edward Towne of Medford, one of the original planners who had returned from the Syracuse meeting with Abbot and Potter, rose and nominated a committee. As prearranged it included William J. Potter, Francis E. Abbot, along with Richard P. Hallowell, H. C. De Long and Hannah E. Stevenson, Theodore Parker's former secretary. This group was instructed to bring in a plan of organization and slate of officers at the afternoon session.

This done, the chairman turned back to the inspirational part of the morning program—that of introducing the platform speakers. John Weiss of Watertown, a "flame of fire" in Frothingham's opinion and his colleague in the young minister's "Hook and Ladder" club of Salem days, was to speak first. Unknown to Frothingham, Weiss, caught in a Boston traffic jam, was fighting his way up the crowded aisle toward the platform and could not be introduced. He turned instead to introduce Reverend Henry Blanchard of Brooklyn, Massachusetts, representing Universalism. Blanchard, after reviewing the history of Universal thought, stated that a broad union of denominations, though desirable, would be impossible. Still he made a plea for a liberal Christian union. Lucretia Mott, the Quaker lady, perennial reformer and perhaps Frothingham's "specimen" for the occasion, chided Blanchard by calling for a broad organization outside of present denominations—a loose federal structure but not a traditional consociation. Next was Robert Dale Owen, then at New Harmony, Indiana, who spoke of the Spiritualists' views of death and immortality.

Between speakers, Frothingham, as chairman, made noncommittal remarks of affirmation and, at times, humorous extemporaneous comments as an introduction to the next speaker. Before Weiss rose to give his address from the view of "left wing" Unitarianism, the chairman made an allusion to his friend's tardy arrival on the platform: "Unitarianism is very apt to be a little late. It was rather late this morning. I hope it will not be late tomorrow." [43] Weiss then spoke about the futile fight at Syracuse over the preamble and launched into a plea for free nonsectarian organization to transcend both old and new Unitarianism. As a sideswipe at Owen, the previous speaker, he ad-libbed a remark that Spiritualism could not be supported or believed in. In acknowledgment, Frothingham agreed, and introduced Oliver Johnson of the Progressive Friends, who added nothing new to the remarks of previous speakers. Next, Francis Abbot gave a paper on science and religion in which he expressed the view that science as a source of truth must be combined with religion as a fact of human nature to form a truly free religion. "New wine" to burst the old bottles as a crusade for religious thought based on his scientific theism was what he called for. David Wasson, introduced by Frothingham as a disputant, took strong issue with Abbot. Between the two, the old line was redrawn between spiritualism and materialism; between the sensationalists (scientists) and the transcendentalists. "Science reveals evil and inhumanity as well as good," said Wasson. We must have a religion of humanity based on "*a priori,* intuitive" guides to religious truth. Thomas Wentworth Higginson, feeling pessimistic that morning, brought the audience to earth with his account of the failure of Unitarianism, Spiritualism, and science. Still they must try, he thought, through free thought meetings.

The last to be introduced and perhaps the one most eagerly anticipated was Ralph Waldo Emerson. As was often the case, he disappointed his audience, apologizing that he had no prepared paper because he came expecting "a little committee" meeting. Yet, in his extemporaneous remarks, he went to the heart of the free religious concept. "The church is not large enough for the man" because the old creeds are outworn. He called for a broad harmony in which intuition and science would be combined so that

> every man is apprised of the divine presence within his own mind—is apprised that the perfect law of duty corresponds with the laws of chemistry, of vegetation, of astronomy, as face to face in a glass; . . . We [will then] have a religion that exalts; that commands all the social and the private actions.[44]

Emerson stated the original purpose of the Free Religious Association founders in his last remark. Never intended to be a new sect or to act as a social reform agency, the purpose was to evolve a universal religion that would exalt the individual in his private acts. They believed the improvement of society would automatically follow.

The essential part of the meeting had been accomplished by midday. After the noon adjournment, the group reconvened, heard the plan of organization, approved of the articles of association, and voted in the slate of officers. The Free Religious Association was born, its object to "promote the interests of pure religion, to encourage the scientific study of theology, and to increase fellowship in the spirit." [45] Membership was to be open to all people interested in free inquiry in religious and philosophical matters. It was to be a Boston organization with yearly meetings during "anniversary week" in that city.[46] Both of these items would cause trouble later when some became disturbed by the theological limitations of the first articles and the geographic narrowness implied in the fourth (see Appendix).

Nevertheless, Frothingham had reason to be proud of the day's work, the result of so many meetings and hours of letter writing of the past half year. There was no doubt that the preliminary planning had been sound—that of small committees presenting the larger group with a definite purpose and plan of organization which they could accept, reject, or modify.[47] These were the tactics that had alienated the radicals from Bellows organization plans for the Association of Unitarian Churches in 1865, but now it was different—they, like Bellows' conservatives, were working with a consensus of their own. For the first time since Divinity School, Frothingham was in a group of congenial free thinkers with whom he could exert influence on the thinking of his times.

FOUR

Observers watched carefully the activities of the newly formed Free Religious Association, wondering just what vintage of "new wine" would be produced. Sidney Morse, who had attended at least one planned meeting, reported the founding of the Free Religious Association in *The Radical,* publishing the articles of organization and covering fully the chairman's opening address. He supported the group by reiterating Frothingham's theme of the need for freeminded people to take a "new departure" in religious thinking.[48] A few days after the Boston meeting Francis Abbot himself expressed misgivings about Frothingham's qualifications to lead such a movement. He confided to William J. Potter, newly elected secretary of the Free Religious Association, that he felt uneasy with Frothingham presiding because of his lack of faith in organization. He was sure he did not fully grasp the idea of free religion which Abbot felt should be as organized as the groups from which the free religionists were departing. "It strikes me as important," he wrote to Potter, "that Frothingham calls this meeting in the Liberal Christian as one not for the organized but for the unorganized." In Abbot's view the Free Religious Association should be tightly organized around a recognized and articulated liberal credo. Frothingham's permissiveness made him uneasy.[49] Eventually this feeling would grow, in spite of surface cordiality, and lead to the break between the two men.

Henry Bellows' *Liberal Christian* observed the founding of the Free Religious Association with an editorial by "CDF" in which that writer faintly praised the efforts of free religion but paid full respects to "the chairman for candor and fairness." [50] Although Bellows was always cordial and fair in his relation with Frothingham, he never really understood or forgave the radicals who founded the Free Religious Association. More than a year after its founding Bellows was still justifying the preamble to the constitution of the Association of Unitarian Churches which had precipitated the break of the radicals and led to the founding of the FRA. Bellows was sure that Christianity was the main channel through which religious progress would come, although he was also sure that this view would be disputed "by the gentlemen who have founded the Free Religious Association." Still it was better, he thought, to have organized on the basis of Christianity and to run the risk of losing the "serious and resolute malcontents on the left wing." [51]

Frothingham himself never really saw any conflict between his radicalism and Christianity. More than a year after the founding of the FRA he attended the Unitarian convention in New York and spoke to this effect. Bellows and the others, such as Clark, Mayo, and Hepworth disagreed, feeling that the radicals who objected to the Unitarian preamble should get out of the organization.[52] It really was not an immediate question of getting out of the Unitarian denomination. Frothingham, along with many of his FRA colleagues, continued to attend the local and national conventions. At each convention there was the usual debate over the controversial preamble with conservatives such as A. D. Mayo and Ezra Styles Gannett, led by Henry Bellows, arrayed against such radicals as Potter and Frothingham. William White Chadwick, Frothingham's Brooklyn colleague, felt oppressed by Bellows' leadership, confiding to his friend William Gannett, son of Ezra Styles Gannett, that if all the conservatives were like Bellows, he could not remain where he was.[53] He was glad that Frothingham in New York often spoke out at the Unitarian conventions against Bellows, the "pious ass . . . in a grand pyrotechnic display." [54] During the immediate years after the preamble conflict began, Bellows led the defense, earning for himself, at least from the younger radicals, the title of "Unitarian Pope." "It seems odd," Gannett wrote to Chadwick, "that people in the East regard him so. Do any people? Or is it superlative self-consciousness on his part?" [55] Frothingham and Chadwick would probably have answered in the affirmative, yet Frothingham never expressed as strong an animosity toward Bellows as did Chadwick, who felt that Bellows hated him "with an almost perfect hatred." [56]

Bellows' colleague, Reverend A. D. Mayo, was less concerned with the radical threat. He wrote in the *Christian Register* of the "Religious Tendencies in the United States." There would eventually be one Christian church in America, he felt. Only a few deluded people would stay out—"self worshippers, who use intuition and literature instead of religion." These independent thinkers would "spin off on their own axis into a spiritual vacuum." [57] This was the only comment that the FRA received in the Unitarian journal.

Fully aware of the obstacles to a free religious movement, both within and outside of the free religious organization, Frothingham devoted the last eleven years of his New York career to clarifying the goals of free religion, of answering its enemies and in stimulating the Free Religious Association members with intellectual leadership. He had able colleagues to be sure, with Potter, Higginson, Chadwick, and Samuel Johnson, though the latter never joined. As for Francis Abbot, Frothingham spent a great deal of his time and energy reassuring him, placating his disaffections and, at times, countering his ideas and plans. As president, the major responsibility for planning the annual meetings in Boston and annual fall conferences in other cities, was his. Much of the administration and planning was done in conference with Potter and the executive board, much through correspondence. Typical of this were letters to Abbot reminding him of the next FRA meeting. Wasson and Weiss were to be "two of my men—I want you for a third," adding gratuitously that his expenses could be paid which "must be a consideration with you. We mean to have a powerful good time . . . and I shall count on your contribution." [58]

Young Gannett, fresh from Divinity School, was asked to speak on the decline of superstition for the same annual meeting in 1870.[59] To James Parton, the historian, there was an occasional note referring to Colonel Higginson's having said he might speak at the New York convention on an appropriate subject. Potter, he told him, was in charge of the details but that he should speak on the subject of "Taxation of Church Property." [60] As secretary, Potter also corresponded with speakers to appear before the FRA conventions. Often his and Frothingham's letters overlapped and reinforced the plea for speaking contributions.[61] To his old friend, Samuel Johnson, Frothingham often turned for aid. The theme for the meeting in the spring of 1873 was to be "Freedom in Religion." The reluctant Johnson agreed, much to Frothingham's relief. He wrote back: "You will strike the grand keynote of the morning. I hate to work so hard an overworked man but we need you—and who that works in our field now is not overworked?" [62]

Leadership was the quality that Frothingham contributed to the Free Religious Association. He dominated the annual spring meetings in Boston between 1867 and 1878 and attended all of the fall and winter conventions held in various cities of the East and Midwest. His chief role was reconciling diverse opinions within the group and interpreting the purpose of the organization to members and nonmembers. At the second Boston meeting in Anniversary Week, 1868, he spoke on the "New Religious Movement." [63] The following year his presidential address reiterated the theme of free religion and its role and problems. A disembodied idea, he said, without a home, is inherently weak. Such groups need unity of purpose if not principle; they need to recognize the coexistence of all religions. Christianity is a "bundle of religions. We can achieve unity under the scientific study of religion. We can never unseat the supreme Ruler of the World however we may call him by different names . . . all the world needs is light." The Free Religious Association should throw light rather than be an arena for "aggressive controversialists." As president of the FRA, he showed more restraint than previously as one of Bellows' "left wing malcontents." His was, in part, a harmonizing role. He often had to function as a mediator while presiding at the FRA meetings and making extemporaneous remarks between speakers he had introduced. At the second meeting in 1869 he was called upon to mediate between the conservative Rev. Jesse Jones, who had spoken on the subject of Christian ethics of Jesus as the heart of religion, and Francis Abbot, who felt the FRA people had no right to call themselves Christians at all.[64]

It is not always easy to achieve harmony among a group of freethinkers such as attended the FRA meetings. For the first few years there was continual debate as to the role of the association. Abbot wanted to turn it into a reform group for taking definite stands on controversial issues and fighting social evils as he saw them. Frothingham opposed this departure as a violation of the purpose of the organization. It became the main business of the spring meeting of 1870 to clarify the role and purpose of the FRA. The report of the executive board raised the issue and Frothingham's presidential address dwelt on it. "What is free religion?" he asked.

> It is [the opposite] of the traditional view that religion belongs to the supernatural sphere. We believe that a rational view of the sphere of the supernatural is in the compass of the mind. Religion is one of the mind's expressions. . . . It is the popular impression that science must be held subordinate to revelation. It is the rational impression that science is revelation.

He cautioned against being "torn asunder by principles." Men need not give up their principles, only their dogmatism, to be free religionists. Mr. Wasson, he reminded them, could disagree with Mr. Abbot without compromising the free religious principle. "We are creedless; we are neither radicals nor conservatives, but rationalists." Nor is the Free Religious Association, he suggested, a reform organization to set up "soup houses and dole out old clothes." Yet, "our rationalism is practical," making "soup houses unnecessary." The theme of the presidential address was followed in the evening session by Rabbi Wise's paper on Judaism, Higginson's on Islamic religion, William Henry Channing on Chinese religion, and William J. Potter on Indian philosophy. In his ever graceful style of moderating, Frothingham closed the session after Potter's speech: "With his benediction from the land of the Brahmins the convention is now adjourned." [65]

Francis Abbot went back to Toledo, where he was by now editing the *Index,* disgruntled at the direction taken by the FRA. "President Frothingham's continual advice to the public to cherish their traditional ideas of amity and charity," he complained to Potter, "[are] objectionable." [66] He was also furious at Frothingham's opposition to taking a stand against obscenity laws. Frothingham, who opposed such laws as thoroughly as did Abbot, considered the issue "irrelevant" to the cause of free religion. Abbot also accused Frothingham, along with Potter and Wasson, of "cowardly, sentimental" use of Christian terminology. Emerson and Parker had freed religion of dogma, Abbot recognized, but it was these successors who have failed to see that science was the vehicle for exploring the freedom Emerson valued. "Neo Christians," he scornfully called them.[67]

Abbot's criticism of the FRA in general and of Frothingham in particular were not fatal to growth of the organization. In fact, at times Abbot may have strengthened Frothingham's natural reluctance to engage issues and strike out at enemies. The annual meeting in the spring of 1871 reflected a good year for the association. The Horticultural Hall lectures, then in their third year, had been received enthusiastically by the public. Although they were planned and publicized by W. C. Gannett, Frothingham was always on hand to open the lecture series as president of the FRA.[68]

Frothingham's lecture entitled "Belief of the Unbelievers" called down the spirit of the infidels of the age of reason—Voltaire, Diderot, Thomas Paine, and Theodore Parker. At the annual meeting in June, the executive board expressed confidence and pleasure in the growth of free religion. There had been meetings in Toledo and Cincinnati attended by Frothingham, Potter, and members of the executive board. In his presidential address, Frothingham felt no need to defend the organization or to redefine its goals. He contented himself by reminding the group that they were no "little closeted group of ministers, literary men, philosophers." "We mean business," he said militantly, but optimistically added that he thought the FRA would become a popular movement which would reach the "working class" to free them from ecclesiastical bonds. Apparently Frothingham was encouraged by the response of audiences in Ohio into thinking that rational religion would become a popular movement. That it never occurred was one of his greatest disappointments.

"Superstition and Dogmatism" was the title of his major paper in the spring meeting. It was a hard hitting attack on supernaturalism in Christianity. "We must give up a few pleasant angels to get rid of our devils by the illuminating daylight of science." [69] Certainly this was enough to ease the suspicions of Abbot.

The Chicago fire in 1872 ended plans for regional meetings there but conventions were held in Detroit and Syracuse. The executive committee's reports of that year presented by Potter noticed the demise of the *Christian Examiner* but praised the *Index* edited by Abbot and observed that the FRA contributed to its support. In the presidential address Frothingham again reiterated the role and purpose of free religion. It was a unifying speech in which he went out of his way to praise the brave Abbot who was always on hand "where bullets fly the thickest." The FRA, said Frothingham, was like the Hebrew tribes "leaving the flesh pots of Egypt," refusing to stop at the oasis for rest. "We are engaged in a war of ideas" against "our enemies and critics." William White Chadwick was then introduced, who spoke against the proposed amendment to put "God" in the United States Constitution. Lucretia Mott, Bronson Alcott, and Cyrus Bartol followed. At times such as this, Frothingham's style was to remain aloof from the specifics of the issue. He simply presided and kept his extemporaneous and prepared remarks to the level of broad principles. It was this very characteristic of Frothingham that led some of his more radical critics, such as Francis Abbot, to suspect his sincerity and commitment to the logical path of rational religion. Ironically, Bellows had distrusted Frothingham for his capacity to change and bolt at a moment's notice, while his radical colleagues were afraid he could not move fast enough.

It could be that he fulfilled his role best while he was pronouncing principles and goals of free religion. It was at the spring meeting in 1872 that he gave his most memorable address, "The Religion of Humanity." It must have inspired the audience for it predated the larger paper which came out as a small book the next year. It was well covered in the press, the *Boston Globe* remarking that "so full of thought was each line and sentence," it would be impossible to condense his essay.[70] The address captured the spirit of radical religion, its objections to Christianity, and its thrust into the broader world cultures for all humanity. Lucretia Mott responded with warm agreement as did Samuel Longfellow, who closed the proceedings of the convention.[71]

The 1873 meeting was one of the "best conventions," [72] according to William J. Potter. Perhaps it was because some of the free religionists could be amused at Bellows' meeting of the Unitarian churches held in Boston at the same time, dealing with procedural matters and pleasantries, according to press reports.[73] Surviving the Boston fire, which destroyed treasurer Hallowell's office and most of the proceedings of the FRA, may have added to the enthusiastic atmosphere. In spite of the disaster, which threatened to end the winter series at Horticultural Hall, six lectures were held successfully, including one of Frothingham's best, "Feuerback and Modern Atheism," which attracted a "large and refined audience, in spite of a falling rain." [74] The durable Lucretia Mott also added spice to the occasion by chiding the men for using warlike words and military allusions in their speeches. Frothingham himself, in his usual presidential address, reiterated the aims of the FRA in matter-of-fact tones.[75] He was not militant, feeling no need to attack enemies or unify friends. He was mellow in an atmosphere of congeniality. There was joy, laughter, serious thought, music, flowers, and eloquence, he recalled of the spring meetings of the FRA. To his own congregation in New York he described the typical scene:

> There . . . was a large upper room decorated with banners . . . and wreaths of flowers. It was filled by a company of men and women who had met together representing the new faith, the new hope of the times. There

were reformers, philosophers, philanthropists, teachers, poets, artists, artisans and workers of every degree. There were old gray-haired men and women who had earned their right to honor . . . [for] their superb achievements for humanity. There were young men and women in the full flesh of youth, with eyes flashing, hearts bright and voices clear. They were talking together—about what? Not about the pentecost at Jerusalem; not about the Christ dead or living. They had no doctrine; they had no creed; they had no commandment. They effected no organization; they built no institution. They were contemplating the better times when the capacities of the human mind should have a chance to do themselves justice; when men and women should no longer be cramped and enthralled by superstition, or bound by tradition; when the natural hopes of the heart should be cultivated and trained to find their legitimate fruition; when reason, trained by science and enlightened by philosophy, should be free to accept all the conclusions of truth. They were inspired. . . . This was their Pentecostal season.[76]

FIVE

The Free Religious Association was in full season for the next four years moving in the direction desired by Frothingham and the majority of the founders of the organization. He had reason to be satisfied, though he never became complacent. The fall meeting was held in New York in 1873, timed to coincide with the meeting of the Evangelical Alliance. At Cooper Institute, Frothingham challenged the orthodox wing of Protestantism in a speech, "Religious Outlook in America." The future would be nonsectarian, he predicted. The country would move, in spite of evangelical efforts, toward a religion of humanity that would be non-Christian. John Weiss, William White Chadwick, and W. C. Gannett were also there to help challenge orthodoxy in its home base of New York City.[77]

At the spring meeting in 1874 new voices were heard. Rabbi Souneshein of St. Louis and Minot Savage, a young radical converted by Frothingham from Congregationalism, appeared as speakers.[78] Other than a few new faces, the pattern of the meetings and the appearance of speakers changed little during the next four years. The *Index*, now published in Boston, by 1874 also housed the office of the FRA. Frothingham, in his presidential addresses, continued to clarify the goals of free religion, stressing nonsectarian creedlessness, recalling the history of the association and tradition it had attempted to change as well as to uphold.[79] At times his address referred to a topical issue to give a point to his presentation. Dr. McGosh of Princeton and his debate with President White of Cornell in New York was used by Frothingham in order to use the orthodox man as a foil. McGosh could not see how an eclectic philosophy was possible—"you have to be either or, not a little of all." [80]

Lucretia Mott returned again in 1875, her last appearance she said, and addressed the group, in her own words, "as an old Quaker woman." [81]

Higginson, who had the capacity for being flamboyantly humorous as well as deadly serious, often entertained the group by friendly jibes at Frothingham, usually austere in public. "I am presiding this morning," he once told the group, "on the orders of President O. B. Frothingham who wishes to make believe he is one of you this morning." [82] At another time he introduced his old classmate with allusions to their early friendship.

> One day at theological school I met my fellow student Frothingham. He was then a comparatively unsuspected, seemingly innocent, virtuous, deserving young man—not one of the million crimes that have since been discovered to coil their fiery serpents around his head had then come to light—he was as good as any of us.[83]

He never let Frothingham get by without an inverted compliment before the FRA convention. However, Frothingham once turned the tables after he had been chosen again as president of the association. Higginson asked him why he had been reelected. Frothingham's reply drew laughter from the audience. He had asked the executive board, he said, "not to choose Higginson so that he himself would not be speedily forgotten." [84]

SIX

By the end of his ninth year as president, it would seem that Frothingham was less inclined to draw the battle lines between free religion and its enemies. In the fall of 1875 W. C. Gannett observed to Chadwick that he noticed at the recent Worcester meeting of the FRA that Frothingham had stressed the "R" in FRA more than ever.[85] Whether this was due to aging or to Lucretia Mott's injunction against a militant stance, or his uneasiness about Abbot and other extreme people in the association, is difficult to say. His presidential remarks in 1876 were a warning to doctrinaire liberals. No one is really free, he suggested, who cannot see the opposition's point of view. The FRA, he continued, was against no church or creed. They were against exclusiveness. To those who recalled the founding of the FRA these seemed like grievous backsliding. Abbot was certainly angered. Even John Weiss, his old and loyal friend, replied with an abrasive speech recalling the battle over the Christian preamble in Syracuse in 1866. Had he forgotten his own famed sermon on Palm Sunday in 1865? "Don't swallow thirty years of history—don't forget the built-in conflict between freedom and religion," warned Weiss.[86] "We have simply looked at the other side of the shield," replied Frothingham in ending the meeting on a harmonious note.

> Forgetting what ecclesiasticism and mistakes and dogma and evil institutions have done in the past and fixing our eyes on the future, turning our gaze inward instead of outward, we have seen how pure and eternal are the principles which are forever re-creating institutions, correcting errors,

abolishing wrongs, and sowing the wilderness of mistakes with the seeds of
truth. The two sides belong to the same thing.[87]

His own father could not have sounded more conciliatory, mild, and
optimistic about the self-corrective elements in Christianity.

It is doubtful if Weiss, Abbot, and the young Felix Adler, soon to
succeed him, were encouraged with the future of the FRA. Nor was this
all. At the 1876 meeting a discussion arose as to why the FRA did not
sympathize with the Liberal League, a reform group, to fight for separation of church and state. Frothingham stated that it did sympathize but
could not officially endorse without compromising its members' views
and violating its own constitution. Mr. John Babcock, editor of *New Age,*
asked why the FRA was not concerned with "sores of society." Did religion
mean merely scholarly discussion in beautiful language?" [88] Old Bronson
Alcott came to the defense of Frothingham's position in familiar transcendental terms. Free religion creates a "spirit and principle which leads
to reform." [89] Here was the issue drawn between the religion of humanity
and the social gospel. No one doubted that human ideas of free religion
would lead to reform. The question was, who would take the lead—and
when. Frothingham was sure it should come from individuals, not organized groups and from experts in the new sciences of society. To him,
for the Free Religious Association to do more than talk and inspire would
be a violation of its purpose. But attitudes were changing and a break in
the tradition appeared to be at hand.

The tenth anniversary meeting was devoted to reviewing the past,
recounting the achievements, and stating the goals of free religion. The
themes were familiar: science and religion [90] and freedom in religion.[91]
Yet there was a difference in the tone struck by Frothingham in his
presidential address, his next to last. A great deal of freedom of religion
had been achieved, he acknowledged, but it was freedom up to a point.
Even in New York, he observed,

> if a person holds certain opinions that go a little too far from the recognized
> center of faith . . . he is chopped from committees, is quietly left out of
> certain societies where he might be of service.

Recalling his own New York experiences, he acknowledged that he had
always been treated with respect, yet

> I can see all the time that I occupy a position alone. Because I am president
> of the Free Religious Association, because I have an independent pulpit in
> New York, somebody else is preferred to conduct this or that public meet-
> ing.[92]

It was a public confessional of disappointment. For the first time on the
FRA platform he sounded the negative note of personal complaint. Was

he disillusioned with radical religion? Was he tired of public criticism and of being ostracized by the mainstream of society? Or was there a growing feeling of dissatisfaction with his leadership of the FRA? There is no clear evidence to illuminate completely any of these questions. In his later career it was rumored that he "recanted" and wrote off his career in radical religion as a failure (see Chapter IX). It is true that he was a reluctant rebel, a man who did not shrink from combat, but who dreaded the possibility of being misunderstood or of hurting others. If his activities after the spring meeting of 1877 are a key to his attitude toward his group, there was no diminishing of his enthusiasm for the FRA. In the fall he was in New Haven, Connecticut, for the regional meeting. In January of 1878 he delivered a lecture in Horticultural Hall in Boston—"The Assailants of Christianity"—a part of the last series sponsored by the FRA. It is interesting to note that he seemed to withdraw noticeably from his earlier unequivocal view that Christianity was doomed as a decrepit stage in the evolution of religious ideas. Abbot was disturbed by Frothingham's implication that Christianity, after all, might be saved, liberalized, and broadened to absorb all contending sects.[93] Allowance might have been made for the fact that he was speaking before a general Boston audience rather than before the more receptive radicals who attended the FRA convention. Frothingham may have hoped to avoid drawing more attention to himself as a man outside the pale of Christianity and at the same time to ease the feelings of outsiders toward the more favorable view of the FRA.

Men of Abbot's turn of mind were not inclined to make allowances for Frothingham's style. Indeed, his mind was a puzzle, his actions and statements sometimes ambiguous, carrying a mixed meaning to his friends and critics alike. Perhaps he saw the handwriting of change on the wall as the spring of 1878 approached. No doubt he had discussed his plan to resign with his close friends, Samuel Johnson and T. W. Higginson, and the loyal secretary of the association, William J. Potter. Yet he revealed the thinking behind his stepping down from the presidency to Abbot, who seemed a better foil for his mind than closer friends. His reasons, he said, were not personal. It was true he was tired, he admitted, but not more than others nor more than he was prepared to be. Mainly he felt that the FRA needed a new chief, a new direction. "I have nothing new to say. I am spent." He felt a new man, a younger vigorous man with enthusiasm was needed. He was sure "Adler could do it." His scholarship and his Jewish tradition would strengthen the FRA. Turning to reasons entirely personal, Frothingham confided to Abbot,

> Moreover I speak frankly. I am not, in my estimation, a good president. I am continually making mistakes, giving offense, committing blunders. My reputation as an *aristocrat* and *man of wealth* is all against me . . . it injures the association.

Furthermore, he felt that a president should be popular and he felt that he was unpopular—more unpopular among the radicals than the conservatives, he felt. He told Abbot this was his greatest burden.

> It grieves me, saddens—almost embitters me to think of it but am forced to think of it and cannot enforce . . . [my] burden upon a cause which in itself has enough to carry on . . . Another man must carry on to do what I can only dream about. . . . I cannot rise to the occasion.

In spite of his own gloom, he thought the FRA was vital and would assume more importance and dignity as time advanced. He closed with a plea to Abbot to stay on the Board of Directors.[94]

By the time the association convened in Boston in May of 1878, Frothingham had either overcome his depression or managed to set it aside. In his last address as president, he heartily endorsed the nomination of Adler, who was absent, and assured the group that his resignation was not a sign of any lack of interest in the work of the association. His presidential address in the morning of May 30, 1878, however, did not stress freedom so much as the constructive, conservative work that needed to be done in religious thinking. The work of the FRA had just begun, he told them, and Felix Adler was the man to lead.

> I am committed to his cause. It is the old anti-slavery cause in a new aspect. . . . Therefore the FRA summons to its banner every true and loyal lover of liberty. . . . [So] that cause that now creeps and totters and falls will be the cause that carries the triumphant march far into the future.[95]

In opening the afternoon session, he reiterated an old theme of free religion. Christianity was like a tree killed by lightning "but not yet visibly dead . . . it was a passing stage in free religion." [96] His morning remarks as retiring president must have had a curiously old-fashioned sound to the younger men. His remark about the death of Christianity four months after his Horticultural Hall address, implying that Christianity could be broadened and made to absorb sectarianism, must have convinced Abbot that Frothingham was totally inconsistent and unreliable as a radical leader.

Felix Adler

(top) WILLIAM CHANNING GANNETT, HENRY W. BELLOWS
(below) JOHN WEISS, SAMUEL JOHNSON

John W. Chadwick

M. J. Savage

(top) THEODORE PARKER, FRANCIS E. ABBOT
(below) T. W. HIGGINSON, SAMUEL LONGFELLOW

(left) GEORGE RIPLEY; (right above) WILLIAM J. POTTER;
(below) GEORGE BARTOL with HENRY BELLOWS

HENRY WARD BEECHER

VI

Cloudy Wine in Broken Bottles: Free Religion and Social Action

T HE *Index*, AN INDEPENDENT WEEKLY JOURNAL closely related to the work of the FRA, was edited by Francis Abbot from 1870 to 1880 when it came under the auspices of the association. Abbot's headquarters was in Toledo, Ohio until 1873 when he moved back to Boston to be free from interference from Asa Butts, the business manager, and to be in closer contact with people of the FRA. *Index* became an official organ of the FRA when Abbot resigned the editorship in 1880. William Potter and Benjamin Underwood assumed the coeditorship until its end in 1886.

ONE

Abbot, a vigorous editor, supported the work of the FRA by devoting a column of space for the "Department of the Free Religious Association." Although this was discontinued after the first year, there was no lessening of coverage of FRA advertising and space devoted to the speeches and writings of the FRA members. It was a lively journal, doing battle with "enemies of free thought" and engaging in interchange of ideas with other liberal journals.[1] The *Index* had a reputation for quality and was respected by friends and opponents alike. Through its final year of 1886 it remained, in Stow Persons' words, "easily the finest liberal journal in America." [2]

Although the *Index* during Frothingham's time as president of the RA was not an official voice of the association, it was closely in tune with its objectives. The two were inseparably connected in the public mind. It is true that Frothingham's name appeared in some connection in nearly every issue from 1870 to 1879. After his retirement and during his sojourn in Europe, news items kept the readers of *Index* informed as to his physical condition and whereabouts. In the same way that the FRA proceedings reflected the memory of Frothingham and his continuing influence, so too did the *Index*, until 1886, keep a fairly steady commentary on the ideas and traditions established by him for the FRA.

Frothingham, though listed as a contributor, had no official connection with the *Index*, but his status as president of the FRA gave him a prominent place in its history. His *Index* work also put him and Francis Abbot into a close working relationship that went beyond the management of the FRA. Two months before the first issue of *Index* appeared in June, 1870, Frothingham wrote to Abbot encouraging him in a "troublesome job" and promised to send him articles to "fill up a gap" but warned him that the *Index* should not be used for "personal views." [3] This, of course, was exactly what the *Index* was used for. After the January issues had appeared he felt that the magazine was making an impact on the "resisters." "Let's keep it that way," he told Abbot. "You are doing manfully." [4] Younger recruits to the FRA had misgivings not only about Abbot's use of the *Index* but about the other contributors. W. C. Gannett, who felt the strongest affinity for the foundering *Radical,* complained to Chadwick that he doubted that any journal could adequately express "natural religion" with Frothingham, capable of so much bitterness, "Abbot's one-ideaness . . . Wasson and Johnson so aloof . . . and Weiss so puckish." [5]

After the first six months of its publication, Frothingham assured Abbot that he had read the issues with great "interest and on the whole, much satisfaction," but he had serious reservations about Abbot's "Fifty Affirmatives." These had appeared as flaming manifestos of religious freedom on the first page of *Index*. Although Frothingham was in basic agreement with their theme that Christianity, now in a disintegrative stage, was a step in the achievement of a universal free religion,[6] he felt that they might be toned down and condensed. The *Index*, he reminded Abbot, should avoid dogmatism and speak to people plainly, unlike the high-toned *Radical.* It should not point in direction, but lead people to "explore the dim ways." [7] His warnings to Abbot were interspersed through the early years of the *Index* with administrative advice, offers of money for its support, and plans for combining with *Radical* magazine. Sidney Morse, editor of the *Radical* and one of the original members of the committee that started the FRA, had long been in financial difficulty. Plans to merge the *Index* with the *Radical* never materialized in spite of efforts through 1873 of the FRA directors to adopt schemes to "save the *Radical.*" [8] A great deal of time was spent in assuring the sensitive Abbot that he was a valued editor and was not being degraded or insulted by fellow free religionists such as T. W. Higginson.[9] There was always the encouraging word to Abbot for a speech he had made, an article he had written,[10] and the advice to "cheer up, hang on" in his work to improve civilization.[11] In Frothingham's opinion, the *Index* continually improved in quality and Abbot did "nobly" as an editor.[12] This was true to a great extent. Even as the relationship between Frothingham and Abbot deteriorated, by 1872 the *Index* gained the respect of a small but intellectual audience of approximately 4,500 readers.[13]

TWO

Keeping the editor encouraged and in a moderate mood was important to the success of the *Index*. Frothingham's main contributions to the journal, however, were articles, editorials, and printed sermons. Virtually every issue of the weekly paper between 1870 and 1877 carried an item written by him. The first issue, January 1, 1870, described the founding of the FRA, giving Frothingham full coverage for his part in the planning of the first meeting in 1867. Two of his sermons were also cited.[14] The next issue carried a communication by Frothingham entitled "Secular Religion." It was a bold statement of the purpose of the "Religion of Humanity." "Life will not accommodate itself to religion, it is religion that must make the first move to accommodate itself to life [to] put on citizen's dress and take its chances . . . or it will be elbowed aside." [15] For the next seven years Frothingham engaged in the battle, already joined in his pulpit, against the "enemies of rationalism." In editorial after editorial in *Index* he defended the aims and procedures of the FRA, acted as peacemaker among his co-free religionists and continued a running attack on such sectarians as Henry Bellows and Henry Ward Beecher.

At one time the *Liberal Christian,* Bellows' paper, chided the FRA for not being active in social reform. Frothingham came to its defense by reiterating the point that it was not a reform group but an agent of rational thought to improve the intelligence and spirit of man.[16] At another time, Rev. Mayo of Cincinnati, Ohio, accused the FRA of demoralizing society. Frothingham's angry answer was to point out that all dissenting groups have been accused of doing this: the Catholics accused Luther; Protestants had accused the Unitarians; now Unitarians accused the FRA of the same thing. On the contrary, thought Frothingham, the Free Religious Association would renovate society.[17] In an editorial, "Call for Courage," he encouraged his coreligionists to bear up under the slights and threats of the critics of free religion and to ignore the "silly women in velvet and lace who say you are a good man but have no religion." [18]

The *Liberal Christian* criticized Frothingham's 1872 Horticultural Hall lecture, "Three Short Studies in Christianity," for not dealing properly with Unitarianism. His defense in an *Index* editorial was the acid statement, "I might have made a study of Unitarianism but microscopical studies . . . are not well adapted to general audiences." [19]

The *Christian Register* was attacked by Frothingham when it was claimed by that journal that the *New York Tribune* was his mouthpiece and ignored the sermons and full churches of other ministers. Frothingham admitted that it was true that the *Tribune* did ignore Bellows, Chapin, Hall, Prentice, Rogers, Montgomery, and sixty or seventy others because "we all know they have nothing to say." [20] Typical of personal attacks and of Frothingham's defense was his reaction to a letter published in *Index* from a Boston Unitarian accusing him of backsliding from the faith of his father.

Angered by the reference to his personal background, he answered editorially that the Unitarians never really followed through with the ideas of Channing, Norton, or Ware, never took advantage of scholarly Biblical criticisms. How could there be backsliding from this? As for his father, stated Frothingham, he was "razor sharp," never afraid to think and inquire, and always agreed with his son in spreading ideas of the new faith. "A son can justify the father only by going beyond him." [21]

Frothingham used the pages of the *Index* to attack Catholic "Jesuitism" as an enemy of freedom of conscience [22] and the Unitarians for backsliding into communion services with Trinity churches.[23] Evangelism, which he hit from his pulpit, also received broadsides in the *Index.* The Evangelical churches "hug specific doctrines and exclude other opposing creeds," wrote Frothingham.[24] Yet they attract the great masses of people due to their appeal to the heart rather than to the head. The popular preacher, however, was not a figure to admire because, he told his readers, "The great teachers have few disciples. . . . Greatness keeps people away. In London Martineau and Marice spoke to scores and hundreds while Spurgeon and Newman addressed thousands. Emerson had but a handful of disciples." [25] As for the great English evangelist, Spurgeon, Frothingham considered his style the crudest form of Bible preaching, offensive to cultivated ears. It rejected art, literature, and intelligence. It "shut out all the gates to heaven but the one that opened out of the back yard." [26]

Warning his readers in the fall of 1875 that the Evangelical team of Moody and Sanky "will soon be upon us," he feared the effect upon nonchurch members of the vapid, trashy message on arid ground from Moody, who "substitutes the fragrant words and saccharine instead of sulfur as in days of old." [27] To arm himself with ammunition to fire at the Evangelicals of New York, Frothingham attended the Hippodrome as a spectator and listened to Dwight Moody preach and Ira Sanky sing. Later he related his impressions in an *Index* editorial, "The Evangelist":

> He is no orator, does not make his points well, misses the effect of his best illustration, tells his stories clumsily, has no humor, no wit, no pathos. *He is simply a galvonic battery.* His head being set flat upon his shoulders, with no neck to limit the flow of blood to the brain, the intercourse between being and cerebellum is close. . . . Sanky sings charmingly sentimental, patriotic love songs. They address the lowest form of sensibility.[28]

The *Index* often printed criticism from orthodox quarters in order to enliven the journal and offer an opportunity for rebuttal. These exchanges often were in the form of excerpts printed from *Liberal Christian* or *Watchman and Reflector* gibing the FRA for creating the impression of being creedless while actually embracing a "liberal creed." [29] When Frothingham entered the fray it was usually to strike back at Henry Bellows' *Liberal Christian* or such orthodox Christians as Rev. McGoch,

Horace Bushnell, Mark Hopkins, and Henry Ward Beecher.[30] So militant was Frothingham at times that he refused to accommodate conflicts by rejecting the olive branch or proferred compliments from fair-minded men like the conservative Unitarians James F. Clark and his old opponent, Henry Bellows.[31] Rather, Bellows was his favorite target. In a letter to Potter he sent notes taken from Bellows' "Lenten Lectures," "so remarkable," wrote Frothingham, "that they ought to see the light." He hoped he and Abbot might "work them up and make a commentary." [32] It was clearly to be a rebuttal of Bellows' Christian view of the Easter ritual.

Final examples of Frothingham's defense of free religion against orthodox criticisms are his editorials "Radicalism and History" and "The Chruch Is Open All Summer." The first was another attack on the *Liberal Christian,* which had unfavorably reviewed John Weiss' new book on American religion. It was full of "metaphysical refinements and overstrained subtleties," claimed the reviewer. Frothingham chided the critic for not knowing enough about the history of Biblical criticism to understand the book. Radicalism, he wrote, rests on history.[33] The second was a bold challenge to the orthodox churches to close up shop in the summer as an experiment; to see if people would come back; to throw them on their own resources; to see if they really needed to go to church. It was a challenge from his free church, "We therefore announce: 'This church is not open all summer.' " [34]

THREE

At the same time that Frothingham was doing battle with groups and individuals hostile to his view of free religion, the pages of the *Index* reflected the growing disagreements between him and Abbot. In spite of disclaimers to the contrary, it was impossible to hide the fact that the *Index* was the voice of the Free Religious Association. All of the editorial contributors were members of the FRA, some holding high office: Frothingham, president; Potter, secretary; Hallowell, treasurer; Higginson, a vice president; and Abbot, editor of *Index* and one of the most vocal members present at the FRA conventions. In spite of Frothingham's unofficial status with the *Index,* his opinions carried great weight as disagreements arose over the policy and future role of the FRA. Increasingly Frothingham took issue with Abbot in the pages of the *Index.*

Frothingham and Abbot had disagreed as to organization and creed from the very beginning. Frothingham continued to raise objections to an exclusive policy for the FRA and a creedal approach for the *Index.* Early in the life of the journal, Frothingham editorialized on "A Predicted Peril." It was a warning against exclusiveness and in opposition to changing the name of the FRA to keep out conservatives. The aims and objectives must be wide open and must welcome unpopularity within its ranks, wrote Frothingham.[35] Abbot's name was not mentioned, but it was clear it was the same type of caution that Frothingham had raised with Abbot from the beginning of the FRA. By 1873 Frothingham felt it was necessary to remind readers (and Abbot) that the FRA and the *Index* were different things. In an editorial, "The *Index* and the FRA," Frothingham tried to disassociate Abbot's attempt to organize the Liberal League and the nonactivist, intellectual aims of the FRA.[36] A series of editorials followed, stating opposition to organization for specific causes and warning against fanaticism. It was clear that Frothingham feared Abbot's dogmatism as much, if not more, than he disapproved of the enemies of free religion.[37] Though Abbot's name was not mentioned in these editorials against dogmatism, in other *Index* communications Frothingham came to grips with Abbot openly. In an exchange of letters, printed in the *Index* in 1871, he and Abbot debated as to the place of Christianity in free religion. Abbot claimed that one must be either for or against, either "extra Christian or anti Christian." Frothingham, characteristically took issue, claiming a moderate position, that the good in Christianity should be recognized even by the radicals.[38] Later, Frothingham warned that radicals should not simply write off all Christian clergymen as ignorant people who blindly cling to an absurd system.[39] Taking specific issue with Abbot's "Demands of Liberalism," published in *Index,* Frothingham disagreed with Abbot's total rejection of the Bible. It should be used as a literary classic and not, of course, as a religious book which the liberal-minded Abbot had criticized.[40] The lines were being drawn between him and the editor. By 1878 the two men read the future differently—Abbot claiming that Christianity was decrepit and dangerous; Frothingham feeling that an enlivened Christianity might have a bright future.[41] Cyrus Bartol supported Frothingham's moderation and cautioned the FRA, though not Abbot specifically, against an overaggressive policy toward established religions.[42] Ironically, Frothingham usually disagreed with Bartol on theological grounds in spite of his early encouragement of the FRA movement.[43]

The conflict between Abbot and Frothingham probably detracted from the effectiveness of *Index* for some readers. One dissatisfied reader wrote to W. C. Gannett, as the Abbot—Frothingham split became evident, that although he liked Gannett's contribution to *Index* he felt "impoverished by OBF" and others of "like characteristics." [44] The *Christian Register* predicted a split in the FRA as a result of Abbot's and Frothingham's disagreements on creedal uniformity. Frothingham, commenting on the *Register* opinion, doubted a split was coming but warned the FRA once more against insisting on creedal conformity but "if a split comes," he wrote, "let it, as a healthy sign." [45]

A split never occurred but the chasm between him and Abbot widened until Frothingham cancelled his subscription to the *Index* in 1878, a move which coincided with his decision to retire as president of the FRA.

During these last five years of Frothingham's FRA activities two issues, the "*Index* troubles" and his part in the Liberal League, clouded their relationship.[46] The *Index* had never run smoothly while Abbot was in Toledo, Ohio. Financial support came from David Lock, editor of the *Toledo Blade*, and Albert Cacomber. Asa Butts, business manager and largest single stockholder, was associated with Abbot in producing the weekly journal. Abbot, never easy to work with, got into difficulties immediately. By 1873, there were mutual accusations of inefficiency and unethical conduct. The officials of the FRA, also stockholders in the Index Association, came to Abbot's rescue when the Board of Directors voted to oust him as editor. By a large proxy vote from the FRA members turned in by Higginson he was reinstated as editor and the *Index* was moved to Boston.[47]

This was only the beginning of the "*Index* troubles." Abbot, being convinced that Asa Butts, the business manager, had misappropriated *Index* funds for personal use, published a circular of accusations in *Index*, signed by the officers of the FRA.[48] Asa Butts then launched a law suit for libel against the signers of the circular. As one of the signers, Frothingham became involved at this point. Even before the circular appeared, Frothingham had cautioned Abbot against forcing a breach with Butts which might destroy the *Index*.[49] After the circular, with the law suit threatening, he was militantly supporting Abbot, promising to meet Butts squarely and "if he attacks, to strike from the shoulder and hit as hard as I can."[50] A month later, with Butts' threat of a suit quiescent, he cautioned Abbot to "be prepared" for the worst.[51]

Although the worst never happened in the form of a libel suit, the issue dragged on for the next three years involving Frothingham in the double accusation, from Butts that he had signed a libelous document, and from Abbot that he was a vacillating and unreliable colleague. Butts had assumed that Abbot had "forged" Frothingham's name on the circular. Goaded by Asa Butts to explain his action of March, 1874, Frothingham wrote a communication to the *Truthseeker* explaining why he had signed the circular accusing Butts of improper conduct. He had read it hurriedly in a New York meeting of *Index* stockholders, he claimed. It was signed by him as an offical of the FRA only and not as endorsing the accusation against Butts.[52] Abbot's reaction was as might be expected. He accused Frothingham of being a treacherous man by refusing to confront Butts with the issue of misuse of *Index* funds. In Abbot's opinion, Frothingham had backed away from his bold stance of four years earlier.[53] Frothingham, much hurt by Abbot's reaction, chided him for not knowing he was not against him in the affair as explained in *Truthseeker*.[54] It was obvious to Butts that Frothingham was innocent of libel against him but was trying to shield Abbot from his attacks in the affair. To Abbot it was clear that Frothingham had not been forthright, that he had tried to straddle the issue and appear in a favorable light to both men.[55]

FOUR

Abbot, always eager to commit the FRA to social causes, led a drive in 1875 to establish the National Liberal League to oppose the growing sectarian impact on secular institutions. The league was formed to oppose the efforts of orthodox Protestant denominations in their efforts after 1873 to legalize Bible teaching in public schools and to get a Christian amendment in the federal constitution.[56] Although Frothingham sympathized with the objectives of the league, he rejected a leadership role and disagreed with the fanatical direction the league took under Abbot's presidency after 1875. Frothingham's part in this development caused him to pursue a torturous zigzag course which baffled and angered Abbot but was characteristic of many other less sectarian-minded men in the FRA. As early as 1872 Frothingham wrote to Abbot criticizing Rev. Mayo's recent lecture advocating the use of the Bible in the schools and requesting petitions for his congregation to sign advocating an "anti-Christian amendment" to the constitution. He encouraged Abbot in leading a movement against sectarianism but disclaimed any desire to be a part of it.

> I can criticize, can judge, can support, but I cannot lead a movement—for I do not *move*. For this reason I cannot share your feeling though, of course, I share your convictions in regard to the constitutional amendment.[57]

The following year in *Index* he editorialized on "Christ in the Constitution" identifying bishops, governors, presidents, and professors at the recent Cooper Union meeting of the National Association for a Religious Amendment to the Constitution, who accused Abbot and others of attempting to "un-Americanize the American people." He defended Abbot but ended with the disarming comment that the group was "not a serious threat." [58] Yet two years later he was being praised by such colleagues as A. K. Stevens for his *Index* editorial, "Concentrate," in which he encouraged liberals to focus upon the issue:

> The release of civil power from ecclesiastical influence and the overflow of authority in the realm of the mind—the complete separation of church and state . . . people are waiting to be led in this effort.[59]

But when the opportunity came in July, 1875, to go to Philadelphia to help organize the Liberal League on a national scale he refused, quipping to Abbot that he hoped he would have a good time. "The city seems to me wholly given over to the centennial. But you may succeed in getting a cock by the ear." [60] When the results of the Philadelphia meeting were published in *Index* it looked as though the National Liberal League was an adjunct of the FRA. Abbot was president and among the twenty-four vice presidents were the names of FRA officers: Frothingham, Potter, Hallowell, and other active members—Minot Savage, Issac Wise, Garlan Spencer, and Robert Dale Owen. The thirty resolutions adopted at the Philadelphia meeting stated the case boldly against sectarian influence in secular life.[61]

Just why Frothingham, so indifferent to the organization of the league, should allow his name to be listed as a vice president, is not clear. Perhaps he dreaded to break ranks with his coreligionists or to offend Abbot further, though he was ideologically allied with those who stood up for checking sectarian influence in schools and political institutions.[62] Nevertheless the Liberal League was the issue that accelerated the alienation between Abbot and Frothingham. After the Philadelphia meeting Abbot complained that Frothingham was losing interest in writing for the *Index.* Frothingham assured him he was not, but gave excuses why he had not been as attentive to the editorial needs. He was writing his history of the transcendental movement and editing articles for a "popular encyclopedia," he told Abbot. As for the Liberal League, he was not suited to it. Young men are needed, he thought, whose "battles are ahead and not behind them." Apparently he was also feeling his age and preoccupied with "depressing thoughts of a private and personal nature." Still, he promised to try to stir himself to talk to Potter about doing more for the League through the FRA.[63]

Abbot, never satisfied with the response of Frothingham or his other FRA colleagues, became more sensitive to their slights, both imagined and real, and resigned from the editorship in 1877. Frothingham attempted to assure him he had not forgotten the *Index* though he admitted he was working with Russell Bellows to "help make the *Inquirer* a radical paper." He was sure it would not conflict with the *Index.*[64] The association had nothing against him, Frothingham repeated in letter after letter. As for himself, he told the temperamental editor, "I am innocent as the newly born child of the least . . . unkindness . . . toward you personally or otherwise." [65] No one had any personal grievance against him, Frothingham wrote, neither T. W. Higginson nor William Chadwick. All felt, he assured him, that his resignation would "stultify and fatally compromise the FRA." [66]

With feelings assuaged, Abbot remained with the *Index* for three more years, but the Liberal League issue remained. It was Abbot's determination to turn the Liberal League into an instrument for political action. In the fall of 1877 the first annual meeting of the National Liberal League met at Rochester, New York. Frothingham, as a vice-president, refused to go because he knew Abbot planned to propose the formation of the "National Conscience Party"—a catchall reform party for civil rights, women's rights, separation of church and state, and universal education. "The ultimate end and purpose of it," wrote Frothingham to Abbot on the eve of the conference, "commands my full sympathy—but my antipathy

to political methods is so great and my faith in political action so small that
I could not go there with any force of conviction." This was his nature, he
said, even though it grieved his best and valued friends.[67]

Abbot, no doubt, was grieved by Frothingham's reluctance to act. Even
more grievous to him was the defeat of his plans for a political party.
Although his plan for political action was accepted at Rochester and won
the support of D. M. Bennett of the *Truthseeker,* the party was never
formed. The extreme freethinkers in the National Liberal League, such
as Bennett, Ezra Heywood, and Robert Ingersoll, attracted the attention
of Anthony Comstock. This self-appointed guardian of public morals,
backed by Protestant laymen and YMCA groups, had been instrumental
in the postal law of 1873 and 1876 banning obscenity in the mails. His
name became a part of speech, "comstockery" being synonymous in
liberal parlance with narrow, fanatical incursions on private freedoms.
After Comstock had instigated law suits for obscenity against Heywood
for his free love pamphlet, *Cupid's Yoke,* and D. M. Bennett for circulating
his "Open Letter to Jesus Christ," it seemed clear that he was not prepared
to make the distinction between freethinking and allegations of pornog-
raphy and atheism. There were no serious consequences to the persons
involved, but the effect of Comstock's attack was to polarize the National
Liberal League. What started out as a group to get repeal of certain postal
laws as a limitation on freedom of speech became, in the public mind
agitated by Comstock, a group of people advocating obscenity, pornog-
raphy, free love, and atheism. Frothingham would have nothing to do
with a crusade against sin led by Comstock. To him and most of the FRA
men this was too closely allied to the evangelical movement and a natural
offshoot of the orthodox campaign they had all fought against since the
Civil War. Yet he continued to support Abbot's attempts to hold the
Liberal League to its original purpose—that of maintaining the
separatism of church and state. He did not hesitate to attend the meetings
of the local New York auxiliary Liberal League and speak before the
assemblies. In March, 1877, he told the New York group that the league
had been misunderstood by the public because it had become involved in
extraneous issues. The Liberal League was conservative, not liberal or
radical, he pointed out. Its one aim was the conservative one of maintaining the separation of church and state; its goal was that of the "anti-
Christian amendment to the constitution." [68] At a later meeting he was
called to the platform and lifted the meeting by his "genial presence" in
"one of his happiest impromptu speeches." [69]

Another general meeting of the National Liberal League was planned
for the fall of 1878 in Syracuse, New York. Abbot was primed to go and
moderate between the extremists who wanted to fight against the "Comstock laws" and reformers such as himself who felt that civil rights,
women's suffrage, and separation of church and state and some control

over obscenity were the main goals. At this point most of the FRA men withdrew over the extraneous issue of the "Comstock laws." [70] Frothingham continued to encourage Abbot by sending money and agreeing ambiguously with him that the postal laws needed revising though obscenity should be checked at the place it occurred. At the same time he disassociated himself from the approaching meeting in Syracuse with a vague reference to Robert Ingersoll as "a tower of strength on your side." [71]

He felt some guilt for not standing beside Abbot at Rochester when the extremists seemed to get the upper hand. With Comstock dominating the league it seemed evident that it would be even more difficult to keep the league on its original track. "What a pity," he wrote to Abbot before the Syracuse conference, that Comstock "will confound the issues and plant blame in the wrong places!" What a pity that all liberals (meaning the extremists) could not see the difference between spiritual liberty and "fleshy license." [72] As predicted, the league split over the Comstock issue at Syracuse in the fall of 1878. Abbot was repudiated by the anti-Comstock extremists who took control of the Liberal League. Abbot and the "moderates" formed a rival group. The result of the schism was the early demise of both groups. After the meeting, which Frothingham did not attend, he wrote an angry letter to Abbot requesting him to remove his name as a vice president of the National Liberal League. The league had been corrupted, he thought, by going out on extraneous issues with which he disagreed. Regretfully but firmly he requested also that Abbot remove his name from the list of contributors to *Index*. [73]

Somewhat mellowed a few days later, he wrote Abbot again, asking him not to publish his note of the previous week. He reiterated his reason for withdrawing from the league and added another—ill health made it necessary to "cut off all but necessary mental effort." [74] This was the first premonition of his approaching illness that would contribute to his decision to retire the following spring. By November, 1878, Frothingham's name was dropped from the Liberal League. A brief account in *Index* recounted the reasons and expressed the hope that if harmony was restored his "interest might revive." [75] But there was to be no more harmony or revival of interest. Abbot, still sore from his defeat at Syracuse and smarting from what he considered Frothingham's defection from liberal ranks, published in *Index* a private note from Frothingham indicating that he had favored the repeal of the "Comstock laws." The implication was that the president of the FRA was guilty of duplicity. He thought one way and acted in another. Frothingham's reaction was a stiff letter accusing Abbot of intolerance and dogmatism. He blasted Abbot for continually "putting the worst construction on the actions of his colleagues." "Self-respect compelled" him to request that his subscription to the *Index* be cancelled. [76]

This was the end for the two men. Given their different temperaments, the break was inevitable. By the end of the year Frothingham would be retired and be in Europe; a year later Abbott would retire from the *Index* and give up programs of political action to pursue philosophic writing and attempts at teaching in the Philosophy Department at Harvard.[77]

There is no doubt that to a man of Abbot's frame of mind, Frothingham was at times devious in his actions and ambiguous in his statements. His Olympian view, his tolerance of opposing views, to Abbot was simply a failure of nerve. Frothingham's wealth, his social status, his complete confidence in his own abilities, and his security with associates were threats to Abbot. Frothingham's success in scholarly writing, his ability to hold groups together—his own free church and the diverse elements in the FRA—were in contrast to Abbot's failures at Dover, New Hampshire, and Toledo, Ohio. But perhaps the two men needed each other during the battles they jointly fought for the cause of free religion. Abbot was an able editor of *Index* and he doubtless kept the reluctant Frothingham moving on a more aggressive course than he otherwise would. Yet it was Abbot's fanaticism that was his undoing and the point upon which his relation with Frothingham broke. By temperament Abbot had more spiritual affinity to the religious fanatics and antisin crusaders than with the religious radicals and social liberals within the FRA. By his own admission he found it easier by 1881 to talk to Anthony Comstock than to O. B. Frothingham. He was, indeed, as Sidney Ahlstrom has pointed out, "the Anthony Comstock of Free Religion." [78]

In contrast to Abbot's failure to guide the Liberal League on a cautious and viable course of action that might have unified the group for political action, Frothingham's policy as president of the FRA seems sound and successful. By avoiding extremes, by insisting on free and open discussion, by avoiding polarizing along ideological lines, by remaining a well-organized group of loosely organized individualists, the FRA and its *Index* magazine served as a broad arena where some of the best thoughts of the age could be expressed. If the FRA promoted a new Religion of Humanity that established a reform spirit in the last half of the nineteenth century, then Octavius Frothingham is indeed a prophet of the Social Gospel which followed.

FIVE

At the twelfth annual Boston meeting May 29 and 30 of 1879, there was a noticeable change of atmosphere and an apparently new departure in the making. The Directors' report mentioned the autumn regional conference in Providence, Rhode Island, but admitted to "less active work than in previous years since the Association came into existence." The treasury was depleted, making necessary the suspension of the winter lecture series in Horticultural Hall. Both John Weiss and William Garrison had died that year. Frothingham sent a message of regrets that due to "broken health" he had retired from liberal religion to seek rest abroad but hoped to soon "return and resume." [79]

Felix Adler, the new president, took hold vigorously, devoting the morning session to a defense of Frothingham's ideas. He rejected the suggestion that his retirement was a sign of his failure and refuted the rumor that he "recanted" his radical views before leaving for Europe a few weeks earlier. Adler saw Frothingham as representing the first stage of free religion—that of individualism, of breaking ground in people's minds. The newspapers had misinterpreted Frothingham's last address, said Adler, in concluding that the first phase which was over was a failure. His last speech was eloquent, thought Adler. "He dwelt upon the necessity of practical work, humanitarian work; he demanded effective organization . . . not even a shadow of a doubt obscured his vision." [80] But the new president was a different sort, more like Abbot, more militant than Frothingham, given to dramatic, extreme, and sometimes exclusive language. He was no harmonizer, no enigma, though perhaps an inspirer to some. All knew what Adler thought and where he stood. The afternoon session led by him was a clear call for a national organization, expanded membership, a journal, and a commitment to social action. Abbot seconded these suggestions with a fighting speech for the need for practical work from the FRA. Higginson disagreed with the expansion of the FRA and attempts to turn it into a social reform group.[81] The line was drawn between the "old and new" guard; a turning point had apparently been reached. With Frothingham retired, Abbot carried on a lively correspondence with Adler proposing ideas for the new approach to social activism, including among other plans one to establish a training school for a radical clergy.[82]

The new departure, however, was more apparent than real. After three years of futile efforts to turn the FRA into a reform organization Adler resigned in 1882, and social action attempts were dropped at this point. Efforts to organize nationally were not successful and there were continual money problems. In spite of the formal merging of the FRA and *Index* magazine in 1880 a strong national voice for the organization could not be established although the *Index* continued publication until 1886. The Free Religious Association came no closer to social action than occasional appearances on their platform of such men as William D. P Bliss of the Church of the Carpenter in Boston, who delivered a fiery address on Christian socialism in 1895.[83] Minot Savage, who moved from Congregationalism through Unitarianism to the social gospel, acknowledged his debt to Frothingham's influence and ideas.[84] Wendell Phillips, active in the post-Civil War battles for economic equality for labor, was a frequent speaker at FRA meetings in the early years of its activities. These verbal calls for social action continued sporadically at the conventions until World War I.

After Adler departed the FRA fell back into the hands of those in the "old tradition" established by Frothingham, Higginson, Towne, and Potter, in spite of Abbot. The annual spring meetings in Boston continued with their usual eloquence but in a self-satisfied atmosphere with much of the old excitement gone. Stow Persons has written that the FRA began to slowly atrophy after 1883.[85] Although the speakers continued to inspire and prophesy better days, it was true that much time was spent in looking back and recalling memories of what seemed to be better days and greater people. In the spring of 1887 William J. Potter, then president of the FRA, presided over a sentimental gathering at the twentieth anniversary. On the platform sat Octavius Frothingham, back from Europe and then permanently retired in Boston. Higginson was there and so was Moncure Conway, and Minot Savage. As the applause for him died down, Potter introduced his old friend, a founder and former president of the association. Frothingham's remarks were brief, humorous, but optimistic. As he looked around at the audience, noticing the large number of Unitarian ministers in the group, he observed that the FRA had accomplished its aim—that of bringing Unitarianism up to the universality of the FRA. "Twenty years of chatter" had done some good, he concluded.[86]

He was back again in 1894 where the meeting was held, fittingly, in Parker Memorial Hall. Memories filled the room as Frothingham sat on the platform with old friends of earlier days—Abbot, Chadwick, and Edna Cheney. Higginson, presiding, introduced him as the man who should be "the presiding officer of the day." In a spontaneous expression of esteem the audience came to its feet as Frothingham rose to speak. It was apparent that his chronic nervous disorder that had contributed to his decision to retire had not fatally affected his powers of speech—certainly not the powers of his mind. It was an extemporaneous speech, "delivered with much of his old fire." Again he was optimistic, predicting the end of sectarianism and congratulating the FRA for helping the churches move toward a universal religion. The reception deeply touched him, he admitted, and he apologized for not being able to "fittingly respond." Yet he must have pleased his old comrades, save Abbot, when he recalled that "my trust is in the logos more than in logic . . . spiritual ideas drive the world forward." His last sentence was couched in militant terms for which Lucretia Mott, had she been there, would have chided him. "Our business is to hold up our banner and march under it ever to the end." [87] It was his last appearance and a fitting epitaph.

It was true that the free religionists had followed his banner since 1867. After he was gone it was as though he continued to lead from the grave. A. N. Alcott acknowledged that O. B. Frothingham had preached the "first liberal sermon he had ever heard." [88] The spring conference in 1896 was devoted largely to memorial addresses to Frothingham, who had died the previous November. Minot Savage read a paper about Frothingham's influence on free thought. Rev. Celia P. Wooly acknowledged having read the works of Weiss, Bartol, Wasson, and Frothingham and being drawn toward radical religion. Rev. E. H. Horton recalled Frothingham's influence on him during his Divinity School days at Meadville Seminary.[89] He had been dead scarcely a year when his former colleagues began linking his name with Emerson, Parker, Lucretia Mott, and Lydia Child as "our great dead." [90] In 1900 Higginson gave a major address to Frothingham's memory, much of which he had given previously before the Massachusetts Historical Society shortly after Frothingham's death. It was one of six addresses around the theme of the convention, "Prophets and Pioneers of Free Religion." [91] At the fortieth anniversary meeting in 1907, Henry Blanchard, a Universalist who was on the platform at Horticultural Hall on Founding Day in 1867, reminisced:

> Octavius B. Frothingham has always stood before me as one of the noblest examples of a consecrated soul. His courage was so great, his earnestness was so deep, his power of language was so admirable that wherever he stood to speak to men they felt that here was not only a gentleman and a polished scholar but an earnest, sincere, devoted man.[92]

Blanchard's comments were typical of the previous ones—glowing eulogistic testimonials to the towering influence of Octavius Brooks Frothingham. But they were the last. Abbot, who had died in 1903, remained silent to the end.

The year 1910 virtually marked the beginning of Frothingham's drop into obscurity. The FRA meeting that year observed the "Parker Centennial" and the fiftieth year since his death. Of all the speeches on Parker, none mentioned Frothingham as his heir nor referred to his 1860 sermon on Parker. Even the aged Higginson, there to give what he knew was his "last speech," was silent about his lifelong friend. John Haynes Holmes, in Henry Bellows' old church in New York, represented a new generation of free religionists who could not be expected to feel close to the old tradition.[93] Only Paul Revere Frothingham, nephew of Octavius, remained to recall his memory in brief references to his "respected and much loved uncle," while functioning as secretary or presiding at FRA meetings.[94]

Little remains to be said about the FRA after Frothingham's generation had passed out of the picture. President Charles Wendt, at the full tide of the "Progressive movement" in 1911, called for more practical work on social problems; in 1912 Rabbi Flescher gave a fighting speech against anticlericism; and Walter Raushenbusch, famed social gospel spokesman, was invited in 1913 to speak on social responsibility of churches, but could not attend.[95] By 1914 it was really all over, World War I having drawn an iron curtain across this and most other humanitarian efforts. No *Proceed-*

ings were published after this date; only programs were printed until 1924, the date of the last meeting. The FRA, with very little shadow and no substance, lived on in a "state of suspended animation" until 1938.[96]

By the time that the FRA ceased to function, it is safe to say that Octavius Frothingham was virtually forgotten. By the severe standards of concrete results, it could be said that his work was a failure. In 1907 Rabbi Stephen Wise asserted before an FRA meeting, "The Free Religious Association will not have done its work until every church in the land shall have become a free religious association. [97] By this test Frothingham, who continually predicted the end of sectarianism, certainly failed in his FRA work. In his own memoirs, written four years before he died, he felt that the FRA had helped liberalize Unitarianism and to infuse an ecumenical spirit among denominations. As for the end of sectarianism, he went no further than to suggest that the rational broad church idea was spreading.[98] However, when in a dark mood, he was sure he had failed. But his successors in the FRA were more generous in their appraisal of his work. Stephen Wise in 1907 congratulated the association for avoiding organization and of being uninstitutionalized. Had Frothingham failed, he asked, because his free church in New York no longer existed or that the free church movement led by him failed to incorporate itself in an enduring institution? He thought not. "The aim of the Free Religious Association," he recalled, "is not so much to establish new churches . . . as to re-establish bases of free, spiritual, universal religion." [99] Frothingham, he felt, had contributed to this. Charles W. Wendt, in addressing the association as president in 1911, was not so sure. In his sketch of liberal religious progress, he thought that the FRA had made little impact on other denominations. Its main impact had been to liberalize Unitarians who now held major offices in the association and could attend without being ostracized.[100] Frothingham had observed this himself on his return to the FRA convention in 1887 (see p.____). The most visible evidence of change in Unitarian thinking came from the Unitarian National Conference in 1882. It was there that the group accepted an amendment to the constitution presented by Minot Savage disclaiming any authoritative test of Unitarianism. The bitter memories of the Syracuse conference in 1866 could be forgotten. In the words of Stow Persons,

> In accepting the amendment Unitarians were tacitly admitting that the Lordship of Christ had become a dead letter. Abbot and Potter spurned this negative commitment hoping for a positive pledge of an allegiance to spiritual freedom, but the majority of free religionists gradually returned to the Unitarian fold.[101]

It could be said with equal validity that after the work of the FRA was done, the Unitarian denomination came into the fold of free religion. Perhaps Henry Bellows was farsighted in his comment to Frederich

Hedge before the Unitarian controversy began. "The real life in our body is in the heretical wing; if we cut it off there is nothing to move with." [102] Frothingham was the leader of the heretics and the prophet of radical religion. Cut off from the mainstream, they moved ahead. It was the Unitarian denomination that had to catch up.

VII

Intellectual Adventure: Historian and Critic

FROTHINGHAM WOULD HAVE, PERHAPS, REJECTED the encomium of prophet. Unlike Higginson, who has been called a dilettante, and Parker, whose learning was more prodigious than profound, Frothingham's intellectual efforts thrust in certain well-defined directions. Unwilling to be confined exclusively to the category of theologian, or even of the spokesman of the "new faith," he wrote biography, intellectual history, and journalistic comments on social questions. He was a critic of the drama and a protagonist in philosophic debates in the leading journals of America. He was an engaged mind that guided his pen, if not his personal activism, in the main currents of intellectual life.

With a large following established in his own church and a series of scholarly theological articles done for the *Christian Examiner,* he had an audience large enough to satisfy most men. Yet in the last months of the Civil War he wrote to Charles E. Norton, editor of the *North American Review,* of the importance of the pen as well as the sermon in educating the public after the war.[1] He would be a part of it.

ONE

His intellectual ventures brought him into contact with the literati of his age—writers, literary hopefuls, and editors. To begin his writing for the *North American Review* in 1864, he presented a translation of Ernest Renan's *Studies of Religious History and Criticism.*[2] Between his biography of Parker and his study of New England transcendentalism, he collaborated with E. L. Youmans in translating M. E. Cazelle's *Outlook of the Evolutionary Philosophy.*[3] Fastidious in his literary tastes, with a drive toward perfection, he often became a prickly and quarrelsome critic. To Charles Elliot, editor of *North American Review,* were the cordial letters requesting books to review or essays to write, assuring him that he could trust his "good taste and delicacy" to cut an article or improve the force of a phrase without the "least sensitiveness on the matter." [4] Yet he could decline to review an author's work as not a good specimen of the person's work and insist on reviewing a book written by a relative.[5] After agreeing to Norton's cutting of the review, he would then complain of the shorter piece, insisting on a "full" review in the next issue of some other author's work.[6] It was an uneasy relationship, between author and editor, yet Frothingham's contributions to the *North American Review,* beginning during his New York career, continued into his retirement years in Boston.

With women seeking to be his literary peers, he was particularly edgy. Caroline Dall of Boston, who Frothingham confided to Francis Abbot made him "choke a little" but admitting she had "more intelligence than any of them," [7] was continually after him for his opinion of her literary efforts while soliciting his support for her reformist schemes. Always cordial, with "kindest regards" to her and her husband, Frothingham devastated her essays and books sent to him with understated criticism for lack of scholarship or a style he considered "flurried here and there." [8] He refused to encourage her plans for a literary journal or reform attempts, rejecting requests for monetary contributions.[9] She accused him of timidity and attacked him in a "letter-written bombardment" for diminishing her literary reputation. Finally he apologized for incidents and remarks of "long ago" which he could no longer recall.[10]

Kate Fields, the biographer of stage figures, drama critic, and would-be literary critic, he considered his "dear friend." She sought him out for his literary opinion of her poems or to help sponsor literary and drama projects.[11] After reading page proofs of one of his editorial efforts, he could not approve of the poetry it contained or "a man [one of the writers] who applauds General Ritter and vilifies General Grant." [12] As to her own poetry, he was kind but brutally frank. "Your poems interest me strongly from the evident power they display. . . . You see, my dear friend—the truth is that your lines contain poetry [but] the whole truth is that they are not quite poetic." [13] He dissected a poem line by line, suggesting different words with the hope that she could improve with practice and patience. He was more patient with her than Mark Twain, who considered her, as a lecturer, "a house emptier." [14] During the depression of the 1870s he discouraged her visionary scheme to establish a Shakespearean Theater. "Money will be needed," he reminded her. "Times are hard [and] money hard to come by for even *human wants.*" The project was a good one, he thought, but doubted if it would be one that "quickens the roots of self-denial in a New Yorker, making him cheerfully resolved to wear his old boots till they drop off his feet in order that he may put . . . a fair coin . . . into the Shakespearean [project]." [15] Although Frothingham remained cordial to Caroline Dall and sincerely friendly to Kate Fields, no literary efforts were forthcoming. His role as mentor to women, reluctantly assumed, was never successful. His temperament seemed not to thrive in the presence of women and, unlike his friend Higginson, he never discovered an Emily Dickinson.

He was content to confide in his friend E. C. Stedman concerning judgment of poetry, and pursue his own writing of books and magazine articles on subjects compatible with his own intellectual tastes.[16]

TWO

It was his major religious work, *The Religion of Humanity*[17] published in 1873, that gave him the reputation among the reading public as an author who expressed high-flown thoughts in an elegant writing style. His own colleagues accepted it as the expression of thc best ideas of the age.[18] Today the book is the most cited of Frothingham's works by intellectual historians attempting to recapture his central ideas. In its day, the book represented to those outside of the Free Religious Movement a fearsome challenge. It was characteristic of the type of writing that stimulated the rather typical remark from a review of one of Frothingham's later books, *Cradle of Christ:* "Mr. Frothingham is *bete noire* to a respectable portion of the reading public . . . he has assumed the ability to see the farther side of things." [19] The book itself was no more radical than his sermons and more moderate in tone. Yet it was his attempt to always see the "farther side of things" that caused him to undertake the writing of history and biography on difficult subjects of a controversial nature.

The *Life of Theodore Parker,* his first major historical work of biography, was a difficult enough subject. Even though the controversies of Parker's time had been either decided or resolved, there was challenge enough in the writing to engage Frothingham's energies at a time when the *Index* and the Free Religious Association might have claimed all of a lesser man's time. It seems incredible that he could have done all of the writing in the summer of 1873. Yet this seems to have been the case. In April Abbot announced in *Index* that Frothingham would write it with the "approval and cooperation of Mrs. Parker," assuring the readers that "it is a noble life in the hands of a most fit biographer." [20] No doubt Frothingham had done much research previously and his personal memories of Parker were a ready source. "Preparation of it was a delight," he wrote Samuel Johnson, "a happier summer I never spent." [21]

The biography itself, almost six hundred pages in length, was a literary triumph but, by modern standards, overlong and crammed with too many quotations. Yet it was an improvement on John Weiss' two volumes published in 1864, which were essentially volumes of letters.[22] Useful for the preservation of many of Parker's letters, Frothingham paid respects to Weiss' work in the preface to his own book. The space devoted to letters in the Weiss biography, he thought, blurred the outlines of Parker's individuality, yet the volumes were invaluable for the serious student wishing details of Parker's life. "The author's aim," wrote Frothingham of his own work, "has been to simply recover and present the person of Mr. Parker with all simplicity, omitting some details which Mr. Weiss' valuable biography will supply to the more searching student." [23] Henry Commager, the most recent biographer of Parker, was more severe on the Weiss biography, judging it "ill digested and wretchedly arranged" but invaluable for preserving some of Parker's correspondence, later lost.[24] The Frothingham biography, which Commager considered the best up to that time, is of interest to us here only as it throws light on the author, as historian and critic.

To capture the atmosphere of Parker's "plebian" origins, Frothingham made the trip to Lexington on foot in the spring of 1873. He searched for the Parker house where Theodore's grandfather departed to muster his small troop of men and ready them for their skirmish with the British. He examined cemeteries and old landmarks of Theodore's childhood. After encountering a native working on the road with a spade, he was disappointed with the rustic atmosphere and the rude attitude of the road worker, who could not recall the name of Theodore Parker or even his grandfather, Captain Parker. His exasperating directions caused a reaction in Frothingham not unlike that of cultured British travelers to rural spots in Western America. "This incident [with the road worker] tells many things," he wrote in the opening of the first chapter, "the limited influence of a great man's name; the power of association to glorify ordinary spots; the absence of neighborly feelings in rural populations; and the crudeness of Society within ten miles of the great city." [25] More at home in Florence, Italy, or Boston than Lexington, Massachusetts, his reaction was typical of the urbane Brahmin that he truly was.

As the biography progressed, he recounted the events of Parker's life and the environment in which he grew. This he did with the accuracy and charm of straight narrative descriptive history. But he was more at home in the realm of ideas—in the intellectual milieu in which Parker fought his battles for religious radicalism and social equality. Of the transcendental environment which surrounded Parker in his early ministry and himself at Harvard College, he wrote,

> The Ferment of Thought . . . was a remarkable agitation of mind that went on in Massachusetts thirty years ago; all institutions and all ideas went into the furnace of reason; . . . It did not seem to be communicated, to be spread by contagion but was rather an intellectual experience produced by latent causes which were active in the air. No special class of people was responsible for it, or affected by it. While in Boston the little group of transcendentalists—Channing, Ripley, Margaret Fuller, Emerson, Alcott, Francis, Hedge, Parker—were discussing the problems of philosophy at the Tremont House and elsewhere, the farmers in the country and plain folks of Cape Cod were as full of the new spirit as they and were reaching, though from the opposite region of common sense, the same intrepid conclusions.[26]

His mysticism concerning the spread of transcendentalism, "in the air," must be discounted as merely symbolic language. However, he showed no snobbery toward plain folks, fully as able as the Boston intellectuals, he felt, to capture the spirit of the age.

Frothingham clearly revealed his own bias in recounting Parker's part in the "Unitarian controversy." Parker was the hero of the battle with the conservatives which included Frothingham's own father, performing as the "Luther" of the radical movement. One is tempted to read into Frothingham's comments autobiographical references related to his own conflicts with the Unitarian associates of his time. He could not resist a dig at the Boston ministers who ostracized, if not excommunicated, Parker in 1843. They had read the German books, he admitted, but continued to "pass on the old theology." They were a self-satisfied group who considered "their work as done." The sect, as such, was torpid.[27] Parker would stir them out of it and be "tried for heresy" for his pains. Frothingham followed the chain of events that led to the incident before the Boston Ministerial Association, chaired by his own father, N. L. Frothingham. His sermon of 1841, "The Permanent and Transitory in Christianity," accused the clergy of emptiness and deceit. Frothingham, armed with newspaper clippings saved by Parker, dealt with the sermon at length but did not bother to mention that the title, not original, was borrowed from the German philosopher, Schleirmacher. A year later (1842) Parker wrote a pamphlet, "Discourses of Matters Pertaining to Religion," which his biographer considered "excellent." [28] The *Dial* article of the same year critical of the Ministerial Association, was followed by the sermon, "The Pharisees," which Frothingham considered allegorical. Apparently the leaders of the Ministerial Association felt the same way. Parker was called in for conversations with Cyrus Bartol, Ezra Styles Gannett, Mr. Waterson, Chandler Robbins, and N. L. Frothingham. This meeting was the famous Parker "Heresy Trial" in January, 1843.[29] The issue was whether or not Parker was a Christian and if he was not, should he withdraw from Unitarianism. Frothingham's treatment of this event is curiously objective. Names are mentioned, such as Bartol or Gannett, but his own father, whose role is played down, is referred to as the "chairman." The meeting ended in an atmosphere of brotherly feelings with handshakes all around. Parker was not asked to withdraw but he was ostracized ever afterward. Pulpit exchanges were denied him and the "chairman," Rev. N. L. Frothingham, quietly took over the administration of the time-honored Thursday lectures so that by invitation Parker would no longer have that platform. "This device," to silence Parker, said Octavius Frothingham, "was ingenious but not handsome." [30] Writing this section of the biography must have brought back the painful Salem days when he and his father were hardly on speaking terms. With obvious admiration, Frothingham discussed Parker's withdrawal from the Unitarian Association and his establishment of the Twenty-Eighth Congregational Society. His description of Parker's congregation could also apply to his own New York group: "The Circles of Fashion were not present, the thoughtful, sensitive, and humane were there in numbers . . . seeking doubters, reformers were conspicuously present." [31]

Nowhere in the biography of Parker was Frothingham as devastatingly critical of Parker as he was in his sermon preached in June, 1860, after Parker's death in Italy (see Chapter IV, p. 82). In the biography he compared him favorably with Channing, Parker's superior in looks, style, and insight, but inferior to Parker in range of thought, imagination, and breadth of human understanding. While Channing was the aristocrat that "trod daintily in high places," Parker was a democrat who "ran swiftly in rough paths." He was greater than Spurgeon, who spoke to thousands but was low in taste, narrow, and lacked learning. While Beecher was equal to Parker in wit—"popular drifts befriended him"—Parker faced unpopular things and told people what they might dread to hear. Beecher, concluded Frothingham, was the Spurgeon of America, Parker the Luther, clumsy but educational and inspirational.[32] He had power of total memory, recalled Frothingham, which gave the impression of genius, yet no genius was there. He was no philosopher, not poetic, nor were his ideas original, yet he used the tools of philosophy and poetry to crystallize thought and to persuade. He founded no church, propounded no creed, was no Luther (in contradiction to an earlier statement); all of his ideas existed before Plato. To Frothingham the most admirable aspect of Parker was his plebian taste in disliking Margaret Fuller, Goethe, and Rousseau, in preferring a "cattle show to a picture show," and in regretting that there was not "a saw mill in all of Rome." [33] Strangely, Frothingham admired a man whose tastes were so different from his own. Yet Parker's interest in "bald truths" and their "practical use" was certainly one that Frothingham shared and demonstrated in his sermons and writings in spite of his high taste in literature.

As the biographer of Theodore Parker, Frothingham kept himself out of the story almost completely. Admirable though his modesty was, it was unfortunate for those interested in recapturing a dimension of his life with Parker. This omission also reduces the reader's view of Parker himself. It is well known that he and Parker were close personal friends, that while in Salem, Frothingham came under his theological influence and Frothingham and his generation looked to Parker as their mentor. Yet, strangely, when John Weiss and Parker's widow carefully collected his letters for the two-volume work, *Life and Correspondence of Theodore Parker* (1864), no Frothingham—Parker correspondence was included. Long passages reproducing conversations are in quotation marks but with no citations. One must guess whether the material in quotes was from memory or from letters later destroyed. Frothingham never used the

personal pronoun, again leaving the reader in the dark as to the full
meaning of certain passages. The possible exception to the omission of
himself from the book is in his chapter on "Specimens of Correspondence." Three items appear—one a "telegraph from O.F.," the others parts
of Parker's letters to his wife. These are nonsense pieces showing rare
flashes of Frothingham's sense of humor:

> Telegraphic from OF—Meetin 'v Sirtl 'n sexn'. Theologic Questyun: Why
> did the Lord make the world? Answer: Nobodi els cood. Wa'nt none reddi
> mad; so he done it! [34]
>
> I saw O.F. the other day with his white hat on. He read a paper before the
> 'cademy, mathematical section, on the trisection of the arc. Who did it first?
> That was the question. O.F. answered the claims of Archamedes, Zeno, etc.,
> No, 'twarn't they. Who was it? Noah trisected the arc for Shem, Ham and
> Jophet. Never was such a family. O.F. recommended that Noah be made
> honorary member of the Academy.[35]
> Nobody misses it. At a meetin' of the Sirtl last night the question came up on
> the antiquity of omnibuses. The usual variety of [wise] opinions were enter-
> tained. But O.F. decided that they were as old as the time of St. Ambrose—
> fourth century. He quoted the well-known rule of that saint, but without
> entire accuracy, for his imagination sometimes supplies his memory with
> facts.

The spoof went on, concluding that the rule was "unity in all things of no
consequence.[36] These vignettes support the reputation he had at Harvard
of being an entertainer among a small group of select friends. They also
anticipate the tone he helped set in the New York Fraternity Club at its
height of activity as he wrote the Parker biography.

There is no doubt that the treatment of Parker's life was weakened by
Frothingham's reticence to include himself as Parker's colleague. "Professionally I stand alone," he quoted Parker as confiding to his Journal in
1851, "not a minister with me. I see no young men rising up to take
ground with me, or in advance of me. I think that, with a solitary exception, my professional influence has not been felt by a single young minister's soul." [37] It is tempting to assume that Frothingham was the exception, yet no further explanation is given. When William White Chadwick
wrote his biography of Parker in 1901 he quoted Parker's statement,
certainly available to Frothingham earlier, expressing pride in the list of
young ministers, following in his tradition. "Johnson at Lynn, Higginson
at Worcester, Kimball at Barre, Longfellow at Brooklyn, Frothingham at
Jersey City, May at Syracuse—pretty good for a beginning." [38] Why did
Frothingham leave the impression that Parker made no impact on him?
Was he modest in leaving out a list of young ministers which included his
name or was he too independent to acknowledge the origin of his inspiration? At the height of his own fame as he wrote of Parker, this may have

been the case. However, at other times in his life, early and late, he was free in his claims on Parker's influence.[39]

As for his father's role in Parker's ostracism, he was understandably in a delicate position. Although his father was dead by 1873, Cyrus Bartol was still active and sympathetic to the Free Religious Association. Ezra Styles Gannett was still allied with Henry Bellows in the Unitarian opposition with enough irritating issues without reviving old ones. Perhaps it was simply filial loyalty that prevented Frothingham from confronting his father's equivocal stand in the Parker episode. Yet how much stronger and historically valid would have been his biography of Parker had he included his judgment of his father, later quoted by Chadwick in his own book on Parker:

> One gentleman, a doctor of divinity, but a man of letters rather than a theologian, a radical in literature but a conservative in sentiment and usage. . . . This gentleman when the question was no longer one of literature, but one of custom and institution and social tranquillity, left the ranks of the pioneers, and fell back upon the old guard. He had gone out for a pleasant reconnoiter; he was not prepared for battle.[40]

Frothingham accused his father of ambiguity. Unable to follow through on his ideas in either direction, to cast Parker out or to follow his radical ideas and support him, he ended by favoring his expulsion from the Ministerial Association.

Frothingham's *Life of Theodore Parker* had its soft spots, but on the whole it was well received for its breadth and objectivity. William Gannett, perhaps typical of the younger colleagues of Frothingham, was favorably impressed with the biography.[41] There were criticisms here and there. The *Boston Transcript* reviewed the book in April, 1874, and attacked Frothingham's version of Parker's "heresy trial." He had been expelled for reasons other than those claimed, the reviewer said. John T. Sargent, with whom Parker had exchanged pulpits after the episode in 1843, defended Frothingham's interpretation and the biography as a valid work of history.[42] After the appearance of the book, Frothingham became recognized as the authority on Parker. After 1874 a great deal of his time was spent defending the book, elaborating on Parker's views or answering inquiries about historical events in his life. Typical of this was the question posed by the English Unitarian journal, the *London Inquirer*, whether or not Parker's works should be included in Christian literature. The perennial question was raised again: Was he a Christian? William H. Channing felt that he was really a Unitarian Christian. Frothingham disagreed.

> I am persuaded . . . that the Christian peculiarity was falling away from his mind and that had he lived, he would have given his support to the Free Religious movement . . . The American Unitarian Association probably saved its corporate life by its exclusion of Parker. It escaped the fate of drowning in a sea of ideas . . . but if the boat sinks, 'tis to another sea.[43]

By modern standards of historical writing, the *Life of Theodore Parker* is not without fault. Though well organized and written in elegant, literary style, the sources are not well used. Some letters are included as in a book of readings in complete form, though not assimilated and sometimes out of context. It could also be criticized for being too eulogistic of Parker, though Frothingham's 1860 memorial sermon could not be accused of this. Yet, by 1874, fourteen years after Parker's death, with the FRA in full power, Frothingham doubtless felt less critical than he had in 1860. His contemporaries felt otherwise. Chadwick, who followed in Frothingham's scholarly steps in 1901 with his own biography of Parker, felt that the Frothingham book was "nothing if not critical." Granted, the criticism was mingled "with lofty, well-considered praise" but also included were "some frank and fearless indications of what seemed to him to be defects." Chadwick paid tribute to Frothingham's critical detachment and objectivity which showed, he felt, the ocean of space between his and Parker's ideas and philosophic method.[44]

The modern observer is forced to say that Frothingham, as historian and critic, is on surer ground in dealing with ideas than when analyzing historical sources of hard facts, requiring synthesis. This would be no handicap to him in his next intellectual adventure. His *Trancendentalism in New England* was presented as part of the centennial year of 1876. While the nation was "gathering up" for the Exhibition before other nations he felt it fitting to attempt to examine some of the roots of the tradition that had helped shape the "national mind." Admitting that he had accepted the task, not voluntarily but willingly, he introduced the book as simply a history of a movement with which he had once fully sympathized. His ardor may have cooled after later speculations and studies, he wrote, but still he felt enough affinity for the subject to do it justice.[45] How he came to write the book is not entirely clear. His intellectual preparation was obvious as was his background and environment. Probably his FRA colleagues, many of whom were the "second generation" transcendentalists, suggested that he undertake it. His personal friendship with the Putnam family may have had some influence. His close friend and confidant, James H. Morse, was invited to his home after the last church session in 1875. He recalled a conversation about the book and Frothingham's misgivings about "delving into papers of living persons," but he planned to take some material to Lenox and "mull over it."[46] There is some evidence that he had been contemplating the book and collecting sources since at least 1870. From his young friend, William C. Gannett, he asked for letters of Levi Blodgett and George Ripley, which he knew had been in the possession of William's father, Ezra Styles Gannett. Yet the date of his request to William Gannett (1870) was written in later by another hand.[47] However, the writing was done in a concentrated summer, of the kind which had produced the Parker biography two years earlier.

Transcendentalism in New England was written almost entirely from published sources, personal contacts, and memories. As Frothingham wrote at the summer home at Beverly Farms, he sat surrounded by copies of *Dial,* Orestes Bronson's *Boston Quarterly,* Emerson's essays, Parker's sermons, and samples of the writings of George Ripley, Bronson Alcott, and Margaret Fuller. Each received a chapter, capturing the spirit of their contributions to the ferment of transcendentalism: "The Seer" was Emerson; "The Mystic," Alcott; "The Critic," Fuller; "The Preacher," Parker; "The Man of Letters," George Ripley. Men of his own generation—W. H. Channing, T. W. Higginson, John Weiss, Samuel Johnson, Samuel Longfellow, and David Wasson—were included as "minor prophets." The name of Henry Thoreau appeared only as a contributor to *Dial* and no mention was made of *Walden,* in print for twenty years by then.

As might be expected, Frothingham, who once considered himself a "pure transcendentalist," [48] left his own name out entirely as he wrote. Transcendentalism was in its late twilight stage when Frothingham and the minor prophets, the young generation of its golden age, were either changing their views or assuming defensive positions against the impact of naturalism, evolution, and materialism. Frothingham's own position, characteristic of his attitude toward complex issues, was ambiguous. In later life he claimed to have given up transcendentalism entirely, yet clearly held views typical of the transcendental mode of thought. He was, as we shall see, accused of "recanting" his earlier radicalism while at the same time claiming to have never withdrawn from any position once taken. But this was all after his retirement. As he wrote in the summer of 1875 with the Free Religious Movement in full tide, he seemed to be outside of the transcendental school looking objectively at the views of his generation of transcendentalists.

> These men, Weiss and Wasson and Higginson, nursed in the transcendental school, thoroughly imbued with its principles, committed to them, wedded to them by the conflicts they waged in their defense when they were assailed by literalists, dogmatists and formalists, look out now upon the advancing ranks of the new materialism as the holders of the royal fortress looked out on a host of insurgents; as the King and Queen of France looked out on the revolution from the Palace of Versailles: the onset of a new era they instinctively dread, feeling that dignity, princeliness, and spiritual worth are at stake. They will fight admirably to the last; but should they be defeated, it is yet possible that the revolution may bring compensations to humanity, which will make good the overthrow of their "diademed towers." [49]

Thus, in stately language, he seemed to disassociate himself from the remnants of transcendentalism, implying that his fellow free religionists were the old guard of a lost cause. Never content to let one of his

judgments stand unmodified by an afterthought, he closed his book with
a generous opinion of the transcendental thinkers.

> Earnest men and women no doubt they were; better educated men and
> women did not live in America; they were well born, well nurtured, well
> endowed. Their generation produced no warmer hearts, no purer spirits,
> no more ardent consciences, no more devoted wills. Their philosophy may
> be unsound, but it produced noble characters and human lives. The philos-
> ophy that takes its place may rest on more scientific foundations; it will not
> more completely justify its existence or honor its day.[50]

Most of the writing was done during his summer vacation in Lenox but
continued during the fall and winter in New York amid all his other
duties. In November he wrote to Emerson, requesting permission to use
his farewell letter to his parish when he left the ministry in 1832.[51] By
spring he had finished, signing the introduction in New York on April 12,
1876. Francis Abbot, in the April 20th issue of *Index*, announced the
imminent publication by Putnam's, predicting that the book "cannot fail
to be a standard work on this very important and very interesting subject." [52] A month later the *New York Times*, usually favorable to Frothingham's activities, hailed the book as a "largely conceived, comprehensive
outline of the history of Transcendentalism. He cannot fail to satisfy all
that desire to see the very pulse of the machine." There were minor
defects, thought the reviewer—Bronson Alcott's birth, wrong by one
year, and the picture of the author on the frontispiece. "It made his eyes
glare like a tiger; an expression which his friends never saw on his face." [53]
A reviewer in *New Age* defended the book against the critical review of
Nation magazine, stating that Frothingham's book should stir fresh interest in transcendentalism, which is still valid and "the hope of the race." [54]
His own cousin, Henry Adams, editor of *North American Review* and
professor of history at Harvard, was more critical. Although he felt that
"very good things are to be culled from Mr. Frothingham's excerpts," he
had overrated the importance of the subject, now a dead philosophy. He
could see little connection between the European and German
philosophers and American transcendentalism and felt that Wordsworth
should not be classed, as Frothingham had, as a transcendental thinker.
Thinking less of Emerson than Frothingham did, Adams felt that the
Divinity School address was not really "epoch making," as Frothingham
stated it, but only "epoch marking." Still he could find no major defects in
the book. He admired Frothingham's style and his "well equipped" background for undertaking the writing. His only real praise, however, was of
Frothingham's synthesis of the European roots and especially his discussion of Fichte.[55]

Most present day historians would agree with Adams as one of the few
new-breed professional historians of the times. The sketches of transcen-

dental prophets, compressed into five chapters, were indeed excerpts, with many long, undigested quotations from printed sources. Modern scholarship has gone far beyond his treatment of these individuals. Had he taken more pains with letters and other primary sources, the book would have been a thoroughgoing history of the subject. It is useful today, however, and still a standard work on the entire movement. It is also significant in the intellectual development of Frothingham for it revealed his remarkable capacity for synthesizing European and English philosophies and interpreting them lucidly for his readers (see chapters II through VI).

A very different kind of intellectual adventure was his biography of Gerrit Smith, the New York philanthropist, abolitionist, and social reformer. He had met Smith at the 1872 FRA convention at Syracuse, then a vice-president of the association. It is possible he and Smith had met on the platforms and in the audiences of Anti-Slavery Society meetings before the Civil War. Among their mutual friends were Senator Charles Sumner, Theodore Parker, and T. W. Higginson. Although he and Smith were not personal friends, Frothingham admired him as a political man for the same reason he lionized Charles Sumner. Smith represented the high-toned militant Christian, crusading against the moral evils of the day.

Smith, being a man of action, was not a subject for an intellectual biography, which made Frothingham's treatment a chronological and narrative descriptive account of his life. Like his other historical works and in the manner of the amateur historian of his time, the book was essentially a compilation of sources. Unlike his *Transcendentalism in New England,* most of the material used came from unprinted documents. Frothingham had the good fortune to be able to spend a summer, probably of 1877, at Gerrit Smith's home in Peterboro, New York. There he was able to sit for uninterrupted days absorbing Smith's letters to and from political and reform leaders of his day, newspaper clippings of events in his life, and a diary illuminating some of Smith's activities.

It was pleasant work, with the run of the spacious, neoclassical house and with the aid and encouragement of Smith's daughter. The biography was, perhaps, unusually eulogistic since it was written in the environment of Smith's personal effects with the family still grieving over his recent death in 1874. While Frothingham attempted to deal with the controversial events of Smith's life, he unavoidably encountered the shadowy events surrounding John Brown's attack on Harper's Ferry. It was common knowledge that abolitionists and social reformers had supported Brown's exploits in Kansas and his later plan to attack slavery by a liberation movement of some sort. Smith, along with such people as Theodore Parker, T. W. Higginson, and perhaps Ralph Waldo Emerson, had talked to Brown prior to Harper's Ferry and had donated money to his cause. It was also well known that Brown had been a visitor at Smith's home in Peterboro just prior to the attack. When the biography of Smith was published in 1877, Smith's implication in the Harper's Ferry attack was made clear in Frothingham's chapter, "Slavery." [56] In it he accused Smith of misleading Brown as to the possible attitude of Northern proslavery Democrats and as to the significance of the New York Democratic "Manifesto," identifying Brown, Smith, and others as being part of a "Central Association" bent on overthrowing slavery and planning high treason. Smith, according to the biographer, was guilty, then, of conspiracy against the United States government.

A storm broke around Frothingham's head. One of Gerrit Smith's colleagues, Lysander Spooner, wrote the author that Smith did not lie to Brown about the threats of the proslave Democrats and that Smith was not a part of a conspiracy.[57] Smith's daughter, who apparently had not read the manuscript, owned the plates from which the printing had begun. She had them impounded and stopped the press at G. P. Putnam's Sons after one thousand copies had been issued.[58]

The embarrassing stalemate was broken after Frothingham revised his chapter on slavery in a second edition which came out a year later.[59] The new edition still included documents proving Smith's close relations with Brown's plans for overthrowing slavery but there were no more implications that he knew of his plans for the attack at Harper's Ferry. "Gerrit Smith's affirmation," concluded Frothingham, that he had no previous knowledge or intimation of John Brown's invasion of Harper's Ferry was made in entire sincerity.[60] The change was actually a minor one since the general impression was left standing that Smith knew of Brown's general plans if not of his specific target at Harper's Ferry. His conclusions after revision agreed with those of F. B. Sanborn, biographer of John Brown.[61]

Frothingham's willingness to retreat from the position taken in the first edition is understandable from a practical standpoint. Smith's daughter controlled the plates of the book. From an intellectual point of view, Frothingham was reluctant to reduce the reputation of a man whose views of humane reform he shared. Also, many of Frothingham's friends were caught in the same embarrassing position with Smith when Brown suddenly fell upon Harper's Ferry. Yet a curious fact of Frothingham's attitude toward Smith emerges from the controversy over the first edition. Even while he was in the process of revising the chapter in question, exonerating Smith in the Brown conspiracy, he answered a letter he had received from Spooner defending Smith's integrity.[62] He disagreed that Smith's actions in the affair were entirely honest. Though the family claimed that he had nothing to do with John Brown, wrote Frothingham, from his own studies of Smith's character he thought him capable of "prevarication" due to his "egotism . . . and his cunning, but I may be all wrong." [63]

Nothing of this part of Smith's character appeared in the biography. Was it because Frothingham was not sure of his ground or did he simply wish to leave out unfavorable parts of Smith's life? He could be accused of intellectual dishonesty or of the less serious charge of simply writing uncritical history. The feelings of Smith's survivors was certainly a controlling factor as was the custom of the age never to speak ill of the dead. He never felt similar restraints, however, when engaged in theological battles and public controversies.

THREE

The journalistic media, which was more appropriate for bold expressions of opinion, was a constant forum for Frothingham during his New York years. In *Nation, North American Review,* and in journals less well known today, he wrote as a drama critic and a commentator on political, religious, and literary subjects.

Nation carried Frothingham's name as a literary editor from the beginning. Founded in 1865 and for a brief time controlled by George Curtis, Henry Bellows, and others, it was brought under the editorship of E. L. Godkin a year later. He expanded the journal from an organ devoted exclusively to civil rights for blacks to one with a broader scope of social criticism.[64] Frothingham contributed twenty-five articles between 1865 and 1876, 1866 being the year of his largest contribution, with eight articles. His first writings in 1865 were critical essays of philosophic works with the exception of the one entitled "The Episcopal Church and the Freedmen." Here he was critical of the church for exploiting the freed slave for sectarian purposes. He took issue with Episcopal bishops who had alleged that black religion was dying out. Frothingham agreed that the religion of the black man was "superstitious and sensuous" but better suited to him than the pomp of the Episcopal church. He made a plea for a nonsectarian effort to help the freedman.[65]

Religious books or essays of religious criticism were usually given to Frothingham to review, which he usually did with a sharp pen.[66] When the occasion arose, he commented on issues of church politics such as salaries of clergymen and the system of renting church pews. These were printed under "Minor Topics" and, as expected, he decried the material and spiritual starvation of clergymen and the elitist custom of renting pews—a slap at the practice in Beecher's church.[67] Horace Bushnell's book, *The Vicarious Sacrifice,* was reviewed by Frothingham in the issue of January 25, 1866. He was a "conspicuous genius in the American church," he wrote, "really a Unitarian but not a rationalist" because he needlessly attempted to preserve the "altar forms" while challenging the Christian myths.[68] When Bushnell died in 1876, Frothingham wrote the obituary, his last contribution to *Nation.*[69]

The Catholic church, of course, could not escape Frothingham's nee-
dling pen. Archbishop Manning's edited work, *A Book of Catholic Essays,*
was reviewed in 1867 after the founding of the FRA. Frothingham saw
Manning's book as a change in tactics against Protestantism from "causis-
try, cunning, and denunciation" to "candid, outright polemics"—a sign of
the times. He rejected the Catholic charge that Protestantism overem-
phasized temporal things at the expense of the spiritual and supernatural.
Not even radicals such as Kingsley and Mill do this; even some Unitarians
hold to supernaturalism "as to their life," wrote Frothingham. In turning
the debate around, he accused the Catholic essays of opposing positivism,
rationalism, and sensationalism.[70]

None of the religious views expressed by Frothingham were original in
Nation magazine. In his sermons he had been saying the same things for
several years. However, during the years immediately following the Civil
War, *Nation* seemed to be the principle outlet for his type of religious
criticism. When *Index* magazine was founded in 1869 there was a noticeable drop in Frothingham's contributions to *Nation.* However, even as late
as 1872 he wrote a review of Henry Ward Beecher's Yale lectures on
"Preaching." It came out in *Nation* under "Notes." Frothingham, a professional friend of Beecher, admired him but did not really approve of his
pulpit tactics, or even consider him a serious theologian. The Beecher
volume, thought Frothingham, was valuable for orthodox students as a
guide to Beecher's "secret"—that of never attempting to preach truth but
to preach to the hearts of men in order to "save" them. Beecher felt that
skeptical, rational men, presumably of Frothingham's turn of mind,
would turn away from soul saving. Frothingham was neutral, stating that
there would be a place for a Beecher type of religious appeal along with
the appeal of the rationalist.[71]

In the Literature Department of *Nation* he reviewed works of philosophy and history. Typical was his critique of Forsyth's *Life of Cicero,* a
competent but dull biography. Frothingham criticized the author for
waving away Cicero's weaknesses as being unimportant and in so doing,
missing Cicero's main strengths.

> We complain of Mr. Forsyth that he owes his hero less than justice by trying
> to vindicate him on grounds of ordinary morality, instead of throwing about
> his person the glory of his illuminated and illuminating mind. He rates him
> too high as an individual; he rates him too low as an intelligence.[72]

The works of Epictetus, edited by T. W. Higginson, pleased him but the
editor, he felt, had "refined" the earthy language of the slave Epictetus
too much and lost the flavor. The language of the editor, he acknowledged, was elegant but less quaint.[73] He was harsh with Leckey's history of
rationalism, which he felt was superficial. The author, "a profound sav-
ant," had written a book "loudly heralded" but disappointing.[74] Nor was

he satisfied with the *Life of Robert Owen* which he reviewed for *Nation*. Taking issue with the author, whose name was not mentioned, Frothingham corrected the author's error in confusing Utopianism with Naturalism. Owen did not believe a man was a pure product of environment and natural law, wrote Frothingham, but rather the opposite.

> They who would meet today the philosophy that teaches that man is the creature of organization and circumstances, the subject of conditions, and the result of law must be prepared to deal not with Robert Owen but with Buckle and Draper.[75]

Modern scholars would agree.

As a contributing editor of *Nation*, Frothingham had the opportunity to comment on personalities and social questions in the forefront of attention between 1866 and 1969. He recognized the end of the *Liberator,* which had done its work and like Garrison, a man of "all conscience," deserved to be retired with thanks. "Popular Leaders" and "Personalities in Politics" were subjects of essays published as "Notes" in the fall of 1866, an off year election.[76] He decried the conditions of American politics often pointed to by other intellectuals: the American leader cannot really lead but must follow mass opinion, must embroil popular causes in order to be elected. In England it was different. Here a political leader was often the educator of the masses, a leader who identified a cause and focused mass attention on it. Wendell Phillips, thought Frothingham, came as close to this type of leader as anyone in America but was too "intellectual and advanced" for the people.[77]

When dealing with social questions he was on less sure ground than when reviewing a work of literature or philosophy. Charity, he felt, did not solve the problem of poverty. The "lower orders," he thought, were in distress due to "want of moral and intellectual culture." Uplift was the answer.[78] He favored reading rooms supplied with "sincere," "warm books," nothing elegant, to lift up the "lower quarter of the city." [79] Not one to crusade against sin, he felt called upon occasionally to deal with the "social evil"—a euphemism for prostitution. Although he used such words as "bad women," "sin," and "moral evil," he disposed of the moral approach used by the fundamentalists. He advocated the licensing of prostitution to keep it off the streets. Yet as to a permanent solution, he could not avoid reverting to the moral approach. "Nothing short of a moral regeneration of individual men and women will go deep enough to touch its roots," adding that he saw no immediate chance of this.[80]

His views of women's rights, expressed elsewhere, also were aired in *Nation* in main articles and minor notes. Women were their own worst enemies, he felt, quoting Lucretia Mott, because they blamed men for putting slavery ahead of women's suffrage and of attempting to shield women from "unpleasant aspects of the world's work." [81] Although he favored women's suffrage he did not think equality at the ballot box meant that there were no differences between men and women. He did not favor the same education for men and women or the same business opportunities. He feared coed colleges and distrusted the ideal of equality of women as the basis of "her humanity." Indeed this was the reason he would maintain a difference in social roles between men and women. He advocated a slow experimental approach to sexual equality. Meanwhile, he was sure that "men will be men and women, women in spite of the theorists." [82] Also, children could be children. "What of their rights?" he asked. Women's rights would inevitably affect children's rights. Would sexual equality bring about public agencies, nurseries, etc., to care for children while mothers worked? What would happen to the family? [83] He had come to grips with a perennial question of an urban society.

Theater going, which had long since lost much of its odium in New York City, if not in Boston, was a favorite pastime for Frothingham. He attended regularly and counted among his acquaintances many of the leading stage personalities. As we have observed, his religious association was hospitable to them and included actors and actresses in the membership of the society. [84] With his high taste in literature and his own skill in forensics, Frothingham was equipped to be a sharp critic of the New York stage. For one year before becoming involved in the organization of the FRA he wrote as drama critic for *Nation*. Edwin Booth just returned to America after his "gloom," and he saw him act in "Richelieu" and "Hamlet." His acting was not to Frothingham's taste. Preferring the "natural" school of acting to the "romantic," he felt that Booth was torn between the two. He should give up the attempt to bring the romantic styles into the modern world, wrote Frothingham, and study the "school of nature" more worthy of the greatest artists of the age. [85] He was also disappointed with the state of the drama in America. It pandered to the lower tastes, he felt, seeking to evoke "side-shaking laughter" and to make money. The theater should not be entertainment, as usually classified in newspapers, but should be an "unfogged mirror" of the society. The theater, to Frothingham, should be an agent to educate and to reflect society, although it should not try to move too far ahead of the tastes and feelings of the audience. To him, the French theater was a model because it was an authentic mirror of France. Let the American stage reflect American life and intelligent patrons would support it. [86]

The big event of the theater season in the fall of 1866 was the American tour of the Italian actress, Adelaide Ristori. The rival of the great French stage figure, Rachel Felix, she stirred controversies wherever she went among the drama critics in America and Europe. Frothingham saw the plays "Medea," "Elizabeth," "Phaedra," and "Judith" and wrote their reviews for *Nation*. They showed that he was thoroughly familiar with the plays and their historical milieu and that he had followed European criticism of the acting of both Ristori and Felix. In "Elizabeth" Ristori was at her best, thought Frothingham, because the part suited her natural temperament. She "was Elizabeth" but her acting was not quite genius, though close to it.[87] For "Medea" she lacked "passionate abandon," while demonstrating all of the attributes of a finished actress. She had all that nature could give her but beauty. She was cold and stiff in the part.[88] In reviewing "Phaedra" he became involved in the controversy over the relative merits of Ristori and Rachel Felix. It is not clear whether Frothingham ever saw the French actress play but he was familiar with French opinions, which, because of some temporary unpopularity at home, rated the Italian higher than their own. Frothingham disagreed. Ristori could not be "Phaedra" because she was

> from first to last, a modern Italian . . . trying to make amends for her natural incapacity to identify her pure and noble self with such a monstrous creature by an affluence of gesticulation and an excess of posturing. . . . Madame Ristori is wanting in passion. It may seem a strange thing to say, but we are persuaded that she is, as compared with Rachel, positively cold. She interests but she does not thrill. Her violent emotions are simulated. . . . In "Elizabeth" she was more successful, because the passions there were sudden and superficial; it was ordinary love, hate or pride, but "Phaedra" was quite destitute of the intense concentration of thought and emotion by which spectators are held spellbound.[89]

His opinion of the performance of "Judith," requiring that she be a "Hebrew Joan of Arc," was similar. Ristori could not go back to that distant land and remote epoch to recover the shadowy image, "so impalpable to a fancy like hers. . . . She did not give us the heroic success of Judean Miriams and Deborahs." As to the contest between the French Rachel and the Italian Ristori, Frothingham ended his critique characteristically with a mediating thought. "In other respects, in sweetness, tenderness, lightness, affluence of fancy, variety of expression, the Italian is the French women's peer." [90] Modern scholarship in nineteenth century drama upholds Frothingham's appraisal that Adelaide Ristori, superb in some roles, was in most heavy, dramatic parts inferior to Rachel Felix.[91]

Although *Nation* was the magazine that engaged most of Frothingham's journalistic efforts in New York prior to the founding of *Index*, he wrote for others. The short-lived *Dial*, edited in Cincinnati by Moncure Conway, carried a series entitled "The Christ of Christianity." Later, Conway, recalling his editorial effort, reminded Frothingham that W. D. Howells had been the poet of the *Dial* and that he had been the theologian.[92] "We were the outpost of Transcendentalism. The Boston *Dial* was the beginning, the Cincinnati *Dial* marked the end." After one year the journal went out of existence.[94]

Henry Bellows' magazine, *Christian Inquirer,* which he founded in 1847, carried Frothingham's name in 1866 along with future FRA colleagues such as William W. Chadwick; Robert Collyer; the conservative Unitarian, Samuel Osgood; A. P. Putnam; and the editor himself, Henry Bellows. He contributed short pieces and reprints of sermons.[95] After the name was changed to *Liberal Christian* Frothingham was no longer a contributor.

Some of Frothingham's most argumentative and opinionated essays were published in the *Radical* which was established in 1865 by Sidney Morse. It had a lively existence until 1872 although its life was also precarious as a journal of limited scope and audience. But before the *Index* was begun in 1869, it was the principle radical journal that published articles of Frothingham, Wasson, Higginson, Longfellow, and others who would found the FRA. At first it was thought that the *Radical,* was to be the organ of the FRA and that later *Index* should merge with it, but none of these plans materialized. Frothingham's articles, which appeared in nearly every volume of *Radical* were on theological subjects. Typical titles were "The New Spirit and the Forms" (June, 1865), "Radicals' Attitude Toward the Bible" (August, 1865), and "Man from Heaven" (June, 1868). Most of his articles were on subjects about which he either preached sermons or had dealt with in more restrained and scholarly fashion in the *Christian Examiner* and *North American Review.* In the *Radical* he apparently felt free to lash out at his conservative opponents. Between 1865 and 1867 he wrote a series on the New Testament, elaborating on the theme familiar in Biblical criticism that "There Are Two Religions in the New Testament." [96]

James Freeman Clark took issue with him in the pages of the more conservative *Christian Examiner,* insisting that Christianity was one synthetic religion and that there were no real conflicts within the New Testament. Frothingham responded with harsh words for the man who had attempted to accommodate the radicals within the Unitarian ranks in 1867 and would later welcome him back into the fold. Clark, wrote Frothingham, was a man lacking in perception and rigidly bound within Christianity. As a "theological peacemaker" he was unable to see the inner contradiction within Christian dogma. "An eclectic is a poor critic," he concluded.[97] As for the enemies of Theodore Parker, he used words never seen in his critical sermon in 1860 nor in his biography of 1874. "The pachyderms of Boston thought it horrid that Parker fired 'minnie balls' at them instead of blowing peas." [98] In spite of Frothingham's usual restraint, his elegant style, and scholarly breadth of writing elsewhere, he obviously relished this intellectual adventure in a journal that permitted combat with words in the realm of ideas. That he thought highly of the journal and that he also wanted to increase his own audience is clear from the advice he gave an unknown person who asked for advice on religious literature. "You could not do better than subscribe to the *Radical.*" [99]

The most traumatic experience of the age for most Americans in the North, except for the Civil War itself, was probably the assassination of President Lincoln. Frothingham, like all who claimed public platforms and pulpits, rose to the occasion and interpreted the event. *Friends of Progress* published his essay, "The Murdered President," in May, 1865. As he wrote on the 3rd of May, Lincoln's funeral train approached Springfield, Illinois. The Civil War was grinding to a close, the armies disbanding. Frothingham had probably seen the "solemn pageant" in New York as the city stood "stunned" in the shock of "horror—almost of terror." The grave theme had been struck by Emerson, four days after Lincoln's death, in his eulogy read in Concord Village. But where Emerson, with cool detachment, could put his finger on his essential humanity and simply say he was "the true representative of the American people," [100] Frothingham, like Whitman, wrote with a tone of personal loss. Angry at the brutal act of the "wretched" occasion and overwhelmed by the popular outpouring of grief, he felt that "nothing like it was ever heard of." No king ever had such pomp of burial—such length of retinue—such overflowing and irrepressible flood of tears. For the pageants of kings, however gorgeous and imposing, are official, but this was spontaneous and popular. The pageants of kings are made up of military, nobility, and clergy. This was made up of people. "How shall we account for this?" he asked. "He was loved as a man and simply as a man," was the answer. Simplicity and humility were the two characteristics of Lincoln that Frothingham used as the subtheme of his essay. The personal description of the man, who physically "protruded from his official skin"; the simplicity that never made him aware "that the world demanded more of him than of ordinary men"; his humility, beyond understanding, approaching "self-forgetfulness," bordering on "saintliness," were captured by Frothingham. Aware of his tribulations while guiding the nation through the war with policies often misunderstood by the best minds, Frothingham capsuled the secret of Lincoln's greatness and, with it, the verdict of history:

> He hoped little, expected nothing. Every difficulty he saw and every obstruction. The whole length of the sandy way lay before his gaze, with scarcely the verdure of a single palm tree along the whole reach of the journey. He was upborne by no transcendent faith in human character, and by no radiant anticipation of natural glory. A man of low temperament and sad nature, he worked and waited, waited and worked, bearing all things, enduring all things, but neither believing all things nor all things hoping: bearing and enduring, oh, how much! Even from his friends. What a history was written on that care-worn and furrowed face—of suffering accepted, sorrow entertained, emotions buried, and duty done! [101]

This was without a doubt his greatest example of intellectual expression from the view of emotions expressed and grasp of the history and psychology of leadership. It was as though the greatness of Lincoln had called forth great writing from Frothingham.

Curiously, Frothingham never wrote for the *North American Review* during Henry Adams' tenure as editor (1870–1877) and no records exist as to why he did not. In 1878, however, he engaged in a written debate with Rev. T. W. Chambers on the subject, "Is Man a Depraved Creature?" [102] Each wrote two essays, going over familiar ground of the controversy between fundamentalism and rationalism. In the same volume, a written symposium on "The Doctrine of Eternal Punishment" appeared, featuring articles by Frothingham, Bellows, President Porter of Yale, and others less well known. The subject was well-worn and rather belatedly debated in the year 1878. Its only real significance is that it afforded an opportunity for Bellows and Frothingham to exchange a final blow in their long personal and philosophic controversy. He gibed at his former mentor (with whom he actually agreed on the subject) who had quoted Matthew Arnold against the doctrine of divine punishment as typical of "liberals who mean to be Christian [but] soon take the debate out of all circles where it can be followed by sober or enlightened argument." [103]

His last offering in the *North American Review* was a group of eulogies and memoirs of people who had been closely associated with the journal: Richard Dana, William Cullen Bryant, John Lothrop Motely, Caleb Cushing, Bayard Taylor, and George Hillard. The article was erudite and gracefully written, showing that he was thoroughly familiar with the work of these men whose activities ranged from literary and historical writing to politics and diplomacy. [104]

By the time the issue appeared Frothingham and his family were on their way to Europe. He had reason to look back on this twenty years in New York with some satisfaction. Few men could match his versatility of mind or claim such a variety of intellectual adventures.

VIII

The Arena of Men:
New York Milieu
1859–1882

UNLIKE SOME INTELLECTUALS BORN AND BRED in Boston, Frothingham had no condescending attitudes toward the social climate of New York City. Although he decried the materialism of the age and was offended by the haphazard growth of the rude, restless metropolis, he found it a stimulating center of action whether for preaching and writing or enjoying the excitement of a circle of friends to share his leisure hours.

New York City, having long since established its supremacy over Boston as the commercial center of the country, was vying for precedence also in publishing and intellectual life. In spite of the fact that Boston remained, through Frothingham's active ministry, the geographic center for the activities of intellectual groups such as the Free Religious Association, the Radical Club, and the *North American Review* and *Atlantic* being published there, New York City was the center that increasingly attracted men and women of ambition and the restless people seeking wider horizons than those provided in Boston. Frothingham was one of these.

He plunged into the activities of the dynamic city as the Civil War approached, deeply involving himself with people and events of these dark years. After Appomattox the influx of immigrants and rural native born, the political corruption in New York and Washington, the economic distress of the 1870s, and the impact of Darwinism all made the New York scene his lively arena of action. He thrived on intellectual combat, needed the stimulation of social life with penetrating minds, and was never happy when idle. His summer vacations he took with reluctance; more at home in the city than the country, he returned early and eagerly each fall. After twenty years, with his work done and health impaired, he left the city with regret.

ONE

Frothingham, his wife Caroline, and nine-year-old "Bessie" had scarcely settled in a temporary home in New York when the news of John Brown's raid on Harper's Ferry broke. This event, shocking or praisewor-thy, depending upon one's view of the slavery impasse, marked another step in a series of events leading inescapably to civil war. There is every reason to believe that Frothingham shared the view of other antislavery people—that Brown was a hero. One can imagine Frothingham with his New York friends discussing this event and others as they unfolded. His home was often the scene of informal meetings of antislavery people of the New York area. Moncure Conway, later a young FRA colleague of Frothingham, recalled a meeting at his house while Kansas was in a state of civil war. Henry Ward Beecher was there and all present were impa-tient at the do-nothing policy of the Buchanan administration, living out its last days in office. Frothingham sympathized with Conway, young and "full of wrath" who blurted out, "Somebody ought to walk down Pennsyl-vania Avenue like the old prophet with his jug and smash it on the pavement and cry out, 'thus shall Washington be destroyed!' " Beecher broke the tension, recalled Conway, with a bit of characteristic humor which brought a relieved round of laughter: "I am afraid that the prophet would only lose his crockery and not hit anybody." [1]

They were no better satisfied with the Lincoln administration in the spring of 1861 with war begun but war aims unclear. Again the group was angry at a vacillating government; again Beecher, though angry, leavened the discussion with "irrepressible" humor. Frothingham, the host at the meeting held in his home, felt that the rebellion should be crushed by striking at its heart—slavery. All agreed to this policy in principle but only Frothingham felt it "practicable" to issue a clear-cut antislavery policy as a war aim.[2]

On the slavery question, as on many social issues, Frothingham fol-lowed no consistent line of action. In spite of his angry impatience with the vacillations of both Buchanan and Lincoln, he declined an invitation of Samuel J. May to speak at the anniversary of the founding of the Anti-Slavery Society. During the "caretaker" administration of Buchanan in the spring of 1860, as the convention summer for the crucial fall election approached, he felt that the "time no longer needed anti-slavery blasts." Wendell Phillips was free, as always, to speak, but he would rather not be on the platform where "superficial forensics" would "fatigue the ear." [3] While refusing to be counted himself, he wrote to Senator Charles Sumner, whose "brave speeches" [4] he had long admired, congratulating him on his "unequivocal stand" against compromise with slavery. The Republican Party, he felt, needed Sumner in the election year when it was looking for a "moderate" presidential candidate. 'If Lincoln goes in, another *less moderate* must also go in with him." He hoped that Sumner, as the Senate's voice of conscience, would be of influence in the new adminis-tration.[5]

Following the military setbacks of the summer of 1862, he made an appeal to his congregation that they compose a letter to be transmitted to President Lincoln, requesting that the government adopt an emancipation policy for the states in rebellion. It was too late. Writing to Senator Sumner in September, he related that the congregation unanimously authorized him to compose a letter to the President, but Lincoln's "proclamation of the 22nd stopped" his pen. Disappointed at not being able to add the persuasion of his group to that of individuals and other organizations in the nation, he was glad the government had at last stated a clear-cut antislavery war aim. Yet to Sumner, he repeated the curious belief, expressed earlier to Henry Beecher and Conway, that a clear-cut emancipation policy would cause the rebellion to collapse.

How much better it might have been! How much better to have emancipated the slaves unconditionally and at once—to have had the use of them during these autumn months, to have knocked the bottom out of the rebellion by a single blow of the hammer—to have saved months of war and perhaps many months of political intrigue! How much better at all events to have made use of the great evil—and to have it over as an act of mercy to the south, not as an act of punishment.

Still he was encouraged by the way the policy of the war was going. "The radical element is alert and prevailing . . . you, God bless you! are among the radicals." [6]

By the following summer, with the rebels contained at Gettysburg, he was already thinking about the problem of suffrage for the blacks. Sumner had forwarded to Frothingham his own article in *Social Science Review* on the civil rights question. He praised his "noble arguments" and assured Sumner that he himself had always in "speech, sermons and conversation" advocated "black suffrage on the grounds of humanity and shall continue to do so." It had been a hectic July, with the Confederate army close by in Pennsylvania, the draft riots in the city, and himself attacked by rioters and relieved of his watch one evening on Fifth Avenue. From the cool and safe vantage point of North Conway, New Hampshire, he expressed to Sumner his eagerness to get back to New York "to the battle." Angered by the experience of the summer, he assured Sumner that his new church, to be dedicated in December, would be a fortress of stone against the enemy with "steel tempered and planks seasoned." [7]

Back in the city in September, he was absorbed in the affairs of his church, then in temporary quarters in Ebbits Hall. The new church building was nearing completion and plans had to be made for the dedication in December. He was too busy to attend the meeting of the Anti-Slavery Society in Philadelphia, turning down an invitation of William Lloyd Garrison, regretting that he would miss the "intellectual and moral banquet." He conveyed his feelings about the noble memories of the "dear faces of people who had worked in the sacred cause. [8]

He probably would not have gone anyway, preferring to identify intellectually with the cause but usually avoiding personal appearances. Once the nation had committed itself to the war Frothingham apparently felt no more need to speak before antislavery groups, although he continued to admire Wendell Phillips' "manly cry" and considered that Garrison had "abandoned his post" when the *Liberator* ceased publication. He did serve as secretary of the American Freedman's Association, collecting funds from contributions sent him from England by Moncure Conway. In this capacity he helped to settle black refugees from the war areas. As the war drew to a close, his feelings, revealed to Conway, were mixed between optimism for the future of the black man, who he felt had vindicated himself magnificently in battle, and anxiety for the American people, "not really awake to the problems of the freedman" or even to the wounded soldiers and families of the slain. Even though he saw terrible problems ahead which the country was not prepared to solve, he was encouraged by the commitment of the nation to "universal and absolute civil and social rights" for the black man. He even believed in Lincoln, he reassured Conway, as well as Congress and the Supreme Court now that Chase was Chief Justice. The people, he was encouraged to write, are now "impatient of all tolerance of the slave system," though not as compassionate as they should be toward the slaves. With Richmond under seige and Sherman's armies sweeping through the South, Frothingham observed to Conway, "We are in the middle of a rushing river of events." [9]

Three months later, with the war closed and Lincoln dead, Frothingham endured the dismal beginning of the postwar reconstruction set off by the struggle for supremacy between President Andrew Johnson and Congress. Curiously apolitical over the issues of civil rights and never on sure ground when discussing politics, he observed again to Conway in England that

> Our politics are in a dreadful muddle—so are our ethics. The war of weapons is over but the conflict of ideas goes on as feverishly as ever . . . the elections [off year of 1867] are going heavily against the Republican Party and Johnson is taking courage. But Congress will still be strong enough to do his business and,

adding a Jeffersonian touch,

> the people will be on the right side whenever the politicians will let them see it. [10]

With the issue of the war settled and the nation at least nominally committed to civil rights for the blacks, he turned to activity more to his tastes, virtually ignoring for the rest of his career the perennial question of black equality. Not that he lost sight of the problem but, characteristic of the politicians and intellectuals of the day, he considered the Civil War a holy crusade, its objective won, and the nation saved. He would become absorbed again in the excitement of New York intellectual life.

He and Conway exchanged thoughts across the Atlantic concerning E. C. Stedman's literary ventures.[11] To Stedman himself he confided that "Longfellow was forever without thought. Emerson had thought without form (except for occasional lines!)." [12] His correspondence with Kate Fields continued in low key, thanking her for gifts of books at Christmas and contrasting her thoughtful attention with that of others of his learned friends—George Ripley and George Bancroft.[13] In the spring of 1876, with a trip to England contemplated, he was pleased with Stedman's high opinion of his history of transcendentalism, admitting that he was afraid the book was "lazy and thin." He was off to England to get ready for the "winter's campaign which will need to be vigorously pushed." [14] On his return in the fall he wrote again enthusiastically to Stedman that he felt encouraged, strong, and revigorated.[15] Then there were the summer vacations back in New England with relatives and old friends—usually at Lenox, Massachusetts, and occasionally in North Conway or Dublin, New Hampshire.[16]

Frothingham's circle of New York friends went far beyond the scope of those engaged in fighting the battles of radical religion. George Ripley, his theological battles over and settled in New York, was a *Tribune* writer and after Greeley's death in 1872 president of the Tribune Corporation. He and Frothingham saw a great deal of each other, after the church services in Masonic Hall, through mutual friends and visits in each other's homes. They both knew Kate Fields, George Bancroft, and Theodore Parker, who was a frequent visitor to New York before his final departure in 1860. Frothingham encouraged Ripley through his early financial trouble while paying off Brook Farm debts. When his wife, Sophia, died in 1865, it was Frothingham who helped him recover from his grief. When Ripley later became engaged to Mrs. Louise Schlozzberger, an Austrian widow, the Frothinghams were part of a small circle of friends to whom he confided the news of the impending wedding.[17] Later he conducted the wedding ceremony. When Ripley died in 1881, Frothingham was abroad and regretted deeply that he could not be on hand to say a few farewell remarks for his old parishioner and friend.[18]

In addition to Ripley were the people of the *Tribune*–Greeley himself, Whitlow Reid, and Lucia Calhoun—in Frothingham's orbit of activities; "a most distinguished group," he considered them.[19] Among the literary people in Frothingham's circle, in addition to Edmund C. Stedman were John C. Holland, better known as Timothy Titcomb, "a copious writer"; Bayard Taylor, novelist, translator of Goethe, and diplomat; and Robert Carter of Appleton's *Encyclopedia*. A Shakespearean actor, Richard Grant

White; Charles. S. Brace, a philanthropist; and E. L. Youmans, a popular science lecturer, added variety to the group. Theologians might be expected in his list of friends. However, Frothingham, for all his militancy against organized religion, included among his friends the editor of the *Evangelist,* Henry Field—a man who could "greet Robert Ingersoll warmly." From Union College was Professor of Biblical Theology Dr. Charles Briggs, and Rev. Hitchcock of Union Theological Seminary. Dr. Washburn of Calvary Church and Isaac Hecher of the Congregation of Paulists were also friends of Frothingham. College professors were also in his circle, including Ogden Rood, Professor of Physics, and Miles Joy, Professor of Chemistry, both of Columbia College. Dr. F.A.P. Barnard, President of Columbia, was usually present both in Frothingham's church and at social gatherings which Frothingham attended. In his memoirs he recalled Dr. Barnard in a colorful *non sequitur* as "the only man I ever knew whose long ear trumpet was never an annoyance." [20]

No reliable record of the interaction of this group exists. Some of the group often met at Frothingham's New York home where they also saw Horace Greeley, Robert Dale Owen, D.E.H. Chapin, as well as two of Frothingham's church trustees, Oliver Johnson and Mary E. Dodge. Others of them must have attended the Sunday evenings at Alice and Phoebe Carey's salon, which was "frequented by the brightest minds," recalled Frothingham.[21] When not preparing sermons or, after 1867, working for the Free Religious Association, he spent his time writing, attending social gatherings, mixing with artists and literary people, serving on committees, and avoiding inconsequential things. As art critic for the *Tribune,* after George Ripley took over as president of the corporation, Frothingham attended showings and artist's receptions at the Dodworth Rooms in company with General Dix and Cyrus Field's sister-in-law.[22] In order to get material for his art reviews he mingled with the crowd and listened to random remarks about the works of art. These, with his own standards of taste, became the basis of his articles. He and George Ripley attended a meeting at Mott Memorial Library on Madison Avenue to help organize a national academy for arts and sciences. An observer reported the event as a gathering of a "strong group" of about sixty people, leaders of thought in the city, at a committee meeting chaired by William Cullen Bryant. O. B. Frothingham, he observed, was "an ultra Unitarian pulpit philosopher and theist in some sense or other. . . ." [23]

Another activity, less consistent with his natural inclination, was an attempt in 1879 to establish a cooperative colony association for setting up a co-op in West Salem County, Kansas. In this enterprise he worked with Felix Adler, Frederick Olmsted, and E. L. Godkin. He was seen occasionally at the American Free Trade League in the company of Henry Demarest Lloyd and Godkin.

His appearance on public platforms in New York City was not an unusual event. However, his speaking on social reforms other than anti-slavery was unusual. In the last few weeks of his stay in New York he appeared at Thackeray Hall to help found the "Society of Moderation." He sat on the platform with "venerable" Peter Cooper, Walt Whitman, and Thurlow Weed. Total abstinence seemed the goal of the crusaders, said Frothingham, but for himself, although he believed in it, he was not one. He indulged in the "moderate use of wines" but admitted that had he never touched a drop, he would have had a clearer mind for more hours of useful work.[24]

At another time he became involved in a controversy that was not to his liking. He had spoken to the New York Harvard Club in the spring of 1870, comparing Dartmouth's and Harvard's approach to education. In part of his discourse he had remarked that Harvard had never succeeded in educating an Indian. The editor of *College Review,* present at the dinner, covered the speech in his journal under the title, "Mr. Frothingham Dislikes Indians." Bitter letters followed, from Frothingham accusing the editor of resorting to the same "vile aspersions of honest representations" typical of the daily press.[25] A day later, with mounting anger, he disclaimed holding any bias against Indians. Harvard, he said, could not claim the same affinity for the Indian shown by Dartmouth but he hoped that his alma mater would admit "red men, black men, and men of every race and color on terms of equality for an education there." Angrily rejecting the accusation of having "peculiar views," his final blast reflected his own sensitivity toward an unsympathetic press. "My enemies have tried to fasten on me obnoxious opinions and you must pardon me if I express amazement at seeing the same thing countenanced by a journal like yours." [26]

His encounter may explain why he turned down the invitations to the Phi Beta Kappa dinner and a request to speak again at the Harvard Club in 1878.[27] To John O. Sargent a cool note conveyed his attitude: "I avoid on principle public dinners especially those at which I am expected to speak. . . ." [28] A year later Henry Bellows accepted an invitation from Sargent to help plan a Harvard Club meeting and the Harvard Club festival.[29] This may have been another reason why Frothingham had no more to do with these affairs.

Absorbed as Frothingham was in the New York milieu, he did not ignore entirely his New England friends. He was associated with them closely in the FRA after 1867. However, in the same year, the Radical Club of Boston was founded which claimed, for a short time, some of his attention. It was an informal group meeting irregularly in Boston at the Chestnut Street home of Mr. and Mrs. John T. Sargent. Emulating the Transcendental Club and the Town and Country Club of pre-Civil War days, members read essays on religion, literature, and philosophy. Spotty records were kept. A single volume put together by Mrs. Sargent after the end of the club in 1880, contains sample essays and accounts of the discussions—all undated. By her account, the membership at the beginning was thirty, expanding to two hundred at the end. There were certainly never two hundred people at the Sargent home at one time. However, the membership list was the roll call of the leaders in the FRA, with such notable additions as Dr. Oliver Wendell Holmes, John Fiske, Benjamin Pierce of Harvard, and Wendell Phillips.[30]

Frothingham, up from New York, occasionally attended. An essay on the Italian saint, Borremo, was his only recorded major contribution, except for a four-line poem given on February 14, 1870, at the club's "Poetical Picnic." It was a stiff little verse, full of "thou's" and "thine," decrying the state of truth—an "outcast stranger" in a lonely world. His essay on Borremo was a graceful piece of literature, graphically describing the Italian countryside and presenting a biography of a man which Higginson said was "not a touched up portrait but a new one." Potter and Cyrus Bartol agreed. Yet there was nothing radical in this.

However, at another meeting Frothingham took issue with both the Darwinists and the trancendentalists in the group. To Nathanial Shaler's paper on Darwinism, he responded that scientific and moral categories are not always in conflict and sometimes not related at all. Immortality is not subject to science. "What right have we to immortality if our mortality bears no fruit?" he asked. "Immortality means growth which is justified in progress." Darwinism and theological distinctions do not destroy one another. Frederick Hedge, the old transcendental minister, gave a paper on "Pantheism," a belief that Frothingham once claimed to adhere to. His response to it had Calvinistic overtones. Pantheism destroys conscience, he said, and eliminates the pull between good and evil, a tension much needed for moral development. Wendell Phillips, who relished a brush with the transcendentalists, must surely have agreed.[31]

It is no wonder that Frothingham's contemporaries, friends and foes alike, had difficulty in following what must have seemed an erratic and inconsistent line of thought. As for Frothingham, he was obviously bored, and his reaction stirred a minor controversy. To Caroline Dall, who blamed him for her exclusion from the group, he admitted in 1871 that his interest, "never deep, ceased long ago and for the past two or three years" he did not know who attended the meetings.[32] Apparently he attended no meetings after 1870 or 1871, shortly before his letter to Caroline Dall. In the fall of 1874 the *New York Daily Tribune* carried an article from "RWL," "The Boston Radical Club, Its Death and How It Came to Die." It died because "left-wing theology killed it," wrote "RWL." Its work was done, a member was quoted as saying. Its narrow philosophy, its pre-Darwinian transcendentalism, was "sublime rubbish" concluded the author.[33]

No one was sure who wrote it. Was "RWL" a nom de plume of a Boston correspondent? Was the Radical Club member quoted, O. B. Frothingham? Was the writer Frothingham himself? It seems quite unlikely. The rhetoric was too strong. Frothingham himself was, at this time, claiming to be a radical and was sensitive about the term "left-wing theology." [34] However, he was fully capable of using such terms as "sublime rubbish" or "its work was done." It is probable also that in 1874 he felt completely beyond transcendentalism and more of an evolutionist. But to plant such an article as a letter to the editor from a Boston nom de plume was not at all like Frothingham's usual direct style of intellectual combat. Moreover, many of Frothingham's most respected friends were still active in the club. As late as the spring of 1874, Christopher P. Cranch, of Frothingham's New York circle, was up for a meeting, recalling that Emerson, Weiss, W. C. Gannett, and Edith Cheney were also there. [35] A few days after the *Tribune* article appeared, he wrote to Mrs. John T. Sargent declining an invitation to attend the club again. His note, polite in the beginning, ended with a mildly facetious tone. He was glad that 13 Chestnut Street was to ring with voices, though strange, and to carry on the "battle against the Romans in the air (like the ancient Germans)." [36]

Perhaps he can be forgiven his disaffection, if not his indirection, for he was at the time totally involved professionally in the FRA and absorbed socially in a much more interesting literary group—the Fraternity Club. George Ripley may have thought of the idea after a church reception at his home in the spring of 1869. James Herbert Morse was there, as were members of Frothingham's church and Frothingham himself. In Morse's records the idea of a literary club was urged on OBF and "he was eager for it." Later, at the home of Lucy Gibbons, Morse's mother-in-law, he was irritated at Frothingham, who seemed to miss the point and "go off half cocked" about public readings for the poor, writing in his diary that "it takes a wrench to bring him back to details." [37] Morse, not known for his patience, was later pleased with results of the beginning of the club. It was to be a club for literary and social purposes, to amuse and instruct the members and give all a chance to express opinions and thoughts. The group, mostly from Frothingham's church, met fortnightly in various homes from October to April. No food and drink was served; reading and conversation were the keynotes and each had a chance to contribute. The record of the club was kept in bound volumes for each year, containing the handwritten essays and poems presented with miscellaneous drawings, cartoons, and hand-done illuminations. [38]

The Fraternity Club was a place where dignified people with public responsibilities could satirize those things they could not in their professional life. They could relax among like-minded people and laugh at themselves and society. George Haven Putnam, with a fuller memory of the club than either Morse or Frothingham, recalled that

sometimes the main essay would be the work of a scholarly writer, and would, with gravity of purpose, present a subject that was entitled to worthy consideration; while at others according to the temperament of the editors, the Journal would be made up of humorous, not to say hilarious, contributions which had no other purpose than amusement.[39]

C. P. Cranch edited the first volume of *Fraternity Papers*. The "Irish problem" was the target of satire. Accompanying an essay on "high art" was a drawing of an enormous statue of George Francis Train, the symbol of the politician: one hundred feet tall, brass from head to foot, an eagle on his shoulder, holding a balloon, as pigeons competed for a perch on his nose. At his feet on a bas relief base lay a tamed Britannia lion. The cost of the statue, in Central Park of course, was one million dollars, to be paid for by the Irish voters.

The next essay panned the clergyman, Protestant or Catholic, who appealed to unthinking people. The cartoon depicted "the cast iron preacher," who preached in "Bogus Hall, on Dark Street." The robot, with hinged jaw and arms, was "one of the most wonderful inventions of the day with sounds, gestures and internal machinery which could be wound up to run for twelve hours—a good invention for enlightening our land."[40] It was patented by "CPC." Some evenings were devoted to nonsense, others to sentimental trivia. At other times, as Putnam observes, serious essays worthy of publication were given. Henry James, the budding writer, gave "Balzac's Letters," which was later published as *French Poets and Novelists* (London, 1878). Howard Hunter's essay on "The Relation of Puritanism to Hawthorne" was also a serious essay worthy of attention by modern scholars (Vol. 8, 1878).

The group was usually composed of the same congenial spirits: Oliver Johnson, Calvert Vaux, Octavius and Caroline Frothingham, Mary Mapes Dodge, George Haven Putnam, C. P. Cranch. Often the evening was enlivened by some members from out of town:[41] T. W. Higginson, James Freeman Clark, Helen Hunt, and Ellen Frothingham. Ellen, Octavius' younger sister, was a frequent visitor to her brother's home in New York. In Boston her Commonwealth Avenue house was very nearly a literary salon. She corresponded with the leading literary figures of the day, was an avid reader, and had literary and linguistic ability of her own.[42] One evening John Weiss, Frothingham's old friend of "Hook and Ladder" days and an FRA colleague, attended. Morse considered him a "singular man—hard to come down to earth." [43]

The second volume of *Fraternity Papers* (1870-1871), commemorating April Fool's Day, was edited by Frothingham's wife Caroline and a Mrs. Sewall. A large drawing of the court jester filled the first pages under the title "Cap and Bells." Frothingham himself set the theme:

Fools day, firmly established in history, serves a human need. Erasmus wrote in Praise of Folly, Parker 'dressed his books in pigskin'; on fools day it is fitting to 'shake our cap and ring our bells in celebration of the folly that runs all the year round, makes each of the twelve months its own and leaves a good many thinking the whole world mad.'

The original joke, of course, was Eve's connubial prank on Adam after being herself outwitted by the snake. Spring itself is a huge joke, tempting birds out only to be frozen; people go out expecting a balmy day and the old fellow laughs in his sleeve "to see them scamper to quarters." A section called "Brevities" were vignettes contributed by Frothingham and others, edited by Mrs. Frothingham: A spoof on housekeeping: "It is an art of letting well enough alone"; an epitaph from Worcester from people, as Frothingham remarked, having exhausted their stock of entertainment: "Under the sod beneath these trees, lies the pod of Solomon Peale. Old Peale is not here but only his pod. He shelled out his soul and went straight to God."

Children, pointed out Frothingham, were the original and perfect fools, in contrast to the adult variety of "darned fools." Children, with their innocent lack of perspective, say unintentionally poignant things that might cause a laugh; a child's prayer: "Dear God help Daddy and make my cat a good cat." Following a few poems, Frothingham ended the literary year with a brief essay on the timelessness of the "Cap and Bells" issue. Using the Easter myth of reincarnation, he closed:

> A piece of bone from a decayed body forms the center of a resurrected body on Judgment Day—so to [hope that our] Cap and Bells paper may go to the Valhalla of good papers, before we become serious—farewell for the summer after your writing labors.[44]

After four years of activity, the club began to lose some of its original spontaneity. Outsiders accused the members of being exclusive, conceited radicals. Many of the insiders felt that its brighter people furnished intellectual entertainment to the average members. At the last meeting of the year, in 1874, Frothingham gave a paper called "Our Club," attempting to refute both criticisms of the group. It was a remarkable thirty-five page essay in his wife's handwriting, defending the quality of the literary output and denying that a few did all the work and that attempts at discussion had led to a "dull level." The essays had been fresh and varied, ranging over topics from Robin Hood Ballads to Herbert Spencer. Nine men and three women had contributed the past year, including Dr. Edward Emerson, Kate Field, Oliver Johnson, James Morse, and George Putnam. Some were brilliant, he thought; all worthy of any magazine. He related to the group the things he had learned from the others (i.e. culture of western cities, his area of ignorance, for example). He was astonished at the industry and brilliance of the amateurs who had done the writing and reading of papers over the past four years "of rich mental entertainment."

He admitted that the discussion of the papers had been the "feeblest part." All seemed to agree to this, which was really the reason for his paper evaluating the club. "Why was it so?" he asked. "Birds will not sing, babies will not gurgle, children will not show off their pretty accomplishments at the time desired—so brilliant people—like jewels, put out one another." [45] His answer was flattering to the club members but there was no real solution. From then on the discussions languished but the quality of the papers held up. The following year Frothingham was president and in Morse's opinion the club appeared at its best under his leadership. [46]

The enthusiasm for the Fraternity Club held up through its last year. James Morse, elected president for the fourth time in 1878, recalled that it was the best winter season and Frothingham's essay on "Culture" was the highlight of the year. [47] Just why the group disbanded is not clear. The last volume, for the year 1878, offers no clues. Morse in his diary says nothing of its demise, nor does Frothingham in his own *Recollections and Reminiscenses.* Perhaps, like the Radical Club, which survived it, it had done its work. Perhaps the people were talked out.

TWO

"Mine has been a career of conflict, where hard words had to be heard and spoken, and heavy blows dealt as well as received." [48] Looking back on his New York years, in spite of his success in his own church and his brilliant social life in the city, Frothingham was disappointed at the reception given him by the popular press. He felt the public image of him was distorted, and that much of what he did was misconstrued in the popular mind. "Because I am radical in theology," he complained, "people think I am radical in everything else and I am beset by long-haired men and short-haired women who expect me to favor their pet schemes." [49]

At first he had received a cordial reception from Dr. Bellows, Dr. Osgood, later turned Episcopalian, and other conservative Unitarians. However, Bellows had expressed mild disapproval of Frothingham's first sermons in Jersey City. [50] As his New York ministry evolved, his sermons there "brought questions to the minds" of the Unitarian leaders, as to his "Unitarian orthodoxy." [51] This was the issue from beginning to end. Just how free was Unitarianism? Frothingham, after leaving Salem, had proceeded as though the denomination was not a sect but a fraternity of minds allowing for a loose association of religious societies, free of ceremonies, sacraments, and liturgy. When he found himself increasingly in disfavor, mildly ostracized, and bypassed in the affairs of the local association of Unitarian ministers, he was hurt to find himself outside of the fellowship and sympathy of the men of his father's generation. He was unhappy, in spite of his growing radicalism, to be exluded in the thinking of his colleagues, from the broader Unitarian tradition which had nurtured them all.

His new church, built by and for his Third Unitarian Society, was to be dedicated in December, 1863. This event brought to the surface the growing alienation between himself and his conservative fellow clergy. When the dedicatory ceremony occurred on Christmas Day, 1863, none of the Unitarian clergy of the city was there; "snubbed," recalled Frothingham, "because it was not a proper church—no sacraments, no ceremonies." [52] Only his father, thirteen years retired from Boston First Church, contributing a hymn for the occasion, was on hand to support him. At the cornerstone laying earlier, Henry Bellows had been offended by what he considered a violation of church practice in New York City—a minor matter of protocol in Frothingham's opinion. Particularly strung by Bellows' boycott, Frothingham accused Bellows of being "petulant and incoherent" in his criticism of the church ceremony. Giving as his reason for not attending the dedication, Bellows wrote that he and Frothingham were essentially different in "ideas of ministerial comity."

Just what the specific grievance was is not too clear but apparently it had something to do with a personal slight, real or imagined, Bellows felt had come from Frothingham's dedication plans. He offered to put the dispute before a third person, Dr. Frederick Hedge of Boston, agreeing to abide by his decision as to whether he had been "incoherent, loose and petulant" in the matter.[53] Frothingham defended himself by citing the precedent of Samuel Longfellow's church dedication in Brooklyn, which he had followed. He denied that he had been divisive or had isolated his church from the others.[54] As for Bellows' plan for adjudicating the conflict, Frothingham thought the matter too small and too personal to involve others. He proposed that the matter be laid to rest.[55] Frothingham's answer downgrading the whole importance of the ceremony must have angered Bellows all the more. Fastidious in matters of liturgy, jealous of his position as leader of the New York Unitarian clergy, he could be a "generous and whole-souled man." [56] Yet for a man who could keep in his private papers a list of his "enemies," he was also capable of bearing ill feeling for a long time.[57]

Although he and Bellows remained openly cordial between their disputes, "Frothingham increasingly found himself occupying a position somewhat similar to that [once] held by Theodore Parker in Boston." [58] His conservative colleagues who had snubbed his church dedication denounced the rational pulpit as "a wolf in sheep's clothes" and declared the tendency of naturalism was to atheism. Frothingham seemed resigned to such criticism.

To Conway, after an unsatisfactory year in the new church building, he complained in a jocular vein that "Bellows blows as usual, putting out a good many sparks he is trying to revive," and Osgood, now Episcopalian, was holding forth on Madison Avenue. "The little tea pot is smoking and

bubbling at a great rate but the people sip their tea, ignoring the tempera-
ture of the water." There was to be an attempt in the spring, he wrote
Conway, to raise $50,000 to organize a "conference of the Western
World" to bring people to the faith of "Channing and Co." "Bellows is
behind it, trying to organize liberality, and believes our people will be
eager" to contribute to it.[59] "The fools are not all in the Cabinet and
Senate, you see, the church has some to spare. . . ." Concerning their
mutual friends he had kinder words; Wasson, he thought, might take
Conway's old church in Cincinnati and Higginson, out of the Army, was
back in Newport to "resume his literary work." For Emerson, much
admired by Conway, he had gentle reproach. He gives the Sunday evening lectures on "Boston topics," ignoring the war, the draft, and our
cities. But things were not going too badly, as the Civil War approached its
end. Four states had already abolished slavery, he informed Conway, and
the true nature of the hated institution had been proved. His own "little
church on 40th Street [Lyric Hall] was not full" but had many earnest
radicals in it, but he was bitter toward his New York surroundings and
envied Conway in London. "I could be content to work forgotten by
flunkies and mobs, and pot houses of my acquaintance if I could have the
position you enjoy in the old land." [60] The struggle between the conservatives and radicals over organization and creed, resulting in the founding
of the FRA, has already been noted (ses Chapter V). The ill will generated
between Bellows and Frothingham over this "schism" in Unitarianism was
never put to rest. Frothingham's FRA activities, his sermons and public
acts drew fire from Bellows, both for professional and personal reasons.

One of the most abrasive popular issues of Frothingham's New York
career was the "McFarland affair," in which he and Henry Ward Beecher
had jointly officiated in a deathbed marriage ceremony between Mrs.
McFarland and Albert Richardson, who had been shot by the aggrieved
Mr. McFarland. Richardson, a *Tribune* writer, had been shot at the newspaper offices in November, 1868, and the marriage took place on
November 25 as Richardson lay dying. The public was fascinated with the
affair for more than one reason and the press, including Bellows' *Liberal
Christian,* took full advantage of it. On the Sunday after the marriage
ceremony both Beecher and Frothingham faced expectant congregations
eagerly awaiting an explanation of their part in the strange affair.
Beecher said nothing but Frothingham, after his previously planned
sermon, made a few informal remarks about his part in the McFarland
affair. The *New York Tribune* (December 6) carried a brief summary of his
remarks, giving his views on divorce and remarriage.

The *Liberal Christian* a few days later carried the event as a news item
under "Religious Intelligence," opposite a lengthy editorial, by Bellows
presumably, on "Marriage—What Is It?" The "ghastly event," he wrote, is
over and everyone must live with their consciences. Beecher, he acknowl-

edged, had "generosity of soul," but Christian ministers have a larger responsibility and must be bound by the moral code of society.[61] Frothingham's answer to this and other press attacks was a polemical sermon on the "Foes of Society." They were the editors who falsify news to make money; who lie and invade privacy to sell newsprint; who avoid their responsibility because they are usually coldhearted, insensitive men.[62] Taking no offense at the pulpit blast, the *Liberal Christian* cited the sermon under "Religious Intelligence": O. B. Frothingham had preached a "timely" sermon and said many "excellent, well deserved" things about "sensational and scandal-loving journals of the time and their editors and interviewers." [63]

Not content to attack merely the press, his next sermon, strangely entitled "Elective Affinities," came out boldly in favor of divorce when needed and, in some cases, remarriage. Marriage, he said, should be freed, as had been government and church, from clerical domination. It is a crime, not a sacred contract, where individuals, no longer harmonious, poison each other. A new chance, a fresh start, should be available provided intelligence instead of passion rules.[64]

The *New York Tribune* quoted parts of the sermon without comment but Bellows, attacking now in the open and quoting from the *Tribune's* excerpts of the sermon, called it "The New Danger." "We are pained," he editorialized on Christmas Day in *Liberal Christian*, "to see that Rev. Mr. Frothingham, in his sermon last sunday morning . . . set forth views hostile to marriage—in favor of free love" striking at the foundations of society.[65] Frothingham's reaction was immediate and angry. The day after Christmas he sent off a note by private courier to Bellows demanding that he apologize for his unjustified attack, claiming that he had been wrongly interpreted from the *Tribune,* Bellows' source of information. Back, by private messenger, came Bellows' query as to why Frothingham had sent him such a communication and a request for a copy of the controversial sermon. Frothingham's reply, a three and one-half page letter, confronted Bellows directly.

> I sent the communication to you mainly because it belonged to you. . . . I did suppose besides that you were concerned in [the editorial management of the L.C.] and shared a portion of the responsibility for what was printed even if you did not contribute with your own pen. I wished to lay open to you personally my feelings in respect to the censor the paper has recently published. Those feelings are very decided. I will not be ashamed to confess that they are keen and bitter.
>
> In the two weeks that I was vilified by every paper in the city, except the *Tribune* . . . I may almost say when my name was coupled with the most opportuning epithets and my character was made the sport of the rabble— not one of you came near me [with] friendly support or sympathy—not one of you sent me a message of good will—not one of you apparently thought it worth while to ask me what my action imported or what my motives and

purposes in them were.

The paper which is your peculiar organ already follows that of the most incompetent journals in the country [and] lends its sanction to the vulgar interpretations . . . mentioning my name in connection with opinions [which] implies moral debasement.

This was simply outrageous . . . for liberal churchmen . . . to spread stupid calumnies. I was hurt and they must hear me say so.

The sermon you allude to does not exist in Ms. It is my custom now to preach without notes and my sympathetic reporter has not copied his report. This is no matter. I do not ask permission to express my views in L.C. I ask for a disavowal of the hasty remarks that were made in advance of any intelligence respecting their character. This may be done either by printing my letter without . . . comment or by publishing an expression of regret at the misjudgement the paper has been guilty of—either will satisfy me. Pardon me if I seem stern in saying that nothing else will—such injustice is not easily repaired.[66]

Whether or not Bellows felt that an injustice had been done, the *Liberal Christian,* on New Year's Day, 1870, carried the editorial, "A Correction." "The Rev. Mr. Frothingham," wrote the editor, using the clerical title he knew Frothingham disliked, "writes the *Liberal Christian* that the report of his late sermon on 'Elective Affinity' in the *Tribune*" was wrong and "the L.C. has drawn wrong deductions." The editor would be glad, he claimed, to correct any errors and publish exactly what was said if the sermon existed in written form. Since it did not, the *Tribune,* usually friendly to Frothingham, would be the logical organ, thought the editor, to correct any errors. Nevertheless, he was glad that OBF did not really doubt the sanctity of marriage even though his discourse, "Elective Affinities," had "an unfortunate title for a Christian sermon." [67]

It is doubtful if the qualified "correction" satisfied Frothingham. There was little doubt that he had been quoted correctly by the *Liberal Christian* by way of the *Tribune*. The sermon in dispute, which Frothingham claimed did not exist, was later printed "by request," [68] but Frothingham never sent him a copy. Apparently he felt a thorough reading of the entire manuscript would not change Bellows' interpretation. The real issue was the wide gap in theological and philosophical views of the social attitude toward marriage and divorce. He knew conciliation was not possible.

Frothingham never really explained to the public, beyond his sermons, his reasons for becoming involved in the affair. Nor would the public have been enlightened by his explanation. Typical of the attitude of other shocked observers was that of George T. Strong, a lawyer in New York, wartime Secretary of the Sanitary Commission, and acquaintance of Frothingham as a trustee of the Mott Memorial Library. To consecrate this deathbed marriage, wrote Strong in his *Diary,* was to make a mockery of marriage. It would also turn the tide of opinion in favor of the aggrieved husband in the pending murder trial. Both Beecher and

Frothingham were accomplices in a sacrilegious act consecrating bigamy, he felt. The free thought that had been characteristic of Frothingham was responsible but

> probably people are prepared for anything from his tribe. It seems a rule that these sensational "free thinkers" of the pulpit and platform such as Beecher, Frothingham, Bellows and others have a screw loose somewhere. They are brilliant, clever, astute talkers, efficient in business—"men of the world" and of affairs far more than ordinary clerics, yet every now and then their commonsense gives way to some flagrant disastrous blunder like this one.[69]

E. L. Godkin, blasting the "cracked-brained reformers" in a *Nation* editorial, felt the same way.[70] With more restraint than shown in his reaction to Bellows' part in the controversy, Frothingham complimented Godkin's editorial, assuring him that he liked the opinions expressed there usually and thought the journal a good one for "genuine entertainment" in spite of the criticism of him in its "McFarland business." He hoped that the "childish controversy would not continue." [71] Of course it did. Godkin, never one to be put aside by what must have seemed an Olympian attitude by Frothingham, picked up the quarrel later at the Century Club, accusing Frothingham of trying to snub him and avoid the McFarland issue. In his own defense, Frothingham's mild reply was a simple denial as to the alleged snub; as for the McFarland business, "any reasonable man," he wrote Godkin, would know that he was not implicated in it as the public imagined, adding enigmatically that "my position [as a clergyman] gave me knowledge of some things" in the matter which justified the action.[72] This was as close as he ever came to explaining his role in the episode. Richardson died, McFarland was acquitted, and there the matter rested. Perhaps the significance of the affair is simply that Frothingham acted out his often expressed antipathy for the legalistic and Pharisaical type of mind. Frothingham had no sympathy for those who cried for McFarland's blood and called for revenge on the doomed Richardson.

The clerical profession, as Frothingham warned the Divinity School graduates in 1868, was not an easy one, nor was it all conflict either. Bright spots, outside of his own congregation and literary circle, were continuing contacts with Samuel Johnson, his visits to Frothingham's home in New York, recalling nostalgic memories, arranging pulpit exchanges through 1870 when he left his church in Lynn, Massachusetts, and looking forward to seeing one another at the FRA meetings.[73] Old acquaintances and friendly visitors from out of town often dropped in to hear Frothingham preach. Samuel Bowles, editor and literary patron from Springfield, Massachusetts, sampled the preachers in New York. He preferred Frothingham rather than Beecher whom he heard "without satisfaction." [74] It must have been satisfying to Frothingham to meet and talk to so distinguished a man, who later described his impressions to Miss Whitney, also an admirer of Frothingham:

> We shall have to be counted converts to your Mr. Frothingham. We went again on Sunday. He was a trifle too radical for Mary, but he on the whole voices my philosophy more fully that any other preacher I ever met. . . . His group is large and growing and attending was my greatest enjoyment in New York. He made me forget my own wants and egoisms.

His appraisal of Frothingham compared him with Parker: "I don't see why he isn't Theodore Parker improved; he has all his philosophy and spirituality and little of his hot temper, gross conceit and bigotry"; ending with a brilliant insight, prophetic of Frothingham's place in history: "Yet because of these lacks he will have smaller power." [75]

On a more personal level were frequent visits from William Lloyd Garrison, his battles over and enjoying a relaxed retirement. The old platform veteran admired both the radical content of Frothingham's sermons and his extemporaneous style of speaking without notes, "standing outside of the desk." [76] At both Lyric and Masonic Halls Garrison always received a warm reception, greeting old friends and possibly dining with the Frothinghams and their circle of friends.[77]

Not all of Frothingham's listeners had a favorable impression. E. L. Godkin, whose mind possessed more precision than breadth, complained to his fellow editor, C. E. Norton, that he had "given up Frothingham in toto." Long before the McFarland affair and while Frothingham was still writing for *Nation,* he had concluded that the "progressive radicals" like Frothingham were really narrow and that traveling the same road with them was uncomfortable. Frothingham is a "snappish dialectician," wrote Godkin to Norton, and "bores one just as much in showing what ought not to be believed as the orthodox in showing what ought." [78]

Henry Ward Beecher, never a close personal friend of Frothingham, could never quite decide how to appraise him. For a man who liked Spurgeon, the English evangelists, and considered himself a "moderate Calvinist," he was by his own admission, "befuddled by the 'vaporous' philosophy of Unitarians." Strictly speaking, he did not consider Frothingham a part of the Christian brotherhood of ministers but felt that he had a moral, if not spiritual force in the community. Yet he had deep reservations about the pulpit radical who could eliminate the threat of sin to hold men in a moral grip and set aside Christ as its redeemer for human weaknesses.[79]

One of Frothingham's most satisfying friends was Edmund C. Stedman.[80] There were no theological conflicts between them and he could always be counted on to help in church affairs. As a literary man he supported Frothingham's plan to present his ideas to "non-church goers." [81] His *Galaxy* article was a special inspiration after "personal trouble" (not explained) and a trip to Europe in the summer of 1876. "As I read it," he wrote to Stedman, "the import of my calling became vivid to me, as often it is not and I felt . . . your generous call to the public in my ears." [82] Caroline Frothingham also included him as one of her favorite friends in the New York circle. He was a frequent guest in the Frothingham home on 36th Street and enjoyed receiving friendly notes and little gifts from Frothingham's wife. They had a warm but stately relationship. "How shall I repay the debt?" (for hand-painted cup and saucer), he once wrote, "where there is a will either you or I will find a way and till then, remember that I am your grateful friend and *beaux Chevalier.*"[83]

Much of Frothingham's time was spent in the routine connected with the life of a minister. Unlike Theodore Parker, who had Hannah Stevenson as a private secretary, there is no evidence that Frothingham had any assistance in the chore of letter writing. During the church year full of events, large and small, there were strangers to write to, invitations for speaking to answer, or letters of introduction to write for young ministers wishing a place in New York City.[84] On vacation in New England, routine affairs pursued him and had to be attended to, whether it was a contribution to the Thomas Paine Bust subscription campaign or a detail concerning his church choir for the fall.[85] Also, there were frequent trip to the Boston area to speak at Parker Memorial Hall, to exchange pulpits with John Freeman Clark, or to lecture to the Waltham symposium.[86]

He was particularly jealous of his summers, not because he enjoyed the country, because it made him lazy and he preferred the city, but this was his time to write, to read, or to travel abroad. In the summer of 1872 North Church in Salem, his first charge, planned its centennial celebration. Former ministers were invited to participate and to deliver brief addresses. Frothingham refused to attend, with rather unfortunate results. Caleb Foote, in charge of the affair, expressed regret and hurt feelings over Frothingham's absence. He took the trouble to add Frothingham's note of refusal to his own remarks in the printed proceedings of the occasion. His note was "not reassuring," wrote Foote, for he had forgotten the agreement to come and was going elsewhere. A trip to Salem from Sharon Springs, New York, in hot weather, he quoted Frothingham as writing, "on that purpose alone was more than I could face." [87] It was not a graceful act but one that showed his aloofness that, at times, bordered on bad manners.

He was really more content in the swirl of events back in New York City. He might be expected to have frequent meetings in his home for small groups on church business and to look forward to entertaining Conway, back from England, to speak at Masonic Hall.[88] There were always the pleasant dinners with a small group followed by a lively discussion of philosophy, theology, or the timely subject of the "Alabama claims," or

Beecher's bigamy trial.[89] Probably less to his liking were times when he and Caroline were obliged to attend receptions at President Barnard's house at Columbia University or a gala affair honoring Bayard Taylor, newly appointed minister to Germany.[90]

Attending ordinations were more in the line of duty as a minister. Frothingham participated in some with enthusiasm. Early in his first year in New York he and Samuel Longfellow, then in Brooklyn, traveled together to Philadelphia to install J. K. Karcher at the Spring Garden Unitarian Church. Frothingham gave the sermon and Longfellow the charge. Both men were able to meet W. H. Furness of Philadelphia's First Unitarian Society, a man who later would work with both of them in the FRA.[91]

When Samuel Longfellow left the Brooklyn Unitarian Church in 1864 he was replaced by William White Chadwick. Just how and why Chadwick was known by Frothingham, Johnson, and Longfellow is not clear. While Chadwick was still in Divinity School he had corresponded with both Johnson and Frothingham.[92] Plans for his ordination were elaborately laid to include an impressive list of radical Unitarians. Bellows and Osgood were there, to be sure, but Robert Collyer of Chicago gave the sermon, Longfellow the charge, and Frothingham the prayer. Both Henry Blanchard, the Universalist, and Samuel May, radical and abolitionist of Syracuse, New York, were there.[93] In relating the plans to Samuel Johnson, who did not attend, Chadwick, with obvious relish, wrote that Frothingham would offer the right hand of fellowship with his "no church" and then he was to "neutralize Osgood." Bellows would be placed where "he can't cut up much." [94]

With Chadwick established in Longfellow's old place in Brooklyn, Frothingham now had a young, liberal colleague to support his efforts in New York. When the time came he proved to be a valued member of the FRA and one of Frothingham's most loyal defenders in times of controversy. Chadwick and Frothingham occasionally exchanged pulpits, as did Frothingham and W. C. Gannett, while the latter was a director of the FRA in Boston.[95] The attitude of the younger men toward Frothingham was a mixture of awe and envy. To fill his pulpit was a big order. Chadwick wrote to Gannett that he "did not enjoy it much . . . for one thing, was conscious of his legs, there being no pulpit—just a lectern," adding that "OB was liked very much by most of his people, not so much by others." [96] After Frothingham's retirement Chadwick, along with Potter and W. C. Gannett, helped transmit his ideas and memory into the twentieth century.

By the spring of 1878 there were unmistakable signs that his New York career was coming to a close. His resignation as president of the FRA, his dwindling interest in writing for *Index* magazine and reluctance to write for other journals,[97] and the end of the Fraternity Club, all heralded the reality of his impending retirement. Sometime during the early fall of this last year, he noticed pains in his back, and his speech and locomotion became increasingly uneven and halting. He was losing his old fluency in the pulpit, his deliberate movements, his graceful gait. These "first dread signs of ataxia," as Higginson later recalled, forced his medical advisors to warn him to give up the strain and responsibility of his position. His congregation gave him a year's leave of absence, hoping that his malady was a temporary one that travel and rest could cure.[98] However, even before the final medical verdict was in, Frothingham knew that his retirement would probably be a permanent one.

Shortly after he submitted his resignation he admitted to Conway in England,

> I am slackening off. Have sent in my resignation and mean to take a furlough of a year at least for mental recreation. A twenty-years ministry in N.Y. will close in the spring. I am fifty-six years old and must consider how I must dispose of the remaining decade or so to the best advantage for the [purposes] I have at heart.[99]

Two weeks later he wrote to W. C. Gannett, then in the West, that he was to leave his parish in May "perhaps never to return to the ministry." [100] To the younger man he admitted what his colleagues had perhaps vaguely sensed: "My resources have been seriously diminished within the last two years."

The strain of the last twenty years had taken its toll. Hard facts had to be faced, painful decisions made. His retirement, announced in February, 1879, was noticed by the leading papers of the city. The eulogies began, in spite of the attempt to pretend he was simply taking a leave of absence. "Frothingham, like Theodore Parker and Emerson," wrote a *New York Times* reporter, had grown "too broad for Unitarianism or any mere theological creed." The leader of the flourishing independent society, whose mental independence is fortified by his independence of circumstances "is ranked by his many admirers as one of the most original thinkers in America." [101] A few weeks later he was the subject of an editorial, "The Tone of Our Modern Life," calling him "our boldest preacher." [102]

During the late winter and early spring of 1879 plans were made for a reception in his honor. Leaders of the intellectual life in New York were invited. His old friends and FRA colleagues from out of town were called upon to participate. Speeches, drawn from accounts of Frothingham's activities and personal recollections of friends, were prepared for the occasion. Higginson, down from Cambridge, arrived two weeks early to assist the trustees in charge of preparations. Staying at Hoffman House rather than with the Frothinghams on 36th Street, he was on hand also to help them through the taxing ordeal.[103] The gala affair promised to be a major social event of the spring, an occasion rarely provided for a retiring minister, particularly a radical one. Certainly Theodore Parker himself got no such farewell as he left his congregation, nineteen years before.

On the evening of April 22, a distinguished group of more than one thousand men and women in full evening dress filled the auditorium of the Union League Club to hear the eulogies and say their farewells.[104] The gas lights, casting a mellow glow, and the flowers tastefully arranged, provided an atmosphere appropriate for the occasion. In a semicircle on the stage sat Frothingham, flanked by nine dignitaries, prepared to speak. Ex-Governor of Utah, Frank Fuller, George Haven Putnam, and Edmund Stedman represented the trustees of the religious society. George William Curtis, editor, orator, man of letters, and main speaker; Felix Adler of the Ethical Culture Society and Frothingham's successor as president of the FRA; Joseph May, Unitarian minister from Philadelphia; William W. Chadwick of Brooklyn; and Frothingham's old classmates and coreligionists, Higginson and Longfellow, made up the platform personalities.

Fuller, rising to open the proceedings, called for gladness rather than sadness on the occasion. He then delivered an expansive speech on Frothingham's contribution to humanity, equating his style and thought with that of Rufus Choate and Edward Everett. Each speaker rose in turn and delivered a eulogy, each different from the preceding one, each dealing with a unique dimension of Frothingham's career. George Haven Putnam sketched the history of their Independent Liberal Church, comparing Frothingham's work with that of Emerson and Parker. He drew a laugh from the audience when speaking of Frothingham's courage as being of such a quality that he feared no one, "not even his trustees!" [105] George Curtis rose to refute the theme of gladness for the occasion, suggested by the presiding officer, but for his own humorous purpose:

> Ladies and Gentlemen, despite what the chairman has been pleased to say, there is always a little that is sad in having to say goodbye, except to bores and bad habits and especially to a man whose going leaves with so many friends a regret that will not be dissipated until he is home again. I confess to a very profound sympathy with our friend Frothingham this evening—not because he is going to Europe but because this is one of those occasions on which a man is obliged to sit still and hear precisely what his friends think of him and before I and the men of this platform are done with him . . . I would not blame him if he quitely slipped out of the back door.

Most of his speech was punctuated with laughter but he ended on a serious note:

> And now my good friends you take leave of a teacher who has stood in the community alone for twenty years and unknown to most of the community has maintained its very cornerstone and its foundations of its continued existence.[106]

Next was Felix Adler whose speech was pungent if not elegant, expressing fears that Frothingham's departure might set liberalism back in religious thought. Refuting this was William Chadwick, Frothingham's younger FRA colleague, who gave him full credit for his influence on his own efforts at liberal religion in Brooklyn.

Higginson, at his best on such an occasion, delivered a humorous address full of clever allusions to people and events in the life he had shared with Frothingham. Entertaining as he was, he came the closest of any that evening to capturing the whole purpose of Frothingham's New York ministry.

> What he has done for you and for me and for all of us is not so much that he has brought us truth, or any system of truth . . . he has set reason above sect and helped us rise above them; he has told me that the word is very nigh us—in our mouth and in our heart—if only we would seek it. . . . He has spared all of you the need of becoming "Frothinghamians." [107]

Stedman and Longfellow followed with graceful remarks of literary quality, adding little to what had been said. The last speaker, Joseph May of Philadelphia, speaking as a Unitarian minister, stated that he regretted Frothingham's split with the denomination but that now (1879) true Unitarianism was really what Frothingham and his Independent Liberal Church had stood for.

The speeches ended. Fuller rose and read letters from those invited but who could not attend. George Ripley was confined at home by ill health. Oliver Wendell Holmes, Samuel Johnson, William Potter, and William Lloyd Garrison could not make the trip from New England. All recalled past events they had shared and expressed admiration for Frothingham's contributions to radical religion. The most poignant came from Emerson:

> Mr. Frothingham has claims on me because of himself but also [for] his father—a noble friend of my youth. It is my clear duty to stay home because old age has tied my tongue and hid my memory.[108]

Certainly there was no applause after that reading, but as Frothingham rose to acknowledge the speakers of the evening the entire audience rose in a prolonged, standing ovation. He began by fending off all praise. Citing his long career of self-scrutiny he turned the praise back to his friends.

> If I had been endowed with the graceful persuasion of my friend Curtis, or the heroic courage of my friend Higginson, or the sweet reasonableness of my friend Potter, or the steadfastness and clearness of my friend Adler, or the joyousness of heart of my friend Chadwick, I should have done much better—so much better—so much better! But I was only myself . . . [in fighting our past battles] the weapon I was forced to use sometimes bent and broke in my hands, wounding me more than my opponent.[109]

He was in no mood, however, to dwell on the conflicts of his career but rather the gains he saw, the optimism he felt: ". . . the spirit in which modern faith comes forward to meet faith of former days [is] not with slogans and war crys, not with the flourish of weapons, but with the still small voice of reason." His only acknowledgement of the profuse praise of the evening was his closing thought couched in terms revealing, in spite of himself, his transcendental past.

> If in these twenty years I have done anything to lighten any burden, to smooth any path, to comfort any spirit, no one should be as grateful for that as I . . . remember it isn't I that have done it, but solemn, eternal forces that work upon us, around us and through us which have condescended to use me as their instrument.[110]

With the applause ended, the chairman's final remarks concluded, chairs were removed and refreshments served for an hour of informal conversation.[111] Old friends greeted one another, exchanged reminiscences, and spoke to out of town acquaintances. The Frothinghams, surrounded by an admiring circle, spoke of their coming trip to Europe, their general plans and indecision as to how long they would stay. Conspicuously absent were Henry Bellows, E. L. Godkin, and Francis Abbot. It had been, in the manner of the nineteenth century, an all-male performance. No wives sat on the stage; no women spoke; no eulogy mentioned Caroline as a part of her husband's successful career. It was after midnight when the last goodbyes were said. Frothingham's New York career was all but over. The brilliant evening had provided laughter, much serious thought, fellowship, and no doubt some tears.

One more thing remained—his farewell sermon.[112] Masonic Temple on 26th Street was more crowded than ever on the Sunday morning on April 27, following the reception at the Union League Theater. A thoughtful, attentive audience listened to him claim he was a transcendentalist of the school of Parker. They followed his criticism of Unitarianism: vague and weak in theology, he claimed, denying that Jesus was a God but undecided as to whether he were merely a man, disclaiming human depravity but insisting that supernatural help was needed to guide humanity, and guilty of establishing a sect based on creedal conformity. This was the reason, he recalled, that he had left it twenty years ago. Not all of his remarks dwelt on the past. His last few minutes were devoted to his optimistic belief that sectarianism would be outgrown and to the hope that the people of the Independent Liberal Church, congregated for the last time, would not disappear into thin air. In a playful but serious aside he exclaimed, "For heaven's sake do not become spiritual tramps!" [113] Never feel despondent, he concluded, never feel hopeless; "that the future years will be better than the last twenty years. . . . The voice of the individual speaker may be silenced forever, but the eternal word will always be articulate." [114]

This was his final word to his congregation, a message that would attract the unfriendly attention of the press and plague his first few weeks in Europe. It would set off a controversy concerning Frothingham's views, not resolved until long after his return to America. But for the immediate future, he could turn his back on the New York controversies, and with the praise of his friends still in his ears, look forward to a relaxed voyage to France with his wife Caroline and their 29-year-old daughter "Bessie."

THREE

The ship was to sail four days after his final appearance at Masonic Temple. In the short time before their departure, there were last-minute letters to answer,[115] the house on 36th Street to be closed, personal belongings and a few choice books to pack, and arrangements to be made for an indefinite absence. Leaving the city by carriage and the Hudson River Ferry, and accompanied by Mrs. Stedman and other close personal friends, they boarded the ship berthed in Jersey. Before sailing time a bon voyage party was held in the main saloon. There were flowers and baskets of fruit from well-wishers. A silver drinking cup and testimonial letters from the Sunday afternoon lecture group and stacks of cards bidding them farewell and improved health arrived with members come to see him off. As the large Cunard liner was tugged from its slip, Frothingham appeared on deck, waving his hat and handkerchief to his friends ashore, as the ship disappeared down the river.[116]

Frothingham, perhaps recalling Theodore Parker, must have watched with mixed feelings as Manhattan Island slipped by and the landmarks of the lower bay dropped over the horizon. One career was probably ending. What would the next phase of his life be like? Would it be in New York or Boston? Or, indeed, would he return to America at all?

By June the Frothinghams were in Switzerland where mail from Stedman waited. Clippings from the *Post* and *Times* recounting his last sermon annoyed him, he acknowledged to Stedman, but he passed it off with a jab at his critics, "who are fools and bigots." Apparently he had not begun to relax noticeably but had made plans to "take springs in France," recommended, he wrote, "in cases like mine of nervous irritability and weakness." [117]

His summer in Switzerland and a trip to France in October, according to Conway, improved his health and spirits. By fall he was looking forward to spending the winter in Rome.[118] It was a disappointment, according to Hannah Stevenson, Parker's former secretary who wrote in a postscript to W. C. Gannett that she had a letter from "OBF in Rome, handwritten, painfully suggestive of weakness and an undertone of depression very perceptible." [119]

By spring, since his health was little improved, he was obliged to turn down the invitation of the *Truthseeker* magazine to represent the Free Thinkers (a New York society of Humanists) at the Brussels conference in June, 1880.[120] In the same month, back in Boston, Francis Abbot was given a retirement dinner complete with spoken eulogies and testimonial letters. No letter came from Frothingham for his old comrade of the FRA battles.[121] At the spring meeting of the association in Boston that year, his old colleague, sensing the state of his health, passed a resolution to assure him he was not forgotten.

> Rev. Mr. Alger—It seems fit that our session should end, not with creed, but with deed, and with a kind deed. I offer the following resolution:—
> WHEREAS, Our late President, Rev. Octavius B. Frothingham, is wandering in foreign lands, with impaired health, and perhaps sometimes with depressed spirits.
> The Free Religious Association holds in grateful and honoring remembrance his long record of historic services in behalf of every noble end, and desire to send him the assurance that they hold him tenderly in their hearts to-day, and wish him great enjoyment in his vacation, a speedy recovery of his strength, and a happy return to his home and work in America.
> The resolution was received with applause, and was passed unanimously, the vote being taken by rising.
> The Association then adjourned to 3 o'clock P.M.[122]

He was back in Switzerland for the summer when he received a copy of the *Index* containing the tribute to himself. In a warm letter to William J. Potter, secretary of the FRA, in publication in *Index* he acknowledged thoughts of his old friends. His interest in the FRA was still high he assured Potter; President Adler had his full support and admiration as did the *Index* and its retiring editor, Francis Abbot. He seemed glad to be thinking about his old association, but in a final thought to Potter he spoke of his own future, giving mixed impressions:

> Respecting myself, there is nothing of interest to tell. It is pretty well understood by this time that I have finally relinquished my post and abandoned my profession—that neither pulpit nor platform will know me again. This resolution is due to no considerations of health. My health is satisfactory, as good as it ever will be—good enough. But I want more leisure than the ministry affords for the pursuit of certain lines of thought which have interested me since I have been in Europe, and the life of a man of letters will be more satisfactory to me. In another career, I can be as useful as in the old one, perhaps more so. My absence will be prolonged a year more, in order that the gulf may be wider between my past and my future. Then I hope to come back better than new.
> Give my kindest wishes to such of our mutual friends as you may see, especially to the supporters of my beloved Free Religious Association; and believe me to be still, as always,
>
> Heartily yours,
> *O. B. Frothingham* [123]

The news was out in America by the fall of 1880. A *New York Times* editor wrote that Frothingham would retire, though his health had improved sufficiently to continue. His inclination toward literature will "serve his cause better" since he had long desired to leave the pulpit and had dropped the title "Rev." for "Mr." as he grew out of Unitarianism and into rationalism.[124] As usual, the press, the public, and even Frothingham's friends were confused. Was it ill health or a desire to begin a new career that caused his retirement and retreat to Europe? Frothingham himself seemed not to be sure as his second year in Europe began.

Little wonder that his congregation could not believe he would not reopen Masonic Temple, or that he got invitations to travel and speak while in Europe. Back in Boston, the people of Parker's Twenty-Eighth Congregational Society, still looking for a replacement, were sure that Frothingham could fill Parker's pulpit and would accept an invitation.[125]

After another winter in Italy, staying first in Rome, then Naples, he resigned himself to his permanent retirement from the ministry but had doubts about his chances for another career. To Conway, who was also in ill health in England, he wrote: "A trip will help you. Shut up shop as I did and move away . . . go to America with unburdened wings . . . and quiet yourself," adding a pessimistic afterthought, "by that time I shall hope . . . for something, as now I scarcely can." [126]

Aside from his own malaise and the cold weather in Rome, of which even New Englanders complain, sad news of deaths came from America. His own brother, Thomas Bumstead Frothingham, of Jamaica Plains died in March, 1880;[127] Weiss had died in July of the first year away; and his old friend and parishioner, George Ripley, made up the depressing list.

A bright spot, of course, was an encounter with an acquaintance or a surprise visit from old friends traveling in Europe. It was pleasant for the Frothinghams, in Venice, to greet Mr. and Mrs. Christopher P. Cranch, the sculptor—poet from his New York congregation, in the spring of 1881. The Cranches brought news from Rome where they had seen Bessie at an art show in the company of the sculptor Mr. Bale, his wife, and "half a dozen art students." [128] Through May, June, and July, the Cranches lingered in Venice, going out to dinner at the Chatham Hotel with the Frothinghams or lunching at their apartment.[129]

Between visits with the Cranches, the Frothinghams went to the "springs" in southern France in May and on to Paris for a visit. From there he wrote Conway that they would summer at a German spa and sail for home in the fall, promising to "pop in" on him in London on the way through.[130] Back in Venice until mid-July, they decided to leave the continent and spend the rest of the summer in Scotland, before sailing home. By now Frothingham was in better spirits. The winters in Italy and summers in Switzerland relaxing, visiting, reading, had arrested the progress of the slow paralysis.

He also now knew what he wanted to do. On the way to Scotland he, Caroline, and Bessie spent a few days with the Conways in London. With Conway he discussed his plans for a literary career. He would begin with a biography of George Ripley. Conway, a transcendentalist himself, encouraged him, as the man best fitted to undertake a biography of the "vice-admiral" of the transcendental, socialistic movement in New England.[131]

After twenty years in New York and more than two years in Europe, it was really New England and Boston that drew him back. In September a small personal item appeared in the *Index* of his "beloved Free Religious Association."

> Mr. O. B. Frothingham has returned to the country and is at present in Boston. We are glad his health is better.[132]

IX

Gentle Knight:
Skeptic or Believer,
1880–1884

Back in America to begin his new life, old questions from his "career of conflict" would not die. Had he become disillusioned with free religion? Had he repudiated transcendentalism for rationalism? Had he, in turn, rejected the validity of rationalism? These, and other questions, were raised by friends and opponents alike. Although his entire New York career had aroused a mixed response from the public, the circumstances surrounding his retirement and especially his farewell sermon raised the question: Has O. B. Frothingham recanted?[1]

ONE

While Frothingham was still on the high seas enroute to Europe, a *New York Times* letter-to-the-editor posed the question: "O. B. Frothingham, who is he, and what is he doing?" Written before he sailed, the letter proceeded to answer the question by a sketchy biography, full of errors of fact, suggesting that he was a "lone, solitary figure" in some sort of "rational, nonsectarian, religious movement." [2] A few days later, an *Index* editorial, presumably written by Francis Abbot, defended Frothingham from another *New York Times* feature article entitled "The Doom of Individualism." Frothingham had admitted in his farewell sermon that his intellectual movement had failed, stated the *Times*. Beecher's *Christian Union* implied the same. The age of individualism is at an end, the age of organization is at hand, Frothingham was said to have preached in his last sermon. Both the *Times* and *Christian Union* assumed that Frothingham, having repudiated transcendentalism, also was disillusioned with free religion. Abbot defended him. By saying that transcendentalism and individualism had fallen short did not mean that free religion was a failure. "Free Religion was not Transcendentalism," wrote Abbot, "and O. B. Frothingham was the best voice of rational religion." [3] William White Chadwick, Frothingham's younger colleague in Brooklyn, also came to his defense in a sermon. "My friend," he said, "must be defended against journalistic misinterpretation. He had not said Free Religion had failed," claimed Chadwick. He had not been a transcendentalist "for the last dozen years," but broke with it and became an "experimentalist, an evolutionist." [4]

It is difficult to see how Frothingham's critics could have construed his farewell sermon as a repudiation of his life's work. Yet, in spite of the effort of some of his defenders, the proceedings of the FRA in the spring of 1879 reinforced that impression. The end of the period of individualism was the theme of his last sermon, a speaker admitted, and was consistent with the change of leadership in the FRA. With Frothingham gone and Adler president, the emphasis would be on more organization, less talk, and more implementation of the ideals of rational religion.[5]

Even his closest friends were confused as to the frame of Frothingham's mind. Chadwick claimed in 1879 that he had not been a transcendentalist for the "last dozen years." Yet two years earlier, Frothingham, in congratulating Samuel Johnson for the article on the subject in the *Radical Review,* wrote glowingly, "As you put the matter, I am a Transcendentalist again . . . a position I have taken and maintain as a preacher." [6] Two years later, with Frothingham in Europe and his farewell sermon being debated, Johnson confessed perplexity to Samuel Longfellow. "In spite of his claims as a Transcendentalist," wrote Johnson, "Frothingham's last sermon did imply a drift away from individualism—a drift," thought Johnson, "of the radical mind toward organization, utilitarianism; a reliance on numbers as contrasted with personal, interior, ideal values." [7] The controversy over Frothingham's changed views had begun in the public press and in private among his old friends. It pursued him across the Atlantic and lay in wait for him when he returned.

TWO

After a few weeks in Boston, Frothingham returned to his New York home in November to work in the *Tribune* files containing George Ripley's papers. While occupied with Ripley, who had also given up a liberal ministry, and in a dark mood with his old career ended, his congregation scattered, Frothingham was interviewed by a reporter of the *New York Evening Post.* "What led you to give up preaching?" he was asked. His answer came out as a feature article, November 12, 1881, under the caption "Radical Thought." The work had become less pleasant, he was quoted as saying, and there was no support from the other members of the clergy. No new men were coming along to carry on. Adler and Chadwick were following the negative path of utilitarianism and materialism. The peripheral work of the radical preacher, complained Frothingham, drew "queer and unpleasant people" to him. He was expected to support all sorts of "wild schemes." Also, he lacked time to study and, as time went on, became more skeptical about free religion. It seemed to "lead to nothing." Creeds would continue, he was sure, as proven by the failure of free congregations in New England. Possibly thinking of Higginson's in Worcester, Johnson's in Lynn, Parker's in Boston, and his own, he confided to the reporter that he envied the holding power of the "working clergy" in Catholic countries, such as Italy. In a word, free thought led to "a dead materialism" which, he was quoted as saying, "I dread as much as any evangelical clergyman." [8]

The next day, a bit alarmed at the tone of the article, he wrote a letter to the *Post* editors. "In the main the account was correct," he wrote, "but somewhat more penitential than I like." Furthermore, he claimed he had not accused his friends Adler and Chadwick of following materialism. Rejecting any implication that he had "recanted," he added the enigmatic comment:

> . . . permit me to say that I have no reason for changing my opinions. It has however occurred to me that they do not contain the whole truth. Certainly, I have not gone back to any position which I have abandoned. [9]

The controversy began. "From Rationalism to Rome" was the title of an editorial in the *New York Times*, usually coldly neutral to Frothingham. Although he was given credit for sincerity of spirit in his sermons, he was flatly accused of changing his religious views. "He has given up belief in the infallibility of his own reason," wrote the editor, and "accepted Papal infallibility!", adding what was probably nearer the truth, "He had said all he had to say on creedlessness—so withdrew." [10]

Robert Collyer of Chicago, an FRA colleague of Frothingham, but no personal friend, accepted the recantation charge. In a sermon, "Octavius Brooks Frothingham's Confession," he mildly criticized him for following the cold reason of Parker and Channing too literally. He was encouraged by O. B. Frothingham's "confession" as a sign that he now realized reason must be balanced with faith in divine power. [11] Collyer confused the issue by implying that Frothingham was returning to transcendentalism and at the same time moving away from the "cold reason" of the more transcendental spokesmen, Channing and Parker. William Chadwick answered Collyer's sermon with a statement of regret if O. B. Frothingham had indeed "confessed" but refuted the charge that he had. Frothingham, he felt, should know as well as anyone that rationalism had grown in strength and evangelicism had grown weaker. Perhaps, he suggested, he had been overpessimistic and lost sight of the progress of rationalism while in "Alpine and Romish" surroundings. [12] *Two Worlds*, a spiritualist paper, explained his recantation from the "magnetic powers of the Catholic Church" which got into him while in Europe, working opposite influences in him. The *Index* tongue in cheek comment on the spiritualist excerpt gave it credit for at least having the "interest of being unlike any other reason for [Frothingham's] alleged change of views." [13]

William Potter, his loyal friend of FRA days, was most serious in rejecting the view that Frothingham had repudiated his radical views. He doubted the truth of the *Post* reporter's attack, written, he claimed, from an interview at which no notes were taken. The article was close to being a fraud and should be refuted at length by Frothingham himself. Since this was impossible, due to Frothingham's health and his attempt to avoid the strain of controversy, Potter visited him in Boston and wrote up for *Index* the results of his conversation:

> Within the last week, I have had the pleasure of three hours' conversation with our friend, and mainly on the themes covered by the published statement. I am sure—and I may say it without undue confidence—that with my knowledge of his mental temperament and past opinions, and my intimacy with his habits of thought and speech, I could write a much more accurate account, from that conversation, of O. B. Frothingham's present religious views than the New York interviewer composed. My account might not be so readable as his, nor so salable. It would certainly be very different in tenor. But I am not going to attempt it.
>
> I came away from our wholly cordial, friendly, and earnest talk with the entire and grateful conviction that he and I stand as near together to-day in our views, sympathies, hopes, as we did during the twelve years when we worked together as President and Secretary of the Free Religious Association. I detected no sign whatever of anything that could be called defection from the liberal ranks; no turning back upon the path, no lessening of conviction in the necessity of religious progress. The Evangelical Protestants and Romanists who are offering him the refuge of their special sanctuaries of belief may spare themselves the trouble. He is not looking in their direction. The only change of mental attitude observable to me was shown on two or three points, and it is evidently, even on these points, more a change of emphasis to his own consciousness than a change of views; for I think all his present views will be found stated somewhere in his published writings. He is, for instance, more dissatisfied than he was formerly, as are a good many liberal thinkers, with the results of materialistic philosophy; and he has less confidence than he once had in science as the solver of religious problems. At the same time, he gives somewhat more credit than he was wont to do to the old churches, with their creeds and symbols, for preserving the religious sentiment and nourishing the practical consecrations of life. And in these particulars, too, he would find not a few liberal thinkers, who are supposed to be in the advanced ranks, in sympathy with him.
>
> But he does not look back to the churches, nor to their creeds nor symbols, nor to any alleged revelation in the past, for the solution of today's great questions. He looks to the future for it, and so he still faces forward. He has faith that it will come in time, and believes that it will come in some grander disclosure of truth, in some larger synthesis of all truths than has yet been discerned. But, because he does not see clearly yet just what it is to be nor how it is to come, he chooses for himself to stop on the line of hope and

expectancy, and wait for more light. There are others of us with him, too, on that line. But few have earned the right to stop by so many years of fruitful labor as he. After thirty-three years of the preacher's toil, with little rest, he might fairly ask to be relieved from the field of active labor without other reason. It is enough if he but stands there to prophesy the coming light. That is encouragement and cheer. But some of us think we do see a little beyond that line of expectancy and hope—see a little of the way by which the coming light is to break. At least we see far enough for the doing of to-day's work, even though it be but to grope, feeling the way, for the removal of obstructions and the opening of windows for the freer access of the new day's light when it shall dawn. Others among us venture to think that the new day is already here, and the skies bright with promise; that the word for the hour has already been spoken, and that the greatest need is a larger and more earnest apostleship to spread it. All these phases and types of mind make up the ranks of religious progress. And all are looking to the future for the realization of their hopes. As to leadership, the Free Religious movement never had a leader nor a claimant for the office. Many individuals, by their abilities and position, have done it distinguished service, among whom Mr. Frothingham will always be held in honored remembrance as occupying a most eminent place. But the movement is led by ideas, not men.[14]

Two weeks later, still angry at the *Post* article, Potter followed up in the *Index* asking the readers to look at Mr. Frothingham's ideas as expressed in his books and sermons rather than believe a reporter's account:

If the wide-spread discussion of Mr. Frothingham's religious views, which the *Evening Post* reporter started, were to lead to a more general reading of Mr. Frothingham's books, it will have accomplished at least one good object. His "Religion of Humanity," his "Cradle of the Christ," his "Transcendentalism in New England," his "Life of Theodore Parker," his volumes of collected discourses, are rich mines of liberal thought. In the department of critical essays on religious problems, his literary work will stand among the first. The grace and easy elegance of his style, the wealth of illustration, the breadth of reading and culture, the critical acumen mingled with the large toleration, the entire freedom from the dogmatic spirit, the lofty moral tone, the perfect intellectual serenity, the fascinating boldness, yet always reverent, with which he invites you to look over the edge of the profoundest abysses of speculation—these are elements which carry the reader of his books irresistibly along, whether friendly to his thought or not. For full and incisive statements of the problems which confront the religious world to-day, for large comprehensiveness of outlook, for fair and candid consideration of all the facts, both those that natural science brings and those that are furnished by the history of religions, these books are almost without a parallel.[15]

Still the controversy of his alleged recantation did not subside. "Every Sunday, the pulpits echo all over the land," said Minot I. Savage of Boston, Frothingham's young FRA colleague:

All the old religious newspapers are chanting paeans of Frothingham's "recantation, the failure of free thought, the death of liberalism." Many of the so-called "free thought" papers ring with taunts and are besprinkled with epithets. Even the daily press heaps on the "confusion more confounded." [16]

Concerned over the misunderstanding of his old friend's views, and perhaps his own, Savage had several talks with Frothingham and got his version of the *New York Post* interview and a firsthand account of his theological position. From the conversations, Savage composed a sermon defending Frothingham. In essence it elaborated what Potter had written in *Index* a few weeks earlier.[17] His conclusions were that Frothingham had changed many of his views of radical religion and had become "more of a pronounced theist" than before, but this did not imply a recantation. The view of Frothingham's ideas in the *New York Post* was utterly misleading, the exact opposite being true, thought Savage. Perhaps the most telling point in Savage's defense of Frothingham was his criticism of the typical reporter and opponent of radical religion. They are always eager, he said, to see Frothingham's natural skepticism and capacity for self-criticism as a sign of his total denial of previous positions. Frothingham himself kept a dignified silence, but authorized Savage's sermon as a true version of his present attitude of thought.[18]

In spite of denials of recanting by Frothingham and his defenders, there was a kernel of truth in the impression given by the *New York Post* interview. Moncure Conway recalled in his own memoir that Frothingham confided to him that after working twenty-five years in free thought he found it "led nowhere—got nowhere" and was mystified by the power of the Catholic priest in Italy. "What this power [is] I cannot undertake to say." [19] Samuel Johnson, writing after the controversy had subsided, admitted to Longfellow:

O. B. Frothingham's recent words and ways I don't wholly understand; though I can see the situation pretty well . . . the whole proceeding only proves to me how impossible it is for a thoughtful man to live off and outside of a transcendental basis; as I think he has been really trying to do.[20]

To Johnson, Frothingham's trouble was that he was caught in a conflict between a half-repudiated idealism and a disappointing rationalism. Yet there was no real confict, he thought, between the rationalism of evolutionary theory and transcendentalism. Frothingham made the same point in 1876 in his *History of Transcendentalism in New England* (p. 217).

Accused of spiritual confusion by both opponents and friends, Frothingham's state of mind in returning to America gave an opening for the critics of rationalism. Reverend Henry A. Braun, pastor of St. Elizabeth's in Washington Heights, used Frothingham's alleged disillusionment for his book, *Age of Unreason.* Written at the height of the recantation issue, Braun attacked Thomas Paine, Robert Ingersoll, Felix Adler, and Frothingham as dangerous men. "The gentle, mild-mannered Frothingham disarms his critics," wrote Braun, "when actually he is the 'Melancthon of American rationalism.' His no-creed, no-devil, no-God theology leads to an individualism that destroys organization and preaches a rationalism that cannot guide the common man." [21] To such critics, Frothingham's comments, both before and after his European sojourn, were signs of a definite repudiation of free religion. What little scholarship has been done on the impact of Frothingham on American religion has reinforced the recantation thesis. Weisenberger, in *The Ordeal of Faith,* (1959) states:

> Eventually scepticism overtook Frothingham himself, for by 1881 he had given up his church work asserting that "it appears to lead to nothing, and may have been grounded on mistaken premises." [22]

In retrospect, it would seem that everyone, including Frothingham himself, lost sight of the primary reasons for his retirement—that of ill health. As events from May, 1879 to November, 1881 began to fall in place, as Frothingham in deep periods of pessimism made certain self-critical remarks, charges of recantation were raised. As his friends, from varying philosophic vantage points, attempted to defend him, and incidentally themselves, the issue became hopelessly confused. Although Weisenberger is probably mistaken in implying that Frothingham gave up his church because he was overtaken by self-doubt, he is close to the truth in using the word "skepticism." M. J. Savage, at the time, had implied as much. It had always been Frothingham's way, indeed a part of his heritage, to proceed as if he was right but be sure there was a chance he was wrong. He doubted as he believed, his beliefs subjected always to the scrutiny of his own skepticism. He was a believing skeptic. From 1879 until 1884, between careers, with his health and future work uncertain, his skepticism became uppermost in his thoughts and utterances.

After a year the controversy had died down, at least for a while. Back in Boston, spending the winter months of 1881 and 1882 at the Vendome Hotel, he could avoid the strain of theological conflict, visit his sister Ellen's Commonwealth Avenue house and enjoy renewed contacts with old Boston friends. But his return to the First Unitarian Church, his father's former charge, was carefully observed by his former opponents in the Unitarian struggles. Many felt it was another sign that he had repudiated free religion and returned to the fold. James Freeman Clark, a man of Parker's generation and a conservative Unitarian with whom Frothingham had broken a few lances, greeted him warmly early in his second year back in Boston. Could Frothingham fill his pulpit, he asked, as in times past when they differed widely on theological matters? How glad he was to note that he had returned to First Church and had "stepped down on our side of the fence." [23] It is almost certain that Frothingham did not accept the pulpit invitation. In spite of the innuendo of "fence-sitting," Frothingham and Clark, whom he once called a "theological peacemaker, incapable of critical thought" (see Chapter III), remained cordial at Unitarian spring festivals and exchanged notes about books of mutual interest and polite inquiries of each other's health.[24] Another tie between the men was the happy event on January 31, 1883, of Elizabeth Frothingham's marriage to William Lincoln Parker of Brookline, at which James Freeman Clark presided.[25]

In the spring of 1883 an event occurred in Boston which the editors of the *New York Herald Tribune* thought newsworthy for Frothingham's former associates in that city. "Mr. Frothingham and His Unitarians" was an account of the Spring Festival of the Unitarian Associates. Frothingham was there and was called upon for an impromptu speech. In a few graceful sentences, without referring to the struggle of sixteen years ago, Frothingham assured the group that he could be counted as one of them again. The old divisions were over; all now could subscribe to the same symbols, free of dogma—open, rational—welcoming new ideas. Recalling the great minds of Unitarianism, he offered generous remarks for Channing, the prophet; his own father, the beautiful writer; Ripley, the scholar; Orville Dewey, the orator; Dr. Bellows, the organizer; and his own "dear friend" and contemporary, Starr King, somewhat of a missionary. Playing on the imagery of a divided Unitarianism of previous years, he reminded them of Dr. Bellows' figure of speech: A bird needs two wings—a left and a right wing. But in earlier days, said Frothingham, the wings beat in different rhythm, trying to propel the bird in opposite directions. Loud applause greeted his final thought, anticipated by the audience: "Now they beat in unison." [26]

The meeting helped him. It was good to be before an audience again and to hear warm applause, this time from former opponents in past controversies.[27] It was good to be back in Boston in the atmosphere of the illustrious tradition which had nurtured him. He would help preserve it with his pen.

THREE

His selection of George Ripley as his first subject for his new career of writing might have had hidden significance. It is true that they had been personal friends in New York and Frothingham, through his book on New England transcendentalism, had a background of material on Ripley at Brook Farm.[28] However, Ripley was a man of controversy who had, like Frothingham, been accused of skepticism, atheism, and worse. In the popular mind, he had recanted his radical views and, after failing in his

Utopian schemes, went to New York for an obscure career as a journalist and minor literary figure. Perhaps there was a degree of self-justification in the choice of his subject.

Making no vast claims for having written a definitive biography, Frothingham introduced the work as a

> memoir . . . to recover the image and do justice to the character of a remarkable man, the pursuit of whose latter years gave him little opportunity to display his deepest convictions, while his singular charm of manner and conversation concealed from all but those who knew him well the recesses of his feelings; a man of letters, a man too of ideas and purposes which left a broad mark on his age, and deserves to be gratefully borne in mind.[29]

After finishing the research on Ripley's *Tribune* years, Frothingham, back in Boston, received encouragement and advice from the editor of the series of which the Ripley book would be a part. "My publisher informs me," wrote Charles Dudley Warner, friend of Mark Twain and collaborator in *Gilded Age*, "that you are about the perspectus of George Ripley's biography . . . a most interesting addition to the Men of Letters series." "Shape the perspectives more on the literary milieu," he advised, "avoiding a straight biographical treatment." [30] Writing on through the winter and spring of 1881–1882, Frothingham apparently thought better of Warner's advice. When the work was published late in the year, the memoir was a comprehensive, if not detailed, coverage of Ripley's life— from boyhood to death—including his ministry, Brook Farm, and years of struggle in New York, none really central to Ripley's life as a literary critic.

However disappointed Warner may have been, the biography, gracefully written and full of brilliant insights into Ripley's private thoughts, served as a valuable guide and source of Ripley's letters, many of which later disappeared. By modern standards, it was "a hastily prepared memoir." [31] Yet Ripley's basic story comes through Frothingham's pen. He was a thoroughgoing transcendentalist, a religious radical of the Parker school, who never recanted, believed with an open mind, but was never a skeptic. "The plunge from pulpit to Brook Farm," wrote Frothingham, "though immediate, was not so headlong as is commonly supposed; on the contrary, it was natural, comparatively easy, almost inevitable." [32] His life was consistent from beginning to end, concluded Frothingham.

The book, coming out shortly after Ripley's death and written by a man the public knew was Ripley's personal friend, was well received, going through four editions in four years.[33] The book also joined the illustrious company of others in the Men of Letters Series: Warner's *Washington Irving*, Sanborn's *Henry D. Thoreau*, Higginson's *Margaret Fuller Ossoli*, O.

W. Holmes' *Ralph Waldo Emerson,* and others. As might be expected, the *Index* carried a long and glowing review, encouraging readers to study the biography of a man who spiritually, if not organically, had been a part of the free religious movement. The writer of the unsigned review went beyond the content of Frothingham's book for material, no doubt interviewing the author himself. For those who had followed closely the controversy over Frothingham's alleged recantation and debated aberration from transcendentalism, the following excerpt must have been interesting reading:

> As a member of Mr. Frothingham's society in New York, Mr. Ripley kept the faith more than his pastor did. The latter says: "He was in no sense or degree a materialist; and, though connecting himself with an independent society of a decidedly radical school, he held fast his faith in beliefs which his minister dismissed. His appeal was still to consciousness of the soul. Of doctrine he had little to say, being content to see them change and pass away; but the substance of spiritual conviction he retained to the last." [34]

As the writing of the Ripley biography drew to a close, Frothingham's old literature professor, Henry Wadsworth Longfellow, died in March, 1882. He was asked by the editors of Houghton Mifflin, Boston, to contribute two chapters to a testimonial volume containing Longfellow's prose works and later poems. "The Man," Chapter VII, and "Apotheosis," Chapter VIII, his part of the volume, were richly detailed essays drawn from personal recollections and painstaking research in newspaper and other contemporary accounts. He described his appearance, his personality, his kindness, the conversations with C. E. Norton about him, the hymn he wrote for the ordination of Frothingham's closest friend, the poet's brother, Samuel Longfellow. Yet it was not all eulogy. Longfellow, in Frothingham's view was a shallow sentimentalist, lacking the capacity for philosophic speculation. A philosophical argument, he quoted Longfellow as once saying, was like running into the forest and ending "up a tree like a squirrel track." His light poetry, never admired by Frothingham, he treated kindly. It would last, wrote Frothingham, in spite of Longfellow's shallow skepticism in religion which might limit his relevance as a poet. His reputation would live, he thought, as long as men and women continue ". . . to weep, to strive, or to love. Such experiences outlast unbelief in God and immortality and will make their voices heard above the din of changing years." [35]

More in keeping with his disposition than writing of a sentimental poet were articles of a more scholarly weight, four in all, appearing in *North American Review* and *Atlantic Monthly.* The first was produced during his first winter at the Vendome Hotel in Boston while the Ripley biography was underway, the other in the spring of 1883 after the winter spent in Washington, D.C. Emanuel Swedenborg, the European mystic, was the subject of his first article, the first of his to appear in *North American Review* for more than a decade. He examined Swedenborg's scientific rather than his mystical side, claiming that the mystic on the material side is deeper than on the spiritual. His vast scientific output bridged the gap between science and theology, a gap that Frothingham himself attempted to span continually in his sermons. Yet he disclaimed ever having read the mystic at the time, thirty years ago, when he was called a Swedenborgian. Perhaps he had absorbed him second hand through Theodore Parker whose theology, he explained in detail, stemmed from Swedenborg. The Christian myths such as heaven and hell, the literal Bible, disclaimed by Swedenborg, wrote Frothingham, are now "commonplaces" freely announced from evangelical pulpits. Yet his views were once radical, influencing Henry James (the elder), and moving Emerson to rank him, "incongruously," stated Frothingham, as a seer with Socrates. But in the opinion of Emerson, recalled Frothingham, "his day is done." [36] His cool neutrality toward one source of his early theological views must certainly have given some encouragement to those who would renew the recantation controversy, then barely subsided.

This could not be said of his next article, published in April of 1883. "Criticism of Christianity" was part of a symposium made up of articles by other clergymen, taking opposing theological views. Back in his old form in the heat of combat, though a war of words, Frothingham took the same radical ground he had held during his New York ministry. His most radical, popular writing, *Cradle of Christ*, [37] became his base of argument again. He examined Biblical criticism past and present, giving Samuel Johnson (recently dead) as an example of a man who did not give up religion just because he gave up Christian myths. He was, Frothingham recalled, "the most spiritual-minded man—a radical of the radicals [declining] to call himself a Christian, [choosing] a universal faith." All of the old symbols—the cross, the cup, the star, the serpent—are universal man-made symbols. Theology of some sort is necessary for the human mind to express itself about religious matters, he admitted, but "religion is compromised" when temporal things are "taken for religion itself." Only a blind defense of Christianity will kill it, not the criticisms. [38]

This was more like the radical his friends had admired and opponents feared four years before. William J. Potter, his most loyal defender, and the one most hurt by the charges of his recantation, could not resist recalling the old debate. Here was something that would surely silence the critics and encourage the friends of free religion. In *Index*, April 12, 1883, appeared Potter's article, "Mr. O. B. Frothingham's 'Criticism and Christianity' ":

> A good many readers have doubtless turned to the last article in the last number of the *North American Review* with special interest. The subject, "Criticism and Christianity," and the name of the author, Octavius B.

Frothingham, made a combination that whetted curiosity. Since the famous sensational report in the *New York Evening Post,* alleging a very important change in Mr. Frothingham's religious views—a change that was very generally interpreted as amounting to a recantation of the views he had been preaching for the larger part of his ministry—Mr. Frothingham has said nothing to the public on religious topics distinctly in his own name. He took occasion to correct in certain particulars the *Evening Post's* report by a brief communication to that journal, and closed that communication with the explicit statement, "I have not gone back to any position which I had abandoned." But, beyond this, he did not choose at that time to make any public explanation of his opinions. Nor did he allow himself to read more than the merest infinitesimal part of the large quantities of matter sent to him in print and in manuscript, wherein other people discussed his opinions from their various points of view and offered him their suggestions and advice. Nearly eighteen months have elapsed since this incident. Within this time, various articles have appeared from his pen in magazines and newspapers, and his biography of George Ripley has been published; but in none of these writings has he taken occasion to consider any of the questions that were started by the newspaper "interviewer." Not until now has he chosen a topic as if with special reference to giving his own views on certain questions involved in that discussion about him. With such a subject as "Criticism and Christianity," he could hardly avoid touching some of the most prominent points then raised concerning his change of religious attitude.

But, if anyone goes to this article in the April *North American Review* with the expectation of finding a clear statement from Mr. Frothingham of his present religious position, such a reader will probably be disappointed. And especially will any reader be disappointed who may take up the article with the thought that it is going to disclose some very great changes in Mr. Frothingham's religious belief. Those persons of the evangelical persuasions who were talking about his having recanted his opinions, and who made haste to tender him the very questionable hospitality of the repose offered in their creeds, will not find much to comfort them in this new utterance. That they are to have the pleasure of welcoming so distinguished a convert to any of their folds, the article gives no encouragement. The only religious body which may reasonably claim, on the ground of this article, more of Mr. Frothingham's sympathy than heretofore, is the Unitarian. The position taken, though only vaguely substantiated, that Christianity in its essential inner principles will survive all critical assaults, made however triumphantly, upon its externals of doctrine and ritual, and that one may not necessarily let go his Christian faith however much doubting the historic authenticity of the New Testament story of Jesus, will be recognized as enough of qualification for Unitarian fellowship, at least on the left wing of that body. But vagueness of the answers given to the questions, What is meant by "Christian faith"?, and What is "the essential inner principle of Christianity"? would incapacitate for affiliation with any other branch of the Christian faith but that which is satisfied if its adherents only keep, on whatsoever grounds, the Christian name.

It will be remembered that, in the brief letter of correction which Mr. Frothingham sent to the *Evening Post,* he said that, while he had seen no reason for changing his opinions, it had occurred to him that they did "not contain the whole truth." And the meaning behind this latter remark, as shown subsequently by the present writer and by Mr. Savage in their statements in the *Index* after conversations with Mr. Frothingham, was that he was disposed to make more account than formerly of a revealing and guiding Power in the world above material nature and above humanity as the origin and sustenance of religions; that is, as he had never been atheistic, that he would more *emphasize* the thought that religion is not merely the aspiration and effort of man toward a Power he conceives to be Supreme, but the actual impartation of that Power to man. The article in the *North American Review* appears to be an expansion of this idea. It begins with a reference to *The Cradle of Christ,* which is regarded as Mr. Frothingham's most radical book, and concerning which he said to Mr. Savage that he desired to change "not one single word" in it, but "would only supplement here and there with additional statements." This essay seems therefore to be designed as somewhat supplementary to that book. He takes nothing from the book, the theory of which was that Christianity was a development of the Hebrew Messianic idea and has very little dependence on the teachings and life of Jesus; but "granting," he says, "the position taken by its writer, the question arises, Why need one abandon his Christian faith?" . . . The rhetoric of the article is strongly Christian. But its argument might be more correctly styled a plea for religious faith than for Christian faith. Though not on this point so clear as we might wish, Mr. Frothingham writes, however, with that easy elegance of style and wealth of illustration which have always been the delight of his readers.[39]

His next article in *North American Review,* "Democracy and Moral Progress," published in July, 1883, revealed his aristocratic attitude toward democracy, reminiscent of De Tocqueville. He began with Walt Whitman's "Specimen Days," calling it a blast at the failure of democracy. Yet it was difficult to conclude about America, wrote Frothingham. It was true that education, now a "common denominator of useful subjects," was no longer an agent of "uplift for the intellectual few." Likewise equalitarianism had clouded the distinction between religious creeds and political principles as to imply that one ideal was as good as another. The popular stage, the newspapers, and the rule of hack politicians was far from uplifting. A parvenu culture, he felt, resulting from the rapid accumulation of great wealth had "cheapened democracy." Thorsten Veblen would say a similar thing in more pungent style a few years later. But Frothingham, never content with a mere jeremiad, also held out hope for democracy. Public opinion, if properly enlightened, would be an agent of democratic progress, he believed. The freedom of the individual, still deeply ingrained, would at last reaffirm the theme of democracy, which was "opportunity and possibility." Democracy was an open, flexible system still in the process of growth. He appealed to the leaders and molders of opinion to give the tendencies of democracy a chance to evolve in the right direction. Reflecting his belief in the developmental theory of evolutionary progress, Frothingham was sure that more progress was possible. "Sentiment precedes intelligence, charity precedes character, and tendency precedes direction." He saw American democracy, with all its faults, as a growing system.[40]

While working on the biography of George Ripley, Frothingham found in his papers a list of twelve names, classified under the heading "Transcendentalism." Assuming that Ripley had intended to imply that the intellectual movement had passed through several stages as represented by the people listed, Frothingham became intrigued with the idea. "Some Phases of Idealism in New England" became the title of his article, published in *Atlantic Monthly*, July, 1883. "Here is the list as existing in his manuscript," he wrote:

> N. L. Frothingham (1820), Convers Francis, John Pierpont, George Ripley (1830), F. H. Hedge, James Walker, Thomas T. Stone, W. E. Channing, J. F. Clarke, R. W. Emerson, W. H. Channing, Theodore Parker. . . . The first two names suggest the literary tendency of the new faith; the third, its application to specific reform; the next four, its bearing on principles of philosophy; the two Channings, J. F. Clarke, and Theodore Parker illustrate its bearing on points of religious opinion; while Mr. Emerson represents idealism pure and simple, apart from all philosophical or sectarian beliefs, from all critical or speculative dogmas.[41]

In this remarkably accurate and compact summary of the transcendental thinkers, Frothingham introduced his essay. Of the twelve names listed by Ripley, he dealt with only eight, omitting discussion of Hedge, Stone, Clarke, and W. H. Channing. His own father received the fullest treatment since he doubted if he were a transcendentalist at all:

> Only by virtue of some general classification can [he] be ranked among [them]. He was not a philosopher, not a man interested in abstruse speculation, not a reformer of society . . . nor an innovator on established ways of thinking [42]

He dealt with all the rest he had chosen for review in a closely reasoned essay, showing intimate knowledge of each man's pattern of thought and their unique contributions to the intellectual movement. Personal sketches, some from memory, added a dimension of depth to the study. This article, by far more penetrating and analytical than his earlier *Transcendentalism in New England,* was at once more critical and less severe in making judgment of the principle transcendentalists. On his own father's part in the Parker "heresy" trial, he threw new light:

> It has been conjectured that Theodore Parker had Dr. Frothingham in mind in his famous discourse on "The Transient and Permanent," where he vehemently rebukes the preacher who said one thing in his study and

another in his pulpit. But this could hardly have been the case, for Mr. Parker was a man of scrupulous honor, and Dr. Frothingham was his personal friend. Besides, it was not true that Dr. Frothingham said one thing in his study and another in his pulpit. He simply did not say everything in his pulpit that he said in his study.[43]

Frothingham attempted to dispose of the popular misunderstanding that the transcendentalists, and Emerson as their leader, worshipped themselves as the source of all benevolence:

> . . . no diligent reader of his books will doubt that Emerson was a theist of a most earnest description. . . . The notion that the soul of man could *create* truth, or do anything but meekly receive it from the divine hand probably never occurred to Emerson. No virtue was more characteristic of him than humility.[44]

For those critics who considered the transcendentalists an organized party with a creed of some sort, Frothingham recalled a conversation with Emerson:

> Shortly after the *History of Transcendentalism in New England* was published, Mr. Emerson said to the author that in his view Transcendentalism as it was called was simply a protest against formalism and dogmatism in religion; not a philosophical but a spiritual movement looking toward a spiritual faith.[45]

There is little doubt that this article, written approximately a year after Frothingham's recantation controversy, was a rebuttal to those critics who accused him of denying the validity of transcendentalism on one hand and of moving toward scientifically oriented materialism on the other. It was comfort to his colleagues of free religion who were hurt by his supposed defection from their ranks. His final words were a tribute to the memory of the older generation who had, in the beginning, stimulated his own revolt against creeds and sects:

> Thus philosophy and faith, thought and feeling, literary and poetic fervor, united to produce that singular outburst of idealism which has left so deep an impression on the New England intellect. The circumstances of the time determined the particular form it assumed. As those circumstances passed away, the fashion of speculation altered, but the old original idealism remained, and will remain when Channing and Emerson are forgotten except as its interpreters. The local and incidental phases that have been noticed are of the remote past. Literature has come into possession of all its rights. Philosophy sits serenely on its throne, unvexed by its old-fashioned controversy with materialism. Reform is no longer obliged to be one-sided, or extreme, or anarchical, but is taken up by reasonable men and women. Religion is released from dogmatism, at least in a measure, the championship of it being left to scholars of whatever denomination. And all this has

been, in great degree, accomplished by men who were once called heretics.[46]

FOUR

During the unsettled years after his return from Europe and before moving permanently to Boston, Frothingham's writings kept him in his rooms at the Vendome a great deal but also gave him cause to circulate in the Boston area, consulting libraries and discussing manuscripts with editors. Down on Tremont Street was the office of the *Index* where B. F. Underwood now did his editorial chores. Potter, in from New Bedford, as coeditor, often met him there, recalling old times and discussing affairs of the FRA, of which Frothingham was still a vice president. The death of his old friend Samuel Johnson in February, 1882, broke Frothingham's long silence in the *Index* after Potter prevailed upon him to write a memorial essay.[47] Close by, though soon to move to New York, William Dean Howells was a central figure of literary Boston, editor of *Atlantic Monthly*, and receptive to Frothingham's manuscripts. From time to time he went out to the Harvard campus to visit Higginson, then moved from Newport, or to attend meetings of the Harvard Committee on Foreign Language to which he had been appointed after his return from abroad.[48]

A short walk from the Vendome took him to First Church which he and Caroline occasionally attended. This aroused much speculation as to Frothingham's views and state of mind. In the spring of 1882, with Ripley's biography in the writing stage, he accepted the invitation to speak by Rufus Ellis, pastor of his father's former church. It was not a sermon but an address on George Ripley. A news account recorded that he spoke with charm, his speech was good, and showed no signs of a "deranged mind, as rumored." [49] So successful was his first public address since retirement, that he appeared a few weeks later, again at Ellis' request, to speak on "Brook Farm." It seemed appropriate, somehow, that the memory of transcendentalism should be kept alive in First Church by the man who wrote its history and admired its principle spokesmen. Frothingham, of course, felt a personal affinity for Ellis whose installation in 1853 at the First Church he attended and offered a prayer.[50] Transcendentalism must have seemed an unduly nostalgic subject in the spring of 1882 with Samuel Johnson, a second generation transcendentalist, dead. In April the death of Emerson removed the major figure of the era. It is strange that Frothingham did not make the trip to Concord to pay his respects to the "seer" and old family friend. Had he been asked to give a eulogy, it is certain there would have been no feelings of dissatisfaction among Emerson's admirers that his last rites had been attended to by strangers.

Frothingham, in his sixtieth year, had reached the time in life when he was obliged to hear news of the death of friends and contemporaries. Weiss, Garrison, and his brother Thomas were all gone by the time he had returned from Europe. News of Henry Bellows' death came in January. Potter, writing in the *Index,* had kind words for him. Though inconsistent and hostile to the preamble of the liberal Unitarians, Bellows deserved, wrote Potter, to be considered a progressive conservative and a "generous foe." [51] Down in New York, Chadwick preached a sermon on the loss of a great figure whose "deep organ tones" would be missed. He had been a liberal voice in Unitarian circles, conceded Chadwick, and had helped form several churches. No mention was made of his part in bringing Frothingham to New York City.[52] Preferring not to comment on the death of his old foe, generous or not, Frothingham kept a discreet silence.

The only permanent home the Frothinghams had during the transitional years between retirement and the Boston period was the summer place at Beverly Farms. Since his father's death in 1870, he had given up summers in the old family place in Burlington, that stately, mansard roofed mansion, built in the 1840s by the Brooks inheritance, being taken over by other members of the family. At Beverly, the Frothinghams were back in the area where, along with Nahant, the aristocracy and intelligentsia of New England summered. A short distance from Frothingham's summer home was the estate of Cousin Henry Adams', and the summer home of his old friend, Oliver Wendell Holmes. The quiet of Beverly and the bracing climate of the New England summer made it an idyllic spot to write, think, and recall the past. Proximity to old Marblehead, across the bay, added authenticity to its New England qualities. Salem, within an easy ride by carriage, was a desired tie to the past that preserved poignant memories of Johnson, who lived there so long, and Frothingham's own start in the ministry.

After a winter in Boston, living in temporary though elegant quarters in the Vendome, Beverly was a delight. Here relatives were reunited and close friends could visit. Bessie and William Parker were frequently part of the group. Young Brooks, Bessie's son from a previous marriage of short duration in New York, was always a center of attraction, as the only grandchild present.[53]

A typical summer at Beverly Farms was late June in 1883. Frothingham had completed his latest article for *North American Review* and *Atlantic.* Herbert and Lucy Morse, close friends from New York days, were invited up for a visit. Arriving by train, perhaps in Salem, they were met by William Parker in the Frothingham carriage. As they turned in the driveway at the "Farms," the Frothinghams waited on the piazza with hearty greetings. After dinner, there was much talk of old times and a long carriage ride into the surrounding countryside. That evening a cousin, Nellie Frothingham, slender and handsome, dropped in to partake of sparkling conversation. The next day the Frothinghams and their guests rode to Salem to look at North Church and visit the Nichols, Frothingham's former church trustee. It was a good visit. Frothingham could relax

from his writing labors of the past winter and confide to close friends his
real thoughts about his recent "recantation" charges. "Mine host was in a
cheerful mood for conversation," recalled Morse of the evening carriage
ride:

> As we left the sea and plunged into the dark forest of pines, he spoke of his
> religious views which had been much misrepresented in the papers. He has
> not changed, he says, in his opinions but only dropped the iconoclastic
> methods which seemed necessary in his pulpit teaching, to cultivate the
> poetic and spiritual or ideal aspect of faith, giving more to his hopes and
> trusting that side of his nature. He had no leaning to any of the churches,
> though he finds enjoyment in going often of a Sunday to his father's old
> church. He is more of a radical, he says, than ever, but less of a materialist.

His latest article in *North American Review,* recalled Morse, expressed his
present feelings,[54] but Samuel Johnson's book, which he was editing,
represented his views better than he himself could express them.[55] The
introduction would have more to say about it. As the conversation developed, Morse recalled that they talked of his transcendentalism period
and its writers, and both agreed that their views "went a little beyond"
what they had found in their late readings.[56]

As the summer slipped away, Frothingham was making plans for his
next writing venture and possibilities of a permanent home. They spent
the fall and early winter back at the Vendome. After the Christmas
season, as the Boston winter closed in, they went to Washington for the
month of January.[57] Not that Frothingham had any close friends in the
capitol city, nor was he on really personal terms with Cousin Henry
Adams, then living on Lafayette Square. Nevertheless, he could sample
life in Washington in the aftermath of Garfield's assassination and observe the workings of the government under Chester Arthur. Probably
more to his liking was the opportunity to do some research on William
Henry Channing, long a Washington, D.C. resident, and the subject of his
next biography. Finding Washington not to their liking, the Frothinghams traveled south for a few weeks in the "Groves" at Magnolia,
Florida.[58] But the climate palled, he was bored, and could not head back
north fast enough—to his friends, his writings, and to Beverly Farms. A
decision had been made, however; the months of temporary living would
end; they would sell the New York house and settle permanently in
Boston. During the few April weeks in New York on the way back, much
remained to be done—books to pack, household effects to dispose of, his
church affairs to terminate. The Morses dropped in and, sitting among
stacks of emptied book shelves and filled crates, Morse heard of
Frothingham's distaste of Washington life and the futility of living in
Florida, while his wife Lucy "got a cozy corner chat with Mrs. F." [59]

George Putnam called to discuss the last problems in disbanding the

Independent Liberal Church. Although the congregation had been disbanded nearly five years earlier, legal barriers prohibited the disposition
of the funds, totaling about fifty thousand dollars. Frothingham was
gratified to hear from Putnam that, by a special act of the legislature, the
funds had been dispersed "among several Unitarian organizations in the
far West." [60]

The last few weeks in New York were full of both business and pleasure,
however nostalgic. With their household dismantled, the Frothinghams
dined often at the Morses, talking not of the past, but of Beverly. He
hoped to see more of Oliver Wendell Holmes as he had in the past, and get
advice for his Century encyclopedia article on Shakespeare. There were
social evenings when the wives, Lucy and Caroline, attended the Philhar-
monic concert while the men went to the Century Club where they met
Edmund Stedman and many literary people down from Boston.[61]

With the last farewells said, and the house on 36th Street emptied and
sold, the Frothinghams headed for Boston, leaving New York City, probably for the last time. In the month before they opened the Beverly Farms
house, the Frothinghams were busy making arrangements for receiving
household items from New York and looking for a suitable location for
their permanent home. It was not a difficult choice. One Eighteen
Marlboro Street, in a neighborhood of graceful "brownstones" of recent
origin, was two blocks from First Church and within walking distance of
the Garden in one direction and Commonwealth Avenue and Beacon
Street in another. Up the street, at 339 Marlboro, lived Bessie and William
Parker and grandson Brooks. It was an ideal spot for a retired man,
seeking seclusion near family and friends, yet in proximity to sources of
intellectual life.

Their decision made and plans announced to friends, they could go to
Beverly Farms for the summer, relax from the ardors of travel and house
hunting, and look forward to continuing, on a more permanent basis, the
new life in Boston.[62]

X

Time to Take in Sail:
Boston Years, 1884–1895

THE BOSTON OF FROTHINGHAM'S LAST YEARS was the city of Edward Bellamy's Utopian hero, Julian West (*Looking Backward,* 1887). The noisy horse drawn traffic, augmented by the first electric streetcars, gave a new look and sound to the Boston streets. The elegant row houses for the elite built in the seventies along the Charles on newly filled ("made land") areas of Back Bay contrasted dramatically with pre-Civil War slums of the poor in the south end. The bitter labor wars of the eighties brought on by the struggle for Union recognition and a share of the wealth of the Gilded Age, the economic recessions climaxed by the panic of 1893, added a new dimension to American society, convincing many socially conscious observers that democracy itself was in jeopardy. But Frothingham, though he had lived through a similar milieu in the New York of the seventies, was far removed from these struggles. While a new generation of political and economic radicals produced literature of social protest and dreamt Utopian dreams of economic democracy, Frothingham seemed unaware that the evolutionary theory he welcomed in his early career as the key to social and intellectual progress had appalling and immediate consequences. He would be content, or at least resigned, to continue the literary career typical of a man whose battles lay behind him.[1]

Up from New York in April of the Frothingham's first year in the Marlboro Street house, Herbert Morse recalled the afterdinner talk with William and Bessie Parker and Frothingham's mood as they sat in the front room study:

> Mr. F. was full of old association reminiscences of theological and literary talk. Dore's picture of the young novitiate with its humble accompaniment of a depraved priest hung in the study over the fireplace, and a picture of the same theme opposite. "These two," says Mr. F., "I keep to remind me of the task I once attempted and to which I gave my manhood." This he said with grim humor. The whole of his past life was, I fear, settled down on his memory as a sort of nightmare.[2]

Morse tended to exaggerate and was given to making snap judgments; however, he sensed the mood of Frothingham's last Boston years correctly. He was to spend the next eleven years looking backward, preserving the memoir of his father's generation and the careers of selected contemporaries. As for his own contribution to religious thought, he had nothing new to say—only his recollections of past battles, won or lost. As always, his skepticism modified his positive belief, leaving it to his friends and critics to appraise his life's work.

ONE

Once settled in Boston, Frothingham's life followed a fairly steady routine—winters at 118 Marlboro Street, near the Lincolns and not far from sister Ellen's brownstone on Commonwealth Avenue; summers at Beverly Farms and, for variety, at Dublin, New Hampshire or, for health reasons, at Saratoga Springs, New York or Newport, Rhode Island. His old friends knew where he could be reached for family dinners or invitations to Harvard College functions or in Boston for literary and social events. With strangers he corresponded about literary topics and sources of theological literature.[3] He and Higginson, out in Cambridge, kept in close touch. In the fall of Frothingham's second year on Marlboro Street they made plans to hold a reception for Moncure Conway's father and daughter during a visit to Boston. Frothingham, regretting that his "winter establishment" was not fully in operation for lack of a cook, offered to entertain them, nevertheless, at 118 Marlboro Street.[4] Throughout the Boston years, he and his old FRA comrade exchanged notes concerning magazine articles and various literary club meetings.[5] When Arthur Stedman, son of Frothingham's former parishioner, began a study of George Ripley, Frothingham wrote offering Ripley's scrap books, then in his possession.[6]

In spite of his alienation from Francis Abbot in 1878, Frothingham maintained his contacts with his former co-worker. After Abbot's retirement from the editorship of the *Index* in 1880, he settled in Cambridge as a writer and part-time instructor in the Harvard Department of Philosophy. They met occasionally at a Harvard alumni function. Their abiding interest in radical religion drew them together in 1889 when both attended a meeting to form a trust fund for publication of liberal thought.[7] These fleeting contacts with old friends and occasional letters from strangers, interested in Frothingham as a literary man and radical theologian, were links to his past career and, in his declining years, a source of satisfaction when satisfactions were few.

In the spring of 1886, despite his involvement in his new writing career, he confided to Herbert Morse that he had regretted leaving New York. In Boston many of his old comrades "were dead or out of touch"; in New York there "was a younger element." The Morses had come on a visit to

discuss a book of poems ("Happy Haven Days") Morse hoped Frothingham would "promote" and perhaps review in some journal. There were
luncheons and dinners at the Parkers, where the Morses slept. Walking
home later in the evening, Morse recalled the first hint of Frothingham's
failing health. "OBF seemed glad to lean on my arm." Yet there was the
pleasant summer at Beverly Farms and, in July, he and Morse traveled to
Cambridge for the annual Phi Beta Kappa dinner and oration. By fall
Frothingham was helping Morse revise a "long poem." [8]

TWO

His "new career" of writing, dealing with well-worn topics and
memorializing deceased comrades, touched on issues still alive in the
minds of Frothingham's friends and critics. The charge of his "recantation," raised after his return from Europe in 1881, was again revived by
some of his last writings. What he had to say gave encouragement to those
who had, all along, denied that he had dropped transcendentalism and
turned away from his religion of humanity.

His first article for *North American Review,* after taking up permanent
residence in Boston, was entitled "The Philosophy of Conversion."
Months earlier he had written to Higginson that the article, soon to
appear, would deal with his alleged "loss of faith in Transcendentalism."
In it he promised to state his views precisely on the validity of this body of
thought.[9] He did just that. Conversion, he wrote, is simply to change your
mind and do differently—reducing the mystery to the level of common
experience. Setting aside the theological view of conversion as a mystical
experience, Frothingham drew on both Emerson, the transcendentalist,
and Franklin, the rationalist, to support his view of conversion. A combination of rationalism and transcendentalism was the key to conversion,
thought Frothingham. Common sense, guided by the inner urge for
perfection led, after all, to a religion of humanity that would guide the
struggle for social justice. Improving society and moving toward a "higher
social and intellectual state" was the true form of conversion.[10]

The meaning here was clear enough: Frothingham would have mankind employ rational processes guided by transcendental goals. In March,
1885, a writer in *North American Review,* Robert Buchanan, attacked
Frothingham's views as being irrelevant and his career for being futile.
The Boston *Sunday Herald* came to his defense, comparing him with
Parker and giving him credit for helping to free Christianity of its shack-
les. He did not recant, wrote the editor, but simply quit when his work was
done.[11] The *Index,* with William Potter and Benjamin Underwood at the
editorial desk, kept a close watch on the issue of Frothingham's recantation. They defended him against the Buchanan article in *North American
Review* and a London *Reformer* article quoting Wilberforce of England,
accusing Frothingham of being an atheist who "deplored the failure of his

work in New York." [12] It was the old battle joined again, which must have invigorated Frothingham, though he remained silent.

His first major work, the editing of Samuel Johnson's last volume of *Oriental Religions,* was published during Frothingham's first year on Marlboro Street. Those who felt that he had recanted his views might have reconsidered after reading Frothingham's introduction to the volume. It was also of interest to those concerned with the theories of history. Defending Johnson against the charge of being an amateur rather than an Orientalist, Frothingham stated that Johnson had analyzed the oriental philosophies wirtten by others in order to find a common theme binding all religions and philosophies together. It was Johnson's purpose to follow a theory. "The historian always has a theory," he wrote. "Gibbon had one; Macaulay had one. Froude has one; an absolutely scientific account of anything complex is not to be looked for. Men with minds will use mind. . . ." [13] As for Johnson's view of the supreme force in religion:

> He did not remand the thought of God to the region of the "unknowable" . . . on the contrary, he began with supreme mind, and saw evidences of its working in all visible manifestations. He was rather pantheistic, decidedly more pantheistic than theistic, but his pantheism had a human cast that brought it close to men's sympathies. [14]

This was good religion of humanity doctrine and very close to Frothingham's own view. He also prepared, by request, a brief testament for James Russell Lowell for *The Literary World,* Vol. XVI, No. 13, June 27, 1885. "In temper and spirit, an American," he hailed his return to America, a nation much in need of his "intellectual refinement." [15]

His choice of William Henry Channing as the subject of his next biography had significance for observers of Frothingham's philosophic and religious views. The nephew of William Ellery Channing, born the same year as Parker, had been admired by Frothingham from his Divinity School years. He had heard him preach, got to know him personally, and became thoroughly familiar with his shading of transcendentalism. He was not of the Parker type who thundered and attacked, wrote Frothingham, but more of a "missionary" at large, an "invigorator, a consoler and uplifter. He was a nourisher of aspirations, not so much an instructor as a healer, an apostle of light and love." [16] In a book review in the *Index,* Sarah Underwood was quick to notice Frothingham's affinity for the avowed transcendentalist:

> . . . that Mr. Frothingham found in the life of Channing a subject on which he could grow consciously enthusiastic is evidenced in many passages in the book. . . . Here was a man without title, preferment, professional rank; floating about from place to place, engaged in unpopular causes, holding opinions which few sympathized with, even when they were comprehended; of no ecclesiastic or literary fame; yet nevertheless he bears the

most searching inspection, and the more keenly he is examined the more
worthy of esteem he appears. Admiration is not too strong a word to use
when describing him.[17]

Yet in describing the intellectual surroundings of Channing, Frothingham had this to say of the influence of transcendentalism—an insight
which escaped the enthusiastic reviewer of the memoir:

> The philosophy of Transcendentalism was purely interior, assuming the
> insight of the soul, and exalting human nature. . . . It suggested belief
> rather than doubt, aspiration rather than inquiry, so that the student might
> sit in his study, planning his sermons, arranging his lectures, blocking out
> his novels, and meditating . . . unanxious.[18]

This statement is close to the criticism Frothingham offered all along for
his father's uncommitted generation of genteel Unitarians. It was in
direct contrast to the impression given in his history of New England
transcendentalism written ten years before:

> The Transcendentalists of New England were the mŏst strenuous workers
> of their day, and at the problems which the day flung down before them.
> . . . They achieved more practical benefit for society, in proportion to their
> numbers and the duration of their existence, than any body of Baconians of
> whom we ever heard.[19]

His contradiction, his second thoughts, his skepticism at his own beliefs,
confounded those who attempted to see a consistent pattern of thought
during his retirement career of writing. However, following the publication of Channing's memoir, Frothingham came out clearly with his views
in "Why I Am a Free Religionist." It was significant for more than one
reason. It not only stated his current attitude toward his career in the
FRA, but it was published in the *North American Review* rather than in the
friendly *Index*.[20] In a few, succinct paragraphs he traced the purpose and
process of the founding of the FRA, mentioning the principal personalities involved, carefully avoiding his own name. It was an enthusiastic, hopeful article. In it there were no bitter memories recalled or disappointments recollected. Twenty years after its founding he appraised its
work:

> It is not claimed that the design of the Association has been carried out, or
> will be in any definite time, though advances toward it have been made in
> the lapse of years; nor is it pretended that the society has accomplished all
> that has been done. Every organization is as much the creature as the creator
> of its period. The thought of the Free Religious Association was in the air of
> the epoch. The passion for scientific knowledge, the demand for liberty, the
> craving after union, the appreciation of goodness is characteristic of the age.
> But prepossessions yield slowly; the passage from dream to reality is long.

The method of sentimentalism prevails when the method of science has vindicated its title to pre-eminence. The application of liberty is painful. Fellowship in the spirit is beautiful, but seems hardly feasible. The supremacy of character is noble, but far off. As to the sympathy, symphony, essential identity of religions, we have our own revelation, say the ordinary sectarians, and that is good enough for us, and every attempt to put Christianity on a level with other faiths must result in dragging it down, not in raising these up. In the interest, therefore, of an exalted, spirituality, the work of the Free Religious Association is more than justified.[21]

Defending the association against charges of being a mere debating society, he reiterated thoughts expressed by himself at many annual meetings:

It has been a standing complaint that the Association *did* nothing, that it was merely speculative, that it consumed the hours in talk, and in somewhat metaphysical talk, too, that it lived in the air, keeping itself aloof from the organized interests of belief. This is, in a measure, true, but it only proves the design of the Association. It was *purposely* speculative. Therein lies the motive of its existence, and to this it steadily adheres, after twenty years of being. It was not a reform club, though eminent reformers spoke from its platform, and individual members held conspicuous positions in the ranks of reform. It was not a philanthropical society, though papers on charity were read at its conventions and were listened to with delight, as well as hearty approval, while beneficent work occupied much of the time of the managers.[22]

In the FRA, Frothingham recognized the two different dimensions of speculation represented by David Wasson, a transcendentalist who believed that man's soul, from where religious impulses came, evolved as knowledge and intelligence, and William Henry Channing, a pure transcendentalist, who believed that premature revelation came from God, that every important truth was communicated in a pantheistic sense from above. In Frothingham's mind, here was the nice combination of pure transcendentalism, rationalism, and evolutionary theory—an eclected body of ideas which came as close as any to being a consistent pattern of thought in Frothingham's own career. "Why Am I a Free Religionist?" His answer was without cloudy ambiguities:

I secure absolute freedom of thought in the study of religious literature, perfect freedom of movement among all religious phenomena, a pure fellowship of religious intention and purpose, a frank confession of the superiority of practical morality to dogma even of the most liberal description.[23]

As for the future of the Free Religious Movement, Frothingham was sure that its work would continue:

The re-enforcement of the highest sentiments of mankind; is not this a crying demand? Does not the age travail in pain till this be accomplished? The sigh of our generation is for unity in all the departments of life. The field of moral sentiment, of ideal principles is the most important. A "Spiritual Peace Society," for this our Association has been called, should be held in honor. It is not a sectarian or denominational question, not a question of Unitarianism or Presbyterianism, of Protestantism or Romanism, but of religion itself in its wide human aspects. It is not a question of belief or disbelief, but of faith in its most vital, that is, its most life-giving sense. The idea is, in the highest degree, conservative. By a logical accident it was launched by radical Unitarians, for they were in the condition to see the beauty, to feel the necessity of it, and in their hands it must remain so long as its fundamental conception is unchanged, but it deeply concerns all who seek the spiritual harmony of men.[24]

One can find no recantation here—only reaffirmation.

The year 1887 was the busiest since leaving New York. The *North American Review* article brought him back into the old arena of debate. As if to relax with a lighter subject, he wrote an introduction to a translation of Leopardi's poems for the translator, Frederick Townshend.[25] Even while doing this and pondering his *North American Review* article, he started his next book—a memoir of David Wasson. To the editors at Lee and Sheppard in Boston, he wrote that he was in the process of editing Wasson's papers and correspondence but that the "hot summer" would probably put a stop to his efforts. His health began to curtail his activities. Instead of going to Beverly Farms, his town house was open all summer, save for a short visit to Lenox, Massachusetts, by the sea.[26]

Apparently the spring of 1887 saw a turn for the worse in his health. In March, Mrs. Frothingham had been to New York without her husband, visiting the Morses and attending a function where Higginson "was the center of admiring ladies." [27] However, a happy family event occurred after her return. Bessie and William Parker had a son, Curtis, born on April 5, the second grandson for the Frothinghams.[28]

The Wasson memoir finally came out in 1889, "unaccountably de-layed," Frothingham complained to Stedman in February, due either to publishing delays or Frothingham's failing energy. For "dear Wasson's sake," he wrote Stedman, he was glad to do the memoir. Although he did not agree with all of Wasson's ideas, he thought they deserved considera-tion by thinkers.[29] Wasson's career had paralleled Frothingham's. Both had been "dismissed" from their first church; both were influenced by Parker. For a brief time, Wasson stood in Parker's vacated place with the 28th Congregational Society, while Frothingham held his independent pulpit in New York. Both wrote for *Radical, Index,* and *North American Review.* Wasson, though never a member of the FRA, was a frequent speaker at the annual meetings. The memoir was sympathetic to Wasson, portraying him in somewhat tragic terms. The collection of essays, not at all complete, were a cross-section of what Frothingham considered Wasson's best. In spite of Frothingham's comment to Stedman prior to the publication of the memoir, it seems clear that Frothingham was in essential agreement with ideas expressed in the essays selected for the compilation. "Nature," "The Prophecy of Man," "Authority," "Unity," "Social Texture," "The Puritan Commonwealth," "The New Type of Oppression," and "The Genius of Women" are sample titles.[30]

In the fall of 1889 Frothingham began to feel his age and the weight of his growing nervous disorder. A few weeks before his sixty-seventh birthday, he wrote to his New York friend, Edward Merril, New York attorney and member of the New York Civil Service Association, "I am afflicted this autumn with a stiffening in my right hand and arm which renders writing awkward and difficult and this is more likely to increase than diminish my errors." [31] To Kate Fields, he regretted that he could not be of more help to her. "My health is uncertain and my working power is weak." [32] In spite of his health, however, he planned to do a sketch of John Weiss as an introduction to a compilation of selected sermons and essays but had to drop the idea due to the hostility of the Weiss family and the fragmentary condition of Weiss' papers.[33]

Disappointed in this, he bore on to his next objective—that of writing a sketch of the Unitarianism of his father's generation. It was laborious work, writing through the fall and winter of 1889–1890, in his front room library study looking out on Marlboro Street. Friends brought in material from nearby libraries. From old colleagues he received letters of former Unitarian figures he was dealing with.[34] Caroline recopied much of his shaky scrawl, making it readable to the editors. Much of the book could be put together from memory of his earlier battles with conservative Unitarians. By spring he had produced *Boston Unitarianism 1820–1850: A Study of the Life and Work of Nathaniel Langdon Frothingham.*[35]

Looking back on his father's generation after forty years, Frothingham was more gentle in his judgment of the conservatives in Unitarianism that he and his Divinity School classmates had been in earlier years, more understanding of his father's frame of mind, and more critical of Parker than he had been in the midst of the antislavery controversy or during the struggle over the Unitarian creed preamble in 1866. Frothingham recalled that Parker was a literal, abrasive, shallow thinker unable to comprehend philosophies alien to his own. He recognized the opposite quality of his father's mind, undogmatic yet firm in conviction. "The true liberal Christian," he quoted his father once as saying, "is he who can, in the first place, believe he may be wrong while firmly convinced he is right." [36] In retrospect, he could appreciate the value of conservative Unitarianism in its struggle with newer scientific theories and German philosophy. In dealing with "Dogmatical Positions" (Chapter IV), he had generous words for the old generation and a modest statement regarding his own views:

It is not at all surprising that these gentlemen feel secure in their doctrinal
and ecclesiastical positions. The opposition was not strong. Mr. Emerson by
far the most important dissident, sang his own song, and cast no reflection
on those who were not in unison with him. Parker's assault was formidable,
but was so much complicated with personal issues as to add to the confidence of his adversaries rather than to diminish it. The *new philosophy* (mine)
visionary and far off, a mist in the air, an almost inaudible note in a
symphony. German opinion had not affected learned opinion to any extent.[37]

The Unitarianism of a generation ago, wrote Frothingham, consisted of
three types, personified by three individuals: William E. Channing and
Theodore Parker on either extreme, and Nathaniel L. Frothingham in
the middle ground. For his father's influence he had nothing but gentle
words:

> To my father I owe what I may have of idealism, of imaginativeness, of
> fondness for literature, in fastidiousness in regard to persons and books, my
> conservatism of sentiment, my freedom of intellectual movement; only the
> wave goes up the shore farther than it did a generation ago, and I have
> spoken in public what he meditated in his study, carrying out what he
> adumbrated.[38]

Frothingham confined his sketch of Unitarianism strictly to the
chronological limit of 1850, thus avoiding the painful break with Unitarianism and founding of the Free Religious Association. Indeed, he
gave the mild, middle ground Unitarianism full credit for breaking the
way for the "new faith." "The insensibly secular cast of their thought
opened the world of poetry and domesticated the best classics among
them. Unconsciously they were Greek and not Asiatic, Western and not
Oriental in their culture." [39] The "new faith," he wrote, was *not* a continuation of Channing and Parker, whose philosophy "would not bear
analysis." This last statement, curious in its implied repudiation of Parker's influence, might also be interpreted to mean that the "new faith" was a
continuation of the middle ground Unitarianism of Frothingham's
father. It might also have added credence to the belief that Frothingham
had recanted his radical position. He offered no supporting discussion;
the statement must stand alone as a judgment of a man in ill health,
looking fondly back after forty years to a tradition which first nurtured
him, then freed him for more advanced thinking. His memoir of Boston
Unitarianism stirred no further debate as to his changed views. The
summer after its publication, the *New York Tribune* (August 5, 1890) ran a
favorable review, recommending the book as a study of "a Boston movement . . . between Channing and Parker."

It was fortunate for Frothingham that his book got a favorable reception. The writing effort had been painful and the progress slow. There is

no evidence that he was able to go to Beverly Farms for the summer. It is more likely that he stayed at 118 Marlboro Street with a short trip for the sea air at Lenox or Newport. As the summer of 1890 came to a close, his paralysis, affecting his speech and locomotion, not to mention his handwriting, continued to progress. His friends attempted to cheer him up through the early winter. His old parishioner of New York days, C. P. Cranch, now in Boston, sent him a collection of "sonnets" he had written to Frothingham twenty years before. In response to Frothingham's letter of appreciation, apparently a melancholy one, he wrote words of encouragement to the suffering and depressed Frothingham:

> You think too humbly of your own work. You have done a vast deal of thorough, critical and biographical work since your ministry in New York, which will long survive, I think. But as a preacher your labors were no less effective, and I am sure you would find that the seeds you then sowed have had a wider and more fruitful result than you imagine. I am truly sorry to hear of your ill health.[40]

A few days later Caroline Dall, his old FRA colleague, putting aside her old animosity for Frothingham, wrote an encouraging letter with suggestions for future writing he might undertake. "Your letter was refreshing," he wrote, apologizing for being so depressed after a "miserable autumn" with an "agony" in his back. "The truth is that I got into deeper waters than I expected and extricated myself by an effort." His latest book had taken much out of him, but he promised to follow Mrs. Dall's kindly suggestion.[41] Kate Fields still had hopes of enlisting Frothingham's aid in her literary projects, but in the winter of 1890 it was a vain hope. "I am giving up all but the absolutely indispensable things," he wrote in asking her to cancel his subscription to her journal (Kate Fields' "Washington"). "You don't need me now anyway," he added. He could not resist, as an afterthought, one more incisive comment about her literary style and his own advancing age:

> I am incurably old-fashioned in my mental habits, and while, in the main, I agree with your conclusions and always am in sympathy with your profession, my instincts are more reserved about modern style-swift, incisive, dashing, smart—is something too much for me.[42]

It was true, even while he was suffering through the fall and winter of 1890–1891, Frothingham continued to delve into the past. By spring he had produced a twenty-five page memoir for the Massachusetts Historical Society of Reverend James Walker, his former Divinity School professor. Much of the essay came from printed sermons, some from Theodore Parker's journals, and a great deal from Frothingham's personal recollections. Walker, as a part of Nathaniel Frothingham's generation, was appraised as a preacher, a professor, and president of Harvard University. His preordination examination in 1816 by a council of ministers intrigued Frothingham. He could not resist recounting the event, probably from memory, of Walker's conversation, as an insight into the working of conservative Unitarianism in those pre-Parkerite days:

> The council declared itself satisfied and the procession moved toward the church. After the exercise there was a dinner at which eighty-four people drank nine decanters of brandy, nineteen bottles of costly Madeira wine . . . and smoked twelve dozen cigars.[43]

In a more serious vein, wrote Frothingham, Walker was a "mild Transcendentalist," familiar with German romanticism but was more English, more practical in his thinking, representing the "palmy days of Unitarianism" and lifting the "tone of the University" while president. As for Walker's influence on Frothingham, it was clear that no radical views came from him. Yet, Frothingham acknowledged Walker's advice to students to avoid shallow skepticism and to do something about their beliefs.[44]

In his own memoirs, written the same year as his essay on Walker, Frothingham had a great deal to recall about the origins of his own beliefs. As the title *Recollections and Impressions* might suggest, it was not an autobiography based on notebooks and a diary, but a recounting of events in his life, called up from memory.[45] As might be expected, his chronology was sometimes out of order and there were minor factual errors. Also, many interpretations of major events in his life were slightly different from his account at the time that they happened. In retrospect, he gave more credit to Parker's influence on his views than in previous writings about him. Due to Parker's contact while Frothingham was in Salem, his "Crisis of Belief" (Chapter IV) came from reading certain books by F. C. Bauer and other German theologians. It was then, Frothingham recalled, that he discarded certain Christian myths such as the deity of Christ, atonement, and the theory of perdition. He had apparently forgotten his Salem Sunday School lectures while still a Divinity School student, which showed he had gone far in discarding such beliefs several years before meeting Parker. A long discourse on his old "friendly enemy," Henry Bellows, was a curious mixture of slightly modified interpretations, both favorable and unfavorable, to Bellows' part in his New York career. He had forgotten apparently Bellows' distaste and uneasiness over the radical views he preached from the pulpit, recalling only that he had received a cordial welcome in New York with never a word of criticism or any opposition to his preachings. Yet in recalling the dedication of his New York church in 1863, he blamed Bellows for snubbing the ceremony entirely on the ground that he did not consider it a "proper church," having "no sacraments, no ceremonies." [46] This memory did not recall the facts in the controversy with entire accuracy.

He was on sounder ground in recalling major developments, made up of large events. The progress of religious thought, as reflected in his own intellectual progress, was an evolutionary process, he felt. His two main sources of inspiration, he acknowledged, were Emerson and Parker. Transcendentalism, he recalled, was a "balm and elixir to me," but when science superceded intuitional speculation, "I began to walk by knowledge steadily, surely, but not buoyantly any more." [47] Never really repudiating transcendentalisn in his memoir, he gave credit both to Dr. Orville Dewey, whose sermons on Beethoven introduced to him the relationship of religion and art, and Robert Ingersoll as a sort of transfigured Thomas Paine who emphasized the human application of religion.[48] Curiously enough, Frothingham never used the term "Religion of Humanity" or made any effort to argue a case for the Free Religious Association having been an agent for religious enlightenment.

However, he was optimistic about the present situation in religion. After quoting Emerson's essay on "Worship," in which he predicted a "new church founded on moral science," [49] he wrote that the broad church principle based on human character and earnestness for social reform was fast being established. Religious progress, his theme of a dozen sermons during his career, would come as people became more rational, as the "visible church [comes to] match the invisible." [50]

It really did not matter if his memoirs distorted some minor events or placed a fact or two in improper order. His image of himself presented in the last section entitled "Confessions" was as accurate as could be given by his most objective critics. He admitted to an undogmatic turn of mind which had gone through the conservative stage and the critical stage. Both frames of mind were inadequate for he who would seek the truth. One must be a "speculative reformer, indifferent to dogma." "Truth exists in layers," he wrote, in the language of the pragmatists, whose day was just then dawning:

> There are truths of the letter and truths of the spirit, there is truth to fact and truth to fancy . . . but it will not do to charge lack of truthfulness upon anybody simply because he does not hold the same opinion with ourselves. . . . Experience has taught me many things—this among others, that there is no final criterion for truth.[51]

Yet it was dead theology and denominationalism he had been fighting and not an arid philosophical battle. His last thoughts were couched in terms more characteristic of him:

> The reign of theology may be succeeded by the reign of charity. . . . We have acquired knowledge, industry, civilization, freedom, enterprise, intelligence, the sense of mutual dependence. . . . When we see the road prepared for the spirit, we may be sure the spirit itself is not far off.[52]

This was his last word on religion and philosophy. Nothing else on any subject came from his pen during the next three years. Meanwhile his life became increasingly difficult, his travels very limited, his handwriting virtually unreadable. There were no more trips for him to New York to visit the Morses. His wife Caroline kept up the social contacts.[53] Yet he sometimes received invitations to attend literary meetings in Boston and requests for information and letters concerning himself or his father's career. These he answered as graciously as he could, sending regrets when necessary, obliging when possible.[54]

As the summer of 1893 approached, he had hopes that he might write again—this time a series of sketches of friends he had known. After a summer in Dublin, New Hampshire, he wrote a publisher he would think it over.[55] It is doubtful if his next, and what proved to be his last, writing was a part of his proposed series of sketches. Back in Boston after the summer of rest in New Hampshire, the Massachusetts Historical Society commissioned him to write a memoir of his cousin Francis Parkman for publication in their *Proceedings*. Working under great handicaps, the preparation of the article was uphill work. The result, however, was a thoroughly researched, brilliantly written forty-two page essay. Although Frothingham knew Parkman personally from Harvard days when Parkman was graduated a year behind him and on summer vacations or at social events in Boston, he consulted documents, family genealogy, and the latest biographical writing on his subject.[56]

Thoroughly familiar with Parkman's works as well as his methods, Frothingham described Parkman's use of French documents, his poor eyesight, his note taking as a reader read them to him in French. By modern standards he was uncritical of Parkman's historical methods. Yet he was able, from his well-read background of American history, to compare his works with those of Prescott and Motley. But essentially it was Parkman, the man, which was the main focus of the memoir:

> He was not a thoroughgoing American, as that phrase is commonly known; not a "democrat" in the usual sense of the word—not a believer, that is, in the raw material of human nature; certainly not a favorer of monarchy or oligarchy or aristocracy as founded on rank, wealth, position, power or any temporal condition whatever. His faith was in cultivated humanity; in man as he ought to be and might be; not in men and institutions as they were.[57]

This attitude, typical of the cultivated Boston Brahmin, could just as accurately be attributed to the author of the essay. Two months after the article appeared, Frothingham wrote regrets to William R. Thayer tht he had only five copies for friends because the essay was written for the society and not published for the public.[58] He also had to defend the article for hinting at Parkman's "psychological problems," stemming from poor eyesight and lack of physical vigor, as they might relate to his interpretation of history.[59]

One of Frothingham's great sources of satisfaction during his last years in Boston was his role as mentor to his nephew, Paul Revere Frothingham. Paul's father Thomas, as we have observed, had died in 1880 while Octavius was abroad. It was natural that he would, after his return, gently take over the guidance of young Paul. Having lost their only son as an infant in 1859, the Frothinghams were glad to watch Paul go through Harvard College and to encourage him in Divinity School. He was a frequent guest at 118 Marlboro Street, as well as at Aunt Ellen's Commonwealth Avenue home, where he was virtually a member of the family circle. This, in a sense, was Octavius' personal reward for having not been in the center of the family circle or Boston area Frothinghams during his New York career. "The family never saw much of him," recalled a grandniece, who knew of him only from family reminiscences, "probably because he was considered a sort of renegade." [60] He spent long hours with Paul in the study discussing literature, philosophy, theology, and the challenge of the literal ministry. No doubt it was Frothingham's influence that drew Paul into the ministry and eventually the Free Religious Association during its last years. "If only I can learn to speak without notes," he wrote in Divinity School, "to stand as Uncle Octave used to and talk right to the people, then I believe I can do something." [61]

When he was graduated from Divinity School in 1889, it was Uncle "Octave" who helped him to be placed in New Bedford, in William J. Potter's vacated pulpit. It would be a big advantage, he advised Paul, to take a liberal congregation, already established, rather than be obliged, as he had been, to build from the ground up. He managed one trip to New Bedford to visit Paul and met Potter's former parishioners. In Paul's early years there, he sent sermons down to his uncle for criticism. "You must be careful of your English, my dear boy, as your Grandfather was," [62] he once wrote after a careful and fastidious analysis of Paul's style. He agreed, however, with his nephew's ideas of theology and opinions on social questions.

In a fatherly way he did not hesitate to give Paul domestic advice. When his nephew married Ann Clapp in 1891, he approved but later, when the young couple were setting up housekeeping in a new house in New Bedford, he wrote sarcastically, "[so] your fashionable wife," whom the family apparently disliked for her parvenu proclivities, "wants a name for her new house. How would 'The Manse' do? The clergy with their usual rapacity tried to appropriate it, but did not succeed. Its primary meaning remains a dwelling with land." [63] As Frothingham's last year approached, with his former colleagues either dead or retired from the liberal ministry, the independent societies long disbanded, he looked more and more to young Unitarians such as Paul Revere Frothingham as the hope of the future. His conversations and letters to Paul in 1894 dealt with the status of denominationalism. It had been his duty, he wrote his nephew, to attack sectarianism, to tear down; now was the time for a new departure, for an enlarged Unitarianism. Recanting a bit on his previous stand for a universal, nonsectarian religion, he wrote Paul, in possibly his last letter to him, that sectarianism was inevitable but, "like a lamp chimney," the separation "should be thin and as translucent as possible." [64]

THREE

Nothing more came from his pen, though he attempted to continue his writing through the winter of 1894–1895. But with the pain in his back a constant misery, his walking and handwriting more and more halting, it was no use. Carrie and Bessie looked after his comfort, saw to the doctor's calls, the hot baths, the special bed and chairs. Son-in-law William brought mail and ran needed errands. Ellen Frothingham looked in regularly and gave him a cheery word. Grandson Brooks, a senior at Harvard, added a fresh dimension to the household when in from Cambridge to visit on Marlboro Street. Eight-year-old Curtis Parker was always welcome when he dropped in to cheer up his grandfather.

Not that Octavius was bitter and disagreeable to his family. He bore up stoically under his growing affliction but was depressed and disappointed in his inability to carry on his writing. It had been his whole life since 1879, and there was so much more to do. Perhaps the summer vacation away from the city would improve him. A long carriage ride or hours in a railroad car were out of the question now; thus the trip to New Hampshire was impossible. It was decided that a vacation by the sea at Newport might help him. He endured the summer of 1895, trying to do a bit of writing in their hotel apartment, meals brought in, sitting long hours in the large wicker chair on the ornate porch, propped with pillows in the sea air with little to do but brood on the uncertain future.

Back in Boston by September, Frothingham made a heroic attempt to carry on, sitting day after day at his library study table, possibly attempting to write the biographical sketches of friends he had previously planned. As the first dull days of November came on, his paralysis took a sudden turn for the worse. He was no longer able to sit up; eating and breathing became difficult. A week before Thanksgiving, the family was alerted to stand by; close friends were called.[65] In the early morning hours of November 27, a day short of his seventy-third birthday, the paralysis, diagnosed as a spinal sclerosis, gripped his vital organs and he died, in a coma, peacefully and without pain.[66]

The next day letters began coming in from friends who remembered him in Salem or New York.[67] The press, probably already prepared, took due note of his passing in curiously irrelevant obituaries. *Nation* ran an article on him, identifying him as an "early contributor." The *New York Times* gave a brief sketch of his life but no real mention of his career at

Lyric and Masonic Hall in New York.[68] Nor did the *Boston Daily Globe* mention his career in radical religion or his work in the Free Religious Association. Instead, he was compared in appearance with the actor, Edwin Booth, and notice taken of his oratorical and writing powers. He was also confused with his father, as a famous hymn writer.[69] Certainly the family could take no comfort from the newspaper farewells to their beloved Octave. But Caroline had comfort aplenty from others. Lucy Morse stayed on until the second day of December.[70] William White Chadwick, up from Brooklyn, was on hand to help Paul Revere Frothingham prepare the funeral ceremony. It was to be, significantly enough, not at his father's First Church two blocks away, but in the Frothingham home, in the front room library, with the coffin placed on the study table where Octavius had done most of his literary work since coming to Boston.[71] On the day after Thanksgiving, November 29, 1895, a small but distinguished group gathered at 118 Marlboro Street as the Beacon Quartette sang "Lead Kindly Light." Charles Francis Adams, Jr. was there, along with Dr. William Everett, Minot J. Savage, George S. Hale, and other younger descendents of Frothingham's old colleagues. Paul Revere Frothingham read "appropriate" excerpts, and William White Chadwick gave the funeral address—a graceful, moving eulogy for his old friend. A hymn written years before by N. L. Frothingham was sung at the close of the simple ceremony.[72] In keeping with Octavius' views of death and disposal of the dead, his body was cremated at Forest Hills and the ashes buried in a private ceremony a few days later at Mt. Auburn Street Cemetery in Cambridge. His remains then lay, appropriately enough, with those of the great statesmen, poets, and theologians of nineteenth century New England. Across Greenbriar Path from the Custis family plot where his infant son also lay were buried the Channings—William Ellery and William Henry.[73]

It was often said that Frothingham was a man of wealth with an indifferent attitude toward worldly possessions. His will, filed two days after his burial, left his estate to Caroline, consisting of a sum of $180,000 and no real estate. When Caroline died in 1900, her estate, willed to Elizabeth Parker, included the Marlboro Street House worth $31,000 and a personal estate of $530,000.[74] It was true that the Frothinghams had been in comfortable financial condition. His estate included the inheritance from Grandfather Brooks' fortune, augmented by royalties from his writings and the Boston home.

Caroline lived on in comfort but failing health. At the annual FRA convention in June, 1900, Higginson was to give a memorial address for her husband. Caroline, accompanied by Bessie, sat expectantly in the audience. Before the tribute could begin, she became ill and was forced to leave without hearing it. A week later she died of a heart attack at her home on Marlboro Street.[75] Most people who had known Caroline

Frothingham would have agreed with the secretary of the FRA, who observed in his annual report of the meeting that "Mrs. Frothingham was . . . a woman of broad views, cordial and winning manners, and in thorough sympathy with the life work of her husband. She was one of the patron members of the association." [76] In the manner of the nineteenth century, when the wife of a prominent man stayed almost entirely in the background, this was the only public comment on Octavius' wife.

In the four and one-half years that elapsed between the death of Octavius and Caroline, many of his possessions were given to members of the family. A little silver vase, given to Octavius by Parker's widow in 1860, went to Paul Frothingham,[77] along with a considerable portion of Octavius' historical and theological library. Ellen received many of his books on literary subjects. All of Frothingham's letters and personal papers disappeared—destroyed presumably by him or later by his previous request when the house was sold. It was an unfortunate but logical outcome of events that his memory was never preserved in First Church where memorial plaques were installed to his father, Emerson, C. F. Adams, Edward Everett, Ellen Frothingham, and Henry Bellows. Yet Frothingham would probably have preferred it that way. Although he attended occasionally, he never actually rejoined First Church. Having rejected ecclesiastical ceremonies and architecture, symbols, and all physical representations, he would have been content to be memorialized in the minds and acts of living people.

FOUR

If the eulogies can be believed, he was indeed virtually canonized by those he left behind. From Chadwick's funeral address, noting his disposition, hostile to dogmatism, and his "brooding" which enriched lives with "noble thoughts and many happy inspirations," to Paul Frothingham's memorial in 1913 giving his uncle credit for allowing him to be "born free," [78] the memoirs all had a consistent theme: Frothingham's brilliance, his oratorical powers, his bold radicalism, his militancy balanced by gentleness toward his adversaries, his undogmatic mind capable of expressing his opponents' views as well as his own; all saw him as the pessimistic-optimist, the conservative-radical, the warmhearted man with a thin layer of ice, the genial but austere personality, and the man with many associates but few close friends. There were no less than six memorials of one kind or another in the eighteen years following his death. The New York Ethical Culture Society hired Carnegie Hall in December 1895, for a memorial service. Bessie and William Parker, visiting the Morses, attended. Felix Adler, George Haven Putnam, Edward Stedman, and Judge Barrett gave addresses.[79] The Massachusetts Historical Society in the December meeting following his death heard a memorial by Reverend Edward J. Young. Charles Francis Adams, Jr. presided and James Ford

Rhodes made a few remarks. The following March Joseph P. Quincy and William White Chadwick read memorial papers before the society.[80] There were also numerous newspaper vignettes on his memory through the years and compiled essays on religious radicals which included Frothingham's contributions to religious thought.[81]

In all of the flood of praise which came from various pens and platforms, it was Thomas Wentworth Higginson who came to the heart of both Frothingham's strengths and weaknesses. He was a "knight of the Holy Spirit"—a gentle knight whose weapon of steel with a silver edge never warped from the heat of battle in its straightforward thrust. But as Frothingham rode his pulpit, "as a war chariot," he displayed

> the defect of occasional overstatement—not of manner but of thought. He owned to this himself but said that oratory was like scene painting—it needed broad effects, not a delicate adjustment of shading. In this respect I think he erred and his printed sermons suffered from it. But then overstatement was in words, never in elocution or gesture. . . .[82]

Minot J. Savage, a younger recruit to free religion, could see more clearly Frothingham's part in the great change that had taken place in American religion:

> The change since I have been here in Boston in the last twenty-two years is something marvelous; it is very difficult for me to understand it—the change in the Unitarian ranks, the change in the ranks of the orthodox churches, quite as marked in one as it is in the other. And it is men like Frothingham who have done a great deal of the work of bringing about this change. For, friends, I am glad of two things. I am glad that Frothingham is recognized to-day as a good Unitarian, just as Theodore Parker is, up at 25 Beacon Street. . . . I am glad, then, that Frothingham went outside, that he raised his lonely flag and stood by it in the midst of misunderstanding, obloquy, what-not, until he compelled the people that were inside to say, "Why, we agree with you; come back and be at home with us." This is the kind of victory that an honest man can be proud of.

The Free Religious Association, close to Frothingham's heart for so long had, in Savage's view, been largely responsible:

> If the Free Religious Association goes out of existence because Unitarianism and liberal orthodoxy are recognizing on every hand the principles that have been its glory, it is only as a star goes out in the dawn, when the sun rises and the whole world is light.[83]

But it was still Higginson who knew best what to say of his old friend. It came at the end of his memorial address in 1900—a fitting epitaph, never heard but also deserved by Caroline:

Never quite fulfilling the great work which he felt to be laid upon him, he won personal triumph and additional development of character from the very contest with obstacles, influenced and even controlled many strong minds, and left behind, among his life-long associates, a personal memory which is sweeter and dearer than fame.[84]

Appendix

ARTICLES OF ASSOCIATION

I. This Association shall be called the Free Religious Association, — its objects being to promote the interests of pure religion, to encourage the scientific study of theology, and to increase fellowship in the spirit; and to this end all persons interested in these objects are cordially invited to its membership.

II. Membership in this Association shall leave each individual responsible for his own opinions alone, and affect in no degree his relation to other Associations. Any person desiring to co-operate with the Association shall be considered a member, with full right to speak in its meetings; but an annual contribution of one dollar shall be necessary to give a title to vote, — provided, also, that those thus entitled, may at any time confer the privilege of voting upon the whole assembly, on questions not pertaining to the management of business.

III. The Officers of the Association shall be a President, three Vice-Presidents, a Secretary and Assistant Secretary, a Treasurer, and six Directors, who together shall constitute an Executive Committee, entrusted with all the business and interests of the Association in the interim of its meetings. These officers shall be chosen by ballot, at the Annual Meeting of the Association, and shall hold their offices for one year, or until others be chosen in their place; and they shall have power to fill any vacancies that may occur in their number between the annual meetings.

IV. The Annual Meeting of the Association shall be held in the city of Boston, on Thursday, of what is known as "Anniversary Week," at such place and with such sessions as the Executive Committee may appoint; of which at least one month's previous notice shall be publicly given. Other meetings and Conventions may be called by the Committee, according to their judgment, at such times and places as may seem to them desirable.

V. These Articles may be amended at any Annual Meeting of the Association by a majority vote of the members present, provided public notice of the amendment has been given with the call for the meeting.

These articles were adopted, and the following officers elected under them:—

LIST OF OFFICERS

President. O. B. Frothingham, New York City, N.Y.

Vice-Presidents. Robert Dale Owen, New Harmony, Ind.; *Thomas W. Higginson, Newport, R. I.; Caroline M. Severance, West Newton, Mass.

Secretary. W. J. Potter, New Bedford, Mass.

Assistant Secretary. Rowland Connor, Boston, Mass.

Treasurer. Richard P. Hallowell, Boston, Mass.

Directors. Isaac M. Wise, Cincinnati, Ohio; Charles K. Whipple, Boston, Mass.; Edward C. Towne, Medford, Mass.; Frank B. Sanborn, Concord, Mass.; Hannah E. Stevenson, Boston, Mass.; and Edna D. Cheney, Jamaica Plain, Mass.

Remarks incidental to the question of organization were made by A. B. ALCOTT, E. C. TOWNE, F. B. SANBORN, LUCRETIA MOTT, Mrs. C. H. DALL, C. C. BURLEIGH, and F. E. ABBOT. The meeting then adjourned *sine die.*

*Elected to fill the vacancy caused by the resignation, on account of numerous engagements, of Hon. Isaac Ames.

Notes

PREFACE

1. *The Register-Leader*, UUA, 25 Beacon Street, Boston, Massachusetts, May, 1967; December, 1967; April, 1969 (examples of this type of inquiry).

CHAPTER I

1. Henry Adams, *Education of Henry Adams*, Houghton Mifflin, 1961 Edition, p. 3.
2. According to Henry Adams, also a grandson of Peter Chardon Brooks, this fortune was "about two million dollars." *Education of Henry Adams*, p. 23.
3. Wolcott Rogers, "The Frothingham Family," *Family Jotting*, Boston, 1939, American Antiquarian Society, Worcester, Massachusetts.
4. Howard Chandler Robbins, *The Life of Paul Revere Frothingham*, Houghton Mifflin, 1935, pp. 1–23.
5. Donald Frothingham U.S.N.R., *Reminiscence and Family Record*, Mrs. Eugenia Frothingham Lombard Collection, Cambridge, Massachusetts, 1953.
6. O. B. Frothingham, *Recollections and Impressions, 1822–1890*, G. P. Putnam's Sons, New York and London, 1891, p. 21.
7. *Ibid.*
8. O. B. Frothingham, *Boston Unitarians 1820–1850: A Study of the Life and Work of Nathaniel Langdon Frothingham*, p. 193ff.
9. G. P. Putnam's Sons, New York and London, 1891.
10. *Education of Henry Adams*, M.H.S., 1918.
11. Boston Latin School Records, *Catalogue of Scholars, 1816–1918*, Rare Book Room, Boston Public Library. Frothingham's years spanned the tenure of two headmasters, both early graduates of the school and later Harvard: Charles Knapp Dillaway (1831–1836); Epes. Sargent Dixwell (1836–1854).
12. Boston Latin School Records, *Rank Books 1834–1839*, Rare Book Room, Boston Public Library.
13. Boston Latin School, *Rank Book 1836–1837*, Rare Book Room, Boston Public Library.
14. The year 1935 marked the tercentenary of the Boston Latin School during which time a "Hall of Fame" plaque was installed in the now existent building on Huntington Avenue, Boston, Massachusetts. Along with others, but not including O. B. Frothingham, appear the names of Cotton Mather, Henry Ward Beecher, Wendell Phillips, Edward Everett Hale, and Charles Sumner. Boston Latin School Records, Rare Book Room, Boston Public Library.
15. Boston Latin School Records, "Order of Performance at Prayer," "Declamations of Public Latin School 1837, 1839." Rare Book Room, Boston Public Library. In 1816 young Waldo Emerson had declaimed on English poetry.
16. Tilden Edelstein, *Strong Enthusiasm, A Life of Thomas Wentworth Higginson*, Yale University Press, 1968; *Harvard College, Catalogue of Officers and Students, 1839, 1840*, Archive Room, Widner Library, Harvard University.
17. Samuel Eliot Morison, *Three Centuries of Harvard*, Harvard University Press, 1936 edition, Chap. IX–XXI.
18. David B. Tyack, *George Tichnor and the Boston Brahmins*, Harvard University

Press, 1967. See Chapter III, "The Cause of Sound Learning."

19. *Ibid.*, p. 125.

20. *Catalogues of the Officers and Students of Harvard College, 1839–1843*, Archive Room, Widner Library, Harvard University.

21. *Ibid.*, p. 22.

22. *Harvard Library Charging Lists 1837–1842*, Archive Room, Widner Library, Harvard University.

23. Harvard College Reports, *Annual Report on Harvard University* (1835–1845 volume), Archive Room, Widner Library, Harvard University.

24. Ann M. Wells, *Dear Preceptor, Life and Times of Thomas Wentworth Higginson*, Houghton Mifflin, Boston, 1963.

25. *Ibid.*, p. 23. Quoted from his *Diary.*

26. Hasty Pudding Club, Sec. Rept. 1836–1839. Volumes for 1840–1843 are missing. Archive Room, Widner Library, Harvard University.

27. Morison, *Three Centuries of Harvard*, 1936, p. 202ff. A lively account of clubs is a brilliant part of this one-volume abridgment of the three-volume work.

28. *College Records*, Vol. 8, Archive Room, Widner Library, Harvard University, p. 180.

29. *University Choir Records*, Archive Room, Widner Library, Harvard University.

30. David B. Tyack, *loc. cit.*, p. 94.

31. *Ibid.*, p. 147.

32. Josiah P. Quincy, "Memoirs of Octavius B. Frothingham," *Proceedings Massachusetts Historical Society*, March, 1890, Vol. X, 1829–1896, pp. 500–501.

33. Frothingham to Longfellow, November 13, 1849, Houghton Library, Harvard University.

34. Frothingham to Longfellow, December 14, 1854, Houghton Library, Harvard University.

35. Frothingham to Longfellow, April 25, 1855, Houghton Library, Harvard University.

36. Samuel Johnson, *Lectures, Essays and Sermons*, with a memoir by Samuel Longfellow, Houghton Mifflin, Boston, 1883. Johnson, a year ahead of Frothingham, recalled this class with Professor Longfellow.

37. Octavius Brooks Frothingham, "Memoir of Rev. James Walker, D.D., LLD," *Proceedings Massachusetts Historical Society*, Vol. VI, second series, May 1, 1891, Boston, Massachusetts.

38. *Exhibition and Commencement Performances*, Harvard College Papers, Vol. XI, Vol. XIV; *Record of College Faculty*, Vol. XI, Vol. XII. Archive Room, Widner Library, Harvard University.

39. *Order of Exercise for Class Day*, July 13, 1843. General Folder of Class Records, Archive Room, Widner Library, Harvard University.

40. Class Book, 1843. MSS bound, Archive Room, Widner Library, Harvard University.

41. *Order of Exercise for Class Day*, Archive Room, Widner Library, Harvard University. Class reunion.

42. *Harvard Commencement Days*, 1642–1916, Albert Mathews, Colonial Society of Massachusetts, Wilson and Son, Cambridge, Massachusetts, 1916, p. 377. Archive Room, Widner Library, Harvard University.

43. *Ibid.* News clipping of unidentified Boston paper, August 24, 1843, attached to 1843 Baccalaureate Exercises.

44. His Phi Beta Kappa key, now in Widner Archive Room, was donated to Harvard Library in 1902 by his daughter, Mrs. William L. Parker (Elizabeth B. Frothingham "Bessie" Parker).

45. Theodore Parker to Convers Francis, September 25, 1842, *Parker Papers*, Rare Book Room, Boston Public Library.

46. *College Papers,* Vol. IX, Archive Room, Widner Library, Harvard University. Norton had been re-offered a professorship at Harvard in 1839, but turned it down with advice to President Quincy as to how to advance theological study at Harvard.

47. Charles Crow, *George Riply: Transcendentalist and Utopian Socialist,* University of Georgia Press, 1967, p. 104.

48. Irving H. Bartlett, *Wendell Phillips, Brahmin Radical,* Beacon Press, 1961, p. 95.

49. Quincy, "Memoirs . . . Frothingham," p. 511.

50. *Palfrey Papers,* Divinity School 1816–1852, Archive Room, Widner Library, Harvard University.

51. Morison, *Three Centuries of Harvard,* p. 243ff.

52. Rev. Ware to President Quincy, January 15, 1842, *College Papers,* Vol. IX, Archive Room, Widner Library, Harvard University.

53. Frothingham, *Recollections and Impressions,* p. 33.

54. Quincy, "Memoir . . . Frothingham," p. 511.

55. Frothingham, *Recollections and Impressions* p. 34.

56. T. W. Higginson, *Cheerful Yesterdays,* Houghton Mifflin, 1898, p. 105.

57. *Ibid.*

58. Mary Thatcher Higginson, *Thomas Wentworth Higginson, The Story of His Life,* Houghton Mifflin, 1914, p. 78; Longfellow and Johnson compiled a hymn book in Divinity School called the *Sam Book,* a "heterodox work [but] now some of the Hymns are in 'respectable' collections." Quoted by T. W. Higginson in *Cheerful Yesterdays,* p. 105.

59. Morison, *Three Centuries of Harvard,* p. 269ff.

60. Johnson, *Lectures, Essays and Sermons, Memoir,* p. 14.

61. *Catalog,* Academic Years, 1842–1843, Archive Room, Widner Library, Harvard University.

62. Jerry Wayne Brown, *The Rise of Biblical Criticism in America, 1800–1870, The New England Scholars,* Wesleyan University Press, 1969. See Chapter 3, "The New Weapon."

63. Johnson, *Lectures, Essays, and Sermons,* p. 11.

64. O. B. Frothingham, *Transcendentalism in New England,* G. P. Putnam's and Sons, New York, 1876, p. 354.

65. *Annual Report of Harvard University 1843–1845,* Archive Room, Widner Library, Harvard University.

66. Johnson, *Lectures, Essays and Sermons,* p. 9.

67. *Annual Reports of Harvard University 1843–1846;* $2,000 was given to the school by a Miss Nancy in 1845; *Society for Promotion of Theological Education, 1843–1844;* small sums of scholarship money were given nine of Frothingham's classmates. Archive Room, Widner Library, Harvard University.

68. *Harvard Charging Lists* 1843–1846, Archive Room, Widner Library, Harvard University.

69. MSS Notes of Lectures Delivered by O. B. Frothingham on Gospels of Matthew and John, the Book of Daniel, and the Apocalypse, 4 Vols. Taken by Miss Eliza Davis Bradlee, Andover Library, Harvard University.

70. As transcribed by Eliza Bradlee from O. B. Frothingham's lecture, Vol. I, p. 2.

71. *Ibid.*, p. 2 *passim.*

72. *Ibid.*, Vol. I, p. 55.

73. *Ibid.*, Vol. IV.

74. *Ibid.*, Vol. IV, p. 31.

75. Letters from Sunday School Class, July 3, 1846, Vol. IV, Eliza Bradlee's MSS.

76. O. B. Frothingham to his Sunday School Class, July 7, 1846, Vol. IV, Eliza Bradlee's MSS.

77. *College Papers*, Vol. XII, 1843–1845, Archive Room, Widner Library, Harvard University.

78. *College Papers*, Vol. XIII, 1845–1846, November 26, 1845, Archive Room, Widner Library, Harvard University.

79. Morison, *Three Centuries of Harvard*, p. 227.

80. April 23, 1847.

81. *Divinity School Visitation Participants*, Archive Room, Widner Library, Harvard University. John Weiss, class of 1843 Divinity School, made a slashing attack on church-state relations in "Religion in Germany." Later he became a key figure in the radical Free Religious Association. James Freeman Clark (1833) gave a bland essay on Robert Hall. Clark, a "liberal churchman," never encouraged radical thought.

CHAPTER II

1. Frothingham to Ellis, January 24, 1852, G. E. Ellis Papers, MHS.

2. "Report of the Committee appointed to inquire into the practicability and Expediency of Establishing Manufacturers in Salem, "Salem, Massachusetts, pamphlets, 1826, pp. 1–31.

3. *Salem Observer*, "Fast Day and the Mexican War," April 8, 1847.

4. *Salem Observer*, September 16, 1847. See Gilbert Osofsky, ed., *Puttin' on Massa*, Harper Torch Book, 1969, for Wells' account, written the same year he spoke at Salem (1847).

5. Frothingham, *Recollections and Impressions*, p. 43.

6. North Church reunited with the original First Congregational Society in 1923. Now Unitarian, it is known as First Church.

7. 1635–1636.

8. *Proprietors Record*, bound volume, 1836–1923, First Church, Salem, Massachusetts.

9. *Salem Gazette*, "Notice of North Church Ordination," March 9, 1847.

10. *Services at the Ordination of Rev. O. B. Frothingham*, "Rightly Dividing the Word of Truth, (Timothy 2:15)," N. L. Frothingham, Salem Gazette Office, 1847.

In Congregational Society Collection, 18 Beacon Street, Boston.

11. *Christian Register,* July 8, 1855. This issue noted that N. L. Frothingham had been reelected vice president.

12. *Harvard Library Charging Lists,* 1837–1838, 1839, 1841, 1842, Archive Room, Widner Library, Harvard University. These books were usually signed in on the withdrawal ledger by "O.B.F."

13. Octavius B. Frothingham, *Boston Unitarian, 1820–1850, A Study of the Life and Works of Nathaniel Langdon Frothingham,* G. P. Putnam's Sons, 1890.

14. Nathaniel L. Frothingham to Emerson, August 21, 1837, June 5, 1838, Emerson Collection, Houghton Library, Harvard University.

15. N. L. Frothingham to Emerson, 1829 (no dates); August 9, 1837, March 21, 1841, October 17, 1844, April 9, 1864, April 21, 1864, May 6, 1867, May 15, 1867, Emerson Collection, Houghton Library, Harvard University.

16. O. B. Frothingham, *Boston Unitarian, 1820–1850,* p. 140.

17. *Ibid.,* p. 200.

18. *Ibid.,* p. 73.

19. *Salem Register,* March, 1847.

20. O. B. Frothingham, *Boston Unitarian, 1820–1850,* p. 92.

21. In September, 1847, when T. W. Higginson was ordained, William Henry Channing preached the sermon, "Gospel for Today," In contrast to N. L. Frothingham's plea for a quiet, conservative ministry for his son, Higginson was urged to challenge and stir his congregation with radical beliefs. William Henry Channing, *Gospel for Today,* William Crosby and H. P. Nichols, Boston, 1847.

22. These houses are still standing. The Bowdich house is now a national landmark and used by a Salem City government agency. The others are maintained by private local agencies and open to the public.

23. *Vital Statistics,* Index 2, 1844–1850, Vol. 42, Massachusetts State House, Boston, p. 204.

24. O. B. Frothingham to George Bartol, September 20, 1847, Washburn Papers, MHS, Boston. The younger brother of Rev. Cyrus Bartol of Boston, an organizer of the Free Religious Association in 1867.

25. *Proprietors Record Committee Report,* bound volume, 1836–1923, First Church, Salem, Massachusetts. This project was done not without some inconvenience. The record shows that a Mr. Bridges was given a new pew because a post was placed in his old one and "damage done to him." A look at the interior of the church today shows two pillars supporting the balcony placed squarely where two pews once were.

26. O.B.F. to George Bartol, September 20, 1847, Washburn Papers, M.H.S., Boston.

27. *Salem Observer,* October 23, 1847.

28. *Salem Observer,* November 10, 1847.

29. Carl Bode, *The American Lyceum, Town Meeting of the Mind,* Oxford Press, New York, 1956, p. 46.

30. Henry H. Oliver, "Historical Sketch of the Salem Lyceum," *Salem Gazette,* 1879. This is the only source of information which Carl Bode also used.

31. *Ibid.*

32. Bode, *The American Lyceum,* pp. 175–188. The building is no longer standing.

33. Henry H. Oliver, "Historical Sketch of the Salem Lyceum," *Salem Gazette,* 1879. Thoreau received $35 (the average) for his appearance; Webster, $100; Beecher, $50; Louis Agassiz, $250; Wendell Phillips, $50.

34. *Salem City Documents, School Report,* "Annual Report of School Committee," February, 1851, Essex Institute, Salem, Massachusetts.

35. *Salem City Documents,* "Annual Report of School Committee," See N. 34, February, 1852.

36. *Ibid.,* March, 1853.

37. *Ibid.,* February, 1854.

38. *Ibid.,* February, 1854.

39. *Ibid.,* February, 1855.

40. *Salem Observer,* September 23, 1854.

41. *Salem Gazette,* 1845–1855.

42. *Salem Gazette,* December 4, 1847.

43. *Salem Register, Salem Observer, Salem Gazette,* 1847–1855.

44. July 19, 1854, appointed along with Rev. W. R. Ellis and three Boston lawyers, *Records of Overseers of Harvard College,* Vol. XI, p. 316.

45. *Essex Institute Historical Collection,* Vol. 23, 1886, p. 119, *Constitution and By-Laws of the Salem Choral Society,* Essex Institute, Salem, Massachusetts.

46. Thomas Wentworth Higginson, *Journals,* No. 12, 1849–1851. In this volume is inserted the printed invitation from Bronson Alcott, 12 West Street, March 20, 1849. On it Higginson penned the curious comment, "Mr. Alcott is an innocent charlatan." Houghton Library, Harvard University.

47. *Ibid.,* May 2, 1849.

48. *Ibid.*

49. Henry Commager, *Theodore Parker, Yankee Crusader,* Beacon Press, 1947, p. 104.

50. *Saturday Club By-laws,* founded 1855, Houghton Library, Harvard University; Johnson Thomas Lynn, *The Early Years of the Saturday Club,* pamphlet, no date, Houghton Library, Harvard University. No names of men of Frothingham's generation appear on the rolls of the Saturday Club.

51. O. B. Frothingham, *Recollections and Reminiscences,* "My Companions," 1891.

52. T. W. Higginson, *Journals,* No. 12, No. 13, Houghton Library, Harvard University.

53. David Wasson to Samuel Johnson, November 15, 1854, Wasson Papers, Essex Institute, Salem, Massachusetts.

54. Wasson to Johnson, December 2, 1854.

55. Frothingham to Johnson, September 24, 1849, Samuel Johnson's Papers, Box 4, Essex Institute, Salem, Massachusetts.

56. Frothingham to Johnson, Boston, July 30, 1850, Johnson Papers.

57. *Salem City Directory,* 1850–1855, Essex Institute (names of members and officers of this group appear almost every year).

58. O. B. Frothingham to Female Anti-Slavery Association, Essex Institute, Salem, Massachusetts.

59. Theodore Parker, *Journals,* Vol. III, 1850–1851, p. 115. One brief entry mentions a visit by O. B. Frothingham about a trivial matter. Frothingham's own *Recollections and Impressions* has more to say of Parker's influence.

60. Hamilton Hurd, ed., *History of Essex County*, Vol. I, J. W. Lewis, Philadelphia, 1889, p. 17; *Proprietors Committee Reports*, 1836–1923, bound volume, 1849–1953, North Church, Salem, Massachusetts.

61. *Massachusetts Historical Society Proceedings*, Vol. X, 1895–1896, Josiah Quincy's "Memoir of Octavius Brooks Frothingham," March 8, 1896, p. 507ff. Quincy states that Octavius B. Frothingham sent back an "admirable series of letters" (now lost).

62. *The First Century of the North Church Society*, Centennial Volume, 1872, Salem, Massachusetts, 1873.

63. *North Church Record, Sunday School Catalogue of Books*, 1856, Essex Institute, Salem, Massachusetts. (15 pages 4″ x 6″ were used to print the list of library books.)

64. Martha Nichols, *Memorial Paper*, read at North Church, Salem, Massachusetts, 1896, MSS, A.A.U. Collection, O.B.F. Folder, 25 Beacon Street, Boston.

65. Various letters, Margaret Brooks Collection, Essex Institute, Salem, Massachusetts.

66. *Ordination of Rev. O. B. Frothingham*, see pp.

67. *First Century*, July 19, 1872, p. 167.

68. Frothingham, *Recollections and Impressions*, pp. 46–48.

69. *Massachusetts Historical Society Proceedings*. Edward Young, "Remarks on the Death of O. B. Frothingham," Boston, 1896, p. 365.

70. O. B. Frothingham to Parker, April 14, 1851 in William Whyte Chadwick, *Theodore Parker, Preacher and Reformer*, Houghton Mifflin, Boston, 1900, p. 302.

71. Frothingham, *Recollections and Impressions*, p. 54.

72. *Ibid.*, p. 60.

73. *Proprietors Reports*, May 14–16, 1854, North Church, Salem, Massachusetts.

74. Henry Commager's *Theodore Parker* has a lively account of the whole Burns affair from the vantage point of Parker's part in the action; Pauline Harrel, *The Rendition of Anthony Burns*, Master's Thesis, Southern Connecticut State College (1969) is a comprehensive description of the events and an analysis of moral and legal aspects of the Anthony Burns affair.

75. "The New Commandment," *Salem Observer* (printer), Salem, Massachusetts, 1854, Box: Frothingham, Massachusetts Historical Society. Delivered June 4, 1854, in North Church, Salem, Massachusetts.

76. O. B. Frothingham, "Theodore Parker," *The Radical*, August, 1869, p. 95.

77. "The New Commandment," *Salem Observer*, Preface, Salem, 1854, Frothingham Box, Massachusetts Historical Society.

78. *The New Commandment, a Review of a Discourse Delivered in the North Church, Salem, Sunday June 4, 1854 by the Rev. O. B. Frothingham*, Henry Whipple and Sons, Boston, Essex Institute, Salem, Massachusetts, 1854. An archivist's notation on the pamphlet mentions the name of James W. Perry, "supposed author." No such name appears in the North Church records.

79. *Ibid.*, p. 17.

80. June 20, 1854.

81. Nichols *Memorial Paper*, MSS in Unitarian Library, 25 Beacon Street, Boston.

82. *Ibid.*

83. O.B.F. to Samuel Johnson, March (undated), 1885, Johnson Papers, Essex

Institute, Salem, Massachusetts.

84. *Salem Observer,* May 19, 1855; *Salem Gazette,* April 31, 1855; *Salem Register,* April 20, 1855.

85. *Salem Observer,* April 15, 1855.

86. *Ibid.,* May 1855.

87. "First Church, The Three Hundredth Anniversary of the First Church in Salem, 1930," address of Stephen W. Phillips, May 28, 1929, p. 74, Essex Institute, Salem, Massachusetts.

88. *Salem Gazette,* July 14, 1847.

89. Conrad Wright, *The Liberal Christians,* Beacon Press, 1970. This contains a useful account of Bellows' contribution to Unitarian organizational development.

90. Frothingham, *Impressions and Recollections,* pp. 64–65. Why Bellows had this much influence with the Jersey City church is unclear.

91. *Ibid.,* p. 65.

92. *Ibid.,* p. 74.

93. *Salem Observer,* May 19, 1855; a notice from the *Christian Inquirer.*

94. O. B. Frothingham, "Uses of the Sanctuary," sermon preached at dedication of Unitarian Church in Jersey City, September 19, 1855, John Gray, New York, 1855. Congregational Society, 18 Beacon Street, Boston.

95. O. B. Frothingham, "Colonization," Anti-Slavery Tract No. 3, Anti-Slavery Society, 138 Nassau Street, New York, 1855.

96. O. B. Frothingham, "Speech Before the American Anti-Slavery Society, New York, May 8, 1856, 138 Nassau Street, New York, 1856.

97. O. B. F. to Samuel Longfellow, November 3, 1856, Longfellow Papers, Essex Institute, Salem, Massachusetts.

98. O. B. Frothingham, *The Last Signs,* June 1, 1856, Ford Collection, Anti-Slavery Pamphlets, New York Public Library.

99. O.B.F. to Ralph Waldo Emerson, June 29, 1855, Houghton Library, Harvard University.

100. O. B. F. to Emerson, August 22, 1856.

101. O. B. F. to Emerson, November (no date), 1856; December 27, 1856; December 26, 1856. The list included Theodore Parker, Rev. Mayo of Albany, T. W. Higginson, Starr King, Samuel Johnson, Frederick Hedge, Wendell Phillips, George W. Curtis, and Rev. Henry Bellows.

102. O. B. F. to Longfellow, December, 1855.

103. O. B. F. to T. W. Higginson, September 4, 1857, Houghton Library, Harvard University.

104. O. B. F. to Higginson, November 3, 1857.

105. O. B. F. to Higginson, February 2, 1858.

106. Mt. Auburn St. Cemetery Records, Cambridge, Massachusetts.

107. John White Chadwick, *Theodore Parker, Preacher and Reformer,* Houghton Mifflin, 1900, p. 302ff.

108. *New York Evening Post,* November 28, 1895, folder of O. B. F., Archive Room, Widner Library, Harvard University.

109. O. B. F. to Henry Bellows, March 2, 1859, Bellows Papers, Massachusetts Historical Society, Boston.

110. O. B. F. to Bellows, May 16, 1859 Frothingham sent the letter from 113 West 34th Street, New York.

Chapter III

1. Conrad Wright, *The Liberal Christians,* Beacon Press, 1970, p. 83ff.

2. *Christian Examiner,* Vol. 41, July, 1846, pp. 56–86.

3. *Christian Examiner,* Vol. 41, September, 1846.

4. *Christian Examiner,* May, 1848. William B. Greene, *The Incarnation, A Letter to Rev. John Fiske.*

5. Octavius B. Frothingham to G. E. Ellis, Salem, January 8, 1851, Ellis Papers, Essex Institute, Salem, Massachusetts.

6. *Christian Examiner,* Vol. 50, March, 1851, p. 20ff.

7. Frothingham to Ellis, Salem, March 19, 1851.

8. Frothingham to Ellis, May 8, 1851.

9. Frothingham to Ellis, May 16, 1851.

10. Frothingham to Ellis, September 15, 1851.

11. Frothingham to Ellis, September 17, 1851.

12. Frothingham to Ellis, September 25, 1851.

13. *Christian Examiner,* Vol. XVI, Series 4, September, 1851.

14. *Christian Examiner,* Vol. XVII, Series 4, January, 1852.

15. *Ibid.,* pp. 2–25.

16. Frothingham to Ellis, November 3, 1851.

17. Frothingham to Ellis, January 24, 1852.

18. Frothingham to Ellis, February 2, 1852.

19. Christian Examiner, *The Christ of the Apocryphal Gospels,* Von Rudolph Hofman (Doctor of Philosophy, University of Leipzig), 1851; review by Octavius B. Frothingham, July, 1852, Vol. 53, p. 81.

20. Frothingham to Ellis, January 14, 1853.

21. Frothingham to Ellis, January 27, 1853.

22. Frothingham to Ellis, February 16, 1853.

23. *Christian Examiner,* March, 1853, Vol. 54.

24. His father's article was entitled "The Word of God"; "Did he speak?" he asked. "No not as such," he concluded.

25. Frothingham to Ellis, March 28, 29, 30, 1853.

26. *Christian Examiner,* Vol. 54, May, 1853.

27. *Ibid.,* p. 453.

28. Frothingham to Ellis, January 31, February 6, June 1, 1854.

29. *Christian Examiner,* "Scientific Criticism of the New Testament," O. B. Frothingham, Vol. XX, July, 1854, p. 95.

30. Frothingham to Ellis, July 30, 1854.

31. *Christian Examiner,* Vol. 58, May, 1855. His father had a poem about "An Asylum" in the same issue.

32. Samuel Johnson to Samuel Longfellow, January 6, 1858 in Samuel Johnson's *Memoir,* p. 52.

33. *Christian Examiner,* Vol. II, Series II, January, 1858.

34. *Christian Examiner,* Vol. 65, November, 1858 (review of three books by Octavius B. Frothingham).

35. *Christian Examiner,* Vol, 70, January, 1859.

36. *Christian Examiner,* Vol. 71, July, 1861, pp. 23–25.

37. *Christian Examiner,* Vol. 71, September, 1861.

38. *Christian Examiner,* Vol. 73, November, 1862, p. 29.

39. *Christian Examiner,* Vol. XIII, 5th Series, July, 1863; September, 1863;

November, 1863.

40. *Christian Examiner,* Vol. XIII, 5th Series, November, 1863, pp. 335–336.

41. *Ibid.*

42. Tichnor and Field, Boston, 1864.

43. *Christian Examiner,* Vol. 76, May, 1864, p. 383 ff. ˈ

44. *Christian Examiner,* Vol. 77, November, 1864.

45. *Christian Examiner,* Vol. 78, January, 1865, pp. 22–23.

46. *Ibid.,* p. 26.

47. *Christian Examiner,* Vol. 79, July, 1865. "Mills Review of Hamilton," p. 301; "The Drift Period in Theology, "p. 26: review of Francis Power Cobbe, *The Religious Demands of the Age,* Walker, Fuller, Boston; Francis Cobbe, *Broken Lights* or *Inquiry into the Present Condition and Future Prospects of Religious Faith,* Trubner, London; Sara S. Hennel, *Thoughts In and Of Faith, Gathered Chiefly from Recent Works in Philosophy and Theology,* Manwaring, London (no dates). This was the lead article.

48. *Christian Examiner,* Vol. 79, July, 1865, p. 26.

49. *Ibid.,* p. 11.

CHAPTER IV

1. Frothingham, *Recollections,* p. 103.

2. *Ibid.,* p. 126.

3. *Ibid.,* p. 125.

4. Printed in *Index,* May 26, 1876, p. 245.

5. James Herbert Morse, *Diary,* Vol. II, February 2, 1871, NYHS.

6. Edmund C. Stedman, *Octavius Frothingham and the New Faith,* G. P. Putnam, New York, 1876, 50 pp. (originally published in *Galaxy* magazine).

7. James Herbert Morse, *Diary,* Vol. XIX, 1913, NYHS, "Conversations at the Century Club."

8. Stedman, *Frothingham and the New Faith*

9. Massachusetts Historical Society *Proceedings,* Vol. X, 1895, Boston, 1896, p. 53.

10. *Boston Journal* printed in *Index,* May 25, 1876.

11. *New York Evening Post,* November 28, 1895 (an obituary).

12. Francis P. Weisenburger, *Triumph of Faith, Contribution of the Church in American Life: 1865–1900,* William Byrd Press, Richmond, Virginia, 1962, p. 33ff. This contains an admirable discussion of the New York church milieu.

13. Stedman, *Frothingham and the New Faith,* Introduction by George Haven Putnam.

14. Peter Dean, *The Life and Teachings of Theodore Parker,* Williams and Norgate, Edinburg, 1877, p. 147.

15. Stow Persons, *Free Religion, An American Faith,* Yale, 1947. This pioneering monograph is an admirable study of the Free Religious Movement and the men who moved it.

16. Stedman, *Frothingham and the New Faith,* p. 24.

17. O. B. Frothingham, *The Cradle of Christ, A Study of the Primitive Christianity,* G. P. Putnam's Sons, New York, 1877, p. 181.

18. Frothingham's "new theology" is best summarized in *Religion of Humanity,*

D. C. Francis, New York, 1873. In it he reasserts themes discussed in his sermons and scholarly writings. This book was intended for reading by the lay public of thoughtful people. Similarly, his *The Cradle of Christ, A Study of the Primitive Christianity*, G. P. Putnam's Sons, New York, 1877, was offered to the public as a simplified version of German Biblical criticism and a summary of Frothingham's criticism of Christianity as an elected and still developing faith.

19. Sidney Warren, *American Freethought 1860–1914*, Columbia University Press, 1943, pp. 96–97. Frothingham may have attended meetings of the Nineteenth Century Club, a free thought group, at the home of the President, Cortland Palmer of New York City, though there is no sure evidence of this.

20. *New York Evening Post*, quoted in the *Christian Register*, August 27, 1859.

21. *New York Evening Telegram*, December 15, 1877; in *Index*, January 24, 1878, Vol. 9, p. 40.

22. OBF, *Instituted and Ideal Religion*, sermon, 1873.

23. OBF, *The Joy of a Free Faith*, sermon, 1873.

24. OBF, *The Radical's Root*, sermon, 1873.

25. OBF, *The Safest Creed*, sermon, 1871.

26. OBF, 1871.

27. OBF, *The Spirit of the New Faith*, sermon, 187

28. OBF, *Clogs and Opportunities*, sermon, 1879.

29. OBF, *The Mission of the Radical Preacher*, 1878; *Why Go to Church*, 1874; sermons.

30. OBF, *Why Does Popular Religion Prevail?*, sermon, 1877.

31. OBF, *The Rising and Setting Faith*, sermon, 1877.

32. OBF, *Revival of Religion*, sermon, 1874.

33. OBF, *The Spirit of the New Faith*, sermon, 1877.

34. OBF, *The Sectarian Spirit*, sermon, 1878.

35. OBF, *Pharisees*, sermon, 1876.

36. OBF, *The Protestant Alliance and Religion*, sermon, 1873.

37. OBF, *The Radical Belief*, sermon, 1874.

38. OBF, *The Struggle for Supremacy Over Conscience*, sermon, 1875.

39. OBF, *The Radical Belief*, sermon, 1874.

40. OBF, "Funeral for Edward and John Ketchum" from A. J. Dugann, *The Fighting Quakers, A True Story of the Civil War*, Bureau of Military Records, P. O. Robins, 37 Park Row, New York, 1866.

41. OBF, *Morality of the Riots*, July 19, 1863, G. D. Francis, New York, 1863, Atheneum, Boston, Massachusetts.

42. OBF, *Saintliness*, sermon, 1874.

43. OBF, *God Is Love*, sermon, 1872.

44. OBF, *Theodore Parker*, sermon, 1860. Perhaps William James had read the sermon when he wrote of Herbert Spencer, "One finds no twilight region in his mind . . . all parts are filled with the same noon-day glare . . . There are no mysteries or shadows." "Memories and Studies," 1912, in Richard Hofstadter, *Social Darwinism and American Thought*, Beacon Press, Boston, Massachusetts, 1944, p. 129.

45. OBF, *Ministry of Reconciliation*, Divinity School Address, July 12, 1868, John Wilson, Cambridge, Massachusetts, Harvard University Archive Room. Also in *Christian Examiner*, Vol. 85, September, 1868.

46. OBF, *Duties and Dreams,* sermon, 186 .

47. OBF, *Flowers and Graves,* sermon, 1873.

48. OBF, *School of Adversity,* sermon, 1871.

49. OBF, *A Plea for Amusement,* sermon, 1874.

50. OBF, *The Disposal of Our Dead,* sermon, 1874.

51. OBF, *Crime and Punishment,* sermon, 1873.

52. OBF, sermon, 1878.

53. OBF, *Charity and the Poor,* sermon, 1874.

54. OBF, *Sowing and Reaping,* sermon, 1874.

55. OBF, "The Moral Crisis in Our Politics, What Our Citizens Must Do, *"New York Times,* November 6, 1871. The Tweed ring had just won another election. Rev. Bellows had also spoken out but his sermon was not carried in the *Times.*

56. OBF, *Beliefs and Practices,* sermon, 1874.

57. OBF, *Suppression of Vice,* sermon, 1874.

58. OBF, *The Let Alone Policy,* sermon, 1861.

59. OBF, *God's Fellow Workers* and *Ebb and Flow of Faith,* sermons dealing with social reform, 1873.

60. OBF, *The Puritan Spirit,* sermon, 1873.

61. OBF, *Creed and Conduct,* sermon, 187 .

62. OBF, *The Hidden Life; The Whole Duty of Man; The Natural Man; The Dimensions of Life;* sermons, 1874–1876.

63. OBF, *Attitudes of Unbelief,* sermon, 1878.

64. OBF, *The Birth of the Spirit of Christ,* 1862; *Radical's Belief,* 1874; *The Agony and the Son of Man,* 1874; *Resurrection of the Son of Man,* 1874; *The Sermon on the Mount,* 1876; *The Festival of Joy,* 1877; *Christmas Eve,* 1877 (sermons).

65. OBF, *Interests: Material and Spiritual,* sermon, 1876.

66. OBF, *The Radical Believer,* 1874. Other sermons dealing with this Frothingham concept of God are *Thoughts About God,* 1876; *Cornerstones,* 1877; *The Holy Ghost, Lord and Giver of Life,* 187 ; *The Living God,* 187 ; *The Overruling God,* 1871; *Dying and Living God,* 187 ; *The Overruling God,* 1871; *Dying and Living God,* 187 .

67. OBF, *Present Heaven,* sermon, 187 .

68. OBF, "Words Spoken at the Funeral of John Hopper," Thatcher and Gladston, New York, 1864, Essex Institute, Salem, Massachusetts.

69. OBF, *Visions of Heaven,* 1872; *Glorified Man,* 1876; *Victory Over Death,* 187 . Other sermons on the subject are *Power of Immortal Hope,* 187; *The Immortalities of Man,* 1871.

70. OBF, *Living Faith,* sermon, 1874.

71. OBF, *The Patronage of Religious Institutions,* sermon, 1878.

72. OBF, *Comfort and Inspiration,* sermon, 187 .

73. OBF, *Reasonable Religion,* sermon, 1876; twelve to fifteen other sermons were preached on the subject of faith and revelation between 1870 and 1878.

74. OBF, *Scientific Aspect of Prayer,* sermon, 187 .

75. OBF, *Prayer,* sermon, 1877; *Office of Prayer,* sermon, 187 .

76. OBF, *Wheat and Tares,* sermon, 1872; *Infidelity,* sermon, 1876.

77. OBF, *The Dogma of Hell,* sermon, 1878.

78. OBF, *Forgiveness,* sermon, 1877.

79. OBF, *Visions of Judgment,* sermon, 1872.

80. OBF, *Religion, Poetry of Life,* sermon, 1873.

81. OBF, *Stories from the Lips of the Teacher,* Walker, Wise and Company, Boston, 1864.

82. OBF, *Stories of the Patriarchs,* Walker, Wise and Company, Boston, 1864.

83. James Miller, New York, 1866.

84. Preface, p. VI.

85. OBF, *Stories of the Patriarchs,* Walker, Wise and Company, Boston, 1864, pp. 22–27.

86. Massachusetts Historical Society *Proceedings,* "Memoir of O. B. Frothingham," by Josiah Quincy, Vol. X, 1895–1896, p. 523.

87. "Mr. Frothingham to Children," *New York Times,* November 29, 1875.

88. Harriet Stanton Blatch; Alma Lutz, *Challenging Years,* G. P. Putnam, New York; 1940 (Introduction by Mary Beard).

89. *Ibid.*

90. Massachusetts Historical Society *Proceedings,* "Memoir of O. B. Frothingham," by Josiah Quincy, Vol. X, 1895–1896, p. 524.

91. *Liberal Christian,* April 6, 1867, Vol. XXII (Editorial). Frothingham felt that women were not yet "ready" for politics; nor were politics ready for them.

Chapter V

1. FRA, *Proceedings,* May 30, 1867, pp. 37–40.

2. FRA, *Proceedings,* 1892, p. 9.

3. *Ibid.,* p. 11.

4. *Ibid.,* p. 12.

5. OBF to Samuel Johnson, December 4, 1866, Johnson Papers, Essex Institute, Salem, Massachusetts.

6. FRA, *Proceedings,* 1892, p. 13.

7. *Ibid.,* p. 12.

8. Theodore Parker to Convers Francis, September 25, 1842, Parker Papers, Rare Book Room, BPL.

9. T. W. Higginson to David Wasson, November 17, 1857, in Mary Thatcher Higginson, *Thomas Wentworth Higginson,* Houghton Mifflin, Boston, 1914, p. 101. Higginson, in writing to his colleagues, continually called for a schematic movement but denied he had the "gifts and training at heart" to lead it.

10. In Conrad Wright, *The Liberal Christians,* Beacon Press, 1970, p. 98.

11. *Ibid.*

12. Stow Persons, *Free Religion, An American Faith,* Yale, 1947, p. 113.

13. *New York Times,* April 7, 1865.

14. *Christian Examiner,* Vol. LXXVIII, May, 1865, p. 421; Conrad Wright, *The Liberal Christians,* Beacon Press, 1970, p. 104.

15. Henry Bellows to R. N. Bellows, April 12, 1865; Conrad Wright, *The Liberal Christians,* Beacon Press, 1970, p. 105.

16. Persons, *Free Religion, An American Faith,* p. 12. Persons states that the struggle to crush the radicals to get denominational unity coincided with attempts to tighten theological lines as well.

17. Persons, *Free Religion, An American Faith,* p. 17. He stated that neither of the young clergymen participated in the conference but sat in the balcony and watched. An observer, reporting in the *Christian Examiner,* May, 1865, stated that

Frothingham made a speech and presented a proposal. The *New York Times,* April 7, 1865, reported the business session in detail, including each speaker, paraphrasing what he said, but did not mention Frothingham's participation. William Potter later recalled that Frothingham, Wasson, and others put up "strenuous resistance" to the preamble at the conference indicating that he, along with a "goodly minority," voted against it. *Index,* September 14, 1882, p. 122.

18. Higginson to Francis E. Abbot, March 16, 1970; in *Index,* April 23, 1870, Vol. I, no. 17.

19. W. C. Gannett to Fox (Unitarian Association secretary), May 30, 1874, W. C. Gannett Papers, Box II, MSS Room, University of Rochester.

20. Samuel Johnson, up in Lynn, Massachusetts, delivered a similar attack on the results of the conference which Frothingham pronounced a "capital sermon." O.B.F. to Johnson, May 21, 1865, Johnson Paper, Essex Institute, Salem, Massachusetts.

21. OBF, "The Unitarian Conference and the Times," April, 1865, *Tract for the Times,* C. M. Plumb and Company Publishers, 274 Canal Street, New York; also published in *Friends of Progress,* May, 1865.

22. OBF, "The Unitarian Conference and the Times." Samuel Bowles to Ann Whitney, April 2, 1866, "It was a sad, bitter and bilious sermon, but yet very strong and pungent," in George Merrian (ed.), *Life and Times of Samuel Bowles,* Century Company, New York, 1885, Vol. II, p. 48.

23. OBF to Johnson, May 22, 1865.

24. OBF to Johnson, December 4, 1866.

25. OBF to H. Bellows, November 29, 1866, Bellows Papers, MHS.

26. OBF to H. Bellows, December 5, 1866.

27. *Liberal Christian,* January 26, 1867.

28. H. Bellows to Cyrus Bartol, February 7, 1967, Bellows Papers, MHS.

29. Charles Lowe to Henry Bellows, February, 1867, Bellows Papers, MHS.

30. Bartol to Bellows, January, 1866.

31. *Liberal Christian,* Bellows' editorial on the Free Religious Association planning meeting, February 16, 1867, p. 4.

32. Frothingham, *Recollections and Impressions,* p. 122ff.

33. OBF to C. E. Norton, February 12, 1867, Houghton Library, Harvard University.

34. Francis E. Abbot to Norton, February 19, 1867.

35. OBF to Norton, May 2, 1867.

36. Norton to Miss Gaskell, July 14, 1867, in Sara Norton and M. H. De Wolf Howe, *Letters of Charles Eliot Norton,* 2 Vol., Vol. 1, Houghton Mifflin, 1913, pp. 295–296.

37. William J. Potter to Caroline Dall, February 8, 1867, MHS.

38. OBF to Abbot, May 2, 1867, Abbot Papers, Archive Room, Harvard University.

39. Abbot to Potter, February 20, 1867, in Sidney Ahlstrom, *Francis Ellingwood Abbot,* PhD Dissertation, Unpublished, Harvard University, 1951, p. 88.

40. FRA, *Proceedings, Report of Meeting,* May 30, 1867, p. 1.

41. Ibid., p. 5.

42. Ibid., p. 6.

43. Ibid., p. 30ff.

44. Ibid., p. 53ff.

45. Article I.

46. Article IV.

47. Frothingham probably had little to do with these details of organizational tactics. Potter, Towne, and Abbot no doubt conceived the plan and got Frothingham, who sympathized with the objectives, to implement it.

48. *The Radical,* Vol. 2, June, 1867.

49. Abbot to Potter, June 18, 1867, in Ahlstrom, *Francis Ellingwood Abbot,* p. 81.

50. *Liberal Christian,* June 15, 1867. In the same month appeared two articles by O. B. Frothingham on innocuous essays: "Social Evils" and "The Sacredness of the Body," *Liberal Christian,* June 8, 1867.

51. H. Bellows, "The National Conference of Unitarian and Other Christian Churches," *Christian Examiner,* September, 1868, p. 319ff.

52. *New York Times,* October 9, 1868 (Report of Unitarian Conference).

53. W. W. Chadwick to W. C. Gannett, June 8, 1869, W. C. Gannett Papers, Box II, MSS Room, University of Rochester. William C. Gannett, while still in Divinity School, had been elected to represent Harvard at the Syracuse conference in 1866 where he voted with Abbot and Towne against the preamble.

54. Chadwick to Gannett, June 2, November 9, 1869.

55. Gannett to Chadwick, November 29, 1869.

56. Chadwick to Gannett, December 19, 1869.

57. A. D. Mayo, "Religious Tendencies in the United States," *Christian Examiner,* July 1869, p. 39ff.

58. OBF to Abbot, May 26, 1870.

59. OBF to Gannett, April 14, May 6, 1870, Gannett Papers.

60. OBF to James Parton, August 3, September 10, 1873.

61. Potter to Lucretia Mott, June 11, 1879; Friends Historical Collection, Swarthmore College; Potter to Caroline Dall, May 7, 1870, May 18, 1871, MHS; Potter to Johnson, November 26, 1874, Essex Institute, Salem, Massachusetts.

62. OBF to Johnson, March 24, April 15, 1873, Salem.

63. *New York Times,* June 1, 1868; a full account was carried. It was a review of the origin and needs of the Free Religious Association, a unifying, inspirational address.

64. FRA, *Proceedings,* May 27–28, 1869, p. 10ff.

65. Ibid., p. 15ff.

66. Abbot to Potter, November 29, 1870, Ahlstrom, *Francis Ellingwood Abbot,* p. 251.

67. Ibid., p. 154ff.

68. Gannett to Andrew D. White (President of Cornell), June 30, 1874, Gannett Papers, Box III, MSS Room, University of Rochester.

69. FRA, *Proceedings,* June 1–2, 1871, p. 20ff.

70. *Boston Daily Globe,* May 31, June 1, 1872, "Local Intelligence" (quarter column on p. 8 each day).

71. FRA, *Proceedings,* May 30–31, 1872, p. 68ff.

72. FRA, *Proceedings,* May 29–30, 1873, Executive Committee Report, p. 8.

73. *Boston Daily Globe,* May 30, 1873, "Local Intelligence." (The notice of the Unitarian meeting appeared above that of the FRA.)

74. *Boston Daily Globe,* January 6, 1873. W. C. Gannett received an enthusiastic

letter from a person who thought the Horticultural Hall lecture peerless for brilliancy and intellectuality. "I feel like putting my hand on my mouth and my mouth in the dust whenever I hear Frothingham, Higginson and other wonders of your association." M. H. Livermore (Melrose, Massachusetts) to W. C. Gannett, November 26, 1875, W. C. Gannett Papers, Box IV, MSS Room, University of Rochester.

75. FRA, *Proceedings*, May 29–30, 1873, p. 8ff.

76. OBF, "The Three Pentecosts" sermon, probably 1876, bound volume, Putnam's Booksellers, p. 187ff.

77. *New York Times*, October 16, 17, 1873, p. 8, 5.

78. *Boston Daily Globe*, May 29, 1874, p. 5.

79. FRA, *Proceedings*, Presidential Address, May 28–29, 1874, pp. 23–24.

80. Ibid.

81. Ibid., p. 15ff. *Boston Daily Globe*, May 29, 1874, p. 8.

82. FRA, *Proceedings*, May 27–28, 1875, p. 15.

83. Ibid., p. 52.

84. *Boston Daily Globe*, June 3, 1876.

85. Gannett to Chadwick, Nov. 23, 1875, Gannett Papers, Box IV, MSS Room, University of Rochester.

86. FRA *Proceedings*, June 1–2, 1876, Report of P. M. Session, p. 80ff.

87. FRA, *Proceedings*, June 1–2, 1876, p. 85.

88. Ibid.

89. Ibid.

90. *Boston Daily Globe*, June 1, 1877.

91. FRA, *Proceedings*, May 31–June 1, 1877.

92. Ibid., p. 19.

93. *Index*, February 21, 1878, Abbot's comment on O.B.F.'s lecture, "Assailants of Christianity," January 6, 1878.

94. O.B.F. to Abbot, May 11, 1878, Abbot Papers.

95. FRA, *Proceedings*, May 30, 31, 1878, p. 25.

96. Ibid., p. 62ff.

CHAPTER VI

1. John Babcock's *New Age* is an example. Generally sympathetic but sometimes a watchdog of the *Index* and FRA, it often supported the ideas and activities of the association. Both Babcock and A. W. Stevens, editorial contributor, were also active in the FRA, *New Age*, April 22, May 13, June 3, June 10, June 17, 1876.

2. Persons, *Free Religion, An American Faith*, p. 90.

3. OBF to Abbot, November 12, 1869, Abbot Papers, Archive Room, Widner Library, Harvard University.

4. OBF to Abbot, February 26, 1879, Abbot Papers.

5. W. C. Gannett to W. W. Chadwick, November 22, 1869, W. C. Gannett Papers, Box II, MSS Room, University of Rochester.

6. *Index*, Vol. 1, No. 1, January 1, 1870.

7. OBF to Abbot, July 5, 1870, March 4, 1873, May 22, 1874, Abbot Papers.

8. William J. Potter to Gannett, July 11, 1872; OBF to W. C. Gannett, June 11, 17, 1873; Gannett Papers, Box III, MSS Room, University of Rochester.

9. OBF to Abbot, January 27, May 20, November 21, 1871; June 8, 1872; April 14, 1873; May 8, November 17, 1873; June 7, 1874, Abbot Papers.

10. OBF to Abbot, March 14, 1874, Abbot Papers.

11. OBF to Abbot, October 6, 1876, Abbot Papers, Archive Room, Widner Library, Harvard University; OBF to W. C. Gannett, December 25, 1875; Gannett Papers, Box IV, MSS Room, University of Rochester. The dispute between Abbot and Hallowell, Secretary of the FRA, Abbot blew up to "about four times" what the matter deserved, wrote OBF to Gannett.

12. OBF to Abbot, April 21, 1877, Abbot Papers.

13. *Index Association Record Book,* Abbot Papers, Archive Room, Widner Library, Harvard University; Stow Persons in *Free Religion, An American Faith,* Yale, 1947, discusses this and other details of the *Index* management. P. 88ff.

14. *Index,* January 1, 1870, Vol. 1, No. 1.

15. *Index,* January 8, 1870

16. *Index,* January 7, 1871, p. 5

17. *Index,* December 23, 1871, Vol. II, p. 405.

18. *Index,* February 11, 1871, Vol. II, p. 45

19. *Index,* "Christianity Again," March 16, 1872, Vol. III, p. 85.

20. *Index,* "Reporting Sermons," May 31, 1873, Vol. IV, p. 225.

21. *Index,* "A Criticism," May 3, 1877, Vol. VIII, p. 211.

22. *Index,* September 16, 1875, Vol. VI, p. 434.

23. *Index,* April 5, 1877, p. 163.

24. *Index,* November 23, 1876, Vol. VII, p. 559; January 4, 1877, Vol. VIII, p. 6.

25. *Index,* "The Right Point," January 4, 1873, Vol. IX, p. 9.

26. *Index,* "Three Short Studies in Christianity," Horticultural Hall Lecture, January 7, January 20, 1872, Vol. III, pp. 17–18.

27. *Index,* October 14, 1875, Vol. VI, p. 487; *Index,* March 2, 1876, Vol. VII, p. 102.

28. *Index,* March 16, 1876, Vol. VII, p. 127.

29. *Index,* May 7, 1870, Vol. I, p. 4; *Index,* June 18, 1870, Vol. I, p. 2.

30. *Index,* November 27, 1873, Vol. IX, p. 484; *Index,* December 4, 1873, Vol. IV, p. 495; *Index,* September 11, 1873, Vol. IV, p. 194; *Index,* November 6, 1873, Vol. IV, p. 447.

31. *Index,* May 10, 1873, Vol. IV, p. 201; *Index,* July 26, 1873, Vol. IV, p. 289.

32. OBF to Potter, April 10 (1871 or 1872), Abbot Papers, Potter sent the letter to Abbot with a note on its back.

33. *Index,* May 6, 1871, Vol. II, p. 141.

34. *Index,* August 10, 1873, Vol. IV, p. 313.

35. *Index,* July 1, 1871, Vol. II, p. 205.

36. *Index,* February 22, 1873, Vol. IV, p. 91.

37. *Index,* July 23, 1874, Vol. V, p. 355; *Index,* December 2, 1874, Vol. V, p. 571; *Index,* December 30, 1875, Vol. VI, p. 619; *Index,* March 1, 1877, Vol. VIII, p. 103; *Index,* March 15, 1877, Vol. VIII, p. 127.

38. *Index,* May 25, 1871, Vol. III (Letters).

39. *Index,* December 16, 1875, Vol. VI, p. 595.

40. *Index,* June 7, 1875, Vol. VI, p. 282.

41. *Index,* February 28, 1878, p. 102 (Letters).

42. *Index*, June 10, 1875, Vol. VI, p. 271.

43. OBF to Abbot, November 23, 1874, Abbot Papers.

44. James Whittier to Gannett, January 31, 1873, Gannett Papers.

45. *Index*, July 1, 1875, Vol. VI, p. 307.

46. Persons, *Free Religion, An American Faith*. This monograph dealt with the administrative difficulties of Abbot and the financial support of the *Index*. Also the background and work of the National Liberal League is a major consideration in Persons' discussion of free religion in America. Understandably, his discussion is comprehensive rather than specific as far as Frothingham's role was concerned.

47. Frothingham was one of the heaviest contributors to the Index Association. By 1874 he contributed $2,360.00 to the Reserve Fund in addition to an undetermined number of shares. *Index Safety Reserve Fund*, 1874, Abbot Papers, Archive Room, Widner Library, Harvard University.

48. *Index*, March 18, 1874.

49. OBF to Abbot, March 11, 1873, Abbot Papers.

50. OBF to Abbot, December 31, 1874.

51 OBF to Abbot, January 14, 1875, Abbot Papers.

52. OBF in *Truthseeker*, April 20, 1878, clipping in Abbot Papers, Archive Room, Widner Library, Harvard University. Abbot had not forged Frothingham's name but knew he was free to use it if he wanted to.

53. OBF to Abbot, August 11, 14, 1878, Abbot Papers.

54. OBF to Abbot, August 27, 1878.

55. Asa Butts controversy, Abbot Papers, Archive Room, Widner Library, Harvard University.

56. Persons, *Free Religion, An American Faith*, p. 114.

57. OBF to Abbot, April 21, 27, 1872, Abbot Papers.

58. *Index*, March 13, Vol. IV, p. 128.

59. *Index*, March 30, 1875, Vol. VI, p. 150.

60. OBF to Abbot, June 10, 1875, Abbot Papers.

61. *Index*, July 13, 1875.

62. Sidney Warren, *American Free Thought, 1860–1914*, Columbia University Press, 1943, p. 109ff.

63. OBF to Abbot, November 5, 1875, Abbot Papers.

64. OBF to Abbot, June 16, 1877, Abbot Papers.

65. OBF to Abbot, June 23, 1877, Abbot Papers.

66. OBF to Abbot, July 15, September 27, 1877, Abbot Papers.

67. OBF to Abbot, October 5, 1877, Abbot Papers.

68. *Index*, March 23, 1878, Vol. IX, p. 246.

69. *Index*, May 30, 1878; *Index*, July 4, 1878.

70. Warren, *American Free Thought*, p. 161ff.

71. OBF to Abbot, June 23, 1878, Abbot Papers.

72. OBF to Abbot, July 23, 1878, Abbot Papers.

73. OBF to Abbot, November 15, 1878, Abbot Papers. OBF had not contributed to *Index* for a year at this time.

74. OBF to Abbot, November 20, 1878, Abbot Papers.

75. *Index*, November 21, 1878, p. 558.

76. OBF to Abbot, January 23, 1879, Abbot Papers.

77. *Scientific Theism*, Little-Brown, 1895; *The Way Out of Agnosticism or Philosophy*

of Free Religion, Little-Brown, Boston, 1890, were two books Abbot wrote after his retirement from the FRA. These obscure works never gained a following. His sense of failure for having never made an impact with his scientific basis of religion contributed to his suicide in 1903.

78. Sidney Ahlstrom, *Francis Ellingwood Abbot,* unpublished PhD Dissertation, Harvard, 1951, p. 250.

79. FRA, *Proceedings,* May 29–30, 1879, Report of Directors.

80. Ibid., p. 77; *New York Times,* May 29, 1879.

81. Ibid., p. 64ff.

82. Abbot to Adler 1878–1882. Letters and Circular, "Address to Friends of Free Religion in the United States," 1879, Abbot Papers, Archive Room, Widner Library, Harvard University.

83. FRA, *Proceedings,* May 31, 1895.

84. Minot Savage, *Social Problems,* Boston, 1883, p. 1; Charles H. Hopkins, *The Rise of Social Gospel in American Protestantism, 1865–1915,* Yale University Press, 1940. Cites Savage's debt to Frothingham for his spirit of reform influence, pp. 109–110.

85. Persons, *Free Religion, An American Faith,* p 97.

86. FRA, *Proceedings,* May 31, 1887, p. 8ff.

87. FRA, *Proceedings,* May 31–June 1, 1894.

88. FRA, *Proceedings,* May 30, 1885.

89. FRA, *Proceedings,* May 28–29, 1896, p. 6ff, p. 91ff.

90. One wonders if there were perceptive ones in the audience who noticed that the memories of the "great," including Frothingham, overlapped on the same platform with the new mode of thought represented by Professor Josiah Royce, spokesman of pragmatism at Harvard University. FRA, *Proceedings,* 1899.

91. FRA, *Proceedings,* January 1, 1900, p. 70ff. Other papers dealt with Roger Williams, Kesib Chunder, Lucretia Mott, Ralph Waldo Emerson, and Theodore Parker.

92. FRA, *Proceedings,* May 31, 1907, p. 67.

93. FRA, *Proceedings,* June 1, 1910.

94. FRA, *Proceedings,* 1913.

95. FRA, *Proceedings,* 1911, 1912, and 1913.

96. George Mills to George Patterson, February 23, 1938; Mills, the last "president of record," wrote to George Patterson of the Unitarian Historical Library, 25 Beacon Street, Boston, Massachusetts. The final records of the slow demise of the FRA are in Charles W. Wendt's copies of the FRA Proceedings in the fragmentary form of newspaper clippings, handwritten notes, all stuffed in Vol. V, the last of the FRA programs, preserved at the Historical Library, 25 Beacon Street, Boston, Massachusetts, until 1970 when they were moved to the Divinity School Library, Harvard University.

97. FRA, *Proceedings,* 1907, p. 38.

98. OBF, *Recollections and Impressions, 1822–1891,* p. 122ff.

99. FRA, *Proceedings,* 1907, p. 30.

100. FRA, *Proceedings,* 1911, p. 8ff.

101. Persons, *Free Religion, An American Faith,* Yale, 1947, p. 155.

102. H. Bellows to Frederick Hedge, December 13, 1864, in Conrad Wright, *The Liberal Christians,* p. 88.

CHAPTER VII

1. OBF to C. E. Norton, October 13, 1864, Norton Papers, Houghton Library, Harvard University.

2. Carlton (publisher), New York, 1864.

3. D. Appleton, New York, 1875.

4. OBF to Norton, November 28, 1863, February 15, 1864, October 13, 1864, February 20, 1864, Norton Papers.

5. OBF to Norton, May 28, 1864, August 8, 1864, Norton Papers (E. L. Frothingham's *Philosophy As Absolute Science*).

6. OBF to Norton, September 9, 1864, October 4, 1864, Norton Papers.

7. OBF to Francis E. Abbot, May 7, 1867, Archive Room, Harvard University.

8. OBF to Caroline Dall, November 26, 1861, December 24, 1861, January 6, 1862, C. H. Dall Papers, MHS.

9. OBF to Dall, January 14, 1862, February 19, 1867. On the back of one letter she penned an angry rejoinder, never seen by Frothingham: "I am glad *not* to be a man if manhood does not bring more courage than this."

10. OBF to Caroline Dall, February 21, 1871.

11. Among Kate Fields' writings are biographies of Adelaide Ristori (1867) and Charles Fechter (1862), *Extremes Meet* (a play, 1877), *New Photographs of Charles Dickens Readings* (1868), and *Ten Days in Spain* (1868).

12. OBF to Kate Fields, November 2, 1868, Kate Fields Collection, Rare Book Room, BPL.

13. OBF to Fields, January 17 (no year, probably 1868).

14. Maxwell Giesman, Mark Twain, *An American Prophet,* Houghton Mifflin, Boston, 1970, p. 409.

15. OBF to Fields, April 11, 1878.

16. OBF to E. C. Stedman, December 17, 1878, Frothingham Miscl., MSS Room, NYPL.

17. D. C. Francis, New York, 1873.

18. *Index,* Abbot, Literary Department, March 15, 1873, Vol. IV, p. 131; Samuel Johnson to Samuel Longfellow, December 29, 1872, *Memoir of Samuel Johnson,* p. 108.

19. "C.W.B.," "Cradle of Christ, A Study of Primitive Christianity," a review, *Radical Review,* February, 1878, Vol. I, p. 787.

20. *Index,* April 17, 1873, Vol. IV, p. 176.

21. OBF to Samuel Johnson, April 15, 1874, Johnson Papers, Box 4, Essex Institute, Salem, Massachusetts.

22. John Weiss, *Life and Correspondence of Theodore Parker,* 2 Vol., D. Appleton, New York, 1864.

23. Octavius B. Frothingham, *Life of Theodore Parker,* Preface, pp. III, IV, James R. Osgood and Company, Boston, 1874.

24. Henry Steele Commager, *Theodore Parker, Yankee Crusader,* Beacon Press, 1947; Little Brown, 1936, first edition, p. 312.

25. Frothimgham, *Life of Theodore Parker,* pp. 1–2.

26. *Ibid.,* p. 125.

27. *Ibid.,* p. 150.

28. *Ibid.,* p. 158.

29. *Ibid.* Frothingham deals with the incident in Chapter VII, "The Unitarian Controversy," reproducing the conversation, though with no citation; Henry Commager, *Theodore Parker, Yankee Crusader*—a "Tempest in a Boston Tea Cup" he calls it—is a lively account of the meeting in the home of Rev. Waterson.

30. Frothingham, *Life of Theodore Parker,* p. 215.

31. *Ibid.,* p. 231.

32. *Ibid.,* see Chapter XII, "The Preacher."

33. *Ibid.,* "Tributes," p. 568ff.

34. *Ibid.,* p. 308 (no date, probably 1852).

35. *Ibid.,* p. 308, to "Dear Old Ladye," June 17, 1852.

36. *Ibid.,* p. 311 (no date, probably 1852 or 1858).

37. *Ibid.,* p. 347, from his Journal, March 27, 1851.

38. William White Chadwick, *Theodore Parker, Preacher and Reformer,* Houghton Mifflin, New York, 1901 (about 1858), p. 287.

39. See Chapters II and VIII of this work.

40. Chadwick, *Theodore Parker, Preacher and Reformer,* pp. 119–120. Chadwick does not offer a citation. Apparently it came through a conversation with Frothingham during the years in New York.

41. W. C. Gannett to W. W. Chadwick, April 17, 1874, Gannett Papers, Box II, MSS Room, University of Rochester.

42. *Index,* April 30, 1874, Vol. 5, p. 213.

43. OBF, *Index,* "Inclusiveness," April 13, 1876, Vol. VII, p. 175.

44. Chadwick, *Theodore Parker, Preacher and Reformer,* pp. 380–383.

45. O. B. Frothingham, *Transcendentalism in New England,* G. P. Putnam's Sons, New York, 1876, Preface, p. iii, ix.

46. J. H. Morse, *Diary,* June 18, 1875, Vol. III, NYHS.

47. OBF to Gannett, September 22, 1870 (date written in later by another hand), MSS Room, University of Rochester.

48. Frothingham, *Transcendentalism in New England,* Preface, p. viii.

49. *Ibid.,* p. 352.

50. *Ibid.,* p. 383.

51. OBF to Emerson, November 19, 1875, Houghton Library, Harvard University.

52. *Index,* "Glimpses," April 20, 1876.

53. *New York Times,* May 16, 1876. This is true, due probably to the glare of illuminative powder used by photographers of the day.

54. *New Age,* September 30, 1876.

55. Henry Adams, "Frothingham's Transcendentalism" in *North American Review,* October, 1876, Vol. 123, pp. 468–474.

56. *Index,* January 24, 1878, Vol. IX, pp. 39–40. The reviewer hailed the book as being honest and sensitive. The author was "at his best."

57. Lysander Spooner to OBF, February 26, 1878, Anti-Slavery Papers, Rare Book Room, BPL.

58. *New York Times,* "A Suppressed Biography," March 13, 1878, p. 5.

59. O. B. Frothingham, *Gerrit Smith,* G. P. Putnam's Sons, second edition, 1879, 371 pp. The prefatory note of this second edition reads, "The second edition of the life of Gerrit Smith differs from the first in one respect. In the portion which relates to John Brown and the attack on Harper's Ferry, the historical facts are

stated simply and without comment. For a final statement as to these the reader is referred to page 254 of the present volume."

60. Frothingham, *Gerrit Smith*, second edition, p. 254.

61. *New York Times*, "A Suppressed Biography," March 13, 1878.

62. Spooner to OBF, February 26, 1878, Anti-Slavery Papers.

63. OBF to Spooner, March 1, 1878, Anti-Slavery Papers, Rare Book Room, BPL.

64. William Armstrong, "The Freeman's Movement and the Founding of the Nation," *Journal of American History*, Vol. VIII, No. 4, March, 1967, pp. 708–726.

65. *Nation*, Vol. I, No. 24, December 14, 1865, p. 742.

66. *Nation*, May 15, 1866, July 17, 1866.

67. *Nation*, January 25, 1866, March 27, 1866.

68. *Nation*, January 25, 1866, p. 117.

69. March 2, 1876.

70. *Nation*, "Notes," October 10, 1867.

71. *Nation*, "Notes," "Henry Ward Beecher on Preaching," October 17, 1872.

72. *Nation*, Vol. 1, No. 2, July 13, 1865, p. 51.

73. *Nation*, Vol. I, No. 16, October 19, 1865, pp. 502–503.

74. *Nation*, December 21, 1865, review of W.E.H. Leckey, *History and Influence of the Spirit of Rationalism in Europe*, 2 Vols., D. Appleton and Company, 1865.

75. *Nation*, March 8, 1866, p. 311.

76. *Nation*, September 27, November 1, 1866.

77. *Nation*, November 1, 1866.

78. *Nation*, "Charities of France," April 4, 1867, p. 272.

79. *Nation*, "The People's Reading," April 2, 1868 (a front page article).

80. *Nation*, "The Social Evil and Its Remedy," February 21, 1867.

81. *Nation*, "Women vs. Women," October 3, 1867.

82. *Nation*, "Is There Such a Thing As Sex?", February 4, 1869 (main article).

83. *Nation*, "The Rights of Children, December 9, 1869 (main article).

84. Implied in sermons (see Chapter III) through no membership lists survive.

85. *Nation*, "The Acting of Mr. Edwin Booth," March 29, 1866.

86. *Nation*, "The Theaters," April 5, 1866.

87. *Nation*, "Ristori," October 11, 1866.

88. *Nation*, "Ristori," September 27, 1866 (Fine Arts section).

89. *Nation*, "Ristori," October 25, 1866, p. 336.

90. *Ibid.*

91. Henry Knepler, *The Gilded Stage*, Constable, London, 1968, pp. 113–117.

92. Moncure Conway to OBF, May 16, 186 , Houghton Library, Harvard University.

93. Mary Elizabeth Burtis, *Moncure Conway*, Rutgers University Press, 1952, p. 69.

94. Lloyd D. Easton, *Hegel's First American Followers: The Ohio Hegelians, John Stallo, Peter Kaufmann, Moncure Conway, August Willich*, Ohio University Press, 1966. Volume I, 1860, was the only issue of *Dial*.

95. *Christian Inquirer*, May 17, 1866, "The Devout Life," delivered by Frothingham at Yonkers Unitarian Church lecture series.

96. *Radical*, October 1867 (a representative article).

97. *Radical*, May, 1869, p. 367.

98. *Radical,* "Theodore Parker," August, 1869, p. 96.

99. OBF to Dear Sir (unknown), New York, December 19, 1866, Essex Institute Collection, Salem, Massachusetts.

100. R. W. Emerson, *Complete Works,* Boston, 1903–1904, XI, p. 335.

101. O. B. Frothingham, "The Murdered President," *Friends of Progress,* May, 1865, pp. 234–239.

102. *North American Review,* Vol. 126, June, 1878, p. 126ff.

103. *Ibid.,* p. 540.

104. *North American Review,* "Absent Friends," Vol. 46, May, 1879, p. 493; *Index,* May 1, 1879, also printed the article.

CHAPTER VIII

1. FRA *Proceedings,* 1898, "Recollections of Moncure Conway," p. 23.

2. Moncure D. Conway, *Autobiography,* Vol. I, Houghton Mifflin, 1907, p. 337ff. Conway, a guest at Frothingham's on his way through New York, had spoken to OBF's congregation and stayed on for this meeting.

3. OBF to Samuel J. May, April 11, 1860, May Papers, Rare Book Room, BPL.

4. OBF to Charles Sumner, March 14, 1855, Houghton Library, Harvard (written from Jersey City).

5. OBF to Sumner, June –, 1860.

6. OBF to Sumner, September 20, 1862.

7. OBF to Sumner, August 3, 1863 (from Washington House, North Conway, New Hampshire).

8. OBF to W. L. Garrison, November 23, 1863, Anti-Slavery Papers, Rare Book Room, BPL.

9. OBF to Moncure Conway, January 1, 1865, Special MSS Collection, Columbia University, New York.

10. OBF to Conway, October 29, 1867.

11. OBF to Conway, February 6, 1875.

12. OBF to E. C. Stedman, May 14, 187 (probably 1874), Stedman Papers, Special MSS Collection, Columbia University, New York.

13. OBF to Kate Fields, January 3, 1867, Kate Fields Collection, Rare Book Room, BPL.

14. OBF to Stedman, June 16, 1876, Stedman Papers.

15. OBF to Stedman, September 20, 1876, Stedman Papers.

16. Eugenia B. Frothingham to T. W. (Col.) Higginson, October 12 (probably 1870), Houghton Library, Harvard. In a letter to Higginson, thanking him for a comment about the Book Eugenia, a cousin of Octavius, added a postscript: "We all missed you in Dublin this summer. Please observe how feminine I am in putting important truths in a postscript."

17. George Ripley to Christopher P. Cranch, Cranch Papers, Box, 1846–28, MHS, Boston.

18. Charles Crowe, George Ripley, *Transcendentalist and Utopian Socialist,* University of Georgia Press, Athens, Georgia, 1967. Professor Crowe implies that Frothingham gave a "stately oration" at Ripley's funeral (p. 263). In Frothingham's own biography of Ripley, it is clear that he was in Europe when Ripley died.

19. *Recollections,* "My Friends," Chapter 13.

20. *Recollections*, p. 226.

21. *Recollections*, "My Friends," Chapter 13.

22. George Templeton Strong, *Diary*, Vol. 3, Alan Nevins and M.K.T. Thomas (editors), MacMillan, New York, 1952, p. 2.

23. *Ibid.*, p. 216.

24. *New York Daily Tribune*, April 12, 1879, p. 1.

25. OBF to Editor of *College Review*, March 10, 1870, Betts Collection, MSS Room, Yale Library.

26. OBF to Editor of *College Review*, March 11, 1870, NYHS. He signed it "your obedient servant," as was his way when angry.

27. OBF to J. O. Sargent, January 12, 1878, MSS Room, NYPL.

28. OBF to Sargent, February 11, 1878, Sargent Papers, MHS, Boston.

29. Henry Bellows to Sargent, February 10, 1879, February 23, 1879, J. O. Sargent Papers.

30. Mrs. John T. Sargent (ed.), *Sketches and Reminiscences of the Radical Club of Chestnut Street, Boston*, Osgood, 1880, Boston. Introduction and membership list, selected essays, etc.

31. *Ibid.*, p. 205–159. Phillips was there; date not recorded.

32. OBF to Caroline Dall, February 25, 1871, Dall Papers, MHS. Dall, angry at being black balled, had bombarded OBF with accusing letters. On the back of this she wrote her own note: "This note shows how little men may know of the institutions to which they give their name and influence." (Written a year later, "CHD, 1872.")

33. *New York Daily Tribune*, October 7, 1874, by "RWL."

34. Sidney Ahlstrom, *Francis Ellingwood Abbot*, unpublished Ph.D. dissertation, Harvard, 1951. Mr. Ahlstrom suspects Frothingham of writing the article.

35. C. P. Cranch, *Note Book* (Staten Island), April 17, 1874. He read a paper and had sat next to Waldo Emerson. Cranch Papers, 1846–1929, MHS, Boston.

36. OBF to Mrs. John T. Sargent, October 14, 1874, in *Sketches and Reminiscences of the Radical Club of Chestnut Street, Boston*, Osgood, Boston, 1880.

37. James H. Morse, *Diary*, Vol. 1, March 13, 1869, MSS Room, NYHS.

38. *Fraternity Papers*, Vols. 1–8 (No. 6 missing), 1870–1878, MSS Room, NYHS. When the club disbanded in 1878, J. H. Morse kept the volumes. In 1951 a descendant returned them to New York from Harvard University Library where they had been stored after Morse's death.

39. George Haven Putnam, *Memories of a Publisher, 1865–1915*, G. P. Putnam's Sons, New York, 1915, pp. 20–21.

40. Cranch, *Fraternity Papers*, Vol. 1, 1869–1870.

41. Morse, *Diary*, March 11, 1871.

42. Ellen Frothingham to Thomas Davidson (two letters, no year—probably about 1875), MSS Room, Yale Library; concerning books borrowed and translations she was doing.

43. Morse, *Diary*, March 15, 1876.

44. *Fraternity Papers*, Vol. 2, 1870–1871.

45. *Fraternity Papers*, "Our Club," OBF, Vol. 5, 1874. The rest of the essay is a literary discussion on the art of conversation.

46. Morse, *Diary*, Vol. III, March 13, 1875.

47. Morse, *Diary*, Vol. 4, January 2, 1878, MSS Collection, NYHS. Vol. 6 of *Fraternity Papers*, containing Frothingham's paper, is missing.

48. *Massachusetts Historical Society Proceedings*, Edward Young, "Remarks on the Death of Octavius B. Frothingham," Vol. X, 1895–1896, Boston, 1896, pp. 363–364.

49. *Ibid.*, p. 366.

50. See "Installation Sermon," "Uses of the Sanctuary," Chap. II, pp. 61–62.

51. Putnam, *Memories of a Publisher, 1865–1915*, "New York in the Sixties—My Church Association," p. 16.

52. OBF, *Recollections and Impressions*, Chap. VII.

53. Henry Bellows to OBF, December 30, 1863, Bellows Papers, MHS.

54. OBF to Bellows, December 30, 1863.

55. OBF to Bellows, December 31, 1863.

56. *Index* editorial, June 2, 1873, p. 233.

57. Bellows Papers, MHS. Dated 1859, the list did not include OBF or any future FRA people.

58. Putnam, *Memories of a Publisher, 1865–1915*, p. 17.

59. This was the conference which established the American Unitarian Association and began the split between conservatives and radicals. See Chapter V.

60. OBF to Conway, January 2, 1865. "My little Lancelot remembers you pleasantly," he assured Conway. Could this be fifteen-year-old Elizabeth Frothingham? His own father, writing from Europe in 1849, asked his wife about "little Ellen," Octavius' fourteen-year-old sister.

61. *Liberal Christian*, December 11, 1869.

62. OBF, "Foes of Society," Ebbit Hall, December, 1863.

63. *Liberal Christian*, December 18, 1869, December 25, 1869, contained a long quotation, with no comment, from the sermon "Foes of Society."

64. OBF, "Elective Affinities," December 11, 1863, Ebbit Hall, New York.

65. *Liberal Christian*, December 25, 1869.

66. OBF to Bellows, December 27, 1869, Bellows Papers.

67. Liberal Christian, "A Correction" (editorial), January 1, 1870.

68. D. G. Francis, New York, 1870.

69. George Templeton Strong, *Diary*, December 4, 1869, April 9, 1870, Vol. 4, pp. 262–283.

70. *Nation*, Vol. 11, May 1870, pp. 300–302.

71. OBF to E. L. Godkin, July 17, 1870, Houghton Library, Harvard.

72. OBF to Godkin, July 24, 1870.

73. OBF to Samuel Johnson, May 23, 1863, December 14, 1864, July 31, 1870, October 21, 187 , December 2, 1872, December 8, 1873, December 30, 1873, Johnson Papers, Essex Institute, Salem, Massachusetts.

74. George Merriam (ed.), *Life and Times of Samuel Bowles*, Vol. 2, New York. "He was feverish, and weary and in a crowd. . ." P. 48.

75. *Ibid.*, Vol. I. p. 409 (about 1864).

76. William Lloyd Garrison to Samuel May, May 15, 1869, Anti-Slavery Papers, Rare Book Room, BPL.

77. Garrison to his son, December 3, 1878, February 20, 1879, Anti-Slavery Papers. He knew in February, 1879, that Frothingham planned to retire.

78. E. L. Godkin to C. E. Norton, February 6, 1866, in Rollo Ogden, *Life and Letters of Edwin Laurence Godkin,* Macmillan Company, New York, 1907, Vol. II, p. 37.

79. Henry Ward Beecher to Rev. Charles Clarke, undated, from Oneanta, New York; Beecher to Mrs. Beecher, undated, from London; Beecher correspondence, Box 54–56, MSS Room, Yale University; *The Christian Union,* Vol. 1, No. 20, May 14, 1870.

80. Mark Twain considered him to be a man with a monumental ego. Maxwell Giesman, *Mark Twain, An American Prophet,* Houghton Mifflin, Boston, 1970, p. 467.

81. OBF to E. C. Stedman, April 19, 186), Special MSS Collection, Columbia University.

82. OBF to Stedman, September 29, 1876.

83. E. C. Stedman to Mrs. Caroline Frothingham, March 12, 1877, Stedman Papers, Bienneke Library, Yale University.

84. OBF to Unknown, April, 1863, H. W. Anthony Bequest MSS Room, NYPL; OBF to Henry Bellows, October 17, 1866, Bellows Papers, MSH.

85. OBF to Mrs. Anthony, July 23, 1867, Houghton Library, Harvard; *Index,* May 25, 1876, p. 245.

86. OBF to Gannett, September 22, 1870, December 13, 1870, Gannett Papers.

87. North Church, *The First Century of the North Church Society,* July 19, 1872, Salem, 1873, p. 127, Essex Institute, Salem, Massachusetts.

88. J. H. Morse, *Diary,* Vol. III, March 17, 1875; Vol. IV, January 2, 1876, NYHS.

89. *Ibid.,* Vol. II, May 24, 1872; Vol. III, June 30, 1875.

90. *Ibid.,* Vol. IV, January, 1877, April 6, 1878.

91. *Miscellaneous Writings and Addresses of Philadelphia,* O. B. Frothingham, "The Practical Uses of Christianity," October 5, 1859, Historical Society of Pennsylvania Collection, Philadelphia.

92. W. W. Chadwick to Samuel Johnson, September 1, 1862, Johnson Papers, Box 4, Essex Institute, Salem, Massachusetts. To Johnson Chadwick wrote that he had heard from O. B. Frothingham "twice during the vacation."

93. Ordination Program, William White Chadwick, December 31, 1864, Essex Institute, Salem Massachusetts.

94. Chadwick Samuel Johnson, November 7, 1864.

95. W. C. Gannett to W. W. Chadwick, December 1, 1873, W. C. Gannett Papers, Box III, MSS Room, University of Rochester.

96. Chadwick to Gannett, March 26, 1872, Gannett Papers.

97. OBF to Gannett, October 29, 1878, Gannett Papers, Box IV, MSS Room, University of Rochester. He sent a check for $50.00 to Gannett to help get *Unity* magazine started but could not promise to contribute to it.

98. Putnam, *Memories of a Publisher, 1865–1915,* p. 19.

99. OBF to Conway, February 1, 1879.

100. OBF to Gannett, February 15, 1879, Gannett Papers, Box V, MSS Room, University of Rochester.

101. *New York Times,* February 17, 1879, p. 4.

102. *New York Times,* April 6, 1879.

103. *New York Times,* April 7, 1879, "Hotel Arrivals."

104. *Proceedings at a Reception in Honor of Rev. O. B. Frothingham,* given by the Independent Liberal Church, at the Union League Theater, Tuesday evening, April 22, 1879, together with a report of the farewell sermon delivered by him at Masonic Temple, April 27, 1879, New York, G. P. Putnam's Sons, 1879.

105. *Ibid.,* p. 21.

106. *Ibid.,* p. 26.

107. *Ibid.,* pp. 36–42.

108. *Ibid.,* p. 51

109. *Ibid.,* pp. 60–61.

110. *Ibid.,* p. 66.

111. *New York Times,* April 23, 1879; *New York Herald Tribune,* April 23, 1879.

112. "Twenty Years of an Independent Ministry," April 27, 1879, in *Proceedings at a Reception in Honor of Rev. O. B. Frothingham,* G. P. Putnam's Sons, New York, 1879, pp. 66–89.

113. Judge George C. Bassett, *Memorial Exercises Ethical Address,* December, 1895, Ethical Culture Society of New York, Philadelphia, 1895, p. 185. His recollection of OBF's last sermon.

114. *New York Times,* April 29, 1879; *New York Herald Tribune,* April 28, 1879. Both carried a paraphrased version of the sermon with long excerpts.

115. OBF to Gannett, April 18, 1879, Gannett Papers. Frothingham wished him well in his new magazine project, *Unity,* and hoped to return and write for it in the future.

116. *New York Times,* Travel to Europe, "Mr. Frothingham's Departure," May 1, 1879.

117. OBF to Sedman, June 17, 1879, from Ragatz, Switzerland, Stedman Papers.

118. *Index,* August 14, 1879, Vol. 10; *Index,* December 11, 1879, Vol. II, Communications from Moncure Conway in England to *Index.*

119. Hannah Stevenson to W. C. Gannett, W. C. Gannett Papers, Box V, MSS Room, University of Rochester.

120. *Index,* June 24, 1880, Vol. II. It was thought by the editor that his ill health kept him away, since his doctor had ordered him to avoid mental exertion and excitement.

121. Abbot Dinner, *Biographical Pamphlets,* June 24, 1880, Young Hotel, Boston, Yale University.

122. *Index,* July 8, 1880, p. 23.

123. OBF to W. J. Potter, St. Moritz, Switzerland, August 14, 1880. In *Index,* Vol. I, September 9, 1880, p. 127.

124. *New York Times,* September 13, 1880, Editorial p. 4.

125. *Index,* March 24, 1881, Vol. I, New No. 38, "The Future of the Theodore Parker Society," p. 460.

126. OBF to Conway, Rome, March 12, 1881.

127. *Index,* March 11, 1880, Vol. II, "Glimpses," Father of Paul Revere Frothingham.

128. C. P. Cranch, *Diary,* March 14, 1881, Cranch Box, 1846–1928, MHS.

129. Cranch, *Diary.* May 5, 7, 13, 18, 24, July 1, 16, 17, 19, 1881.

130. OBF to Conway, May 27, 1881, Special MSS Collection, Columbia University.

131. *Index,* Moncure Conway's "London Letter," August 25, 1881, Vol. II, p. 94.

132. *Index,* September 29, 1881, Vol. II, No. 13.

CHAPTER IX

1. "Twenty Years in the Independent Ministry," Masonic Hall, April 27, 1877.

2. *New York Times,* "E.L.A." to Editor, May 6, 1879.

3. *Index,* "The Doom of Individualism," May 9, 1879, Vol. 10, p. 222.

4. W. W. Chadwick, "The Failure of Transcendentalism and Individualism," sermon, May 15, 1877; in *Index,* June 5, 1879, Vol. 10, p. 266.

5. *Index,* "The FRA Meeting of 1879," June 13, 1879, Vol. 10.

6. OBF to Samuel Johnson, November 19, 1877, Essex Institute, Salem, Massachusetts.

7. Samuel Johnson to Samuel Longfellow, June 29, 1879; in Samuel Longfellow (ed.), *Memoirs of Samuel Johnson.*

8. *New York Evening Post,* November 12, 1881; also reprinted in *Boston Transcript,* November 14, 1881.

9. OBF to Editors of *New York Evening Post,* November 13, 1881; in *Index,* "A Correction by O. B. Frothingham," November 24, 1881, p. 250.

10. *New York Times,* Editorial, "Rationalism to Rome, "November 23, 1881.

11. *New York Herald Tribune,* Account of Sermon, November 28, 1881.

12. *New York Herald Tribune,* November 28, 1881, Chadwick's rebuttal of Collyer's sermon.

13. *Index,* December 22, 1881.

14. *Index,* "Mr. Frothingham and His Alleged Change of Views," December 1, 1881, p. 256.

15. *Index,* "Mr. Frothingham's Theological Position, Past and Present," December 15, 1881, p. 276.

16. M. I. Savage, "O. B. Frothingham and His Supposed Change of Base," sermon, *Index,* December 22, 1881, pp. 294–296.

17. *Index,* December 1, 1881, p. 254.

18. *Index,* December 22, 1881, p. 296; reprinted in *New York Evening Post, Boston Transcript,* and *New York Times.*

19. M. D. Conway, *Autobiography,* Vol. II, p. 445. Probably a conversation while in England, 1879–1881.

20. Johnson to Longfellow, p. 139.

21. Henry A. Braun (D.D.), *The Age of Unreason,* New York, 1881; essay: "The Rationalism of O. B. Frothingham and Dr. Felix Adler."

22. Francis Weisenberger, *The Ordeal of Faith,* 1959, p. 23. No source quoted.

23. James Freeman Clark to O. B. Frothingham, December 14, 1882, Houghton Library, Harvard.

24. OBF to Clark, May 4, 1887.

25. Suffolk County Vital Statistics, 42nd Registration, Vol. 345, p. 11.

26. *New York Herald Tribune,* June 15, 1883, p. 8.

27. Apparently not all of the Unitarians in the audience were willing to let bygones be bygones. An unsigned article in the "official" journal, Christian Register, disagreed that free religion and Unitarianism were the same thing. Cited in *Index,* June 14, 1883, p. 594.

28. See Chapter VIII, "George Ripley—The Man of Letters," O. B. Frothingham, *Transcendentalism in New England,* New York, G. P. Putnam's Sons, 1876.

29. O. B. Frothingham, *George Ripley* (Men of Letters Series, Charles Dudley Warner, ed.), Boston, New York, Houghton Mifflin Company, 1882, Chapter I, p. 1.

30. Charles Dudley Warner to OBF, December 4, 1881, Warner Papers, Bienneke Library, Yale University (from Avignon, France).

31. Charles Crowe, *George Ripley,* Athens, Georgia, University of Georgia Press, 1967, p. 292.

32. Frothingham, *George Ripley,* p. 108.

33. Fifth Edition, 1886.

34. *Index,* "Book Notices," February 1, 1883, p. 370.

35. O. B. Frothingham, "The Man," "Apotheosis," *The Complete Prose Works and Later Poems of Henry Wadsworth Longfellow* (Part 45), Boston, Houghton Mifflin; Cambridge, Riverside Press, 1883, p. 1407.

36. O. B. Frothingham, "Swedenborg," *North American Review,* June, 1882, Vol. 134.

37. 1877.

38. O. B. Frothingham, *North American Review,* April, 1883, Vol. 136, p. 196ff.

39. P. 482.

40. O. B. Frothingham, "Democracy and Moral Progress," *North American Review,* July, 1883, Vol. 137.

41. O. B. Frothingham, "Some Phases of Idealism in New England," *Atlantic Monthly,* July, 1883, p. 13.

42. *Ibid.*

43. *Ibid.,* p. 15.

44. *Ibid.,* p. 12.

45. *Ibid.,* p. 22.

46. *Ibid.,* p. 23.

47. *Index,* March 2, 1882, Vol. 2, p. 410.

48. *Records of Overseers of Harvard College,* Vol. XI, Archive Room, Widner Library, Harvard. In 1882, Higginson joined the Committee. Pp. 16–18.

49. Newspaper clipping (unidentified), Frothingham Mscl. Folder, Archive Room, Widner Library, Harvard.

50. Richard Pierce (ed.), *Records of First Church,* Vol, 41, Colonial Society of Massachusetts.

51. *Index,* February 9, 1882.

52. William White Chadwick, *Sermon on Henry Bellows,* Second Unitarian Church, Brooklyn, New York; New York, D. W. Green, 1882.

53. Elizabeth had married Henry T. Brown, a member of her father's church trustees, in approximately 1873. This ended in divorce for unknown reasons. Harvard Class Book, Class of 1843, Class Memorabilia, stated by O. B. Frothingham in 1882, Archive Room, Widner Library, Harvard.

54. "Criticism and Christianity," April, 1883.

55. Johnson's volume on Oriental religion, not then published.

56. James Herbert Morse, *Diary,* Vol. 6, June-July, 1883, NYHS (all above from this source).

57. *Index,* December 27, 1883, Vol. IX, "Personal Items," p. 310.

58. OBF to George William Curtis, February 18, 1884, Houghton Library,

Harvard.

59. Morse, *Diary,* Vol. 7, April 1, 1884.

60. George Haven Putnam, *Memories of a Publisher, 1865–1915,* G. P. Putnam's Sons, 1915, p. 20.

61. Morse, *Diary,* Vol. 7, April 30, 1884, NYHS.

62. *Salem Register,* May 19, 1884; J. H. Morse, *Diary,* Vol. 7, July 23, 1884.

CHAPTER X

1. He never changed his views on women's suffrage which he considered "unnecessary and inexpedient." Women should not be spoiled by the vote but must be educated as a preparatory training for participation in worldly affairs. This contradictory statement was written in 1886 in "Women's Suffrage, Unnatural and Inexpedient," Pamphlet, Collection of New York Association Opposed to Extension of Suffrage to Women, compiled in New York, 1896.

2. J. H. Morse, *Diary,* Vol. 7, April 9, 1885, NYHS.

3. OBF to (name not given), November 15, 1884, answering a request for the address of James Martineau, the English religious radical, Lee Kohn Memorial Collection, MSS Room, NYPL; OFB to (name not given), May 18, 1889, sending his autograph and an article about Longfellow, A. W. Anthony Bequest, MSS Room, NYPL; OBF to "Mr. Brooks," October 12, 1890, about his "Series" and Higginson's article in *The Visitor* magazine, Houghton Library, Harvard.

4. OBF to Higginson, October 7, 1885, Conway Papers, Special MSS Collection, Columbia University.

5. OBF to Higginson, June 13, 1886, May 5, 1887, Houghton Library, Harvard.

6. OBF to Arthur Stedman, April 14, 18, 1887, Stedman Papers, Special MSS Collection, Columbia University.

7. Abbot Diary, November 18, 1887, in Sidney Ahlstrom, *Francis Ellingwood Abbot,* Unpublished Ph.D. Dissertation, Harvard, 1951, p. 289.

8. Morse, *Diary,* Vol. 7, April 22, July 8, 1886; Vol. 8, October 11, 1886.

9. OBF to Higginson, May 23, 1884.

10. O. B. Frothingham, "The Philosophy of Conversion," *North American Review,* October, 1884, Vol. 139, p. 324.

11. *Boston Sunday Herald,* March 26, 1885.

12. *Index,* March 12, 1889, Vol. V, No. 37 (new), p. 437.

13. O. B. Frothingham (ed.), "Introduction," Samuel Johnson, *Oriental Religions and Their Relation to Universal Religion,* Vols. VII–XXIX, Boston, Houghton Mifflin, 1885, 782 pp.

14. *Ibid.,* Introduction, p. xvi.

15. OBF to Edward Abbott, Editor, *The Literary World,* June 15, 1885, Abbott Memorial Collection (Bound), Special Collections Room, Bowdoin College.

16. O. B. Frothingham, *Memoir of William Henry Channing,* Boston, Houghton Mifflin Company, Riverside Press, 1886, pp. 424–426.

17. *Index,* Book Notices, Review by Sarah A. Underwood, December 2, 1886, p. 273.

18. Frothingham, *Memoir of Channing,* p. 149.

19. Frothingham, *Transcendentalism in New England,* p. 140.

20. O. B. Frothingham, "Why I Am a Free Religionist," *North American Review*, July, 1887, Vol. 145, pp. 8–16.

21. *Ibid.*, p. 13.

22. *Ibid.*, pp. 12–13.

23. *Ibid.*, pp. 14–15.

24. *Ibid.*, p. 15.

25. *The Poems of Giacomo Leopardi*, Translated by Frederick Townshend, Introduction by O. B. Frothingham, New York, G. P. Putnam's Sons, 1887.

26. OBF to (name not mentioned), May 17, 1887, MSS Room, NYPL.

27. Morse, Diary, Vol. VIII, March 13, 1887.

28. *Suffolk County Vital Statistics*, 46 Registration, Vol. 374, p. 104. Curtis Parker died at age twenty in 1907.

29. OBF to Edmund Stedman, February 5, 1889, Stedman Papers, Special MSS Collection, Columbia University.

30. David Wasson, *Essays, Religious, Social, Political: Memoir by O. B. Frothingham*, Boston, Lee and Sheppard, 1889.

31. OBF to Edward Merril, November 1, 1889, Merril Papers, Special Collection, Bowdoin College.

32. OBF to Kate Fields, November 4, 1887, Kate Fields Collection, MHS.

33. OBF to Merril, August 30, 1889, November 1, 1889, November 4, 1889, December 18, 1889, February 4, 1890, February 5, 1890.

34. OBF to C. E. Norton, February 24, 1890, Houghton Library, Harvard (thanking him for a letter he needed and a "little book").

35. G. P. Putnam's Sons (Knickerbocker Press, New York and London), 1890.

36. *Boston Unitarianism*, p. 73; also cited on p. 24 of this book.

37. *Ibid.*, p. 70.

38. *Ibid.*, p. 232.

39. *Ibid.*, p. 253.

40. C. P. Cranch to OBF, November 20, 1890, Cranch Papers, Box 1846–1929, MHS. Ironically, Frothingham would write an obituary of Cranch three years later in the *Boston Transcript*, William Russell to Elizabeth Cranch, January 2, 1893.

41. OBF to Caroline Dall, December 9, 1890, Dall Papers, MHS.

42. OBF to Fields, December 10, 1890.

43. Massachusetts Historical Society, *Proceedings*, Vol. VI, 2nd Series, May, 1891, pp. 443–468, "Memoir of Reverend James Walker, D.D., LL.D.," by O. B. Frothingham, p. 447. Frothingham had become a member of the MHS, by invitation, in 1887, Frothingham Collection, MHS.

44. *Ibid.*, pp. 463–468.

45. Frothingham, *Recollections and Impressions*.

46. *Ibid.*, Chapter VIII.

47. *Ibid.*, p. 138.

48. Moncure Conway in his *Life of Thomas Paine*, New York, G. P. Putnam's Sons, 1892.

49. Frothingham, *Recollections and Impressions* p. 270.

50. *Ibid.*, p. 288.

51. *Ibid.*, pp. 293–294.

52. *Ibid.*, pp. 300–302.

53. OBF to Mrs. Rogers, March 26, 1892, MSS Room, NYPL; "Carrie is in New

York," he wrote, but would soon return "to receive your kind invitation."

54. OBF to (unknown), February 2, 1872, (agreeing to attend a meeting of some kind), MSS Room, NYPL; OBF to (unknown), December 23, 1892, (sending a letter of his father's written to his mother from Switzerland in 1849), Frothingham Collection, MHS.

55. OBF to (name not given), April 25, 1893, MSS Room, NYPL.

56. OBF to Mr. Gilden, January 18, 1894, (requesting the November issue of *Century* for Lowell's paper on Parkman), *Century* Collection, MSS Room, NYPL.

57. Massachusetts Historical Society, *Proceedings,* Vol. VIII, "Memoir of Francis Parkman," O. B. Frothingham, March 1, 1894, pp. 520–562, p. 546.

58. OBF to William Roscoe Thayer, May 3, 1894, Houghton Library, Harvard.

59. OBF to Thayer, May 5, 1894.

60. Interview with Mrs. Eugenia Frothingham Lombard, Cambridge, Massachusetts, November 11, 1968.

61. Howard Chandler Robbins, *The Life of Paul Revere Frothingham,* Boston, Houghton Mifflin Company, 1935, p. 23.

62. *Ibid.,* p. 48.

63. *Ibid.,* p. 50.

64. *Ibid.,* December, 1894, p. 53.

65. Morse, *Diary,* Vol. X, November 23, 1895. Lucy Morse, called by Bessie, arrived to be near Caroline during the last ordeal.

66. *Massachusetts Vital Statistics,* Index to Deaths, No. 36, Vol. 456, p. 468, State House, Boston, Massachusetts.

67. Mrs. E. Healey to OBF's brother (probably Edward), November 24, 1895, written at Hotel Vendome, Frothingham Folder, UUA Collection, 25 Beacon Street, Boston, Massachusetts.

68. *New York Times,* November 28, 1895, p. 5, adjacent to Alexander Dumas' obituary.

69. November 27, 1895.

70. Morse, *Diary,* Vol. X, December 15, told of O. B. Frothingham's last days and "Mrs. F's condition."

71. News clipping, unidentified, Frothingham Folder, UUA Collection, 25 Beacon Street, Boston, Massachusetts.

72. News clipping, unidentified, Frothingham Folder, Archive Room, Widner Library, Harvard.

73. Mt. Auburn Street Cemetery Records, Lot No. 665, December 1, 1895.

74. *Suffolk County Court House Probate Records,* Boston, Massachusetts; will of O. B. Frothingham; will of Caroline C. Frothingham.

75. *Massachusetts Vital Statistics,* Index to Deaths, No. 896, 1900, No. 311, State House, Boston, Massachusetts.

76. FRA, *Secretary's Report for 1900,* UUA Collection, 25 Beacon Street, Boston, Massachusetts.

77. *Suffolk County Court House Probate Records,* 1920, 1921; will of Paul Revere Frothingham. The vase, with the inscription, "T.P. 1846, O.B.F. 1860, P.R.F. 1896" was willed to the Massachusetts Historical Society. Many of his books went to the Harvard Department of History.

78. William White Chadwick, "Funeral Address," in the *Free Church Record,* Vol. IV, No. 1, February, 1896, UUA Collection, 25 Beacon Street, Boston,

Massachusetts; FRA, *Proceedings,* 1913, Paul Revere Frothingham's remarks.

79. *Ethical Address, Memorial Exercises in Honor of Octavius Brooks Frothingham,* Series II, No. 10, December, 1895, S. Burns Weston, Philadelphia.

80. All published in Massachusetts Historical Society, *Proceedings,* Vol. X, 1895–1896 (published by the Society), Boston, Massachusetts.

81. *New York Evening Post,* November 28, 1895; *Boston Herald,* July 13, 1898; Joseph Henry Allen, *Sequel to Our Liberal Movement,* Roberts Brothers, Boston, 1897; Samuel Elliot (editor), *Heralds of the Liberal Faith,* "Octavius Brooks Frothingham," by Paul Revere Frothingham, Unitarian Association, Boston, 1910.

82. *Prophets of Liberalism,* Six Addresses Before the Free Religious Association, Thirty-Third Annual Convention, June 1, 1900, James West Company, Boston, p. 22.

83. FRA, *Proceedings,* Twenty-Ninth Annual Meeting, May 28–29, 1896, Boston, pp. 21–22.

84. *Prophets of Liberalism,* Six Addresses Before the Free Religious Association, Thirty-Third Annual Convention, June 1, 1900, James West Company, Boston, p. 73.

General Bibliography

BOOKS

Adams, Henry, *Education of Henry Adams,* Houghton Mifflin Company, 1961 Edition.

Bartlett, Irving H., *Wendell Phillips, Brahmin Radical,* Beacon Press, 1961.

Bellamy, Edward, *Looking Backward,* Modern Library Series, 1887.

Bode, Carl, *The American Lyceum: Town Meeting of the Mind,* Oxford University Press, New York, 1956.

Braun, Henry A., *The Age of Unreason,* New York, 1881. (Essay, "The Rationalism of O. B. Frothingham and Felix Adler.")

Brown, Jerry Wayne, *The Rise of Biblical Criticism in America, 1800–1870, The New England Scholars,* Wesleyan University, 1969.

Burtis, Mary Elizabeth, *Moncure Conway,* Rutgers University Press, 1952.

Chadwick, William White, *Theodore Parker, Preacher and Reformer,* Houghton Mifflin Company, 1901.

Commager, Henry Steele, *Theodore Parker, Yankee Crusader,* Beacon Press, 1947.

Conway, Moncure, *Life of Thomas Paine,* G. P. Putnam's Sons, New York, 1892.

Crowe, Charles, *George Ripley, Transcendentalists and Utopian Socialists,* University of Georgia Press, 1967.

Dean, Peter, *The Life and Teachings of Theodore Parker,* Williams and Norgate, Edinburg, 1877.

Easton, Lloyd D., *Hegel's First American Followers: The Ohio Hegelians, John Strallo, Peter Kaufman, Moncure Conway, August Willich,* Ohio University Press, 1966.

Edelstein, Tilden, *Strong Enthusiasm, A Life of Thomas Wentworth Higginson,* Yale University, 1968.

Emerson, Ralph Waldo, *Complete Works,* Vol. XI, Boston, 1903–04.

Frothingham, O. B., *Stories from the Lips of the Teachers,* Walker, Wise and Company, Boston, 1864.

———, *Story of the Patriarchs,* Walker, Wise and Company, Boston, 1864.

———, *Child's Book of Religion,* James Miller, New York, 1866.

———, *The Religion of Humanity,* D. G. Francis, New York, 1873.

———, "In Temper and Spirit, An American" (James Russell Lowell) for *The Literary World,* June 27, 1885.

———, *Life of Theodore Parker,* James R. Osgood and Company, Boston, 1874.

———, *The Cradle of Christ, A Study of Primitive Christianity,* G. P. Putnam's Sons, New York, 1877.

———, *Transcendentalism in New England,* G. P. Putnam's Sons, New York, 1876.

———, *Gerrit Smith,* G. P. Putnam's Sons, Second Edition, 1879.

———, *George Ripley* (Man of Letters Series, Charles Dudley Warner, ed.), Houghton Mifflin, Boston, New York, 1882.

———, "The Man," "Apotheosis," *The Complete Prose Works and Later Poems of Henry Wadsworth Longfellow,* Houghton Mifflin, Riverside Press, Cambridge, Massachusetts, 1883.

_____ , *Memoir of William Henry Channing*, Houghton Mifflin, Riverside Press, Boston, 1886.

_____ , (ed.), *Essays, Religious, Social, Political* by David Wasson, *Memoir* by O. B. Frothingham, Lee and Sheppard, Boston, 1889.

_____ , *Boston Unitarians, 1820–1850: A Study of the Life and Work of Nathaniel Langdon Frothingham*, G. P. Putnam's Sons, Knickerbocker Press, New York, London, 1890.

_____ , *Recollections and Impressions, 1822–1891*, G. P. Putnam's Sons, New York, London, 1891.

Giesmar, Maxwell, *Mark Twain, An American Prophet*, Houghton Mifflin, Boston, 1970.

Higginson, Mary Thatcher, *Thomas Wentworth Higginson, The Story of His Life*, Houghton Mifflin, 1914.

Higginson, Thomas Wentworth, *Cheerful Yesterdays*, Houghton Mifflin, 1898.

Hopkins, Charles H., *The Rise of the Social Gospel in American Protestantism, 1865–1915*, Yale, 1940.

Johnson, Samuel, *Lectures, Essays, and Sermons* (with a *Memoir* by Samuel Longfellow), Houghton Mifflin, Boston, 1883.

_____ , *Oriental Religions and Their Relation to Universal Religion*, Vols. VII–XXIX (O.B. Frothingham, "Introduction"), Houghton Mifflin, Boston, 1885.

Knepler, Henry, *The Gilded Stage*, Constable, London, 1968.

Leopardi, Giacomo, *The Poems of Giacomo Leopardi*, Translated by Frederich Townshend, Introduction by O. B. Frothingham, G. P. Putnam's Sons, New York, 1887.

Morison, Samuel Elliot, *Three Centuries of Harvard*, Harvard University Press, 1936.

Ogden, Rollo, *Life and Letters of Edwin Lawrence Godkin*, Macmillan, New York, 1907.

Oliver, Henry, *Historical Sketch of the Salem Lyceum*, Salem Gazette, 1879.

Persons, Stow, *Free Religion and American Faith*, Yale, 1947.

Renan, Ernest, *Studies in Religious History and Criticism*, Carlton Publishers, New York, 1864.

Robbins, Howard Chandler, *The Life of Paul Revere Frothingham*, Houghton Mifflin, 1935.

Rogers, Wolcott (ed.), *Family Jottings, The Frothingham Family*, Boston, 1939, American Antiquarian Society, Worcester, Massachusetts.

Savage, Minot, *Social Problems*, Boston, 1883.

Stedman, Edmund C., *Octavius Frothingham and the New Faith*, G. P. Putnam's Sons, New York, 1876.

Tyack, David B., *George Tichnor and the Boston Brahmins*, Harvard University Press, 1968.

Warren, Sidney, *American Freethought, 1860–1914*, Columbia University Press, 1943.

Weiss, John, *Life and Correspondence of Theodore Parker*, 2 vols., D. Appleton, New York, 1864.

Wells, Ann M., *Dear Preceptor, Life and Times of Thomas Wentworth Higginson*, Houghton Mifflin, Boston, 1963.

Weisenburger, Francis, *Triumph of Faith, Contribution of the Church in American Life, 1865–1900*, William Byrd Press, Richmond, Virginia, 1962.

———, *The Ordeal of Faith, The Crisis of Church-Going America*, Philadelphia Library, 1959.

Wright, Conrad, *The Liberal Christians*, Beacon Press, 1970.

INSTITUTIONAL RECORDS

Boston Latin School Records,
    Catalogue of Scholars, 1816–1918, Rare Book Room, BPL, Boston.
    Rank Records, 1834–1839, Rare Book Room, BPL, Boston.
    Declamations of Boston Latin School, 1837–1839, BPL, Boston.

Channing, William Henry, "Gospel for Today," William Crosby and H. P. Nichols, Boston, 1847, (T. W. Higginson's ordination sermon).

Ethical Addresses, Ethical Culture Society of New York, December, 1895.

Essex Institute Historical Collection, Vol. 23, 1886, "Constitution and By-Laws of Salem Choral Society," Essex Institute, Salem, Massachusetts.

First Church, "The Three Hundredth Anniversary of First Church in Salem, 1930," Address of Stephen W. Phillips, May 28, 1929, Essex Institute, Salem, Massachusetts.

Free Religious Association, *Proceedings*, 1877–1913.

Frothingham, O. B., "Colonization," Anti-Slavery Tract No. 3, American Anti-Slavery Society, 138 Nassau Street, New York, 1855.

Harvard College,
    1. *Catalogue of Officers and Students*, 1839–1840, 1843, Archive Room, Widner Library, Harvard.
    2. *Library Changing List*, 1837–1842.
    3. *Annual Reports of Harvard University*, 1835–1845.
    4. *Hasty Pudding Club, Secretary's Report*, 1836–1839.
    5. *College Records*, Vol. 8.
    6. *Exhibition and Commencement Performances*, Vol. XIV.
    7. *Harvard College Faculty*, Vols. XI, XII.
    8. *Class Record: Order of Exercise, Class Day, July 13, 1843*.
    9. *Class Book*, 1843.
    10. *Harvard Commencements*, 1842–1916.
    11. *College Papers*, Vol, X, 1842, 1843, 1945, 1846.
    12. Palfrey Papers, Divinity School, 1816–1852.
    13. *Catalog*, Academic Years, 1842–1843.
    14. Divinity School Visitation Reports.
    15. *Records of Overseers of Harvard College*, Vol. X.

Hurd, Hamilton (ed.), History of Essex County, Vol. 1, J. W. Lewis, Philadelphia, 1887, "Proprietors Committee Report," 1836–1923, North Church, Salem,

Massachusetts.

Index Association Record Book, Abbot Papers.

Lynn, Johnson, Thomas, *Saturday Club By-Laws, The Early Years of the Saturday Club,* Houghton Library, Harvard (no date).

Mt. Auburn Street Cemetery Record, Cambridge, Massachusetts.

New York Association Opposed to Extension of Suffrage to Women, O. B. Frothingham, "Women Suffrage, Unnatural and Inexpedient," Pamphlet, New York, 1896.

North Church,
   The First Century of North Church Society, Salem, 1873, Essex Institute, Salem, Massachusetts.
   Proprietors Record, 1836–1923, First Church, Salem, Massachusetts, Essex Institute, Salem, Massachusetts.
   Sunday School Catalogue of Books, 1856.
   Proprietors Report, May 14–16, 1854.
   Services at the Ordination of Rev. O. B. Frothingham, Nathaniel Langdon Frothingham, "Rightly Dividing the Word of Truth," Salem Gazette, 1847, Congregational Society, 18 Beacon Street, Boston.

Probate Records, Boston, Will of O. B. and Caroline Frothingham; Paul Revere Frothingham.

Proceedings at a Reception Given in Honor of Rev. O. B. Frothingham, Independent Liberal Church, Union League Theater, April 22, 1879, G. P. Putnam's Sons, New York, 1879.

Prophets of Liberalism, Six Addresses Before the Free Religious Association, Thirty-Third Annual Convention, June 1, 1900, James West Company, Boston, 1900.

Report of the Committee to Inquire into the Practicability and Expediency of Establishing Manufacturers in Salem, Salem, Massachusetts, 1826.

Salem City Documents, *School Report,* "Annual Report of the School Committee," February, 1851, 1852, Essex Institute, Salem, Massachusetts; Directory, 1850–1855.

Suffolk County Vital Statistics, 42nd Registration, Vol. 345, County Court House, Boston.

Vital Statistics, Index, No. 2, 1844–1850, Vol. 42; Index No. 30, Vol. 456, State House, Boston.

SERMONS

O. B. Frothingham sermons:
   The Rising and Setting Faith and Other Discourses, G. P. Putnam's Sons, New York, 1878.
   Knowledge and Faith and Other Discourses, G. P. Putnam's Sons, New York, 1876.
   The Spirit of the New Faith, G. P. Putnam's Sons, 1877.
   Belief of the Unbelievers, G. P. Putnam's Sons, 1876.
   Sermons, 4 Vols., D. G. Francis, New York, 1871, 1873, 1874, 1875.
   Sermons, 8 Vols., Bound, No Date, No Publisher, J. Wade Caruther's Collection.
   The Safest Creed and Twelve Other Discourses, Asa Bults and Company, New York, 1874.

Visions of the Future and Other Discourses, G. P. Putnam's Sons, New York, 1879.

"The Last Signs," June 1, 1856, Ford Collection, Anti-Slavery Pamphlets, NYPL.

"Uses of the Sanctuary," Jersey City, September 19, 1855, Congregational Society, 18 Beacon Street, Boston.

The Morality of the Riots, D. G. Francis, New York, 1863, Atheneum, Boston.

The Unitarian Convention and the Times, C. M. Plumb and Company, New York, 1865.

Elective Affinity, D. G. Francis, 1869.

"The Practical Uses of Christianity," *Miscellaneous Writings and Addresses of Philadelphia,* Historical Society of Pennsylvania Collection, Philadelphia.

The New Commandment, A Review of a Discourse Delivered in North Church, Salem, Sunday, June 4, 1854, by Rev. O. B. Frothingham, Henry Whipple and Sons, Boston, Essex Institute, Salem, Massachusetts (author anon).

William White Chadwick, *Sermon on Henry Bellows,* D. W. Green, New York 1882.

LETTERS, MEMOIRS, MANUSCRIPTS

Abbot Dinner, *Biographical Pamphlets,* Yale University.

Abbot, F. E., to C. E. Norton, Houghton Library, Harvard University.

Ahlstrom, Sidney, *Francis Ellingwood Abbot,* Unpublished Ph.D. Dissertation, Harvard University, 1951.

Beecher, Henry Ward (Miscellaneous Letters), Beecher Correspondence, MSS Room, Yale University.

Blatch, Harriet Stanton and Alma Lutz, *Challenging Years,* G. P. Putnam's Sons, New York, 1940.

Brooks, Margaret, Collection (various letters), Essex Institute, Salem, Massachusetts.

Chadwick, W. W., to W. C. Gannett, Gannett Papers, MSS Room, University of Rochester.

Conway, Moncure D, *Autobiography,* Vol. I, Houghton Mifflin, 1907.

Cranch, C. P., *Note Book* Cranch Papers, MHS.

Elliot, Samuel (ed.), *Heralds of the Liberal Faith,* "Octavius Brooks Frothingham" by Paul Revere Frothingham, UUA, Boston, 1910.

Fraternity Papers, vols. 1–8, MSS Room, NYHS.

Frothingham, Donald (USNR), *Reminiscence and Family Record,* 1953, Mrs. Eugenia Frothingham Lombard Collection, Cambridge, Massachusetts.

Frothingham, Ellen, to Thomas Davidson, Davidson Papers, MSS Room, Yale University.

Frothingham, N. L., to Ralph Waldo Emerson, Emerson Collection, Houghton Library, Harvard University.

OBF to Edward Abbott, Abbott Memorial Collection, Special Collections Room, Bowdoin College.

OBF to F. E. Abbot, Abbot Papers, Archive Room, Widner Library, Harvard University.

OBF to George Bartol, Washburn Papers, MHS, Boston.

OBF to Henry Bellows, Bellows Papers, MHS.

OBF to Moncure Conway, Conway Papers, Special Collection, Columbia University.

OBF to George William Curtis, Houghton Library, Harvard University.

OBF to Editor of *College Review,* Betts Collection, MSS Room, Yale University.

OBF to Editor of *College Review* and J. O. Sargent, Miscl. Papers, NYHS.

OBF to Caroline Dall, Dall Papers, MHS.

OBF to G. E. Ellis, Ellis Papers, MHS; also Essex Institute, Salem, Massachusetts.

OBF to Ralph Waldo Emerson, Houghton Library, Harvard University.

OBF to Female Anti-Slavery Society, Essex Institute, Salem, Massachusetts.

OBF to Kate Fields, Kate Fields Collection, Rare Book Room, BPL.

OBF to Mr. Gilder, Century Collection, MSS. Room, NYPL.

OBF to E. L. Godkin, Godkin Papers, Houghton Library, Harvard University.

OBF to T. W. Higginson, Houghton Library, Harvard University.

OBF to Samuel Johnson, Samuel Johnson Papers, Essex Institute, Salem, Massachusetts.

OBF to Henry Wadsworth Longfellow, Houghton Library, Harvard University.

OBF to Samuel Longfellow, Longfellow Papers, Essex Institute, Salem, Massachusetts.

OBF to Samuel J. May, May Papers, Rare Book Room, BPL

Frothingham Miscellaneous Folder, Archive Room, Widner Library, Harvard University.

OBF, Ministerial Folder, AAU Collection, 25 Beacon Street, Boston, Massachusetts.

OBF, *Notes of Lectures Delivered by O. B. Frothingham on Gospels of Matthew and John, Book of David, and the Apocalypse,* 4 Vols. (MSS) by Eliza Bradlee, Andover Library, Harvard University.

OBF to C. E. Norton, Houghton Library, Harvard University.

OBF to James Parton, Houghton Library, Harvard University.

OBF to J. O. Sargent, Sargent Papers, MHS.

OBF to Edmund Stedman, Stedman Papers, Special MSS Collection, Columbia University.

OBF to Charles Sumner, Sumner Papers, Houghton Library, Harvard University.

OBF to (Unknown), Lee Kohn Memorial Collection, A. W. Anthony Bequest, New York, MSS Room, NYPL.

Harrel, Pauline, "The Rendition of Anthony Burns," M.A. Thesis, Southern Connecticut State College, New Haven, Connecticut, 1969.

Higginson, Thomas Wentworth, *Journals,* Houghton Library, Harvard University.

Merriam, George (ed.), *Life and Times of Samuel Bowles,* Century Company, New York, Vol. II, 1885.

Morse, James Herbert, *Diary,* Vols. II, XIX, NYPL.

Nichols, Martha, "Memorial Paper on O. B. Frothingham," OBF Folder, AAU, 25 Beacon Street, Boston, Massachusetts.

Norton, Sara and M. H. DeWolf Howe, *Letters of Charles Eliot Norton,* Vol. I, Houghton Mifflin, Boston, 1913.

Parker, Theodore, to Convers Francis, September 25, 1842, Parker Papers, Rare Book Room, BPL.

Parker, Theodore, *Journals,* Vol. III, 1850–1851, AAU, 25 Beacon Street, Boston, Massachusetts.

Potter, W. J., to Lucretia Mott, Friends Historical Collections, Swarthmore College, Philadelphia, Pennsylvania.

Potter, W. J., to Caroline Dall, Dall Papers, MHS.

Putnam, George H., *Memories of a Publisher, 1865–1914,* G. P. Putnam's Sons, New York, 1915.

Ripley, George, to Christopher P. Cranch, Cranch Papers, MHS.

Sargent, Mrs. John T. (ed.), *Sketches and Reminiscences of the Radical Club of Chestnut Street,* Osgood, Boston, 1880.

Spooner, Lysander, to OBF, Anti-Slavery Papers, Rare Book Room, BPL

Strong, George Templeton, *Diary,* Vol. I, Alan Nevins and M.K.T. Thomas (Editors), Macmillan, New York, 1952.

Warner, Charles Dudley, to OBF, Warner Papers, Bieneke Library, Yale University.

Wasson, David to Samuel Johnson, Wasson Papers, Essex Institute, Salem, Massachusetts.

PERIODICALS

Atlantic Monthly

Boston Dailey Globe

Boston Sunday Herald

Chadwick, William White, "Funeral Address for O. B. Frothingham," *Free Church Record,* Vol. IV, No. 1, February, 1896, AAU Collection, 25 Beacon Street, Boston, Massachusetts.

Christian Examiner

Christian Inquirer

Christian Register

Friends of Progress, OBF, "The Murdered President," May, 1865, BPL.

Index

Journal of American History, William Armstrong, "The Freeman's Movement and the Founding of the Nation," Vol. VIII, No. 4, March, 1967.

Liberal Christian

Massachusetts Historical Society, *Proceedings,*

    OBF, "Memoir of Rev. James Walker, D.D.," Vol. VI, 2nd Series, May 1, 1891, Boston.

    OBF, "Memoir of Francis Parkman," Vol. VIII, March 1, 1894.

    Josiah P. Quincy, "Memoir of Octavius B. Frothingham," March, 1896, Vol. X, 1892–1896.

    Edward Young, "Remarks on the Death of O. B. Frothingham," Vol. X, 1892–1896.

Nation

New Age

New York Evening Post

New York Herald Tribune

New York Times

North American Review

Radical, The

Radical Review

Salem Gazette

Salem Observer

Salem Register

Truthseeker

Index